OUR MAN IN PANAMA

HOW GENERAL NORIEGA
USED THE UNITED STATES
—AND MADE MILLIONS
IN DRUGS AND ARMS

JOHN DINGES

RANDOM HOUSE ⌂ NEW YORK

Library of Congress Cataloging-in-Publication Data

Dinges, John.
Our man in Panama : how General Noriega used the United States—and made
millions in drugs and arms / John Dinges.
p. cm.
ISBN 0-394-54910-4
1. Noriega, Manuel Antonio, 1936–   . —Ethics. 2. Panama—Politics
and government—1946–   . —Moral and ethical aspects. 3. Corruption
(in politics)—Panama. 4. Panama—Relations—United States.
5. United States—Relations—Panama. 6. Generals—Panama—
Biography. 7. Panama. Guardia Nacional—Biography. 8. Heads of
state—Panama—Biography. I. Title.
F1567.N67D56 1990
972.8705—dc20   89-42769

Manufactured in the United States of America
24689753
First Edition

FOR TOMÁS, SEBASTIÁN AND CAMILA

CONTENTS

A NOTE ON SOURCES

On February 5, 1988, U.S. prosecutors in Tampa and Miami, Florida, announced separate indictments on drug-trafficking charges against General Manuel Antonio Noriega, the military ruler of Panama. On December, 20, 1989, the United States invaded Panama to remove Noriega from power and to enforce that indictment. Never before had the United States indicted a foreign official of Noriega's rank and power. Never before had such an array of U.S. power been employed against an objective so personal rather than political. The charges against Noriega, and the invasion, were even more astounding in light of his undisputed history of close cooperation with the United States in military, intelligence and drug enforcement matters.

In reconstructing the history of that cooperation and of Noriega's association with drug activity that is almost as long-standing, I have attempted to apply a strict standard of verification and corroboration of sources in order to avoid passing on the myriad of lurid, unsubstantiated tales and downright lies that clutter the public record about Noriega. With few exceptions, the major actors in this story, notably Noriega's enemies in the Panamanian opposition, Noriega himself, and even U.S. officials, have in greater or lesser degree been guilty of distorting the record. In Panama, fabrication of documents and gross exaggeration have been common not only in the press, which is largely government controlled, but among some of the opposition figures upon whom U.S. journalists have most relied. In the United States, "revelations" about Noriega have at times been based on putative intelligence reports related by anonymous sources. In at least one case, according to an influential Panamanian opposition journalist, a U.S. congressional staff member with access to classified material on Noriega seemed to encourage him to embellish, telling him: "Put down whatever you want and it will be true."

In the notes at the end of the book, I have attempted to be as explicit as possible in evaluating the credibility of the sources I used and in explaining why I find other sources or particular accounts unreliable. Certain evaluations are in order at the outset: After a close examination of the investigations that led to the indictments against Noriega, I found no basis to question their general conclusions. At the core of the Tampa and Miami indictments, respectively, is the testimony of two convicted drug smugglers, Steven Michael Kalish, an American, and Floyd Carlton Caceres, a Panamanian. I found their testimony to be strongly corroborated by other evidence, and I consider them to be credible in relating the key allegations of Noriega's involvement in drug trafficking. I have drawn heavily on the stories of both men—as told by Carlton in congressional testimony and classified depositions I obtained and as told by Kalish in many hours of interviews with me in addition to his public testimony. In my opinion, virtually the entire legal case against Noriega rests on their credibility.

Conversely, at no point does the book rely on the uncorroborated testimony of the former Panamanian consul in New York, José Blandón, whose dozens of hours of public testimony and press interviews have more than any other single witness colored U.S. media perceptions of the Noriega affair. Although Blandón undisputably had a major political role in Panamanian events and had inside knowledge of many major events in Panama, a significant number of his allegations defy confirmation and in some cases are implausible or demonstrably false. In at least one case, I believe the Miami prosecutors were led into a significant error by writing charges into the indictment at the last minute based on the uncorroborated testimony of Blandón.

My investigation was greatly aided by more than two thousand pages of secret U.S. government documents that were declassified under the Freedom of Information Act. Documents released by the State Department and the Department of Defense were invaluable in providing contemporary reports of events in Panama that could be compared to the accounts of officials recalling the events—and U.S. policy decisions—from hindsight.

Finally, another indispensable body of material on Panama is found in the four volumes of hearings and two-volume report by the Senate Foreign Relations Subcommittee on Terrorism, Narcotics and International Communications, chaired by Senator John Kerry of Massachusetts. The Kerry hearing material must be used with care, however, since witnesses' accounts are presented uncritically, with little independent corroboration or cross-checking of evidence. The testimony of one Kerry hearing witness, money-launderer Ramón Milian Rodríguez, for example, was rejected outright by the investigators who prepared the Miami indictment, and the U.S. attorney's office in Miami took the unusual step of issuing a public affidavit describing Milian as "wholly without credibility" and a witness whose use in criminal proceedings would "violate our ethical obligation to present truthful and reliable information."

Through this thicket of half truth and misinformation, I have been guided by personal interviews with more than one hundred participants on all sides of the Panamanian question in the United States and Panama. I have weighed their information according to their ability to present firsthand accounts and to corroborate the independent knowledge of other participants. In the final analysis, the reliability of the account presented in this book rests on the skeptical care in investigation and the standard of credibility I have held up for my sources. For that, and for any errors, I must assume sole responsibility.

OUR MAN IN PANAMA

CHAPTER 1

```
罠||||||||||||||||||||||||||||||||||||||||||||||||||||||||||||||||||||||||||||||||||||罠
```

THE RAID

```
罠||||||||||||||||||||||||||||||||||||||||||||||||||||||||||||||||||||||||||||||||||||罠
```

MAY 1984

Combat, not cocaine, was on Major Augusto Villalaz's mind as he guided the squadron of Huey helicopters low over the jungle. They had taken off just after sunrise from Garachiné, the Indian village that housed the last outpost of the Panama Defense Forces (PDF) on the Pacific Ocean side of Darién Province. Twenty minutes later the three helicopters were near the target landing zone. The squadron of young soldiers seated behind Villalaz shifted their weapons as his chopper slowed and banked into a wide circle. Villalaz scanned the green below. There it was, just as it had been described to him: a hole in the unbroken canopy, a shaft 160 feet deep where a few giant trees had been cut down to clear an oblong landing pad on the jungle floor.

The helicopters roared in an open V formation over the opening and swung back around to prepare for the descent. This was the most dangerous part of the mission. If a guerrilla force was waiting below, it would not have a better moment to open fire. It was not for this that Major Villalaz had joined the military. Neither he nor anyone else in the attack force had ever been in combat. His routine duty was to ferry General Manuel Antonio Noriega and other top officers around the world in the Panama Air Force's Boeing 727.

The soldiers crouched grimly at the open doors on either side of the aircraft. Most carried MI6 assault rifles; one carried a 7.62-mm machine gun, another a grenade launcher. This was what their trainers had called a "hot LZ approach." But it was no training exercise. In thirty seconds, they expected to be in a real firefight.

Intelligence about the camp had come in several days before. The captain of a shrimp boat trawling in the Gulf of Panama, within sight of the coastal ridge known unglamorously as the Serranía del Sapo—the Toad Mountains—had reported a suspicious cargo ship anchored close to shore. Two helicopters had been seen shuttling pallets of bulky supplies from the ship to the beach, then from the beach to a spot in the hills several miles inland. The Colombian border was only fifty miles to the southeast, but the Serranía was an unlikely spot for any legitimate export-import business.

There seemed to be only one explanation. For months, PDF troops in Darién had been on the alert for Colombian guerrillas seeking a haven in Panama. The most active groups, the Nineteenth of April Movement (M-19) and FARC (Revolutionary Armed Forces of Colombia), were tough fighters with an arsenal of the world's best assault weapons. The rebels had recently begun an uneasy truce with the Colombian government, and the Colombian military had warned their Panamanian counterparts that the groups might attempt to establish military bases across the border in Panama to evade the restrictions agreed upon in the truce.

The three Hueys dropped swiftly into the clearing; the soldiers, eleven in each chopper, leaped into the blowing debris and scrambled to establish a protective perimeter among the stumps lining the landing field. The abrupt shadow of the huge trees created a dusklike dimness. But there was no gunfire, no sign of resistance. Off to the side of the landing field was a small helicopter—a French Alouette—covered with camouflage netting. Camouflage for a second helicopter was piled nearby. Dozens of fuel barrels were hidden just beyond the cleared area.

Through the trees, Major Villalaz could see the zinc roofs of several low buildings. He followed a path that had been heavily traveled but so recently cleared that machete marks still showed whitely on vines and small trees. After a few dozen yards, the path became a raised walkway constructed of sheets of marine plywood, pine two-by-fours and hefty posts cut from trees.

The first building—consisting of a plywood platform, tree columns and a roof covered with corrugated zinc sheets—housed five Lister (Onan) diesel-powered generators. Rolls of wire and barrels of fuel filled the hut. Wires strung on poles carried electricity to five or six other buildings, including a kitchen and mess hall and two sleeping cabins with twenty-five or thirty hammocks each. Villalaz noticed that the packing crates for the generators were still stacked nearby. Large black letters on the crates identified the supplier as an equipment distributor in Medellín, Colombia.

By this time, PDF soldiers had posted sentinels and were waiting for orders. Captain Francisco Alvarez, the platoon leader, and a group of soldiers were inspecting the largest two buildings, when Villalaz walked up. If it weren't already obvious from the generators and walkways, the curious installations in the two buildings were conclusive evidence that this camp had, in fact, nothing to do with guerrillas. Hanging from the roof of each structure, about six feet off the floor, was a forty-by-six-foot plywood frame with a bank of one hundred twenty 150-watt electric bulbs. A deep, metal-lined tray of the same dimensions, like a display table in an open-air plant store, had been built beneath the lights. The camp residents had spread out some clothes under the lights, apparently to dry. Draped over the rim were some pants and an extra-large red T-shirt with the word YES in six-inch stylized lettering.

Just past noon another helicopter landed in the now-crowded clearing. Several men in PDF officers' uniforms got out. With them was a civilian with short-cropped graying hair: James Bramble, the chief drug sleuth for the United States in Panama. As the Drug Enforcement Administration's (DEA) agent-in-charge, Bramble ran an international antinarcotics operation out of the U.S. embassy. He was within two weeks of wrapping up what he had considered a productive and harmonious two-year stint working with Noriega's narcotics control people to plug the flow of cocaine and cocaine money through Panama.

Getting out of the helicopter with Bramble was Inspector Luis Quiel, Bramble's main contact with Noriega and the PDF. Bramble liked and respected Quiel. He was bright and hardworking, a soldier's soldier, a crisp professional who seldom wasted words. Still in his early thirties—a decade younger than Bramble—Quiel had been appointed by Noriega to head the PDF's special antinarcotics unit. That made him a member of Noriega's inner circle, one of the trusted younger officers who bypassed the chain of command and reported to no one but the general.

Quiel had called Bramble the previous afternoon, Friday, May 18. "For your information, we have discovered a clandestine operation in the jungle, in Darién," he said. "We think it's guerrillas, but it could be Colombian narcotraffickers, too. We're not sure. We'll keep you posted." Bramble carried his two-way radio with him the rest of the day. Early the next morning, Quiel had contacted him again; the camp looked like it might be a cocaine laboratory. "General Noriega wants us to fly you down there to look it over," Quiel had said.

As Bramble began to explore the camp, he unwrapped a sandwich and munched on it. No question this was a cocaine factory. He was once again astonished at the speed and ingenuity of the cocaine entrepreneurs. He calculated that construction had begun less than a month before, perhaps as few as twenty days. In that time, the crew of carpenters and electricians had landed in virgin jungle and had built a processing facility that in a few more days would have been turning out enormous amounts of cocaine hydrochloride. But the raid had caught the traffickers before they had brought in the raw cocaine paste and chemicals to put the factory into operation. A careful search turned up no cocaine or by-products.

The long banks of light bulbs and trays were no mystery to Bramble. Impure cocaine paste was dissolved in ethyl ether and other chemicals, carefully filtered and then dried in the trays under the powerful lights into the snowy final product ready for consumption in the United States. The process required skilled workers, known as *cocineros,* or cooks, and was extremely dangerous because of the combination of toxic, volatile ether and heat. A factory this size was probably capable of producing perhaps a ton of cocaine a month. Water for the process was provided by plastic pipes running several hundred yards through the jungle to a collection basin rigged up at the base of a waterfall. The engineering was first rate, Bramble thought. In fact, the factory was better than anything he had seen in Latin America.

The builders had taken advantage of the natural setting to achieve almost total concealment. From the air, nothing of the camp had been visible until the helicopter was directly overhead. Even then it could easily have been taken for a field cleared by an Indian farmer. The upper canopy of giant broadleaf evergreens was barely visible; shorter trees formed a second canopy fifty feet above the ground. Between the two layers was an incredible luxuriance of rain forest plant life—ferns, mosses and bromeliads whose roots never touched the ground but drew moisture and nutrients from the air and from their contact with the trees. A few feet above the cocaine factory's roofs, the world's most voluptuous orchids crowded each other in a promiscuity of glamour rarely seen by human beings. Most of the Serranía's animal inhabitants—snakes, monkeys, lizards and birds of a thousand varieties—lived a high-rise existence in the trees, indifferent to the intruders. There was not a second of respite from the animals' screams, clacks and thumps mingled with the ticking and rustling of insects.

The ground around the buildings had been cleared of vines and undergrowth. But by erecting everything on stilts, the builders had left the thick mat of dead leaves and brush relatively unscarred and unlikely to create visible erosion or telltale muddy runoff—a primary consideration in a forest with a monthly rainfall of ten to fifteen inches.

Bramble took detailed notes and some photographs for DEA files and flew back to Panama City in time for dinner that night. For him, this was an important break, a new blow against the Colombia-based network of cocaine traders that had only recently become the DEA's primary criminal target in Latin America. In 1984, names of Colombian traffickers like Carlos Lehder Rivas, Jorge Luis Ochoa Vásquez and Pablo Escobar Gaviría had been on the DEA's most-wanted lists for less than two years and were unknown to the general public. The Medellín cartel was not yet a term in common parlance, even inside the DEA. Bramble and his colleagues could still only guess at the scale of the Colombian organization, but recent events had opened their eyes. In March, acting on DEA information, Colombian police had raided a factory complex known as Tranquilandia in the Colombian Amazon, seizing 13.8 tons of cocaine as well as ledgers documenting mass production of 27 tons the previous seven months.

The Darién factory, with construction and processing techniques that were unmistakable trademarks of the same Colombian enterprise, was clearly a replacement for the destroyed Tranquilandia complex. The economics of the Darién operation were staggering. The whole installation, according to Quiel's later painstaking calculations based on captured receipts and pay vouchers, cost about $500,000 to build. That investment would have been recouped easily in the first week of production. Even at falling 1984 prices for freight-on-board cocaine, the Darién factory would have returned at least $5 million per month. On the street in New York or Los Angeles, a month's production could have been sold for upward of $120 million.

Over the next two days, PDF troops searched the jungle and on Tuesday captured the first of twenty-three Colombian residents of the camp. They had not gone far; some had staggered back to give themselves up. The prisoners included a peasant woman hired as a cook. The rest appeared to be construction workers, not dope smugglers. One prisoner identified as the camp foreman, Otalvaro Cabrera Medina, had a record of involvement with the Medellín cartel. His name showed up in DEA files in connection with the Tranquilandia bust two months before.

The Panamanian press was told about the raid only after all the Colombians were in custody. The progovernment papers and television gave it ample but not overblown coverage as another triumph in Panama's war against drugs. The opposition paper, *La Prensa,* did not dispute that interpretation. In a press conference, Captain Alvarez, who had led the attacking soldiers on the ground, described the operation in a straightforward battle report, mentioning the names of all the participating units and their commanders, but giving few details about the installations or the raid itself. Alvarez stressed that early reports indicated that the site might have been a guerrilla camp and that during the raid there had been full cooperation between the intelligence services of Panama and Colombia.

A few days later, on Saturday, May 26, Major Villalaz—the lead pilot in the Darién raid—was summoned to a new assignment. He loaded the twenty-three prisoners in an Air Force plane and flew them to El Dorado International Airport in Bogotá. He watched as they walked down the ramp and into the terminal "as if they were any other international travelers." No police met them. They were free.

General Manuel Noriega personally approved the orders to raid the suspected guerrilla camp but did not otherwise play a direct role. After the fact, however, he was quick to take credit with the United States. In two meetings with visiting high-ranking U.S. officials, Noriega made a point of bringing up the successful raid. Vice Admiral Robert F. Dunn, commander of U.S. naval forces in the Atlantic, perhaps bewildered by all the talk of drugs at a purely courtesy meeting, signed the "distinguished visitors' book" with a note congratulating the PDF for its good work in the war against drugs.

The second U.S. visitor, on June 5, was Carlton Turner, the Reagan administration's narcotics coordinator. Noriega summoned Inspector Quiel to give a full narration of the Darién raid. The progovernment *Matutino* reported Turner's parting comment to Noriega, that he considered Panama a "key country in the eradication of drug trafficking."

U.S. officials had ample reason to be pleased with Noriega's antidrug team, independent of the Darién raid. Since April, Panama had played a key role in the DEA's newest battlefront against cocaine production: the tracking and confiscation of so-called precursor chemicals, substances such as ethyl ether that were not themselves narcotics but that were indispensable in the refining of cocaine paste into powder. The DEA called it Operation Chemcon, and Panama's help in locating and seizing chemicals shipped through their country was crucial. In mid-June the Panamanians had moved in on a warehouse and confiscated the largest cache of cocaine precursor chemicals ever located, more than six thousand 55-gallon drums. Newspapers published photos of PDF detectives with gas masks destroying the ether by emptying the barrels into deep ditches.

Yes, these were times of great satisfaction and accomplishment for

Manuel Antonio Noriega. After decades in the shadow of his charismatic mentor, General Omar Torrijos Herrera, and two years of internal jockeying after Torrijos's sudden death in 1981, Noriega was indisputably, though still insecurely, on top. It was still less than a year since he had become *comandante* of the PDF and had promoted himself to Panama's first brigadier general. With sheer abundance of effort, energy and organizational agility, he cemented the loyalty of his officers. By expanding, reorganizing and "professionalizing" the military and reincarnating the National Guard as the more elevated Panama Defense Forces, he was able to please both the United States, which was financing the upgrading, and his officers, who reveled in the rapid promotions and prestige.

Panama in 1984 was undergoing rapid change, and Noriega saw himself as the vehicle of that change. He headed a military-dominated government that was in the process, it claimed, of turning power over to civilians. There had been elections, won amid charges of fraud by Noriega's candidate, Nicolás Ardito Barletta. But opposition parties were again organized and the press was free to print pretty much whatever it wanted. Still, the memories of sixteen years of military rule had left a quota of fierce bile among those excluded from power. Even before Torrijos's death, Noriega had been running the intelligence apparatus, the secret police. And he had masterminded a system of repression that was seldom brutal but nevertheless skillfully applied and never dismantled. The nasty little secret in Panamanian politics was that Noriega could keep his opponents in check with very little violence. He repressed his enemies in ways that isolated and humiliated them. Opposition leaders identified their humiliation as Noriega's doing, and he was the personal target of their wrath. Whenever they could, opposition leaders resurrected old charges that Noriega and others in the Torrijos régime had been involved in drug trafficking, charges that first arose in the 1970s and that had been neither proven nor disproven; they had simply languished from too much repetition and too little substantiation. Noriega brushed aside these accusations with his constant smile.

But one man seemed to have been able to get under Noriega's skin. Hugo Spadafora was not of the opposition; he was a Torrijista, a loyalist to the Torrijos revolution, a recognized friend of the Panama

Defense Forces. A few months before the Darién raid, in March 1984, Spadafora had cried "shame . . . that Noriega's activities for years now are soiling the uniform of the members of the Defense Forces, activities involving drug trafficking, arms trafficking and political manipulation."

Spadafora's charges threatened Noriega in his own constituency, in the masses of middle and lower middle class Panamanians who had benefited from the Torrijos revolution. Noriega had gone to great lengths to win their respect and had succeeded. It would never be the respect based in love that a child proffers a father, never the warm, unquestioned devotion most Panamanians felt for Torrijos. Noriega would not be loved; few would refer to him with other than grudging admiration. Those who did not hate him recognized his power to deliver to his friends and harass his enemies. The obeisance they paid him was street respect. His initials spelled MAN in a country where most people know at least some English. He was the boss. About him the highest compliment was rendered, most often with the appropriate gesture of a cupped, upturned hand: *"Ese hombre, sí que tiene cojones"*—"This guy has got balls."

To the three men in the penthouse of the Bank of Boston high rise, on Panama City's broad Vía España, no earth tremor had ever been as rattling as was the news of the Darién raid. The factory bust had taken them by surprise, and in their business no surprise was pleasant.

César Rodríguez and Steven Kalish had driven Kalish's Mercedes 500 SEL from their San Francisco district homes. Enrique "Kiki" Pretelt, the only one wearing a suit and tie, could have walked the short distance from Joyería Pretelt, his jewelry business on the street level of a nearby bank building, but as usual his driver dropped him off. The three men met in the Tower Club, a restaurant and bar owned by Rodríguez.

Each man had a distinct style of announcing to the world that he was rich, new-money rich, private-Learjet rich, own-your-own-nightclub rich. Kiki Pretelt was understated elegance, $4,000 European tailored suits, a $3,000 Cartier watch and deliberate Spanish cadences intended to evoke the sophistication of Castile but actually closer to the speech of a Colombian coffee magnate. Steven Kalish was the only one who was handsome, with an athletic stride and an open friendliness that made women follow him around even before they discovered that he had so much money. He dressed casually in light slacks and knit shirt, all designer labels but not flashy. He still wore his hair parted down the middle, as he had since high school in a Houston suburb in the late 1960s. It was not so long as it had been in those hippie days, and it was not trimmed by his girlfriend of the moment; now it was styled at the best salon in Panama, at $150 a session, including manicure. Rodríguez and Pretelt knew Kalish's real name but called him by the name on his Panamanian diplomatic passport, Frank Brown.

César Rodríguez liked flashy gold chains around his neck and expensive shirts open several buttons down his chest. He had dark, curly hair, a mustache that dropped just below his lip and slightly hooded eyes. Six years ago, when he was flying weapons to the Sandinista revolution, he had been lean and snapping with energy. Now his paunch pushed against his shirt and his face was pudgy. Lately, too much alcohol and cocaine had given him stomach trouble and a bleary gaze. He had the shady look of a movie gangster. He had become one.

The three men were supposed to know what was going on in Panama, especially what was going on with drugs. General Noriega was their partner. They were continuously in Noriega's company in the evenings—drinking, partying, talking about their next business deal. No one was closer to Noriega, no one knew better how things worked in Panama. Yet they hadn't even known of the existence of the cocaine factory.

Steven Kalish felt angry and betrayed. He was a fugitive from a Texas conviction for marijuana smuggling, and he was in the middle of arranging a 400,000-pound shipment from Barranquilla, Colombia, to the United States. Rodríguez and Pretelt had talked him into using Panama as his base of operations. They were his channel to the top, to Noriega—and Noriega was the guarantee of the kind of climate Kalish needed to do business. Panama was low profile: no production, no violence, no evidence U.S. drug people could lay their hands on. Panama was merely a money-laundering haven and a discreet transshipment point, and that was the way it was supposed to be. A major installation like the Darién factory was not part of the mix. Its capture might spur the DEA to try to discover what really was going on in Panama.

The three men had to find out who had allowed the plant to be set up, who had been paid off. But most of all they had to find out why the protection had been withdrawn, why the PDF had raided the lab. The only man who could give any answers, they knew, was Tony Noriega himself.

It took several days to get to see him. They couldn't just call his office and make an appointment. They waited until they found him at night out partying, more than a week after the raid. They managed only a brief conversation alone. Noriega was cryptic, as was often his style. He said he had ordered the seizure of the camp and implied that he was not involved personally with allowing the lab to exist. He said he had not condoned it or accepted money for it. He reassured Kalish that things would be all right, that the raid had nothing to do with their personal business relationship. Kalish noted a caginess in Noriega that distressed him. He could get no specifics, no direct answers before Noriega moved away.

Kalish was only mildly assuaged. In his gut he still trusted him. Noriega might not be telling the whole truth, but Kalish felt his protector was acting in the best interests of himself and his partners. And Kalish was also relieved that the cocaine laboratory was gone. It wasn't his investment, and on second thought, its dismantling had perhaps placated the DEA and decreased the chances of a crackdown in Panama like there had been in Colombia.

Noriega traveled frequently, and major upheavals in Panama had a way of happening while he was out of the country. On June 17, a month after the Darién raid, he and an entourage of senior colonels climbed aboard the Air Force Boeing 727 and took off on a long trip publicly described as official visits to France, Great Britain and Israel. The officers included his inseparable aide, Lieutenant Colonel Julián Melo Borbua; Lieutenant Colonel Elías Castillo, chief of military operations; and Lieutenant Colonel Lorenzo Purcell. Noriega left the PDF and the country in the charge of Colonel Roberto Díaz

Herrera, who as chief of the general staff was the PDF's second ranking officer.

A few days after Noriega's departure, Kalish got a visit from a Colombian trafficker. César Cura was a mid-level drug entrepreneur from Medellín, a middleman between kingpins Pablo Escobar and Jorge Ochoa and their U.S. buyers. "Mid-level" meant he exported perhaps 1,000 kilos of cocaine a month to the United States. But he also dealt in Colombian marijuana, and that was how he had come to know Kalish. He was, in fact, as close as Kalish had ever gotten to direct contact with the Medellín cartel. Cura said a representative of the cartel wanted to meet him and had some information to offer and perhaps a favor to ask. "I don't know the details, Brown," he said, using Kalish's cover name. "And I don't know what is going on, but there's something that they think you need to know and they want to talk to you." Kalish was flattered to be asked. He had grossed $20 million from drug smuggling over the past year, but he knew that to the cartel he was only a small-time operator.

Cura brought the cartel's envoy to Kalish's house, introduced the two men and left. Luis Guillermo Angel had the dress and demeanor of a diplomat. He told Kalish that his friends called him "Guillo"— and made it clear that Kalish was in that category. Angel said he had learned his flawless English as an exchange student in the United States.

He and his people had a problem, Angel said. The organization had sent him to Panama to oversee the construction of the Darién factory and to ensure the safe passage of the ether shipments, some of which were destined to go to the factory. Both operations had been busted and his organization wanted some quick and clear answers. "We paid $5 million to protect those operations, for security," he said, "and we're a little upset." Angel said he had been living at the Caesar Park Marriott Hotel in Panama City for several months and had spent a lot of time at the Darién plant, flying helicopters in and out.

"Maybe you could do us a favor. You're running operations in Panama; we're running operations in Panama. You have your contact to the top; we had ours. Obviously, ours was not so good. We need to get through to get some satisfaction. How good is your channel to Noriega? Who are you paying?" Angel said.

It was an intentionally blunt question, a favor asked with a friendly insistence Kalish was not in a position to refuse. It was the classic offer of "silver or lead"—riches if he accepted, destruction if he refused. And Kalish was ambitious. He knew he was being offered a unique opportunity to get inside the cartel, to get a piece of the cocaine action and the really big money. All he had to do was put Angel in touch with Noriega.

"Noriega himself is our contact," Kalish said. "We don't deal with intermediaries. But I think it's crazy to think Noriega was getting your money. If he took it, he wouldn't have had the lab busted. Listen, we've got to go talk to my partner César Rodríguez about this. Let's see what we can find out."

They got in Kalish's Mercedes and drove the five blocks to Rodríguez's house. Halfway there, along 78 Street, they passed Noriega's family residence. Noriega's house did not stand out in the affluent neighborhood, although it was the largest, with almost a half block of grounds. The house was white stucco with a tiled roof and enclosed courtyards in imitation of a Spanish colonial hacienda. In one corner of the lot, visible from the corner of Third Avenue C, was a finely appointed aviary—parrots, macaws and other tropical birds. Nothing identified the grounds as belonging to the most powerful man in Panama except a tastefully decorated ceramic tile imbedded near the main car entrance. It bore the simple legend "Noriega."

Rodríguez's house was smaller but more pretentious—a two-story salmon pink Spanish colonial pseudomansion with a cast-iron fence surrounding it and a small water fountain in the cobblestone front court. Inside, the expensive furnishings had a glassy, unused look. César Rodríguez brought Kalish and Angel into one of the living rooms he used as an office. Two other Panamanians arrived, Gabriel and Olmedo Mendez. They were nervous and greeted Angel obsequiously, with elaborate apologies and assurances that everything could be worked out. Kalish later learned that the two men had acted as agents for the Colombians in arranging the ether shipments and had received some of the protection money.

Angel was immediately in charge of the meeting. Speaking mildly, he said his people had paid $5 million on the understanding that they were buying protection from Noriega. The person who took their money, he said, glancing toward the Mendez brothers, evidently did not or could not deliver. "My people are very anxious to find out why the labs and ether were seized, and why things don't seem to be working out as they were presented to us. You know how these people are in Medellín. You know how we operate. We aren't going to stand by with millions of dollars in losses when we already paid $5 million without someone answering for this.

"Now you people say you deal directly with Noriega. Our own avenue to Noriega has been shown to be worthless, worse than worthless. We would greatly appreciate it if you could put us in touch with the people we need to talk to about this."

"No problem," Rodríguez said. "Noriega's out of town, but we'll get this straightened out with his best people." He got on the phone to Lieutenant Colonel Julio Ow Young, the G2 chief. A half hour later, two PDF officers in civilian clothes drove up and came in. Kalish recognized one as Inspector Luis Quiel. Quiel had been to his house for drinks once or twice. Having made the contact, Kalish excused himself. It was no longer his business, and he didn't want the mess to become his business. Besides, they had been talking in English up until then because of Kalish, and Spanish had taken over as soon as the two officers walked in.

Late the next afternoon, Angel showed up at Kalish's house again. He brought along an associate, José Eduardo Zambrano, who he introduced as the accountant, the money man, in the cartel's Panama operations. He said that the meeting the night before had gone on long after midnight and that he hadn't gotten back to the hotel until after three A.M. Kalish got the impression he had been on the phone and in meetings all day. Certainly he had reported to Jorge Ochoa, his boss, who at that time was in Spain. He was grim as he dropped a new bombshell of information.

"We paid the money to Colonel Melo. He was our contact with Noriega. We thought it was a sure deal because you can't get any closer to Noriega than Melo," Angel said. "We talked to Melo. He says Noriega double-crossed him and ordered the busts to impress the DEA. He says we should get rid of Noriega, eliminate him, you know, so Melo can take over as head of the PDF."

Oh, my God, thought Kalish, you don't want to kill Noriega. He's my connection to Panama. This is really getting out of hand. How did I get mixed up in this? I don't even deal in coke. Here I am in the middle of the biggest marijuana operations in my life, and this mess gets dropped in my lap.

Kalish didn't quite understand why he merited such confidences from Angel or what he should do about it. The revelation about Melo confused him, made him wonder about his own connections. He barely knew Melo, who was one of the officers around Noriega who kept away from Kalish and his drug-related friends. Kalish tried to convince Angel that Melo was a rogue elephant, that it was Melo who had double-crossed the cartel, not Noriega.

"Assassinate Noriega? That's crazy," Kalish said. "He told us he didn't know about the lab. Now I don't know if he's lying, but it stands to reason he didn't know. Why would he have busted the lab and lost all that business with you? Melo is the problem, not Noriega."

"No, no, no," Angel assured him. "We told Melo it was crazy. Ochoa is adamantly opposed to it. We have no interest in setting up a dictatorship in Panama. It's absurd."

Kalish knew he had to get the information, however absurd, to Noriega as quickly as possible. César Rodríguez could handle it. He took Angel and Zambrano to César's house and left. The next morning he got a frantic call from Angel's wife, who was staying in the Marriott with her two children. "Where is Guillo? He didn't come home last night. You've got to find him!"

Kalish raced to César's house and found him in bed. He woke him up and demanded to know what had happened. Rodríguez was groggy, languid. Two nights of stress and no sleep had aggravated his ulcer. "G2 came again. And as soon as they heard the story about Melo wanting to assassinate Noriega, they arrested everybody," Rodríguez said. Zambrano and Angel and the two Mendez brothers were all in custody.

Kalish's first reaction was a groan; his second was fear. He could imagine no greater disaster. His first major dealing with the cartel and he gets them arrested. "We've got to get them out, fast," Kalish said. "Angel is my responsibility. I'm going to get some serious pressure from these people."

César mumbled that he was going to take care of it and shut his eyes in exhaustion.

When Kalish got home, he started making calls. The first calls were to ensure his own protection. He felt caught in the middle, and he didn't know who might hold him responsible for what had happened. He hired a half dozen experienced bodyguards to station themselves around his house armed with Uzi machine pistols. By midafternoon, he learned that César Rodríguez was so sick he had been admitted to the hospital. When he got to the hospital, César was half conscious and barely recognized him. He was relieved to find Kiki Pretelt at the hospital.

"My God, Kiki, you're never going to believe this." They went to Pretelt's office to talk.

"Kiki, here's the problem, I did this in good faith. If they don't release those Colombians, they are going to kill me, they're going to kill César, they're going to kill you. If you deal straight with them, you won't have any problems, but if you betray them or cheat them, they will kill you. It's a known fact. Sooner or later, they get you.

"Okay, here's what we've got to do. You've got to get Noriega on the phone and talk to him. Explain that these people have to be released immediately. Explain that they told us about Melo and the assassination talk in good faith, to warn Noriega, to help him out."

Noriega was easy to reach. Pretelt dialed 282338, Noriega's private line at PDF headquarters. Noriega carried special uplink equipment whenever he traveled to ensure immediate, secure communications with his office. Noriega took the call in Paris, a few days after his official interview with French president François Mitterrand.

In Panama, the arrest of the Colombians created a delicate problem for Colonel Roberto Díaz Herrera. In Noriega's absence he was officially in command, but he bore the responsibility uneasily. His relationship with Noriega was defined by rivalry and coconspiracy. While serving shoulder to shoulder for two decades, Noriega and

Díaz Herrera had shared many drinking parties but few confidences. During Torrijos's life, they disputed over who had more intimate access to their leader, and neither could be sure the other had not come out ahead. Díaz Herrera took an early advantage—he had entered the National Guard two years before Noriega, which gave him seniority; he was also Omar Torrijos's first cousin—but early along the way, Noriega had slipped past him. Now, with Noriega the commander in chief, Díaz Herrera found it galling to serve as number two. He and Noriega needed each other to hold the expanding Defense Forces together and to keep a grip on the changing civilian political scene. They were allies on the most fundamental issue: that no amount of democratization would be allowed to weaken the stability, power and perquisites of the military institution they had inherited from Torrijos.

Several years later, Díaz Herrera would remark about the strange coincidences surrounding Noriega's extended trips abroad. Something major and sticky always seemed to crop up in Noriega's absence. The Melo imbroglio was one of the first situations he was thrust into with the uncomfortable feeling that he was being kept deliberately in the dark. Díaz Herrera was suspicious by nature, a political animal who always watched his back. His greatest worry was not that a fellow officer might be involved in drug trafficking but that Noriega might be setting a trap to discredit him and ruin his chances to become Noriega's successor.

Díaz Herrera was first confronted with the Melo problem a few days after Noriega and his entourage had left for Europe. Lieutenant Colonel Marcos Justine brought him a bizarre story. Justine was the PDF's fourth-ranking officer, just behind Díaz Herrera and Melo. He held the key post of G3, head of PDF administration and finances. Justine said that two friends of Melo's, Gabriel Mendez and Ricardo Tribaldos, had come to him shaking with fear and had said they were in deep trouble with the Colombian "mafia." They said they were partners with Melo and that he had failed to carry out a contract with the Colombians. They were vague, according to Justine, but made allusions to drugs and to political contributions. The two men put a large suitcase in front of Justine and opened it. It was full of U.S. dollars. They said it contained $2 million, and they begged Justine to take it off their hands and return it to Melo's Colombian contacts.

Justine told Díaz Herrera he didn't know anything about Melo's private business affairs and didn't want to get involved. He said Mendez and Tribaldos took the money away in the trunk of their car.

Even in wide-open Panama, businessmen did not drive around with suitcases full of $50 bills. Díaz Herrera knew the two men must be in big trouble, and it clearly wasn't the police or the DEA they were afraid of. Determined not to get involved, Díaz Herrera ordered Justine to inform Noriega about the money directly by phone.

That call was one of a series to Noriega about Melo and the dispute with the cartel. It is safe to assume that Lieutenant Colonel Ow Young and Inspector Quiel informed Noriega about their first meeting with Angel. But it was the second meeting, the talk of assassination and the arrests that moved Noriega and his men to action.

One of the first moves was an attempt to build evidence that Noriega had no knowledge of Melo's dealings with the cartel. Quiel arranged for one of his Colombian prisoners to place a call to Melo in Paris. As tape recorders rolled and Quiel listened in, the prisoner—it could not be learned which one—asked Melo directly whether he had obtained Noriega's authorization for the operation of the Darién laboratory. Melo said no, he had not even broached the subject with Noriega.

Noriega and his party, including Melo, then flew to Israel for a scheduled five-day visit. From there he called Díaz Herrera. "Roberto, they tell me Melo is mixed up in this scandal. I'm sending him back home so you can investigate what his responsibility was," Noriega said. Díaz Herrera tried to pass the buck back to Noriega. He argued that Noriega, as Melo's commanding officer, was in a much better position to interrogate Melo and straighten out the mess. But Noriega said that Melo would be on the next plane to New York and that he should be picked up there, taken to Panama and placed before a trial of his peers—his fellow officers.

For Díaz Herrera, the Melo business was becoming as sticky and stringy as eating a ripe mango without a knife. Díaz Herrera had used his high position to enrich himself, as had virtually every PDF officer above the rank of captain, but he had been careful to steer clear of such criminal activity as drug trafficking. He was determined not to allow himself to be saddled with opposition charges that he was covering up for drug activity he had no part of.

When Melo arrived on a commercial flight from New York, Díaz Herrera convened the entire general staff, the *estado mayor,* in the officers' mess at PDF headquarters. It was just after lunch and a usual time for the officers to meet.

Díaz Herrera seated Melo at the opposite end of the table from himself. The informal trial began with some desultory questioning centering on two issues: the assassination plot and the $5 million in payoffs. Melo said the alleged plot was an invention by criminal minds, and he asked them to recall his record of loyalty to the PDF and especially his personal service to Noriega. He wiggled and dodged the questions about money. Those were legitimate Colombian businessmen, he began. They wanted to make a contribution to the PDF's favored candidate in the recent presidential campaign. Of course they expected favors down the road. If there is any money missing or that should be returned, it is the fault of those slippery characters Tribaldos and Mendez, he said. They took a big chunk of it. He denied it had anything to do with Darién and the shipments of ether.

Díaz Herrera made a sign to Lieutenant Colonel Ow Young, of G2, who was seated at the table. Ow Young, a slight, humorless man of Chinese descent, brought in his prisoners, the Colombians whose arrest and interrogation were the source of Noriega's charges against Melo. Guillermo Angel and José Eduardo Zambrano strode in and remained standing in front of the table, facing Melo. They were not there to answer questions but to accuse, not to beg for freedom but to demand retribution.

Zambrano, looking straight at Melo, stated that he personally had given the money to Melo. (Later, PDF investigators claimed that the Colombians had been so blatant about the payoff that they had driven into the parking lot at command headquarters to deliver the suitcases with the $5 million to Melo.) Then Zambrano opened up on Melo, as if he were a boss dressing down an employee.

"Usted es un chiquillo! You, you are just a boy. I thought we were making a deal with a man. You made all sorts of guarantees, but they

didn't last very long, did they? You are a *chiquillo* who doesn't understand how serious it is to do business with our people. We made a big investment and we don't like losses."

Díaz Herrera watched Melo's face fight to maintain control. Melo started to speak, his voice caught and he remained silent. The other officers looked away, squirming at the spectacle of a fellow officer's humiliation. Then Angel addressed the table. "I'm sure you will know how to make this right. For starters, we want the money and confiscated equipment back, as soon as possible," he said softly. Then he and Zambrano were escorted out by Lieutenant Colonel Ow Young.

Díaz Herrera wondered at the scene he had just witnessed. At Noriega's orders, a Colombian drug trafficker, supposedly in custody of G2, was given a forum to dress down a colonel as if he were a boss scolding a hireling. During the time since the Colombians' arrest, Ow Young, dealing directly by phone with Noriega, had given Díaz Herrera only the sketchiest reports about what was going on. Díaz Herrera ended the meeting with a "verdict" that Melo be stripped of his rank and expelled from the PDF without pension. After the meeting, he took Justine aside. "About that business with the suitcase that you told me about," he said, "since you are the one they came to, you take care of it from here on out." A short while later, one or several suitcases were brought to the officers' mess and several officers sat around the table counting piles of money.

Steven Kalish, barricaded in his house out of fear the cartel would take revenge on him for getting their people arrested, practically shouted with joy when he saw a PDF Land-Rover pull up and Angel get out. With him were Zambrano, Inspector Quiel and another PDF officer. Angel was carrying a suitcase.

Kalish gave them all coffee and something to eat. When they were alone, Angel thanked Kalish for his help as a mediator. He opened the bag to show it was full of cash—$2 million, he said, as a down payment on the total owed. He said that Noriega had ordered total restitution of the cash and helicopter captured in the raid and that they were working on getting back some of the confiscated ether. Later, he paid Kalish and his two partners $500,000 for their help. They joked about how close the affair had come to being a total disaster to all. Several days later, Kalish gathered up Angel, his wife and two children and flew them to Aruba.

For Kalish and Angel, talking cocaine deals on the beach in Aruba in the first days of July 1984, the episode was over. But in Panama, the press and the public were getting the first incomplete accounts of what had transpired. The controversy over drug trafficking that five years later would be a firestorm had just reached the brushfire stage.

The first tip was the publication on June 30 in the PDF's Order of the Day that Lieutenant Colonel Julián Melo Borbua had been dishonorably discharged. The next day, Colonel Díaz Herrera released a statement saying that Melo had been shown to be "linked with persons involved in international drug trafficking." He said that Melo would be placed at the disposal of civilian authorities for possible prosecution.

The opposition paper, *La Prensa,* noted that "it is the first time in the history of the Defense Forces that a member of the military of Melo Borbua's rank has been discharged because of such charges." Once *La Prensa* and the opposition tabloid, *Extra,* got their teeth into the story, they did not let go. For weeks, stories and editorials accusing the military of drug crimes competed with stories accusing the military of rigging the May presidential election. As usual, facts were hard to come by, but that did not deter the free-swinging opposition press. *La Prensa* claimed to have sources who could tell them what went on in the very meetings between Melo and the Colombian drug bosses, and not surprisingly the results were damning for Noriega. Melo, according to "reports obtained by *La Prensa,*" told the drug dealers that their business arrangements in Panama had collapsed "because Noriega had betrayed them."

The press smelled cover-up when Díaz Herrera announced that he had established that no other members of the PDF were involved with Melo and that Melo, as a former member of the Defense Forces, would face the charges as "just another citizen." The civilian attorney general, Isaac Chang Vega, followed with a disingenuous pronouncement that his first knowledge of the case was from the press. He said Melo was being charged with "illicit association to commit a crime," rather than drug trafficking, because "not a gram of drug has been found."

With Noriega still out of the country, Melo under house arrest and the opposition marshaling its attack, on July 5 another bombshell landed in Panama, this time launched from Colombia. *La Prensa* bannered a story picked up from *El Tiempo,* the Bogotá newspaper, reporting that the most-wanted members of the Colombian cartel, including Jorge Ochoa and Pablo Escobar, had been in Panama for much of the month of May. The drug traffickers, ensconced in suites at Panama City's best hotels, had met with former Colombian president Alfonso López Michelsen and with the Colombian attorney general, Carlos Jiménez Gómez. The traffickers were offering a deal. In its simplest form, the deal called for Colombia to waive prosecution and extradition proceedings against the traffickers; in exchange the traffickers would return billions of dollars of their riches for investment in Colombia. The cartel did not, as has erroneously been reported, offer to pay off Colombia's international debt in exchange for exoneration, but the brazenness of the bribe was not lost on the Colombian press and political circles, which torpedoed the incipient deal with withering sarcasm.

In Panama, the meetings fueled the first public uproar since the 1970s about drugs and allegations of official complicity. It was left to Guillermo Sánchez Borbón, *La Prensa*'s premier columnist, to draw together all the strings into a circumstantial case pointing to PDF complicity. True, conceded Borbón, a lab had been captured, ether confiscated and a high officer dismissed. But no one, he pointed out, was in jail. All those captured at the Darién raid had been released without charges, Melo faced charges no more serious than a traffic ticket and the world's biggest drug smugglers had been sitting out an international manhunt unmolested in Panama. A statement by the Alliance of the Democratic Opposition, the opposition political coalition, said that the recent events "suggest a vast network of complicities under the protection of the most powerful official personalities, who have not shirked from staining the prestige of the nation or the professional integrity of the Defense Forces." Another *La Prensa* column tied in a June 15 seizure at Miami International Airport of a Panamanian cargo airliner, INAIR, loaded with almost

3,000 pounds of cocaine hidden in freezers. "To judge from the news in the press . . . Panama has turned into a hub of international narcotics trafficking," the front-page editorial concluded.

At this time the country's most powerful personality, General Noriega, was winding up his busy tour. The main public business was ended when he departed from Israel after a meeting with Prime Minister Yitzhak Shamir on June 27. He held protocol meetings in London on July 2 and 3. But despite Díaz Herrera's urging that he return, Noriega refused to cut short the trip. In addition to the publicly scheduled stops, Noriega had arranged a high-level secret trip to meet with Fidel Castro in Cuba. Additional officers and civilians, who had flown directly to Cuba from Panama to provide staff support for the meetings, included Captain Felipe Camargo, and political adviser José Blandón, who showed up in official photos with Castro.

Whatever secret business was conducted in Cuba, Noriega considered it more important than returning to regain control of a situation involving drug charges that would dog him until finally plunging the country into chaos. Blandón, by later turning against Noriega and testifying about his former boss to Congress and a Miami grand jury, would be a major vehicle for making the charges against Noriega stick. Among many other accusations, Blandón would allege that during Noriega's secret stopover in Havana, Castro met with both Noriega and Blandón to offer detailed advice about how to resolve the dispute with the Colombian cartel—but that account is uncorroborated and inconsistent with other accounts and facts.

Noriega finally arrived in Panama at 11:45 the morning of July 6, after an absence of almost twenty days. He had ordered Díaz Herrera to receive him with an elaborate military ceremony. The press was alerted and was there in force for the arrival and promised press conference. The general projected energy and confidence as he stepped down the ramp of the Boeing 727 to march between long lines of crisply disciplined troops. For the coming moment, at which he would confront the most serious accusations of corruption ever directed at the Panamanian military, Noriega eschewed his uniform and dressed in gleaming white—from his straw hat and open-necked shirt to his loose linen trousers and ivory loafers. Inside a hangar, behind a long table at which he arrayed a dozen of his top officers, Noriega presided over the press conference. To his right, Díaz Herrera; to his left, Marcos Justine. Two dozen other officers and civilian advisers filled the space behind him.

Noriega bantered easily with the press, chiding them good-naturedly when they insisted on questioning him almost exclusively about the Melo affair. But he was clearly prepared and seized the offensive.

"Panama," he said proudly, "reaffirms its refusal to let anything prevent it from destroying the barrels of ether or the cocaine labs. [Applause.] This is our doctrine, this is the principle of the Defense Forces. . . . We know that the countries in which the military have made pacts with the drug traffickers are still at a dead end, that the results of the drug trafficking go against society, and that he who takes a peso or a dollar from drug trafficking is entering a dead-end street. Drug trafficking leads to death."

Melo's criminal activities had damaged the entire "Panamanian family," he said, but the Defense Forces could be proud of how the affair was handled: "No one told us we had a drug trafficker in our midst. No one discovered that someone had infiltrated our ranks. We ourselves as a Defense Force, our intelligence services, are the ones who set the trap. We were looking for a shark, but we got a goldfish.

"Therefore, we cannot have any grudges, nor can anyone point at any of the other members of the force, because they had nothing to do with this incident. The children of the members of the general staff do not have to feel ashamed or have any complexes. On the contrary, they can hold their heads up because never in the world or at any time has there been another armed forces that speaks of and points out its own defects."

He was interrupted several times by hearty applause from the largely progovernment press and his own military colleagues. A few weeks later, applause arrived from the United States: "Dear General Noriega: I would like to take this opportunity to congratulate the members of the National Department of Investigations (DENI) for their efforts in the investigation resulting in the largest ethyl ether seizure ever made in the Americas," the letter began. It went on to thank Luis Quiel and other officers by name for "their professionalism, pride, and dedication to the suppression of drug trafficking. . . ."

The letter was signed William French Smith, Attorney General.

CHAPTER 2

THE KID
FROM TERRAPLÉN

This is the image that has stayed with a man who knew Manuel Antonio Noriega personally and professionally for almost thirty years: Noriega has a drink in his hand, Johnnie Walker Black Label, ice, just a little water. It is long after midnight, and he has been drinking for many hours, so his eyes are red rimmed, but they gleam with focus and energy. Noriega is talking, or rather he is interrogating. The other person cannot loosen the hold of Noriega's attention until he has explained all, told all, turned over the subject of conversation to every angle of scrutiny. Noriega questions again, then listens, a not unfriendly smile on his face. He gazes sideways and up from under heavy eyelids, as if skeptical or indifferent, and the ice in his drink clinks back and forth, back and forth, a metronome of encouragement or reproach, depending on the adequacy of what he is hearing. A barely visible gesture, a slightly raised finger, activates a hovering aide, a West Point graduate, to produce within seconds a fresh scotch. The party will go on until Noriega decides it is over. No one of his inner circle of officers will leave, no matter that their wives have long since stopped trying to conceal exasperation and yawns of fatigue.

The topics will be wide ranging and often intriguing, from Eastern philosophy to theories of extraterrestrial life, as Noriega probes a new acquaintance for areas of expertise, fixes on what knowledge he stands to gain, then questions his target to exhaustion. When it is over, he will have dominated the conversation but betrayed almost nothing about himself. He is always the intelligence officer, always at work and on alert. He is friendly, at times self-effacing, yet suspicious of friendships. He has created, defined and strengthened a circle of loyalists in civilian and military life, yet has shied away from ever defining himself, as if he were a stellar black hole absorbing immense amounts of energy but reflecting no light.

In that negative space he has given his enemies a free hand to paint him as the epitome of evil, goading them on to greater fulminations, appearing to glory in the exaggerated power imputed to him. Murderer, torturer, rapist, pederast, deviate, communist, thief, addict, drunk, dope smuggler, devil worshipper—all these epithets had been hurled at him even before he took power. A U.S. newspaper in 1978 headlined its profile of him THE NAME THAT STRIKES INSTANT TERROR. Once he laughingly obliged when an interviewer asked to inspect the crown of his head for the satanic sign of 666. Only one insult could cause him to flinch: *"cara de piña,"* pineapple face, the reference to his cruelly scarred face from a life-long battle with acne.

In one of the few instances when Noriega appeared to bare his soul, he did it with astonishing hubris. At the time of his promotion to head of the National Guard in 1983, he granted a rare interview to *La Prensa* reporter Migdalia Fuentes. He slipped around questions about his youth and family. When she asked, "Who really is Manuel Antonio Noriega?" he answered, *"Ego sum qui sum,* I am who am. I am Manuel Antonio Noriega. I always have been. I have my personal characteristics. There is nothing enigmatic about me." Not only did Noriega unabashedly describe himself in God's words to Moses from the burning bush; he used the expression to the same effect: to conceal his innermost essence while implying the possession of vast power.

In the interview he went on to say that his reputation for inspiring fear came from his former job as Torrijos's chief of intelligence. His disclaimer, of course, only reinforced the image of the all-knowing, all-powerful hatchet man who, since Torrijos's death, lacked even the relative restraint of his more humane mentor. It was as if a dark-skinned J. Edgar Hoover had succeeded John F. Kennedy as president of the United States. He had files on everyone, on former and current presidents, on the kickbacks and shady dealings of even the most upstanding businessmen. No matter that no one had seen the files; it was the certainty of their existence and the threat of their use that gave Noriega power. His enemies even spread the story that he had once kept General Torrijos himself prisoner for several days, a story that defies confirmation but is nevertheless persistently spread.

Noriega is like a malevolently smiling Wizard of Oz, blowing the smoke and whistles and pulling the levers to manipulate his own image from behind a curtain. It is the smile and the wink that infuriate most. The smile can be open, almost timid, disarming, and the wink that often accompanies it intimates that somehow we are all in a big joke together, one that we all get, enemy and ally alike, but that we will play all the way through, feigning appropriate gravity.

It is as if Noriega is saying, "Hey, why all the fuss and worry. How could anyone be afraid of me? Underneath, I'm still just the slum kid from Terraplén."

From the time in 1513 when Vasco Núñez de Balboa took a thirty-mile hike across the isthmus and found the ocean he named the Pacific, Panama has been a point of transience, a place to pass through rather than to be from. Transshipments of gold from Peru to Spain brought Panama City to life as a small port nestled on a point of volcanic rock curling out into the Bay of Panama. The first railroad across the isthmus was built in 1855—in time to accommodate the tens of thousands of fortune seekers rushing from the American east coast to prospect for California gold. The rail link reduced the Atlantic-to-Pacific crossing from three arduous days by mule to four hours.

The jetty and public market built around the railroad's Pacific terminus became the hub of Panama City. And the name Terraplén was given to the maze of narrow streets, plazas and rickety buildings adjacent to the market. Two-story rooming houses of vertical wooden framing were home to those who worked the port, from petty tradesmen and stevedores to prostitutes, all serving the flow of passengers and goods that were Panama's ever-renewable source of riches. By the time Manuel Antonio Noriega was born on February 11, 1936, there was a canal, and the main rail and port traffic had shifted to its mouth, a mile to the west. The bayside neighborhood of Terraplén was seedier but still raucous when "Tony" Noriega was growing up.

Details of his early life are sketchy. His father was said to be an accountant, Ricaurte Noriega, who earned a modest income doing the books for small businesses. His mother, María Moreno, worked as a cook and laundress. It is unclear whether she and Noriega's father were ever married, although as was customary Ricaurte Noriega acknowledged paternity, giving his son the full name, Manuel Antonio Noriega Moreno. Both parents were gone from his life—the circumstances of their departure could not be learned—by the time Noriega was about five. He was raised as an orphan by a relative or godmother he has referred to as Mama Luisa.

In Terraplén, Noriega's poverty did not stand out. Neither did his dark skin. He was born a mixture of black, Indian and Spanish blood that Panamanians call Creole. Later in life, Noriega would point with pride to his humble origins, even commissioning a small book about himself to be published with the title, *El Criollo de Terraplén* ("The Creole of Terraplén"). The neighborhood bustled with activity, and there was no shortage of odd jobs for a boy willing to hustle for spending money. Noriega worked the streets selling newspapers. Without roaming more than a mile from home, the young boy could touch Panama's major centers of power: A few blocks east along the bay was the Palacio de las Garzas, the presidential palace, and the elite Union Club. Walking west, he would come to National Guard headquarters. From there he could walk along Fourth of July Avenue, bordering the unapproachable world of the American-controlled Canal Zone, then loop past the National Legislature on his way home.

Growing up among foreign sailors and prostitutes and with a daily life punctuated with drunkenness and violence, Noriega became street smart without becoming a tough. He was small for his age and tended to be the one the rougher kids picked on. His survival depended on outthinking and outtalking those who threatened him.

But he was caught and beaten enough that by the time he was a teenager he often carried a small pistol.

Mama Luisa, a schoolteacher, instilled bookishness in her young charge as a way to get ahead. A high school classmate remembers him as always neatly dressed and one of a rare breed of students who read all the books assigned and recommended by teachers. His older half-brother, Luis Carlos, also pushed him toward intellectual pursuits—and introduced him to politics. From 1952 to 1955, Manuel Antonio attended the National Institute, considered the best public high school in Panama. The school was also within easy walking distance of Terraplén, near Fourth of July Avenue. At some point during high school, Noriega went to live with Luis Carlos in a rented room. Luis Carlos had also attended the National Institute and was still active there as an organizer for the Socialist party.

Manuel Antonio was a quick recruit to the Socialist party's youth wing. The party was led by one of the great names of Panamanian politics, Demetrio Porras, whose father, Belisario Porras, had created Panama's first broad-based political movement, in the early part of the century, by organizing blacks and urban workers. In the 1950s, Demetrio Porras's party was the nurturing ground for idealistic youth rebelling against the Spanish-blood oligarchy, known derisively as the *rabiblancos,* or "white tails," who controlled most of Panama's economic and political power. The Socialist party's anticommunism and European-style social democratic platform did not make it immune to red-baiting, and the party was banned from electoral lists in 1953. U.S. military intelligence reports later referred to the Socialists as "Marxist oriented" and noted with suspicion Noriega's affiliation.

Noriega did not stand out as a leader in the movement, preferring instead to stick to his books and graduate near the top of his class. But he wrote and published nationalist poems and articles attacking the U.S. presence in Panama as an affront to Panamanian sovereignty. He also took part in rock-throwing attacks against Panamanian police, a fact that was also noted on later U.S. intelligence reports.

His relationship with the Socialist movement was not solely idealistic, however, and may have served as his introduction to the double-dealing that was to characterize most of his adult military career. According to a longtime political ally, Socialist leader Porras was giving Noriega a stipend of $15 a month, perhaps out of compassion for the bright young man without parents, perhaps as an investment in Noriega's political future. The money went a long way in Panama in the 1940s and ensured that Noriega could stay in school. And he soon found another way to profit from his Socialist connections: According to U.S. and Panamanian sources, he allegedly served as a "double agent" who provided inside reports to U.S. intelligence agencies on the activities and plans of his leftist comrades.*

In his graduation yearbook Noriega listed "president of the Republic" among his ambitions, but he indicated no interest in the military. Members of the National Guard were considered more policemen than professional soldiers; only in 1953 was the Panama National Police officially upgraded to become the paramilitary National Guard, and in any case Noriega aspired to become a medical doctor and eventually a psychiatrist. He felt, however, that he faced a stacked deck: A poor mulatto youth trying to compete with the sons of Panama's elite, his failure to gain one of the coveted openings at the University of Panama Medical School remained a permanent source of resentment. In his battles against the opposition thirty years later he would taunt the upper-class *rabiblancos* by saying that their greatest mistake was hoarding all the medical school openings for themselves. Instead, Noriega took courses in medical laboratory technology, hoping for an opportunity to switch into medical school.

In 1956, a former National Institute classmate, Boris Martínez, encountered a disgruntled Noriega working at Santo Tomás Hospital taking blood samples. Noriega told Martínez he had run out of money and could no longer sustain a full course load at the university. He said he had switched to teacher training in science. Martínez spoke enthusiastically about his own career choice. He was about to

---

*During the 1988 campaign, presidential candidate George Bush appeared to confirm this early intelligence relationship when he said, "Seven administrations were dealing with Mr. Noriega. . . . There was no evidence that Mr. Noriega was involved in drugs, no hard evidence, until we indicted him." *The Washington Post,* Sept. 26, 1988. That statement placed Noriega's first U.S. government contacts during the 1953–1960 Eisenhower administration.

graduate from military school in Mexico* and expected to qualify for a commission as a second lieutenant in the Panamanian National Guard. This encounter may have given Noriega the idea for his way out of the life of obscurity that he could see looming ahead.

He had only one political connection to call upon, and he used it. His half-brother, Luis Carlos, had received a political appointment as a minor official in the Panamanian embassy in Peru. Among the meager patronage Luis Carlos was able to dispense were scholarships to Peru's Chorrillos Military Academy. He got one for Manuel Antonio.

In 1958, wearing the somewhat dandified French-style uniform of the Peruvian academy, Noriega began his career studying military engineering. While there, he got to know another Panamanian officer candidate, Robert Díaz Herrera, who was studying at the Peruvian Police Academy. The Panamanians felt like second-class citizens among the Peruvians, with their proud military history going back to the wars of independence against Spain; and unlike the Panamanian candidates, many of the Peruvian students were sons of the most upper-crust families. They made fun of Noriega's unpolished manners, pocked face and Negroid features—seldom seen in that part of South America. Peruvian attitudes were also a source of pain for Noriega's half-brother, Luis Carlos: His open homosexuality, which had been accepted with little more than occasional snickers in Panama, became a matter of scandal in less tolerant Peru and marred his fledgling diplomatic career. According to Díaz Herrera, Noriega overcompensated for the ridicule his brother was suffering and adopted a "supermacho" exterior of talking gruff and carefully disguising all signs of weakness. For all of the handicaps he faced in his four years in Peru, however, Noriega managed to forge many lasting friendships among the Peruvian students and would return for regular reunions with them even after they had all become high-ranking officers.

When Noriega returned to Panama, in 1962, he immediately joined the National Guard as a common soldier. He received his commis-

---

*Panama did not at that time have its own military academy and depended on institutions in other Latin countries to train its officer corps.

sion as second lieutenant in September of that year and was assigned
to Colón, Panama's second largest city and the Atlantic opening to
the canal. His commander in the Colón garrison was the handsome
son of a schoolteacher from Veraguas Province, Major Omar Torrijos Herrera.

"En el país de los ciegos, el tuerto es rey," goes the typically
sardonic Spanish saying. "In the land of the blind, the cross-eyed
man is king." In the 1960s the Panamanian National Guard lacked
intellectual vision, and men like Torrijos and Noriega quickly recognized each other as beacons of intelligence and idealism above a sea
of mediocrity. Torrijos, at thirty-three only a few years older than
Noriega, was a visionary with a passion for geopolitical strategy and
social conflict rather than for military struggle. His one involvement
in combat, as a young lieutenant in the late 1950s, marked him for
life. Torrijos was ordered to hunt down and crush a group of student
revolutionaries. He later reflected on the incident in a letter to Senator Edward Kennedy:

> I was wounded, the most seriously wounded, and also the most
> convinced that these young slain guerrillas were not the real cause but
> rather the symptom of discontent. I also thought, as I read their
> proclamation, that if I hadn't been wearing a uniform, I would have
> joined them in the trenches. This was where my determination arose
> that if one day I would direct our Armed Forces, I would unite them
> with the best interests of the country.

Torrijos had absorbed his brand of eclectic Latin American class
analysis while a student at the Santiago Normal School, the provincial teachers college in his small home city. Juan Materno Vásquez,
a black student leader, organized a group of students in a literary
discussion group called the Youth Idealist Vanguard. Torrijos and
the others studied the works of José María Mariátegui, whose books,
written in the 1920s, gave an authentically Latin American interpretation to the ferment of the Russian Revolution. They read many
other Spanish and Central American poets and novelists and learned
the ABCs of Marxism from the *Communist Manifesto.* Other teachers, refugees from Spanish fascism, contributed their insights about

the ideals and failures of Republican Spain's experiment in radical
social change. The result of this ideological mishmash was the left-of-
center pragmatism Torrijos would propagate years later with such
simplistic but effective slogans as "We believe not in class struggle
but in struggle in the classroom" and "We are not against the rich;
we are for the poor."

Like Noriega, Torrijos had entered the military as perhaps the only
outlet available for his ample ambitions of personal advancement, and
only remotely to promote his still-vague ideas for social change. The
two men complemented each other. Noriega was calculating and
utterly amoral; Torrijos was intuitive and passionate. Noriega's intellect was oriented to tactics; Torrijos was inclined to grand strategies.
Noriega loved to draw flowcharts, to master the organizational in-
tricacies of a task; Torrijos set goals and objectives according to
deeply held principles and values. Torrijos became Noriega's military
mentor, protector and guru, and for the next four years, Torrijos made
sure that Noriega was always assigned to his command.

Notwithstanding Torrijos's inchoate radicalism, the Panamanian
National Guard in the early 1960s was hardly a caldron of intellectual
idealism. Noriega's first job was to supervise the patrol cars of the
traffic police; most traffic tickets were paid on the spot, as bribes to the
patrolmen rather than as fines to the public treasury. English and
Spanish were mixed in the stock phrase for offering a bribe, *"Dame un
chan-say,"* or "Give me a chance," which more accurately translates
as "Give me a break." A several-dollar bribe was not mandatory, but
was always lower than the cost of the fine, and the "chance" was
seldom passed up. Noriega's troopers kept track of the seedy bars,
whorehouses and cheap gambling joints that serviced the sailors on
leave while their ships waited their turn to pass through the canal.

The world to officers like Torrijos and Noriega was filled with
petty corruption, hard drinking and sexual exploits. The environment was not unfamiliar to a street veteran like Noriega, but for
some reason, his first years in the National Guard were unhappy,
conflict-ridden times of struggle with his internal and external de-
mons. Without the rapport and protection of Torrijos, it is unlikely
the young second lieutenant would have survived as an officer. Even
by Panama's lax standards, Noriega was in trouble almost from the

first days of his assignment to Colón. He was mean when he was drunk, and he was drunk almost every night. Sex was easy and cheap for a swaggering officer prowling the portside bars, but Noriega gained a reputation for mixing violence with sex. One incident made the papers briefly before being hushed up. A streetwalker charged Noriega with raping and beating her in a patrol car after she was placed under routine arrest. Torrijos got Noriega out of that mess, but in January 1963, barely three months after his commission, Noriega's drinking and brutality were so out of control that Torrijos punished him with thirty days' confinement to quarters.

A few months later, Torrijos was given a new, more prestigious command as chief of the National Guard's North Zone on the border with Costa Rica. The zone encompassed the provinces of Chiriquí, Panama's richest agricultural region, and Bocas del Toro, where the vast banana plantations of the United Fruit Company were located. Noriega was transferred with him and again put in charge of the traffic police.

Torrijos also arranged for the transfer of Lieutenant Roberto Díaz Herrera, who was his cousin and a protégé whose intelligence and knack for practical politics he valued. Noriega and Díaz Herrera renewed the friendship they had established in Peru, but it was a relationship always tinged with rivalry. Díaz Herrera perceived that Noriega, who was several years older, resented the fact that the younger man was already a first lieutenant and addressed Torrijos with the familiar Spanish tú instead of the formal Usted still used by Noriega. Off duty, they spent time together drinking and chasing women. Díaz Herrera recalls Noriega making an open play for a woman he was seeing. When he called Noriega on it, Noriega said, "I want her. How important is she to you?" Díaz Herrera replied, "Today a lot, tomorrow who knows." The upshot was that Noriega waited six months, until Díaz Herrera gave him the go-ahead, then offered the woman a job in his section in order to win her as a lover.

Noriega made little attempt to conform to the conservative mores of the province and the small-town atmosphere of its capital, David. And he had not left his darker urges behind in Colón. This time it wasn't a portside prostitute, but an adolescent town girl he forced to have sex with him. The girl's parents were not rich, but they were assertive enough to seek the help of a priest and a prominent physician, who denounced the rape directly to the commander in chief of the National Guard, Colonel Bolívar Vallarino, in Panama City. They demanded criminal charges and Noriega's removal from the National Guard. Again, Torrijos stepped in. He met with Noriega's accusers and, using his friendship with the physician, got them to accept a far lesser punishment for Noriega: exile to a remote outpost in Bocas del Toro for several months until the community's outrage had cooled.

Back in Chiriquí in an election year, 1964, Noriega was disciplined again for misconduct with a political color. Chiriquí was the home of Arnulfo Arias, a coffee farmer and two-time president who combined populist politics with baiting the military. Arias was gearing for another run for the presidency against the party of the current president, Rodolfo Chiari. Chiari's party pressed Torrijos to harass the "Arnulfistas," as they were called, in an attempt to break their political momentum. Torrijos assigned the task to Noriega.

Noriega's men arrested dozens, including many prominent citizens such as teachers and lawyers and farmers; unlike the student radicals Torrijos helped to wipe out in the 1950s, the Arnulfistas were part of Panama's mainstream. Some prisoners said they had been tortured; others said they had been raped in the prisons by common criminals. When reports of mistreatment leaked out, there were protest marches. Torrijos publicly claimed that the mistreatment was an aberration and would be investigated. Privately, he confided to a fellow officer that Noriega was responsible for the brutality and would be disciplined. Noriega was relieved of duty for ten days; this slap on the wrist was not made public but became part of the U.S. Army Intelligence file on Noriega.

Torrijos may have indeed seen Noriega's potential as an intelligence officer during the young lieutenant's brief foray into political repression, but after three years in the National Guard Noriega had failed to measure up to whatever expectations Torrijos had for him. Still drinking heavily and rapidly gaining a reputation as a thug, Noriega had yet to win his first promotion. In an attempt to help him shape up, Torrijos sent Second Lieutenant Noriega to take a jungle operations course at the U.S. Army School of the Americas in the

Canal Zone. The streets of Terraplén had not prepared Noriega for the rain forest. He performed miserably in practical tests that required mastery of jungle survival techniques, finishing 147th out of a class of 161. In the key course, Jungle Navigation, he received only 5 of 100 points—he must have gotten very, very lost.

Then, in 1966, Noriega abruptly pulled together his personal and professional lives. He got his first full-time assignment as an intelligence officer, he got his promotion to first lieutenant and he met a bright young high school teacher named Felicidad Sieiro, the daughter of Spanish immigrants who had a small business in David. Felicidad translates, appropriately, as "happiness," and Noriega's relationship with her, perhaps more than any other single factor, put him on track. They married and had the first of three daughters in 1967.

An even more felicitous match was Noriega's new job as intelligence chief in the Guard's North Zone. Torrijos had at last found a productive job for his erratic protégé; Noriega had discovered a vocation that suited and fulfilled him perfectly. His main task was to penetrate and disrupt the socialist-oriented unions that had organized most of the twelve thousand banana workers on the plantations of the United Fruit Company. Noriega possessed the uncanny ability to absorb information, size up the options available to an adversary, place himself in the other person's shoes and astutely anticipate probable courses of action. The Chiriquí intelligence section under Noriega was Panama's first serious intelligence operation and was the immediate antecedent to the full-fledged national intelligence branch, G2, which gained importance after 1970.

Just as Noriega's career was relaunched, however, Torrijos was promoted to a staff job at general staff headquarters. His replacement in Chiriquí, and Noriega's new chief, was Major Boris Martínez, a former classmate of Noriega's at the National Institute. Martínez cracked down on Noriega's drinking and kept him working hard in the intelligence section. Martínez was a fervent anticommunist and he found no lack of enthusiasm from Noriega on that score. Noriega went back to the School of the Americas in 1967 to take the military counterintelligence and infantry officers' courses—this time graduating near the top of the class. From his counterintelligence instructor he earned the comment: "outstanding."

There are plausible reports that Noriega at this time reestablished his activity as a double agent, sharing with U.S. agencies his intelligence product on the potential "leftist threat" of the banana workers. The existence, if not the content, of his relationship with the U.S. military is confirmed in a 1976 U.S. Army Intelligence report on Noriega. At one point the document notes that "his record of association with U.S. military goes back at least 15 years" and elsewhere that "Noriega has maintained a friendly and cooperative relationship with U.S. military personnel since prior to joining the GN [National Guard] in 1962."

The lives and careers of National Guard officers like Torrijos, Noriega and Díaz Herrera mattered little as yet in the overall scheme of things in Panama, but this would soon change. Torrijos's rise from obscure provincial guardsman to charismatic national leader was a uniquely Panamanian story, involving the country's volatile mix of racial, class and nationalistic politics against the backdrop of the overweaning presence and influence of the United States.

Until Torrijos, the power centers in Panama were the presidential palace, the *rabiblanco* elite and the U.S. embassy. Since 1903, Panama had been ruled as a kind of businessman's republic: Civilian presidents, usually sponsored by the previous incumbent, followed each other in and out of office. Violence was seldom part of the equation, and in the few instances when the military stepped in to shore up or kick out a leader, it was in the Latin American tradition of tipping the scales in support of a more favored political faction. There had been only one president from the ranks of the National Guard: José Antonio Remón, who was assassinated in 1955. The presidents and power brokers tended to come from a pool of men with the same few last names.* They were all white, of European

*There were, for example, two presidents each named Arias and Arosemena, three named Chiari. The Arias family controlled coffee, the Arosemena shipping and the Chiari sugar. Other powerful names included the Duques and Eletas (publishing), the Boyds (cattle and importing), the Galindos (construction materials, containers) and the Delvalles (sugar).

descent, in a country whose population of less than two million people is almost 90 percent mixed race, or *mestizo*. Collectively, they were the oligarchy and did not shy from describing themselves with that term. All major participants, their families and business partners belonged to the by-invitation-only Union Club, whose grand dining rooms and drinking halls overlooked the Pacific from a majestic perch on Panama Bay, not far from the presidential palace.

Although elections were held like clockwork and an opposition candidate occasionally won, vote rigging by the incumbents was taken for granted. A "Panamanian victory" was an election margin so large it could not be thrown out by government-controlled vote counters, and it was not unusual for the vote counters to try for two weeks or more before conceding that an unfavored candidate had indeed won. The slogan was "It's not who wins that counts; it's who counts that wins."

The system was corrupt, but hardly more corrupt than many in Latin America. The poor were less hopeless, the rich less baronial, the elite less lily white, the military less repressive. Politics had barely recognizable ideologies and resembled more the art of the deal. The threat of communism, so much a concern in other countries, consisted of the Moscow-line People's party, with about five hundred members, most of them easily identifiable intellectuals at the University of Panama. Unions were weak, peasants were unorganized and the Catholic Church minded its own business. Panama's national life existed as the perishable fruit around the durable center that was the Canal and U.S. investment.* The symbol of the nearly total intertwining of Panama's economy with that of the United States was, and remains, the U.S. dollar, which circulated as Panama's national currency.

But in the late 1960s the comfortable, irresponsible rule of the oligarchy began to collapse; the motivating causes were quintessen-

*Of the three largest employers in Panama, two were under U.S. control: the Panama Canal and the Chiriquí Land Company (United Fruit), with more than ten thousand employees each. Only the bloated Panamanian government bureaucracy had more. No other Panamanian enterprise was even close. U.S. direct investment in Panama was by far the greatest in Latin America on a per capita basis.

tially Panamanian, having more to do with personal ambition than political ideology. Indeed, the leaders of the oligarchy had tried to adjust to the wave of heightened social urgency that was sweeping Latin America. Fearful of the threat of a Castroite revolution and nudged to reforms by the American-sponsored Alliance for Progress, Liberal President Roberto Chiari, who had won a "Panamanian victory" in 1960, attempted a low-cost housing program with U.S. AID funding. His successor, Marco Robles, went even further, proposing business tax reform that for the first time would have taxed even Chiari's protected sugar refineries. But the modest reforms caused howls of recrimination. Amid charges that the Liberal technocrats had turned against the business elite, the oligarchy split down the middle.

So it was that in 1968 the wild card of Panamanian politics, Arnulfo Arias, was elected to the presidency for the third time. Arias was Panama's caudillo, "leader" by virtue of sheer popular magnetism rather than political program or organization. Arnulfo (the use of his first name denoting respect and affection) had attained his first presidency in 1940 as a professed admirer of European fascism and promptly engineered the adoption of a new constitution enshrining authoritarianism, nationalism and disenfranchisement of many non-whites. He had also tried to throttle the National Guard, which overthrew him in 1941 while he was in Cuba visiting his mistress. The United States had greeted Arias's ouster with undisguised satisfaction, fearing he had Nazi sympathies; in 1949, he was reinstalled in the presidency after a dubious recount of the 1948 election, then impeached after trying again to change the constitution and impose authoritarian rule.* In resisting his overthrow in a bloody shootout

---

*The Arias presidency was also associated with Panama's first narcotics trafficking scandal. Walter LaFeber, *The Panama Canal* (Oxford University Press 1979), p. 112. "Having obtained United States support in late 1949, Arias spent public funds lavishly to build a supposedly impregnable political base. The budget deficit reached $7 million. The Arias family naturally received its share. The President forced owners of choice coffee lands to sell out to him, then built a twenty-seven-mile highway and a bridge on the lands at taxpayers' expense. He put a similar squeeze on Panamanian bankers. A huge narcotics and gold smuggling operation developed under the alleged leadership of his favorite nephew, Antonio 'The Druggist' Arias."

with the National Guard, Arias established an undisputed reputation for *cojones* among Panamanians but earned the undying enmity of the National Guard.

Arnulfismo swept to victory in 1968 with the support of farmers, the middle class and antireform elements of the oligarchy, running an artfully populist campaign that positioned him as both antireform and antioligarchy. On assuming power on October 1, Arias immediately reverted to the same high-handed, autocratic tendencies that had aborted his previous régimes.

But it was not his ambivalence toward democracy that caused his final downfall. Four days into his presidency he launched a frontal attack on the National Guard. He removed most of the general staff by retirement or assignment to "diplomatic exile" in foreign posts. Lieutenant Colonel Omar Torrijos, who was first in line for National Guard commander, was told to pack his bags for El Salvador for an assignment as military attaché. Arias and his supporters had not forgotten Torrijos's repressive actions against them a few years earlier.

Under the perceived threat of seeing the National Guard reduced to a subservient institution at the whim of a civilian ruler, Torrijos and several officers led a coup against Arias. The overthrow was bloodless, and Arias was forced to take refuge in the Canal Zone before flying again to exile in Miami. He had been in office only eleven days.

The officer corps rallied almost unanimously to the military rebellion. The Chiriquí garrison, under the leadership of Major Boris Martínez, set the plan in motion by seizing the city of David. The public explanation for the coup—that Arias was leading the country into a dictatorship with the participation of Nazis and Communists—was baseless, but served to reveal the ideological confusion of the military. In fact, the National Guard had not acted on behalf of any civilian faction or ideology but simply out of self-preservation.

A junta was quickly assembled, but Torrijos, as new National Guard commander, and Boris Martínez were really in charge in an uneasy power-sharing arrangement. The junta promised elections, but when that promise was shown to be empty after three months, the civilians in the government resigned. Panama faced the mounting reality of permanent military dictatorship.

Arnulfo loyalists launched a guerrilla uprising in Chiriquí that was to last for a year. The new régime filled the jails with politicians, shut down the press and banned political parties. And members of the junta fought over the reins of power. Martínez, convinced that Torrijos was too soft and would open up the military to corruption, began to project himself as a messianic leader who was both anti-Yankee and anticommunist. Without Torrijos's approval, Martínez went on television to announce a radical land reform program. The next morning, February 25, 1969, Torrijos moved against him. He gathered his officers in his office, then summoned Martínez. When Martínez entered, he was handcuffed and gagged. By noon, he was on a plane for Miami.

Torrijos groped for a program less likely to antagonize the United States, while reaching out to create and consolidate a base of civilian support. That base, he knew, could never again grow out of the cabals formed over dinner and scotch at the Union Club. He expropriated the club's posh bayside property and converted the grounds into a recreation center for officers and their families. Torrijos extended a hand down rather than up, to those of his own background and that of the great majority of the National Guard troops: the middle-class teachers and government clerks, the Antillean blacks who Arnulfo had once rewritten the constitution to exclude, the mestizo and mulatto workers who had never had a political movement, let alone a government, of their own.

The military coup put Lieutenant Manuel Noriega's career on the fast track. Suddenly, the task of intelligence officer in Chiriquí became crucial to the National Guard's survival in power. He was under Martínez's command the day of the coup and participated in securing the city of David and Chiriquí Province, Arias's most important power base. When a group of Arnulfistas attacked a military outpost on October 11 to begin guerrilla resistance to the takeover, Noriega was given the duty of tracking down the rebels and their supporters. Promoted to captain, he assumed command of the militarily powerful North Zone, which included Chiriquí. With typical thoroughness, Noriega wiped out the rebellion by the end of 1969. The unprecedented campaign of repression resulted in dozens of deaths and reports of torture.

By mid-December 1969, Torrijos felt confident enough to embark on a junket to Mexico for a few days of relaxation. His entourage included three cronies: his friend, Demetrio "Jimmy" Lakas, who was head of Social Security and would be named president in 1970; a young black officer, Major Rubén Darío Paredes; and Fernando Eleta, the television and publishing magnate who was one of Torrijos's few allies among the oligarchy. The group attended the Clásico del Caribe horserace—in which two Panamanian horses were running—and Torrijos arranged to meet his favorite comedian, Cantinflas.

They were in Mexico only two days when a coup began to unfold in Panama. The morning of December 15, Lieutenant Colonel Ramiro Silvera and Lieutenant Colonel Amado Sanjur, who ranked just below Torrijos, took control of National Guard headquarters and announced that they were in charge. Torrijos, they said, had become too powerful and was leading the country into a procommunist dictatorship. They cited recent statements by Torrijos in favor of compulsory unionism and his appointment of "communists" to the government, a reference to the Labor Minister Rómulo Escobar Bethancourt, a former member of the People's party.

Like most barracks coups, virtually the entire scenario was played out over the phone. First the plotters called key garrisons around the country to inform them that they had taken over. The majors in command of troops were then faced with defining themselves, either for Torrijos or for the new commanders. Each officer then looked to his most trusted comrades to see which way to go, the cardinal rule: put off a decision just long enough to make sure one ended up on the side of the winner. The importance of each officer was measured by how many troops he had under arms. Not a shot need be fired in anger; the final tally would determine whether Torrijos or his challengers had the greater force of arms. Silvera and Sanjur may have assumed that their task was simple and that Torrijos would be unable to muster his forces by long distance.

Indeed, Torrijos, in his hotel in Mexico City, found that his calls to Panama were not put through. He tried frantically to charter a plane back to Panama. Finally his friend Fernando Eleta used his connections with a telephone satellite company in Washington, D.C., to put through a call to National Guard headquarters in David. Torrijos described the call in a later interview: "I reached Noriega at the number 237021 in David. Noriega said that even if he had to make the province independent he would be waiting for me in David. . . . 'Come quickly, and don't call anymore, because here we have burned our ships in favor of the true commander of the Guard, which is you.' "

By four in the afternoon, Torrijos and Paredes arrived in El Salvador in a Mexican airplane. A delegation of four Panamanian majors was waiting at the airport. Three of the officers said they had been dispatched by the plotters to arrest Torrijos, but they pledged their loyalty to him. As dusk was gathering, Torrijos and his small group of supporters had to find a pilot willing to make the four-hour flight to David. The Mexican pilot who had flown them to El Salvador was unfamiliar with Panama and unwilling to land at night in an unlighted airport. The problem was solved when they located an American pilot who had flown many times into David and was willing to go along as navigator to guide the Mexican pilot. At 8:17, Torrijos, Paredes and the two pilots climbed into the two-engine plane and took off into the darkness.

In Panama, the telephoning continued. Noriega spoke several times during the early morning to Sanjur and Silvera, who at one point assured him that Noriega's brother, Luis Carlos, had been named the new minister of labor and had accepted the post. (That appointment was cited years later to show that Noriega's loyalty to Torrijos was not total and that he may have vacillated in those early hours between Torrijos and the coup leaders. Paredes added to the speculation in an interview in which he said he reached Noriega from El Salvador and "noticed something strange about his replies . . . as if they had a gun on him.") But by noon Noriega was in touch with several other officers who expressed their loyalty to Torrijos and planned to ensure Torrijos's return to power after his landing in David under Noriega's protection.

Late that afternoon, Noriega proclaimed his decision in a short speech to his troops at the David garrison:

> Without beating around the bush, señores, I will tell you that some bad members of the National Guard, in conspiracy with individuals whose illicit businesses and interests have been hurt by the Revolution, have given a coup to overthrow General Omar Torrijos, who at this moment is in Mexico.
>
> But I have gathered you here to tell you it is my decision not to turn over this barracks; and here we will wait for General Torrijos and fight to the last man.

The two-engine Aerotaxi carrying Torrijos approached the airport from the south at about one A.M. on a cloudless, moonlit night. From El Salvador the pilot had flown south and east far out over the Pacific, then turned inland to cover the last twenty-five miles to David. When radio contact was established, Noriega gave the order to light torches and turn on the headlights of dozens of trucks, jeeps and cars along the runway. The plane made a pass and then touched down smoothly. It had fuel remaining for only twenty more minutes of flight.

Noriega saluted as Torrijos opened the door and climbed down off the wing of the plane. Then they embraced, as soldiers around them fired their rifles in the air and shouted, *"Viva el Comandante Torrijos, Viva!"* By six A.M., as Torrijos made contact with key units around the country, the coup dissolved and Torrijos's loyalists in Panama City arrested the major plotters.

On two hours' sleep, Torrijos and most of Noriega's Chiriquí garrison set out for Panama City in an unhurried caravan of cars, buses and military vehicles. In town after town, they were greeted by cheering crowds and more cars joined them. When the motley caravan reached the Bridge of the Americas over the canal, the entrance to Panama City, they found it lined with tens of thousands of well-wishers.

Torrijos's triumphant return captured the imagination of the masses of Panamanians and came to symbolize a new, nationalistic

Panama taking its destiny in its own hands. Torrijos became almost overnight a revolutionary leader who invited comparison with Fidel Castro of Cuba and Gamal Abdel Nasser of Egypt. The day, December 16, would be celebrated in Panama as *El Día de la Lealtad,* the Day of Loyalty, the real anniversary of the revolution that was to transform Panama over the next decade. And it was thanks to the loyalty of Manuel Noriega, more than any other man, that Torrijos was that day propelled onto the stage of history. Noriega was confident that his loyalty would not go unrewarded.

CHAPTER 3

OPERATIONAL CONTROL

In August 1970, Manuel Noriega was promoted to lieutenant colonel and given command of G2, the newly expanded intelligence branch of the National Guard. Noriega, at thirty-four, was now one of the top half dozen officers in Torrijos's inner circle. His troubled period as a junior officer was behind him, and the change was palpable. It had taken him seven years to make captain, then only a year and a half to become one of the youngest members of the general staff. He was goal-directed, efficient, aggressive, and he worked around the clock. He imposed an exhausting work schedule on his subordinates and kept them in line with sarcastic reprimands in front of their peers.

The sloppy uniforms and lax discipline of the past gave way to crisp salutes and double-time execution of orders. "My Colonel, order me" was the standard officers' response when spoken to by Noriega and his peers. Noriega, even more than Torrijos, set the dress code with his neatly tailored fatigues and custom-made boots. Few officers, however, imitated Noriega's one sartorial quirk of bending down the sides of his flat officer's cap into a semicircle.

In the first years after Torrijos had consolidated power, Panama was a tightly run military dictatorship. Politicians unwilling to cooperate in the reformist program of the new régime were arrested or forced into silence or exile. At one time, his jails held as many as sixteen hundred political prisoners—an enormous number in such a small country. A new constitution was written, proclaiming that "Brigadier General Omar Torrijos Herrera, commander in chief of the National Guard, is recognized as Maximum Leader of the Panamanian Revolution." The constitution created a subservient Assembly of Municipal Representatives that met one month a year to rubber-stamp Torrijos's programs. These programs included agrarian reform and a radically rewritten labor code establishing a minimum wage and compulsory collective bargaining. For the first time, the government stepped in with heavy regulation—and invest-ment—in the previously laissez-faire economy.

While Torrijos dispensed the carrots, Noriega—as head of all political police, intelligence and immigration—had the job of wield-ing the stick. Two incidents established Noriega's reputation for ruthlessness. In early 1970, a mentally ill man hijacked a commercial airplane and diverted it to David airport. Noriega refused to allow the aircraft to be refueled. Then, after the hijacker had apparently agreed to surrender, Noriega's men went aboard the plane and coldly executed him. No more hijacked planes landed in Panama for many years.

In the second case Father Hector Gallegos, a young Colombian priest working at an agricultural cooperative in Torrijos's home province of Veraguas, disappeared in June 1971. His independent work with peasants was seen by the National Guard as a threat to its own efforts at rural organization and had hurt the interests of a local merchant who happened to be Torrijos's relative. A peasant had witnessed uniformed men in a National Guard jeep take the priest prisoner. As head of the political police, DENI, Noriega most likely would have been the commander of the soldiers who took Gallegos into custody. The priest's body was never found.

A year later, a priest colleague of Gallegos's said that a National Guard soldier told him what had happened: According to that ver-sion of the event, Gallegos's skull had been fractured from beatings he had received after his arrest. While undergoing emergency sur-gery in the Military Hospital, he had suffered a cerebral embolism that had left him paralyzed. To avoid the scandal of allowing the disabled priest to appear in public, Torrijos had ordered him killed. His body had been thrown from a helicopter far out at sea.

Torrijos put Noriega in charge of the "investigation," the effect of which was to seal off any further information about the case and to attempt to discredit any reports blaming the National Guard. Noriega provided the Panamanian justice minister at the time, Juan Materno Vásquez, with false information that Materno used in a television appearance in which he exonerated the National Guard.

Torrijos also relied on Noriega for help in shaping international policies and entrusted him with handling major tasks in Panama's sensitive relations with the United States. In mid-1970 Noriega traveled to France, England and Israel to arrange weapons purchases for the expanding National Guard. About the same time, he became a member of the Counterintelligence and Counterespionage Organization, an international network of intelligence agencies.

Then, as G2, Noriega was initiated into his official liaison relationship with U.S. intelligence agencies. This was a giant step up from the occasional "asset" role he had played before, in which he had offered information on request and had been paid, usually around $50, on a case-by-case basis. Now he had an official institutional link that included access to large sums of CIA contingency funds. The money was virtually unaccountable in the CIA's budget and was invisible from outside the CIA. It was officially justified as support for "institutional cooperation," but in fact it was a slush fund turned over to the head of the "cooperating" intelligence agency to do with as he desired. Noriega was expected to use the money to enhance G2 programs and to pay agents who produced intelligence for the CIA. But there were no invoices or budgets; indeed little distinguished the payments, which have been estimated at more than $100,000 in some years, from an outright bribe for Noriega's cooperation.

Noriega and G2 also had a close but more open relationship with U.S. Army Intelligence. The point of contact was the liaison branch of the 470th Military Intelligence Group of the U.S. Southern Command, Southcom, the complex of U.S. bases in Panama, home to about nine thousand U.S. troops. The 470th had a dual task: to gather intelligence on Panama, ranging from threats to the Canal to internal National Guard politics; and, probably more important, judging from the resources devoted to it, to establish informal friendships and social access to key National Guard officers. To that end, the unit's headquarters at Fort Amador in Panama City was outfitted with a luxurious bar and lounge. An open invitation was extended to the Guard's officer corps, and the bar gained a wide reputation for its raucous Friday night happy hours, which Noriega often attended. All of the liaison officers spoke near perfect Spanish and most were of Puerto Rican or Chicano origin. They organized baseball and beer parties with their G2 counterparts.

Noriega was quoted by one of the officers of the 470th as saying "the best way to control your enemies is to maintain close contact." He had made the comment to justify his increasingly intimate relationship with Cuba, but it said a lot about his attitude toward contacts with the United States as well. Despite the back-slapping and drinking bouts, the Panamanians were deeply suspicious about U.S. motives toward the Torrijos régime. They had well-founded reports that U.S. officials had been involved with the conservative officers who tried to overthrow Torrijos in December 1969. One U.S. officer, Efrain Angueira, had met with a principal plotter, Lieutenant Colonel Amado Sanjur, only hours before the coup attempt began. Torrijos had considered Angueira a close friend and had felt deeply betrayed. After the coup, Sanjur and several others escaped from a high security jail in a sophisticated commando operation and turned up in the Canal Zone before going into exile in Miami. After that experience, Torrijos shunned all but the most official contacts with U.S. officers. He refused to set foot inside the "occupied" Canal Zone and put strict limits on his senior officers' contacts with U.S. officials.

Noriega was entrusted with the task of being the funnel through which most of the military relationship was conducted. He became close friends with Arturo Esparza, a San Antonio Texan who worked as a civilian employee in the 470th liaison group. They called each other "Art" and "Tony," and Noriega was the godfather of one of Esparza's children, an act that in Latin America denotes the strongest of bonds between men. Esparza's intelligence reports on Noriega, based on a six-year relationship, showed an adversarial relationship but revealed Esparza's deep respect for Noriega and his remarkable foresight about Noriega's future. According to a long biographical report that Esparza prepared for the Defense Intelligence Agency:

> Noriega is intelligent, aggressive, ambitious and ultranationalistic. He is a shrewd and calculating person [deleted].* . . . He has a keen mind and enjoys verbal "jousting" matches with U.S. contacts. He is a persuasive speaker and possesses rare common sense. [ ] he is considered to be a competent officer with excellent judgement and leadership ability. . . . It should be of no surprise to some day find this officer in the position of Commandant of the GN (National Guard) and perhaps a dictator of PN (Panama), provided he survives the typical Latin American military/political machinations.
>
> In the event of a confrontation between the US and PN & current regime, Noriega would be a capable adversary, but it is believed he would endeavor to maintain a limited liaison contact with certain US officials, as has been his policy in the past. . . . The organization of his G2 office reaches out to all sectors of the public domain and provides collection of raw data and intelligence which permits Noriega to be the best informed individual in PN. . . . He is a man of action and not afraid to make decisions.
>
> He is respected by friends and feared by enemies. . . . He depends upon his intelligence organization and close relationship with Torrijos for the maintenance of power. . . . His personal financial status appears excellent. [ ] Although his record of association with US military goes back over 15 years, he is becoming increasingly distant towards the US. He maintains open channels with Cuban, Soviet, Chilean and other political representatives in PN. He is probably the second most powerful man in PN and, therefore, possesses almost unlimited military and/or political potential.

Meanwhile, another U.S. agency was discovering that Noriega had a potential for more than military prowess. In 1970, the Bureau of Narcotics and Dangerous Drugs (BNDD), the predecessor to the DEA, established a new office in Panama and staffed it with two young, Spanish-speaking agents, Bill Place and Rubén Monzon. Armed with a strong mandate from the Nixon administration, which

---

*Brackets indicate material deleted from documents released under the Freedom of Information Act (FOIA).

had declared a "war on drugs," the BNDD was ordered to lead that fight abroad by going to the source of illegal narcotics supply. The mandate specifically directed them to seek out not only the drug traffickers but also to identify and stop any foreign government officials who were protecting and assisting the traffickers. The two agents were told they could count on the full cooperation of the U.S. embassy and the CIA station in Panama.

Place and Monzon were not diplomats; neither were they intelligence agents. Each had been trained as a policeman and brought a beat cop's directness and energy to his work. Although nominally under the supervision of U.S. Ambassador Robert M. Sayre, the agents kept their activities to themselves and their superiors back in Washington.

In February 1971, they set a trap to catch their first big fish. They arranged a baseball game between one of the Canal Zone teams and a team of Tocumen airport employees. Their target was Joaquín Him González, chief of Tocumen's air traffic controllers and deputy chief of Panama's civil aeronautics authority. Place and Monzon had been developing a case against Him González for months. Informants in the United States said he was the man you had to pay off in order to fly drugs in and out of Panama—and Panama, they had discovered, was a major transshipment conduit for heroin and cocaine reaching the United States from South America. Him González was an avid baseball player and unofficial captain of the airport team, and he personally made the call to the Zonian team to confirm the game.

Sunday morning, February 6, Him González, wearing his baseball cap, walked onto one of the neat fields just inside the Canal Zone boundaries near Fort Amador. His jaunty air turned to a look of panic as he recognized Monzon standing on the sidelines, pointing him out to the Zonian police. Him González started to run in a desperate attempt to reach the safety of Panamanian jurisdiction, only several hundred yards away. He didn't make it.

Once in jail, he asked to make two phone calls: one to General Torrijos and one to Foreign Minister Juan Tack. The messages were the same: "Get me out." For the Americans listening in, the calls reinforced the somewhat nervous realization of how big a fish it was they had in their net.

The arrest caused an outburst of anti-U.S. feeling. General Torrijos made a dramatic appearance on television, accusing the United States of kidnapping a Panamanian citizen. The ruse involving the Canal Zone was another example of U.S. disrespect for Panama's sovereignty. If Him González was not released, Torrijos said in a barely veiled threat, Panamanian authorities would go into the Zone and free him themselves.

The normally mild-mannered Ambassador Sayre erupted in angry phone calls to Washington. "It was a serious incident," he said later, "because I was not informed about it. And if the State Department had been informed they didn't tell me. And I might say the [Canal Zone] governor didn't know anything about it either."

Not only had the agents not consulted him about this novel use of the Canal Zone, but they had violated an understanding with the Panamanian government. "One of the commitments the BNDD had made [in setting up the Panama office] was that if they had any indication that a Panamanian official was involved in drug trafficking, they would tell the Panamanian government," Sayre said.

In Washington, bureaucratic lines were being drawn. The State Department and the Department of the Army favored defusing the incident by releasing Him González. State was concerned about a new round of Canal Treaty negotiations that were about to begin. A central issue was the kind of legal jurisdiction the United States would retain, under a new treaty, over Americans and Panamanians inside the Zone. The last thing the United States wanted to press on the Panamanians was its theoretical right to entice a Panamanian citizen into the Zone and arrest him on charges originating in the United States. For State, it was a classic case of the need for diplomatic concerns to prevail over international law enforcement.

The U.S. Army, which had recently signaled its willingness to move major parts of its Panamanian military command structure back to the United States, was horrified to be confronted with the possibility of having to defend the Zone from a Panamanian incursion.

On the other side was BNDD and its superiors in the Department of Justice. "We were pretty naïve" about the implications of targeting foreign officials, said Gerry Strickler, who was supervising the two Panama agents from BNDD headquarters in Washington. "We had no idea of diplomatic protocol."

Strickler and his boss, Andrew Tartaglino, flew to Panama to lend some muscle to their field agents' arguments that Him González was a major player in the narcotics network. The next morning, they met with Ambassador Sayre, then drove with him to the Panamanian Foreign Ministry to meet with Foreign Minister Juan Tack. Also present was Lieutenant Colonel Noriega, whose G2 command included drug enforcement.

The U.S. team built its case. Him González was an important symbol of the U.S. war on drugs. He was known in drug ports all over the world as the man to see if the merchandise was to move safely through Panama. The indictment against him was airtight. They had made sure it wasn't just an informant linking him to drug transactions: A BNDD undercover agent accompanying Him González had witnessed him approving a Texas pilot's plan to obtain a hundred kilos of cocaine. The undercover agent had gotten Him González to discuss past and future shipments, and as a show of good faith, Him González sent a sample of cocaine to the United States. Another piece of evidence involved a Chilean trafficker in Texas who asked an undercover agent to help him place a call to Panama to arrange a shipment. The call was to Him González.

The Panamanian foreign minister, looking sidelong at Noriega every few moments as if for approval, said that the evidence against Him González was not the issue. The issue was one of sovereignty. How could sovereignty have any real meaning if U.S. agents, acting on their own, could arrest a Panamanian citizen in Panama for crimes that had not been committed in Panama?

Noriega then moved the discussion to a more practical level. Must our citizens worry every time they go into the Canal Zone that some secret U.S. legal process has made them subject to arrest? What if, he said, the United States gets Him González back to the States and he begins to talk and say outrageous things? For example, he might say that General Torrijos is involved in these things. Then what if the general goes into the Zone to show the Canal to some tourists, and he is arrested and put on a plane to the United States?

The U.S. officials assured Noriega that they would never take such action against General Torrijos. But Strickler—recalling that he had seen intelligence reports linking Noriega himself to drug activity—

wondered whether Noriega's hypothetical example might not have more relevance to Noriega than to his boss.

After the meeting, Sayre continued to recommend against defying the Panamanians by deporting Him González. The matter dragged on for almost two weeks as the Washington bureaucracy made up its collective mind. Finally, State backed down and Tartaglino and Strickler began the tricky process of transporting their prisoner. They arranged for a U.S. helicopter to fly Him González the four miles between the Zone and Howard Air Force Base, having been warned that it was too risky to transport the prisoner by car even such a short distance over roads patrolled by Panamanian military police. Southcom officials signaled their displeasure with the whole affair by refusing to provide an airplane to fly Him González out of Panama. Strickler called his Washington office, which got the White House to send down a plane from the presidential Air Force One fleet.

On board the plane, Him González found himself in an incongruous situation. He was in shackles, he had lost the battle to stay in Panama and yet he was in the most luxurious airborne setting he had experienced in his life. He, Strickler and Tartaglino were flying in space meant for presidents, vice presidents and members of the Cabinet. The plane had couches, beds and a complete office and conference room.

Tartaglino sat across from Him González and began to berate him. The more he talked, the more upset he got. "You disgust me," he said, "bringing drugs to corrupt American youth." His face grew redder as the epithets got wilder. He called him a "child-killer," he drew a comparison to Hitler. In a 1978 affidavit Him González described the scene: "During the flight from Panama to Dallas, Mr. Tartaglino lashed out with every kind of insult against the Panamanian government and against me personally, against high officials such as then-Chancellor Juan Antonio Tack and especially against President Demetrio Basilio Lakas. Then he threatened to personally testify before the federal court in Dallas if I did not cooperate with them in this case. He said he would ask for the maximum sentence of forty years and there was no way I would ever return to see that piece of earth called Panama."

After two hours, Tartaglino said that Him González had made him sick and he went to lie down in one of the airplane's beds. Strickler took over. In the classic good cop, bad cop tactic, Strickler was sympathetic; he said Him González was in serious trouble but that there might be a way out. The affidavit continued: "It would be to my advantage, Strickler told me, to cooperate with the BNDD and give them names that I had to know of Panamanian officials who were involved in drug trafficking. . . . In exchange for my cooperation and a guilty plea to the charges against me, they would help me get a light sentence and I would be released on parole early and could remain living in the United States with their help."

Him González maintained his innocence and refused to cooperate with the BNDD's efforts to develop a case against higher-ups in the Panamanian government. He was convicted in Dallas U.S. District Court and sentenced to a relatively light five years.

The Him González case convinced the BNDD agents that official complicity in drug trafficking ran broad and deep in Panama. Now, when Rubén Monzon got informants' reports pointing to Noriega, he followed up vigorously. The BNDD had penetrated a boat charter service operating out of Miami. Informants in the service tipped BNDD to intercept a boat that they said had been hired by drug dealers to pick up a load of marijuana in Panama. After their arrest, the smugglers told BNDD that the man they paid off to move the marijuana out of Panama was a colonel with a pock-marked face. They said they had an address book with his name and direct telephone numbers. The name they pointed out was Colonel Tony Noriega.

The case was strong against Noriega, and BNDD agents at the time said it could easily have been pressed to indictment. Not only had the arrested smugglers told of meeting and paying off Noriega, but the BNDD informants who rented them the boat—men with a track record of providing credible information to DEA—offered solid corroboration.

But in the early 1970s the idea of indicting the head of the intelligence service of a friendly country was beyond the pale. The international mechanisms that had to be brought into play to charge and extradite a foreign official—particularly in a case linking him to a

crime that had been committed in the United States, not Panama—
were complex and cumbersome. The Justice Department was not
comfortable with the possible repercussions of such government-to-
government jurisprudence. No one seriously believed Noriega would
ever be extradited, and the alternative to extradition was the kind of
extrajudicial kidnapping or trickery already used in the Him González case. The Miami U.S. attorney's office decided against pursuing
the indictment.* "There was zero interest in indicting people outside
the country," one of the BNDD agents said.

The case against Noriega languished in bureaucratic faintheartedness, but the agents pressed on against another Panama-based narcotics ring. On July 8, 1971, a young Panamanian stepped off Braniff
flight 906, arriving at New York's JFK Airport from Panama City.
When Customs officials asked Rafael Richard to open his suitcases,
he refused and showed them a Panamanian diplomatic passport. He
said he was the son of Panama's ambassador to Taiwan and claimed
diplomatic immunity. The officials weren't impressed.

An inspector opened the luggage and found plastic bags containing 155 pounds of heroin. Richard hadn't even bothered to put a layer
of clothes over the drugs. It was a major seizure for those days,
significant enough for a front-page story in *The New York Times*. If
the drugs had been sold on the street, they could have brought about
$20 million.

Over the next few days, Richard and an accomplice, Guillermo
González, began to talk. They had run five previous loads of heroin
to New York, each about 150 pounds. Never before had Richard been
stopped. His diplomatic passport, clean-cut youth and upper-crust
bearing had placed him above suspicion, and on previous trips he had
been whisked through without inspection.

Guillermo González said that Panama was the last leg of a heroin
pipeline that started in processing labs in Marseilles, France, and
involved Spain, Argentina, Paraguay and Peru. How had he moved
it through Panama? He had a high-placed friend named Moisés
Torrijos, older brother of General Omar Torrijos and currently

---

*The head of the Miami office's criminal division at the time was Neal Sonnet. In
1988, as a private attorney, Sonnet was hired by Noriega to defend him.

Panamanian ambassador to Argentina. González, whose account was corroborated by Richard, said Torrijos's role was simple but vital. When a shipment was arriving from Paraguay or departing to the United States, they said, the elder Torrijos would go with them to the airport and walk them through Panamanian customs. There were never any questions.

The two men also said Torrijos used his contacts at the Foreign Ministry to get Richard his diplomatic passport. Guillermo González said he knew Moisés Torrijos because he had once worked as his chauffeur.

The evidence against Moisés Torrijos was relatively flimsy, but Richard and González were quickly brought before a federal grand jury in New York to lay the groundwork for a possible indictment. Federal prosecutors alerted their superiors at the Justice Department that they were developing a politically sensitive case.

BNDD and Customs had developed three major cases in only a few months, and more intelligence was coming in every day. Within a week after the Richard and González arrests, BNDD officials went to the State Department to brief officials there about what they had learned. At State's request, they put their most important findings in writing. Operations officer Gerry Strickler prepared a memorandum dated July 28, 1971, that listed intelligence gathered on fifteen prominent Panamanians, including Moisés Torrijos and Lieutenant Colonel Noriega. The memo quoted a political exile—a man with an axe to grind—as saying he had information that Noriega had "overall operational control" of officially sanctioned traffic in Panama. Another report said that Noriega personally ordered the release of a drug trafficker caught red-handed with cocaine. Over the next two months, there were other major seizures of marijuana, heroin and cocaine that had passed through Panama.

The case for Panamanian official complicity in drug trafficking could no longer be ignored, and the Nixon White House began to translate the concern about Panama into a plan of action. Strickler was asked to present the incriminating information at a special briefing at the National Security Council (NSC). The meeting included two NSC officials and two CIA officials, all with special responsibilities for interagency narcotics coordination. The officials listened and volunteered little about their intentions, but Strickler left the meeting puzzled by one of their questions.

"They asked me for my candid opinion as to whether the United States would be better off if Torrijos were removed and replaced by someone else. I said no, that we probably would be better off with a known quantity like Torrijos, than with someone else," Strickler later said. "There was no doubt what they meant by remove."

What the officials were contemplating was disclosed in 1973 in the midst of the Watergate scandal. Former White House counsel John Dean, testifying before the Senate Watergate Committee, said that the White House contracted E. Howard Hunt, one of the Watergate burglars, to assassinate Torrijos. Dean said Torrijos was targeted because of his "uncooperative attitude" toward the Panama Canal treaty negotiations and because his government was allowing heroin to flow through Panama on its way to the United States. According to Dean, the assassination plan was aborted before the hit team reached Panama.

BNDD chief John Ingersoll was pursuing his growing concern about Panama on a separate but ultimately similar track. He presented a report to the House Subcommittee on the Panama Canal. Narcotics enforcement was especially difficult in Panama, the report said. There were a dozen deep-water ports and over a hundred airfields able to handle smugglers' light aircraft. The report summarized the seizures involving Panamanian officials but, unlike the briefing to the State Department and NSC, did not list Noriega and Moisés Torrijos as suspects. It noted that some elements of the Panamanian National Guard were cooperating in the effort to stop the trafficking but that the overall picture was discouraging. "It is clear that the Republic of Panama has not and is not paying sufficient attention to narcotic enforcement activities to achieve noticeable results. This may be due to high level apathy, ignorance and/or collusion. Unless the Republic of Panama is sincerely willing to put forth the necessary effort to combat the traffic, the Republic will continue to serve as a conduit through which vast amounts of illicit drugs are funneled enroute to the United States."

The State Department agreed to Ingersoll's recommendation that he travel to Panama to present the evidence personally to General

Torrijos and to underline the seriousness of U.S. concerns. The BNDD chief made the first of three trips to Panama in September 1971. According to a posttrip memo to Attorney General John Mitchell, Ingersoll complained to Torrijos that "in my opinion, Panama could have cooperated to a greater extent. During this private meeting, General Torrijos's aides made several telephone calls and it was apparent that General Torrijos and his senior staff members had received misinformation with regard to past cooperation." But Ingersoll did not mention the U.S. intelligence linking Noriega to drug trafficking, nor did he bring up the case that federal prosecutors were building in New York against Torrijos's brother, Moisés. Torrijos expressed "disgust" that narcotics were flowing through Panama and readily agreed to a stepped-up program of U.S. assistance in narcotics enforcement, including an immediate training course for the National Guard's central narcotics unit, which would more than double in size. The agreement shuttled the problem back into Noriega's hands.

Ingersoll came back impressed with the apparent sincerity of Torrijos's moral revulsion against drug smuggling. It was the same impression Torrijos would convey to almost all U.S. officials who dealt with him: personal outrage at any kind of illicit drug use and a determination to stop any trafficking through his country. But as reports of new transshipments continued, U.S. alarm about Panama only increased. Torrijos was insisting that all information about drug running by Panamanian officials be turned over to him so that he could crack down on the offenders. But U.S. officials did not trust Torrijos enough to do that. "There was frustration all over the place," recalls then Ambassador Sayre, who accompanied Ingersoll on all his meetings with Torrijos. "One of BNDD's problems was that if they provided information to the Panamanian government about Panamanian officials doing things, they had no real confidence in what the Panamanian government would do with that."

In the meantime, more intelligence was received, making it clear that Noriega was the real problem in Panama. Noriega was a special case. He wasn't just another corrupt official taking a payoff or facilitating a drug shipment. He was the dead center of any narcotics enforcement effort by Panama, if there was to be one. "He was the second highest authority in Panama. As long as he was in the number two spot, we would never have reliable cooperation," Strickler said.

The idea of indicting someone of Noriega's position seemed too farfetched to be practical, and the Nixon administration was pressing Ingersoll for results. In the anything-goes atmosphere of the Nixon Justice Department under Attorney General John Mitchell, Ingersoll decided on drastic action. He convened his top BNDD operations officers in early January 1972 to come up with a plan of action to get Noriega out of the drug-trafficking business. One BNDD officer present described the way Ingersoll's request was passed on down the line. "They [the officers who had met with Ingersoll] said Ingersoll wanted a plan. It should include everything, from the far out to the most basic, it should include the ultimate. When it was done, the first item on the list was to wipe him [Noriega] out. That was followed by the reasons why that wasn't such a good idea, that it would be inappropriate and unnecessary."

The options paper came to light in 1978 during a secret Senate session to discuss the charges of drug trafficking in the Torrijos régime. In the heavily redacted transcript of the *Congressional Record,* Senator Birch Bayh, chairman of the Senate Select Intelligence Committee, described the plan as "immobilization" and listed the five options in the written report, of which a sanitized version was made public:

> The options considered in January and February of 1972 included the following: linking the official [Noriega] to a fictitious plot against General Torrijos; leaking information on drug trafficking to the press; linking his removal to the Panama Canal negotiations; secretly encouraging powerful groups within Panama to raise the issue; and "total and complete immobilization." . . .
>
> At the time Ingersoll ordered preparation of the options paper, he was under White House pressure to be more aggressive in international narcotics control. The most extreme options were immediately rejected, but some were put into action. A Department of Justice inquiry in 1975 concluded that no illegal activity resulted.

That the assassination option was given short shrift is confirmed by every BNDD official willing to comment on the plan. Ingersoll has said little about it except to insist it was rejected out of hand. Three of the other four options, however, appear to have been tried in the subsequent months, although it is impossible to say that all of the ensuing events were the result of some BNDD master plan.

A 1975 Justice Department investigation known as the Defeo Report contains information that is consistent with the idea of involving Noriega in a bogus assassination plot against Torrijos. The report, which examines allegations of corruption in the BNDD and its successor, the DEA, discovered at least one instance in which BNDD officials conveyed intelligence to Panama about an alleged assassination plot against Torrijos. It could not be learned if the alleged plot was real or invented or if Noriega was identified as the alleged perpetrator. But the two men named by the Justice Department probe as "develop[ing] information of a plot to kill General Torrejos [sic]" were Phillip Smith and William Durkin, both of whom were also participants in drafting the options paper for Ingersoll.

In a leaked portion, the Justice Department report says, "Smith testified that this information was quickly passed on to the CIA for transmittal to the Republic of Panama. Smith said that he was later informed that the plot had been verified and neutralized. . . . It was alleged that a discussion concerning assassination involved the possibility of killing Mr. Noryago [sic] . . . and that Smith and William Durkin actually proposed that he be killed." The report provided no additional information on the alleged plot, but said, "A review of the files does not reveal Smith's position as to discussion concerning Mr. Noryago."

The second option put into action involved leaks to the press. But it backfired and involved the United States in another serious diplomatic incident with Panama. The leaker was Congressman John Murphy of New York. Murphy was chairman of the House Subcommittee on the Panama Canal and a fervent opponent of attempts to negotiate turning the Canal over to Panama. He saw in Torrijos a dangerous leftist and enemy of the United States—an idea inculcated in him by his good friend, Nicaraguan dictator Anastasio Somoza. Ingersoll had confided his frustrations about Panama to Murphy's committee, and Murphy saw a chance to use the drug allegations to torpedo the Canal negotiations. Murphy traveled to Panama in February with the idea of holding hearings in the Canal Zone; Ambassador Sayre had to talk the brusque congressman out of trying to subpoena Panamanian officials to testify at the hearings, but a report surfaced in the Panamanian press that Murphy intended to force an appearance by Foreign Minister Juan Tack.

Tack was enraged at Murphy's arrogance and signaled his displeasure by failing to appear at a luncheon at Ambassador Sayre's residence—the purpose of which was to smooth things over. Only one Panamanian official of the four invited did show up, and he was clearly embarrassed that he had not gotten the word to boycott the event. "We received instructions that nobody was to see John Murphy," said Fernando Manfredo, a former ambassador to the United States. The snub was deeply felt by Murphy, who had recently married and had brought his bride with him to Panama.

Murphy found a way to retaliate. During the visit, he was briefed by BNDD officer Bill Place. When he returned to Washington, Murphy passed on what he had learned to columnist Jack Anderson. Anderson's March 14 column for the first time named names: "American narcotics agents have implicated the foreign minister of Panama and the brother of Panamanian dictator Omar Torrijos in a scheme to smuggle hundreds of pounds of heroin into the United States," the column began. Moisés Torrijos was linked to the July 1971 heroin seizure at Kennedy Airport through his former bodyguard, Guillermo González, it said. Foreign Minister Tack, Anderson revealed, "signed the dubious diplomatic passport" used by Rafael Richard in the smuggling trip. Anderson added insult to innuendo by describing the foreign minister as a handsome man "who looks like an American movie star idol, but talks like a Mafia overlord."

The Panamanian reaction was immediate. Tack called U.S. Ambassador Sayre the same afternoon that the column crossed the wires and informed him that the three American BNDD agents had twenty-four hours to leave Panama. Sayre sympathized somewhat with the Panamanian outrage. "I always thought that Murphy's allegations against Juan Tack were because he thought Tack snubbed him in front of his brand-new wife in Panama and he had to get even some way," Sayre now says. The evidence against Tack was flimsy.

It depended entirely on the fact that Tack had signed a drug smuggler's passport—not surprising since all Panamanian diplomatic passports required the foreign minister's signature.

Although the Anderson report did not mention Noriega, the leaks were intended to put pressure on Torrijos to "get rid of Noriega," a BNDD insider said. "We gave the intelligence reports to Murphy to raise the profile of Panama and to surface the facts of Panamanian official involvement in drug trafficking."

A third tactic was to persuade prominent Panamanians to go to Torrijos to complain about the damage Noriega's continued presence would do to Panama's long-term interests. According to press reports, this was also done.

What effect all of these dirty tricks and pressure tactics had on Torrijos is not known. Clearly nothing happened to diminish Torrijos's reliance on Noriega or to damage Noriega's own ties to other U.S. intelligence agencies. But there is no doubt that—whatever the cause—U.S. perceptions about Panama and drugs changed radically in mid-1972.

eemingly overnight—only a few months after two U.S. agencies toyed with the idea of carrying out assassinations in Panama—the hardline mandate to go after top officials disappeared. Ironically, the new policy had its first impact just as those favoring the hard line were celebrating a victory: On May 16, after almost a year of political vacillation, the Justice Department sought and obtained an indictment charging Moisés Torrijos—General Torrijos's brother—with drug trafficking. The indictment was a carefully guarded secret, but for those working inside the drug enforcement agencies, it appeared to break new ground. It was a bold attempt to bring to justice a high-ranking foreign official and one of the first times drug conspiracy charges were brought against a foreign official not yet in U.S. custody.

The next step logically would have been to lure Torrijos into U.S. jurisdiction and arrest him. A Him González–style capture would have been relatively easy since Moisés Torrijos was a regular visitor to the Canal Zone. Instead, the opposite happened. Over the next half-year the U.S. government went to extraordinary lengths to avoid a situation in which Moisés Torrijos or any other Panamanian official would be captured or prosecuted.

Sayre and the State Department, as usual, were the architects of the softer new policy. Sayre worked hard to persuade Torrijos to allow the BNDD office to be reopened, and by early June, Torrijos had dropped his ban on BNDD activities in Panama, and a new BNDD officer, Edward Heath, had reopened the Panama office.

In late June, John Ingersoll made his fourth trip to Panama. He was under orders from his superiors in the Justice Department, "with the concurrence of concerned agencies," to inform General Torrijos that there was a warrant for his brother's arrest. A meeting took place the morning of June 22 at Torrijos's beach house near the Rio Hato military base. According to the BNDD memo on the meeting, Ingersoll stressed that the federal indictment was sealed in New York. Secrecy was intended to prevent the suspect from knowing about the charges until he was arrested, but in this case it would serve to prevent Panamanian embarrassment. "If Ambassador Torrijos enters the United States," Ingersoll said, "he will be arrested and prosecuted. This information is limited to a few individuals in the United States government, and we hope General Torrijos will be able to deal with the matter before it becomes public knowledge. I am passing it on in the hope you will investigate the matter further, recall your brother [from his post as ambassador to Argentina], and persuade him to remove himself from the illicit drug business."

Ingersoll then delivered the mild scolding he had administered in previous visits: "Panama must mount a strong law enforcement effort and strengthen Customs controls to deny Panama revisitory [sic] to drug traffickers. Narcotics enforcement is in your government's best interest. Failure to do so effectively could result in further embarrassment to your government."

But the Moisés Torrijos matter was still far from resolved. In December 1972, CIA station chief Joe Yoshio Kiyonaga informed Ambassador Sayre that Moisés Torrijos and his wife were on board a passenger cruiser, the *Verde,* that was scheduled to dock at the port of Cristóbal, Panama, well inside the U.S.-controlled Canal Zone. The CIA also passed on the information to U.S. Customs agent Leland Riggs, who planned a stakeout at the port to arrest Torrijos.

But Sayre saw Moisés Torrijos's arrival in the Zone as a trap set by his brother. It was all too convenient, he thought. "There was no reason for Moisés to be on this boat," Sayre said. The elder Torrijos always flew in and out of Panama on his frequent trips. Sayre was convinced Torrijos was setting up a spectacular international incident to demonstrate that U.S. control of the Canal Zone constituted an egregious violation of Panama's sovereignty. "What was going on," Sayre said he reported to Washington, "was that the Panamanians—Torrijos—were trying to develop a case to take to the meeting of the U.N. Security Council that was to take place in Panama City in February 1973."

Sayre said he received orders from Washington to "confront" Torrijos on the matter. He got word to Torrijos that the United States was aware his brother was on the ship and would be in U.S. jurisdiction when it arrived in Cristóbal. "Torrijos wouldn't see me himself," Sayre said. "He sent [President] Jimmy Lakas over to see me. He came over to the residence. We sat down in the library, and I told him we just didn't appreciate these kinds of tactics. I asked him to cut it out. Torrijos was having a party somewhere with his cronies and Lakas went over and told him."

Torrijos contacted his brother, who left the ship in Caracas, Venezuela, and took a commercial airliner to Panama. When the *Verde* arrived, Mrs. Torrijos disembarked alone in the Canal Zone with all the couple's luggage.

What had happened to reverse the tough U.S. crackdown on official complicity in Panama, a policy so strident it engendered plans and discussions about solving the problem with assassination?

Ambassador Sayre's explanation is simply that the case against Torrijos's brother was weak. "The reason the BNDD and Ingersoll were willing to tell Torrijos about it was they did not have enough evidence to get a conviction. They only had one witness. That's it. They didn't have anything else." But the case did have value as a way to put pressure on Torrijos, and that was the way it was ultimately used. Its merits aside, the Moisés Torrijos case was treated as a political football almost from the first moment it was discovered he was the brother of the Panamanian head of state. It was further politicized during the 1978 congressional debates over the Canal treaties. The case was finally and quietly dismissed for lack of evidence in 1980.

Other evidence indicated that the turnaround on Moisés Torrijos was part of a broader U.S. policy decision to ease off on the pursuit of Panamanian officials. A State Department official said he had been told by Sayre in October 1972 that drug enforcement efforts should continue in Panama despite a "high level agreement between the United States and the Panamanian governments not to upset each other's domestic political apple carts." The alleged agreement came as the Nixon administration was coasting to reelection and Torrijos was orchestrating the election of a showcase legislature.

Drug enforcement did continue in Panama, but Noriega was undergoing a radical transformation from target-suspect to trusted collaborator. In this metamorphosis, his new, official relationship with the CIA may have come into play as Noriega began to prove his usefulness as an international covert operator for the United States. In the same time period that two branches of the U.S. government were contemplating killing Torrijos and/or Noriega, other U.S. officials were enlisting their help to bail out a CIA dirty tricks operation gone bad.

On December 15, 1971, a Cuban gunboat attacked the trawler *Johnny Express* near one of the Bahama Islands. The *Johnny Express* and a sister ship, the *Leyla Express,* were both flying Panamanian flags of convenience. And both were being used to launch speedboats manned by Cuban exiles to carry out machine-gun attacks on Cuban fishing villages. Panama became involved in the incident shortly after the *Johnny Express* came under fire. The high-seas battle was conveyed live by ship-to-shore radio telephone to, among others, the Panamanian ambassador to Washington, Fernando Manfredo.

"I received a call from Teófilo Babún [the owner of the Miami-based Bahamas Line, which operated the *Johnny Express*]. He said a Panamanian flagged ship was being attacked—he wanted me to call the State Department and have them send planes to defend our ship. To convince me, he patched me through to the captain on the ship. I could hear machine-gun fire. I put him on hold and called Torrijos in Panama to ask what I should do. He said 'No way. Don't get the Americans involved. Don't give them any excuse to attack Cuba.' "

Without a pretext to request U.S. protection, the shipowners ordered the captain, José Villa, already seriously wounded, to surrender. Cuban officials announced the seizure along with charges that the *Johnny Express* had played a part in a CIA-sponsored raid in October on the coastal village of Boca de Sama, in which several civilians had been killed.

President Nixon got involved in efforts to free Villa, a Spaniard living in Miami. Nixon invited Villa's wife to the White House and posed with his arm around her shoulder. Although Panama did not have diplomatic relations with Cuba, Torrijos agreed to a U.S. request to send a diplomatic mission to mediate. Meanwhile, CIA station chief Joe Kiyonaga received instructions from Washington to ask Noriega to go to Cuba as Torrijos's personal emissary.

The operation was conducted with the kind of compartmentalization and dual-track secrecy that would characterize the Noriega-U.S. relationship for the next two decades. The overt, diplomatic mission to Cuba was carried out by Rómulo Escobar Bethancourt, one of the former Communists whose presence in Torrijos's cabinet had occasioned the 1969 attempted coup. But according to William Jorden, an NSC aide who would become U.S. ambassador to Panama in 1974, it was the added clout of Noriega's mission that, more than a year after his capture, convinced Castro to release Villa. Both Escobar Bethancourt and Noriega flew to Cuba and escorted Villa to Panama. In keeping with the agreement with Castro, Panama brought espionage charges against Villa, reams of legal paper were generated and, after sufficient delay to save face all around, Villa was freed and allowed to return to Miami.

The mission may not have been the first task Noriega performed for the U.S. government, but it was up to that time by far the most important. Many years later, Noriega still carried the mission as a credit in his account with the United States. In an interview in late 1987, Noriega bragged about the incident as one of the favors for which the United States still owed him gratitude.

Jorden, who later wrote a highly respected account of the Canal treaty negotiations, saw irony in Noriega's mission for the United States. "Thus, Panama's links to Castro commenced in 1971 at the request of the U.S. government," he wrote. "By 1974, Torrijos was ready to use that connection as a trump card in the treaty game."

.   .   .

The change of colors was not solely on the U.S. side. Noriega apparently put the profits of drug deals behind him and set out to convince the world that Panama would become the "enforcement center for fighting drug trafficking in Latin America." Noriega took closer personal charge of all drug enforcement activity—with a grip he was not to loosen as long as he was in power—and proceeded to prove to U.S. officials that his usefulness far outweighed the suspicions of the past. In 1973, in an event that would have its echo in the Darién cocaine factory seizure eleven years later, Noriega's men detected, seized and destroyed a functioning heroin laboratory, the first example of narcotics production in the country.

The circle of Noriega's rehabilitation was completed in a *New York Times* story, September 22, 1973, headlined PANAMA PRAISED FOR DRUG CURBS. The story quoted Noriega as vowing a "war to the death" on traffickers and said U.S. officials "are publicizing their satisfaction at the latest events in Panama," which had been moving vigorously to make major seizures of cocaine and marijuana. In reference to past suspicions of official complicity, "United States sources now say that no real evidence against Mr. Tack or any other Panamanian Government official was ever turned up, and the United States officials have reportedly apologized to Mr. Tack."

It was as if the evidence against Noriega had never existed. For the next ten years, drug enforcement officials apparently raised no serious questions about Noriega's complicity in drug running. On the other side of the ledger, Noriega began to pile up credits with U.S. law enforcement personnel for his unstinting cooperation.

A case can be made that Noriega was following the pattern he had set years before: a spell of good behavior to curry favor, resulting in solid achievement and ascension, followed by a paroxysm of greed and brutality as he tested his limits of opportunity. The crisply dressed "A" student at the National Institute had won his teachers' approval by reading extra books, then had taken money from politicians to throw rocks at the police; the aspiring National Guard officer had sacrificed for years to win his commission, then had gone on rampages of drunkenness, rape and brutality; he had leapfrogged over his fellow officers to become head of G2 as a reward for his loyalty to Torrijos, then had become an outlaw profiting from drug smuggling.

At some point, Torrijos would always tighten the reins and Noriega would again be the capable, dedicated staff officer. Just as Torrijos covered for Noriega in the Colón rape case, it is reasonable to assume that in 1972 Torrijos followed through on the requests from U.S. officials and privately called Noriega on the carpet about the drug accusations—not because Torrijos himself was morally upright, but because he had more important goals for Panama, and more important tasks for Noriega.

CHAPTER 4

THE TREATY GAME

To the world, the Panama Canal was an engineering marvel; to the increasingly nationalistic Panamanians, the U.S.-controlled canal had come to represent the looting of a natural resource by a colonial power, a gash dividing Panama against itself and preventing true nationhood—"a stake in our heart," as Torrijos once called it. The problem was not the Canal, but U.S. control, and Torrijos set out to make the United States so uncomfortable in Panama that it would leave of its own accord.

Lieutenant Colonel Manuel Noriega was never to play a public role in Torrijos's plans to recover the Canal. His assignment was darker: to provide intelligence and counterintelligence. And when needed, Noriega conducted covert operations to back up Torrijos's plans. As Torrijos played the game on the table, Noriega was in charge of the dirty tricks.

The U.S. governor of the Canal Zone, General David Parker, tells this story of Noriega's tactics—and of his willingness to put himself personally into the fray. In late 1972, drivers employed by the Canal Zone's private bus company went on strike and received the enthusiastic support of the Torrijos government. The drivers were Panamanian, but the buses operated almost exclusively inside Zone boundaries. The bus company's status as a Canal Zone enterprise independent of Panama City's public transportation network was one of the many nettles between the Zone administration and Panama.

The bus company tried to break the strike by hiring new drivers, but strikers sequestered the buses by driving them, one by one, outside Zone boundaries to a rendezvous point on National Guard property. A few drivers rejected the strike and continued on their routes. As one of these buses was picking up passengers along Fourth of July Avenue, the Zone borderline, two men in National Guard uniforms got on, pointed their guns at the driver and forced him to take the bus to the strikers' rendezvous. General Parker was furious at the violation of Canal Zone immunity. Zone intelligence identified one of the gunmen as Lieutenant Colonel Noriega himself. There was talk of bringing felony charges against Noriega in the Zone's independent court system, but nothing came of it. In the end, the striking drivers were fired and all given new jobs by the Panamanian government.

The spectacle of a military officer holding up a bus driver in his own country, and a representative of a foreign government contemplating hauling him into court over it could only have happened in Panama—the product of a U.S.-Panamanian relationship born in gunboat diplomacy and perpetuated in insensitivity. For seventy years, a treaty neither negotiated nor signed by any Panamanian governed the operation of Panama's principal economic resource and granted the United States virtually absolute power over a vast strip of Panama's most vital territory.

When the U.S. warship *Nashville* steamed into Cristóbal harbor in November 1903, it did not cause the Panamanian secession from Colombia, to which country it then belonged; the rebellion had been brewing for much of the previous sixty years. But the U.S. action, ordered by President Teddy Roosevelt, sealed the futility of Colombian attempts to put down the uprising and all but guaranteed the success of the Panamanian movement. The real bullying happened after Panama won its independence. Teddy Roosevelt did not create Panama, as has been sometimes asserted, but it is difficult to exaggerate the high-handed U.S. maneuvering that led to that new nation's agreement to allow the United States to build the Canal.

The treaty so one-sidedly favored U.S. interests that one U.S. senator considering it for ratification commented, "We have never had a concession so extraordinary in its character as this. In fact, it sounds very much as if we wrote it ourselves." He was wrong. The final draft was almost entirely the words of French businessman Philippe Bunau-Varilla, representative of the French-owned Panama Canal Company. Bunau-Varilla had not worked in Panama since contracting yellow fever eighteen years before, but was able to finagle the new Panamanian junta's authorization to act as "plenipotentiary" to negotiate on behalf of Panama. He threw out the draft offered by the U.S. secretary of state as too lenient toward Panama and substituted a treaty that doubled the size of the area where the Canal was to be built and gave the United States power to act as "if it were sovereign" in the area. Compensation to Panama was a flat $10 million—most of which was immediately turned over to tycoon J. P. Morgan to be invested in New York City real estate. Thereafter, the United States paid Panama $250,000 each year as payment to lease the land, build and operate the Canal and construct military bases that would remain the largest outside U.S. soil until World War II.

No one argued that it was fair. For Panama, the treaty was perceived as the price of the U.S. guarantee of its newly won independence from Colombia. For decades, there was little serious prospect for modifying the arrangement. Through two world wars and the growth of the United States as a world power, the "special relationship" was for Panama an inexorable fact of life. Like the ten inches of rain that fall each month in Panama during the summer, the treaty was something Panamanians often cursed but couldn't live without and were powerless to change.

Panama indeed prospered from the arrangement. The Canal and related services allowed Panama to develop as a middle-class trader society that avoided some of the most egregious inequities of the rest of Central America. But politically and militarily, Panama remained a dwarf, a comprador nation forced to tolerate the occupation of its land by U.S. forces—troops that intervened against other Latin American countries as early as 1914, when Canal-based Marines were dispatched to Mexico as part of the U.S. campaign against Pancho Villa. For much of the century, the U.S. military force was far larger than Panama's own National Guard, which was relegated to little more than police and border patrol. The relationship was an affront to Panamanian national pride, and demands for new treaties were heard as early as the 1930s.

Still, no serious effort to change the treaties was entertained by the United States until an outbreak of violence in 1964 exposed U.S. vulnerability. The uncontrolled rioting of that year marked a continental divide in the U.S.-Panamanian relationship. For the first time, U.S. troops and Panamanian citizens, with the unofficial but nevertheless real support of their government, fought and died in the Canal Zone and surrounding areas.

The fighting began over the flying of flags. Panamanians insisted that, even though their government had no real control there, the Canal Zone was sovereign Panamanian territory. U.S. authorities had granted the right to the symbolic flying of the Panamanian flag inside the Zone, but five hundred rabidly anti-Panamanian Zonians gathered to prevent the exercise of that right when several hundred Panamanian students marched into the Zone on January 9 and tried to raise their flag outside Balboa High School. First there were insults, then shoving. In the scuffle, the silk red, white and blue Panamanian flag was torn. The students retreated, their nationalism inflamed.

The clash ignited Panama as nothing before in the country's history. As word of the insult to the Panamanian flag spread through the city, tens of thousands of Panamanians took to the streets. Thousands marched down Fourth of July Avenue, which marked the Canal Zone boundary, forcing U.S. troops to defend the Zone from foxholes with live ammunition. Panamanian snipers pelted the Tivoli Hotel, just inside the Zone, where U.S. troops had set up headquarters. Investigators later reported that the firing had reached a rate of five hundred shots an hour. U.S. sharpshooters returning fire picked off several Panamanians in an apartment building across the road, including an eleven-year-old girl killed by accident. The rioting lasted for three and a half days. The National Guard withdrew to barracks and made no attempt to control the rioters. When it was over, workers patched over two thousand bullet holes in the façade of the Tivoli Hotel. The toll was shocking: At least eighteen

Panamanians and four U.S. soldiers had died; 200 to 300 Panamanians and 156 North Americans had been injured.

Panama's president Rodolfo Chiari broke relations within twenty-four hours of the flag incident and later renamed Fourth of July Avenue "Avenue of the Martyrs." Secretary of the Army Cyrus Vance proclaimed that the riots were the work of outside agitators, communist agents trained in Cuba; President Johnson dispatched to Panama his gruff Latin America adviser, Thomas Mann, a hardliner who had participated in the U.S. operation to overthrow Guatemala's democratic government ten years earlier. Relations were never again to return to the tepid duality of passivity and paternalism. But out of belligerence would grow a truly bilateral, albeit persistently unequal, relationship.

The crisis spurred the Johnson administration to begin negotiations. Although admitting in late 1964 that the talks were aimed at "an entirely new treaty"—a historic breakthrough—the U.S. side assumed a carrot-and-stick strategy that revealed it had not abandoned a fundamentally strong-arm approach to Panama. Almost simultaneous with the announcement of talks, the United States proclaimed its intention to make the Panama Canal obsolete by building a sea-level canal. It was thought that nuclear devices would greatly speed and cheapen excavation of the new canal, an idea the Panamanians found chilling. The most likely site of the new project was not Panama but Nicaragua, then under the Somoza dynasty, the United States's most unconditional ally in Central America. The message to Panama was unequivocal: Take the deal you're offered while you still have a canal to bargain over.

Three treaties were drafted by 1967 but had no serious prospect for acceptance by either side. LBJ's preoccupation with the Vietnam war and his subsequent declaration that he would not seek a second term orphaned the treaties on the U.S. side, and in Panama, criticism of the weakness of the treaties was so great they were not even presented for approval to the National Assembly.

After Torrijos came to power in the 1968 coup, he officially buried the corpse, declaring the draft treaties so flawed that they could not serve even as a starting point for new negotiations. In Torrijos, the

United States had encountered a fair match. For him, the mandate to recover the Canal was absolute. "I don't want to be in the history books; I want to be in the Canal," is one of his most often quoted sayings. *("No quiero entrar en la historia, sino en el canal.")*

Talks resumed in 1971 and 1972, but settling the Canal issue was abysmally low on the list of Richard Nixon's global objectives. Such was U.S. insensitivity that in the middle of negotiations Nixon nominated an outspoken treaty opponent as ambassador to Panama. (The nominee, former Ohio Republican Congressman Frank Bow, died of a heart attack before assuming the post.)

The lackluster negotiations convinced Torrijos that only a geopolitical offensive, bringing to bear the growing strength of the Third World movement, would capture Washington's attention. So in 1973 Torrijos launched the Panama Canal as an issue on the world stage. He first solidified a phalanx of support from his most influential Latin American neighbors. Self-conscious of his own status as military ruler, Torrijos forged personal friendships with the presidents of Costa Rica, Colombia and Venezuela to gain legitimacy as a peer among the region's most respected democratic leaders. The renewal of relations with Cuba covered his left flank at home and gave him an ally among the more radical nations of Asia and Africa. His Latin American base secure, Torrijos traveled to Europe to make Panama's case to the United States's most strategic allies.

Noriega went along on almost all the trips, including one to Cuba. After the Cuba trip, he gave the CIA a detailed briefing. He stressed that Torrijos's purpose was to mark off the clear differences between Panama's nationalistic reform and Cuba's socialism. He quoted a comment from Torrijos's visit to Santiago de Cuba: "Every country has its own brand of aspirin," he said. "Panama's brand is Bayer." The reference to the American product was an unmistakable signal of Torrijos's desire to cultivate its ties with the United States. It was vintage Torrijos, Noriega explained. When in Panama he punched with his left; when in Cuba, he used his right.

At the United Nations, Panamanian Ambassador Aquilino Boyd lobbied incessantly for the convening of a special session of the Security Council to be held in Panama City to discuss "problems of colonialism and dangers to peace in Latin America." The U.S. ambassador to the United Nations, George Bush, fought the idea vigorously, to no avail.

The Security Council meeting in Panama, March 15–21, 1973, was a master diplomatic ploy by Torrijos. The government hosted the meeting in the National Assembly, a modest structure several blocks from the Canal Zone whose outside walls are covered with a striking bas-relief depicting the "martyrs" of 1964 facing the rifles of diabolically portrayed U.S. soldiers. The meeting's focus, inevitably, was on the Panama Canal. Panama deftly maneuvered the passage of a Security Council resolution favorable to Panama, whose wording was just tough enough to mousetrap the United States into a self-isolating veto.

Noriega, as usual, played the heavy. The new U.S. ambassador to the United Nations, John Scali, predictably became the target of animosity by the Third World representatives. In his speech he gave Panama an unwelcome reminder of supposed U.S. generosity, lecturing the Council on a long list of benefits accruing to Panama from U.S. aid and operation of the Canal. William Jorden, then an NSC official, recounted that Noriega called Scali at the U.S. embassy on the day the Security Council was to vote on the Panama resolution: "He told Scali he had a message from his government. 'If you are going to veto the resolution, you better do it at the airport,' he said ominously. Scali exploded. He told the Panamanian he was going to cast his vote in the council chamber in front of everyone."

To angry boos from the audience, that was what Ambassador Scali did. The episode was deeply embarrassing to the United States; the world was left with the picture of an irascible U.S. ambassador defending the indefensible. After the Security Council meeting, the idea that the United States could continue to maintain its uneven relationship with Panama was no more tenable than England's hold on the Suez Canal in the anticolonial euphoria following World War II. Although denounced in the United States as counterproductive to Panama's cause, the U.N. meeting appeared to have its intended effect: It grabbed U.S. attention and raised the cost of U.S. inaction on Panama. That is the conclusion Jorden reached: "[T]he embarrassment of the Security Council meeting . . . sounded an alarm loud enough to get [Secretary of State] Henry [Kissinger]'s attention. His geopolitical mind recognized that an explosion on our own doorstep, while it might be contained, would not add luster to U.S. prestige or improve Washington's ability to cope effectively with larger issues. It would have done for us about what an outburst of violence and a general strike in Eastern Europe would have done for Brezhnev." Three months after the meeting, President Nixon's report to Congress on foreign policy showed how well Torrijos's tactic had worked.

"For the past nine years, efforts to work out a new treaty acceptable to both parties have failed. That failure has put considerable strain on our relations with Panama. It is time for both parties to take a fresh look at this problem and to develop a new relationship between us—one that will guarantee continued effective operation of the Canal while meeting Panama's legitimate aspirations." Soon after, Nixon named veteran diplomat Ellsworth Bunker to head the U.S. negotiating team. The savvy former ambassador to Vietnam would not leave the post until the treaties were signed.

By 1976 U.S. and Panamanian negotiators began to make real progress, but they agreed to disagree for the time being on the two main sticking points: the duration of the treaty and the continuing U.S. right to defend the Canal militarily. To complicate matters further, the negotiations became a focus for demagoguery in an American election year, particularly after Republican underdog Ronald Reagan declared during the primary campaign: "When it comes to the Canal, we bought it, we paid for it, it's ours, and we should tell Torrijos and company that we are going to keep it." He also denounced the existence of a "secret" U.S. commitment to give Panama sovereignty over the Canal. For a dozen years it had been the most public of U.S. policy objectives to reach an agreement with Panama based on the recognition of Panamanian sovereignty, but Reagan's rhetoric made the Canal a rallying cry for the U.S. conservative movement. Even after Gerald Ford won the Republican nomination, all sides recognized that a final agreement on the Canal would have to wait for the next U.S. administration. "We had to stand down on the negotiations of the furor raised by Ronald Reagan," one of the U.S. officials said. "We knew we couldn't conclude a treaty, so we concentrated on secondary issues."

During the negotiating period, Torrijos kept the pressure on with frequent rallies and a few violent demonstrations. Pitching rocks through the windows of the U.S. embassy and United States Information Service office became a kind of national sport, and the local press kept score by counting how many windows were broken in each incident (eighty in an August 1974 attack; eighty-five in September 1975). After such demonstrations, the U.S. ambassador, with appropriate indignation, protested at the slowness or lack of police protection and sent a bill for the damage to the Panamanian government, which it unflinchingly paid.

It was generally accepted among U.S. officials that Noriega's G2 had a hand in organizing the demonstrations, and he gained a reputation in some U.S. quarters as a hardliner. But at the same time, Noriega was turning the intelligence he was generating about the unrest into negotiable credits with his friends at the 470th Military Intelligence Group. "This guy was too good to be true," one veteran U.S. officer commented with conscious irony. "He was telling us all about the students' plans for demonstrations before they happened."

Noriega and the United States were also engaged in an intense game of spy versus spy as both sides attempted to gain an intelligence advantage in the negotiations. The activities of the United States are still highly classified and very few details can be learned about them. What is known is that the cloak-and-dagger tactics, when discovered by the Senate Select Intelligence Committee in 1976, caused such alarm that the committee convoked a special investigation to determine to what extent the clandestine operations may have tainted the outcome of the treaty negotiations.

Starting in the early 1970s, the U.S. military and the National Security Agency (NSA) had been using the Canal Zone and U.S. bases in Panama to gather continentwide electronic intelligence. The first U.S. listening post had been established in Panama in 1938; by the 1970s eavesdropping capabilities had so vastly expanded that not only radio frequencies but telephone conversations were also included. For example, a U.S. soldier stationed in Panama in 1973 told of keeping track of intimate details of political party affairs in Chile—three thousand miles to the south—during the government of Socialist President Salvador Allende, who was overthrown and killed that year in a CIA-encouraged coup. Although the United States is not known to have ever consulted with Panama about these or any other military installations, there was a gentlemen's agreement between Panama's G2 and the U.S. intelligence services that the surveillance was not targeted on Panama. But the Canal negotiations raised the stakes. With the prospect that property and installations worth hundreds of millions of dollars would be transferred, the agreement was forgotten.

The United States moved first, setting up a telephone bugging network that one U.S. official described as leaving the upper levels of the Panamanian government "wired for sound." The intercepts were churning out hundreds of hours of official conversations, at least some of them pertaining to the Canal negotiations. Then, sometime in early 1976, a U.S. soldier walked into Noriega's G2 headquarters with a packet of transcripts under his arm and offered them for sale.

The soldier, who has never been reliably identified, was described as a Puerto Rican army sergeant. The soldier was thought to be a sympathizer with the Panamanian cause. According to one account, however, he was only out for the money and first offered the transcripts to the Cubans, who turned him down. He gained access to the transcripts through his job in a communications unit. One source described his job as "receipting" the transcripts—a kind of librarian function keeping track of which intelligence officers checked out and returned the transcripts.

Noriega bought the transcripts and asked for more. The conversations that U.S. operatives had bugged were of officials talking to each other and to their wives and girlfriends. Torrijos's main residence at Farrallón just outside of Panama City on the coast was blanketed. Every phone call for months was logged. The listeners had got a titillating earful of Torrijos's love life, but few details about the treaty negotiations. They also had tuned in on hours of homey chatter between Torrijos's elderly cook and her daughters and grandchildren.

In espionage parlance, Noriega had "turned" the U.S. intelligence operative and obtained a "mole" inside the U.S. intelligence apparatus. Once the sergeant had begun to provide the documents, Noriega, as the competent intelligence officer he was, upped the ante. He offered more money for more transcripts and asked what other materials the sergeant could obtain. At about the same time, Noriega recruited at least two or three other U.S. soldiers to provide him with classified information. Noriega's G2 was also considered to have its own extensive telephone bugging operation—a simple matter since Panama owned the telephone company.

The cases became known as the Singing Sergeants affair. Before they were discovered and stopped, according to U.S. officials, the Puerto Rican sergeant and the other moles—about whom few details are known—had turned over "the entire take" from the electronic surveillance operation, including not only the Panamanian targets but targets all over Latin America. In addition, they turned over secret technical manuals about NSA systems. The most damaging information turned over was a list of NSA communications targets in all of Latin America, a document that amounted to a guidebook to U.S. electronic surveillance in the continent.

By April 1976, U.S. intelligence officials realized that their spies were being spied upon. One official recalls that they became suspicious of the Puerto Rican sergeant because he was living lavishly, far above a noncommissioned officer's standard. The official Army investigation was begun April 23 in response to "a request to initiate a counterintelligence investigation concerning a possible leak of classified defense information." It was the first of four investigations cver the next two years, titled respectively Canton Song I, II, III and IV, all involving similar breaches of security to Noriega's G2.

But little came of the investigations. The Army decided that punishing the sergeants was not so important as finding out exactly how much U.S. intelligence information had been compromised. A deal was struck: The soldiers were given dishonorable discharges and immunity from prosecution in exchange for cooperating in assessing the damage. That decision to grant leniency raised hackles in the NSA, which wanted the soldiers tried for espionage—a move that would also have made public Noriega's role in recruiting and paying them. According to *The New York Times*'s reporters Stephen Engelberg and Jeff Gerth, NSA chief Lew Allen, Jr., brought the matter to the attention of George Bush, who had moved to a new job, as director of central intelligence. Bush refused to challenge the Army decision not to prosecute the soldiers and told Allen that he did not have the authority as CIA director to overturn the Army's handling of the case.

Whatever the validity of Bush's qualms about authority, he apparently did nothing to question the CIA's relationship with Noriega and G2's status as a friendly intelligence agency. As the Singing Sergeants investigations proceeded, so did the U.S. bugging operations. The U.S. spying became even more necessary as a tool to penetrate the Panamanians' spying. By the end of the year, the layers of espionage and counterespionage were approaching comic book absurdity: The United States was conducting counterintelligence against Panamanian counterintelligence against U.S. bugging.

While the NSA, the Army and Bush's CIA fretted in Washington about the tolerable parameters of friendly intelligence relationships, in Panama the dirty tricks took a nasty turn. In late October 1976, a few days before the U.S. elections, a wad of *plastique* molded into a soap dish exploded under an empty car parked near the U.S. commissary, just down the hill from the main Canal Zone administration building. The bomb had been placed near the gas tank—not under the driver's seat—and its clock mechanism was set to go off in the middle of the night. The placement and the timing seemed intended to minimize the chance of injuring anyone. The car belonged to William Drummond, a Canal Zone policeman who was the most visible and vociferous leader of Zonian opposition to the treaties. Within forty-eight hours, two more bombs went off under parked cars in the Zone.

The bombings were effective propaganda. Although no one was hurt, the attacks were a frightening reminder of what U.S. officials had long known: Zone facilities and American personnel were impossible to protect from a hostile Panama. After three quarters of a century of Panama's unhappy but relatively peaceful endurance of the quasi-colonial U.S. presence, the bombings were the first unequivocal acts of terrorism against U.S. targets.

The U.S. investigation of the bombings determined that the bomb components were of U.S. manufacture but that the materials could easily have been obtained by the National Guard. There were two theories, neither of which could be confirmed. Many Panamanians believed that Zonian opponents of the treaty had set off the bombs to sabotage the negotiations, while most Americans were equally convinced that the Panamanian National Guard carried out the bombings to intimidate Drummond and other outspoken residents of the Zone.

A few days later, intelligence reports began to arrive on Ambassador Jorden's desk. Sources inside the National Guard were saying that some National Guard members had been exhibiting detailed knowledge about the bombings. For Jorden, the information was solid: "We had very good reason to think the perpetrators were members of the National Guard." Most likely, it had been carried out by highly trained "antiterrorism" specialists under Noriega's command. U.S. Army and Canal Zone security filed reports saying that a Panamanian-born U.S. soldier with expertise in explosives and electronic detonation techniques had obtained the C-4 *plastique* and had trained the Panamanians who carried out the bombings. The same soldier was under investigation in the Singing Sergeants case as a possible mole providing classified information to Noriega.

Jorden went directly to General Torrijos's office at National Guard headquarters. "It was probably our most unpleasant meeting. I told him about the incidents, and that we had reason to think his people had done it. I didn't say he'd ordered it, but it had happened, it was a mess and had to be dealt with." Jorden also gave a pointed warning: Any repetition of the incidents would have "serious consequences" for the treaty negotiations. When Jorden left, Torrijos summoned Aquilino Boyd—now the foreign minister. Lieutenant Colonel Noriega and Lieutenant Colonel Díaz Herrera were also there. Torrijos was grim. He sat hunched forward, his elbow on the arm of his chair; his thumb vigorously rubbed his nose—a personal tick that his associates recognized as a sign of anxious anger.*

"Bill Jorden was just here; he read us a telegram from Henry

---

*Some in the Panamanian opposition were anxious to confide that Torrijos was addicted to cocaine and that the nose rubbing was an indication of that. Most people I talked to who knew Torrijos personally, including U.S. intelligence officials, consider the charge baseless.

Kissinger accusing the National Guard of being responsible for acts of terrorism. This is very serious," Torrijos said. "The Americans are threatening to cut off all talks on the Canal." Torrijos wanted Boyd to take charge of drafting and delivering a response.

Boyd turned to Noriega. "I need your assurance that none of our people was involved in this."

Noriega was emphatic. "Nobody of ours," he said. The other officers nodded agreement.

Boyd flew to New York. The incoming Carter administration— not hamstrung, as were the Republicans, by the right wing's anti-treaty rhetoric—had expressed its willingness to turn the Ford administration negotiations into a real treaty. Boyd's mission was to ensure that the outgoing administration did not use the U.S. intelligence about the bombings to characterize the Torrijos government as a "terrorist" régime and an unreliable treaty partner.

From New York, Boyd called his friend, CIA director George Bush. For the delicate task at hand, Boyd's access to Bush, and Bush's job, was a felicitous coincidence. Bush was the highest official in Washington with whom Boyd had what Latins call *confianza,* the personal trust that allows difficult problems to be worked out candidly and confidentially. A few years earlier, when Panama was successfully pushing the Canal issue to the top of the U.N. decolonialization agenda, George Bush and Aquilino Boyd were ambassadors to the United Nations. They would later be described as close friends, but theirs was not a tennis-and-small-dinners relationship. It was professional, diplomatic; a friendship born out of mutual respect as adversaries, but one that might never have occurred at a time of less international assertiveness by Panama.

Boyd was the embodiment of Panamanian nationalism, combining upper-crust oligarch status with devotion to Torrijos and to the cause of the Panamanian recovery of the Canal. He was a descendant of Irish immigrants who had become rich in Panama's boom during the California gold rush. His grandfather, Federico Boyd, was a leader of the revolt against Colombia at the turn of the century. Federico, arriving in Washington on November 18, 1903, to help negotiate the Panama Canal Treaty, is said to have slugged the aristocratic

Frenchman Bunau-Varilla when he was informed that Bunau-Varilla had rushed to sign the treaty two hours before. Aquilino Boyd had led defiant marches against the U.S. occupation of the Canal Zone in 1959, long before Omar Torrijos gave public expression to his own nationalistic fervor. Boyd's passion for the recovery of the Canal grew from within, from the sense that it was his destiny to recover what his grandfather had lost.

In 1972, Boyd and Bush had attended the special session of the U.N. Security Council held in Addis Ababa, Ethiopia, home of the Organization of African Unity. The meeting was called to focus world attention on the problems of the Third World, and Boyd adeptly moved the Canal issue into that focus. Whenever an African or Asian representative spoke against European holdover colonialism, Boyd rose to excoriate the United States for its occupation and control of Panama's canal. After the day's session, Boyd and Bush continued their debate in the hotel. Bush was angry that Boyd had not warned him that he intended to bring Panama into what the Americans had expected to be a routine exercise in anti-imperialist bashing by the Asians and Africans.

For Bush—as Boyd tells it—the meetings were the beginning of an education. Bush was flabbergasted to learn that racial segregation had existed until recently inside the Canal Zone and that many vestiges still remained. Boyd told him of the separate pay scales according to which the mostly black Panamanian Canal workers were paid only one-fourth that earned by U.S. citizens. Bush refused to believe, until he checked it out in Washington, that overt Jim Crow conditions had been allowed to flourish in the Zone after the civil rights movement had obliterated their overt signs in the American South.

Back in New York, after the U.N. meeting in Ethiopia, Boyd and Bush met again for a long talk about the Canal, this time in the patrician Lotus Club on Manhattan's Upper East Side. Bush brought with him the Nixon administration's special ambassador for treaty affairs, Robert B. Anderson. Boyd felt he had gained Bush's confidence and had converted his basically negative attitude toward the prospect of returning the Canal to a grudging respect for the political necessity and inexorability of a new treaty. Bush's greatest misgiving, one that he never ceased to express in his meetings with Boyd, was his fear that the United States would end up negotiating away its right to a "physical presence" in Panama. The U.S. military, he said, needed the bases in Panama as a forward presence to promote stability and to ward off leftist inroads in the rest of Latin America.

When Boyd called on Bush in early December 1976, he hoped he could count on that kind of understanding from the CIA director to help put the bombing accusations to rest. He told Bush that Torrijos had suggested that the matter be dealt with directly by the heads of intelligence of both countries. Noriega, Boyd said, was flying to Washington; would Bush agree to meet with him?

On December 8 Bush arrived without entourage for lunch at the Panamanian embassy just after noon. Noriega was waiting with Boyd and Panamanian Ambassador Nicolás González Revilla.* Boyd sat next to Bush, across from Noriega, and acted as interpreter. Noriega stiffly repeated denials of Panamanian involvement in the bombings. He said that U.S. Ambassador Jorden, who had conveyed the charges, had refused to provide proof. Noriega complained that he and Ambassador Boyd were placed in the difficult position of answering accusations based on evidence they were not allowed to see.

Bush remained laconic. "I'm listening. I'm listening," he said.

Noriega's questioning betrayed that his main concern was to pin down the CIA's intelligence source inside the National Guard. The bombing evidence clearly originated with the CIA, Noriega said. "Did you get the information from General McAuliffe [commander in chief of Southcom] or did you get it from the agent the CIA has planted inside the National Guard?"

Boyd translated the question and relayed Bush's answer: "We got the information from our man in the field." In each man's mind, the

*An Army Intelligence report on Noriega's trip to Washington referred to it as "unrevealed official business." The report also said he was traveling with a close associate, Whitgreen (probably Carlos). Whitgreen was later indicted in Miami for arms trafficking (see p. 106). FOIA release: 470th MI Group Information Report, Jan. 5, 1977.

exchange was refracted by prisms of knowledge about the intelligence operations he was conducting, operations both with and against the other. Bush knew Noriega knew about the U.S. bugging operations, but did Noriega know the U.S. knew? So far, Southcom and the CIA had concealed their detection of the Singing Sergeants' operation. Noriega was announcing he knew that the CIA had penetrated the National Guard and was implying he knew the identity of the agent. Bush was confirming the penetration—giving the CIA credit rather than McAuliffe's army intelligence unit—but offering nothing to help Noriega pin down the leak. The U.S. source could have been simply the product of the telephone intercepts. Or it could have been an American mole in his own organization. Or—a possibility American intelligence officials would later examine—it could have been that the CIA was receiving information from the very agents Noriega thought were working for him, that the Singing Sergeants were singing a double and triple song.

Bush has never commented publicly about that meeting or any other aspects of the CIA's relationship with Noriega while he was director. In his short tenure at the CIA, Bush had had several occasions to review the U.S. relationship with Noriega. The Singing Sergeants espionage investigation was one that would have required his personal attention the previous April. At about the same time, another major inquiry involving the CIA and Noriega is thought to have crossed his desk. The Justice Department investigation of narcotics intelligence collection, known as the Defeo Report, fully documented the United States's unsuccessful attempts to prosecute Noriega in 1971 and 1972. The report, still highly classified, described at least one of the inchoate assassination plans against Noriega and Torrijos. Such major charges against a man considered to be one of the CIA's major sources in Latin America almost certainly would have been brought to the attention of the CIA chief.

Bush would also have been fully briefed about Noriega's relationship with the CIA, which had flowered after he became head of G2 in 1970. The CIA file on Noriega would have described his help on the release of José Villa from Cuba* and his valuable intelligence on

*See above, pp. 69–70.

Torrijos's trip to Cuba about the time Bush took over as CIA director. Bush had his reasons to pass up the opportunity to upbraid Noriega about the bombings. Ambassador Jorden says the meeting ended in a draw: "Bush listened courteously, never said what he really thought, and moved on to other matters. He was telling the Panamanians as subtly as he could: 'Let's drop this subject—as long as it does not happen again.'"

The four men finished their coffee and moved into the embassy solarium, which gathered the warmth of the early afternoon sun. Whatever Bush thought about Noriega's possible involvement in drugs and espionage and terrorism against the United States, his next question bluntly set straight his real priority. Torrijos was a military dictator who encouraged rather than repressed social reform, and he had recently visited Cuba. "Is Torrijos a Communist?" Bush wanted to know.

Boyd, himself a dedicated anticommunist despite his anti-Yankee radicalism, relished the translation of Noriega's reply: "Torrijos isn't communist, I'm not communist, and neither is the Panamanian people." The meeting ended with Bush writing in his pocket calendar two points Boyd and Noriega asked him to convey to President Ford. Panama wished the negotiations to go forward quickly in the new administration, building on the work of the Ford administration's negotiators. And General Torrijos recognized that the United States had legitimate security interests in the Canal.

A few days later, Boyd received a package from CIA headquarters by special messenger. In it was a memento of their meeting, a picture of a smiling George Bush with the inscription, "To Aquilino Boyd, With friendship and much respect, George." The CIA's signal of friendship for Noriega was even warmer. He spent the rest of his time in Washington as a house guest of Bush's deputy director, Vernon Walters.

By the time Jimmy Carter became the thirty-ninth president of the United States, and the thirteenth president to administer the destiny of the Panama Canal, there was already considerable momentum toward final agreement on the new treaties. Boyd's mission and

Noriega's visit had removed any obstacles there might have been in the handoff from the Ford to the Carter administrations. Carter had subscribed to the findings on Panama of a blue-ribbon commission on U.S.-Latin American relations, chaired by Wall Street lawyer Sol Linowitz. Linowitz's report called Panama "the most urgent issue . . . in the Western Hemisphere." Carter named Linowitz his new special ambassador for the treaty negotiations, to work alongside Ellsworth Bunker. On January 21, 1977, his presidency less than twenty-four hours old, Carter issued Presidential Review Memorandum 1 directing the secretary of state to compile a quick review of all aspects of U.S. interests and objectives "with regard to concluding new canal treaties with Panama."

Perhaps it took a president with Jimmy Carter's quixotic tendencies to place Panama finally at the top of the U.S. foreign policy agenda. The renegotiation issue, all considerations of enlightened self-interest notwithstanding, had always been a policy without a constituency. Polls had consistently shown strong public resistance to giving up the Canal, and no interest group stood to benefit directly from a new arrangement. On the contrary, if there was a constituency at all it was the small but vocal Zonian community that had lived in undisturbed comfort and security for more than half a century. The Zonians—the ten thousand U.S. Canal workers, many of whom did not speak Spanish—were well into their third generation and had developed a microculture of their own. The Canal Zone even had its own delegates to the U.S. presidential nominating conventions. The Zonian constituency had cultivated a number of strong right-wing supporters in the U.S. Congress by successfully identifying retention of the Canal with the fight against communism. They portrayed the treaty as another post-Vietnam retreat by those too timid for the full exercise of U.S. power in the world. Among the most vocal were Senators Jesse Helms of North Carolina and James Eastland of Mississippi and Representatives Daniel Flood of Pennsylvania and John Murphy of New York.

But Carter's problem was far broader than the handful of ideological conservatives. Only a year before, thirty-eight senators—four more than needed to block ratification of any treaty—had introduced a resolution opposing a new treaty and asserting U.S. sovereignty over the Canal Zone. For Carter, expending his postelection honeymoon in the fight for justice for Panama seemed a thankless task.

Carter's reasons, as spelled out in his book, *Keeping Faith,* were based more on realpolitik than on altruism. "[T]hough we could not talk about it much in public," he wrote, "the canal was in serious danger from direct attack and sabotage unless a new and fair treaty arrangement could be forged." His military advisers had reached the conclusion that the Canal could be defended only in a "cooperative effort with a friendly Panama." The use of military force to continue U.S. control was out of the question, as it was estimated that it would require at least one hundred thousand soldiers to protect the Canal in a hostile environment. The continuing stalemate on the Canal was also a major obstacle to other foreign policy priorities. It was "driving a wedge" between the United States and its best friends among the Latin American democracies. "They were being forced to take sides between us and Panama and they were not supporting us. This issue had become a litmus test throughout the world, indicating how the United States, as a superpower, would treat a small and relatively defenseless nation that had always been a close partner and supporter."

Compared to the enormous political obstacles, the actual work of finishing up the negotiations was relatively straightforward. A solid basis for agreement had been left by the previous administration. During the summer of 1977, Linowitz and Bunker worked rapidly with their Panamanian counterparts, Rómulo Escobar Bethancourt and Carlos López Guevara.

One issue remained in dispute: money. How much would the United States pay immediately as part of the settlement, in addition to the fees and annuities to Panama from the actual operation of the Canal? The Panamanians had floated figures as high as $1 billion. The U.S. negotiators tried to explain that it was politically impossible for the United States to even appear to be paying a bonus to Panama for the privilege of receiving the Canal from the United States. The United States would not even entertain the notion of lease payments for the many Southcom bases in Panama, notwithstanding the many millions of dollars the United States paid each year for similar bases in the Philippines and other countries. Various formulas were discussed to allow an increased flow of cash to Panama under the guise of U.S. foreign aid payments, but nothing remotely approaching the sums the Panamanians were demanding. International precedent favored the Panamanian demand for compensation, but the North Americans had unassailable political reality on their side. The negotiations turned hostile, and some negotiators seriously thought that the treaties might be derailed so near the final goal.

It was in this charged atmosphere that the U.S. bugging operation and Noriega's successful counterintelligence again became a factor. The incident began with a routine press breakfast by negotiator Linowitz on July 14. Although the session was off the record, a leaked version quoted Linowitz as blaming the Panamanians for snarling the talks with excessive monetary demands—the amount cited in the story was $5 billion, an outrageous figure far in excess of the Panamanians' actual requests. To make matters worse, the reports said that the treaties under consideration would leave the United States free to "intervene" in Panama to protect the Canal. That mischaracterization of perhaps the most sensitive issue in the talks left the Panamanian negotiators sputtering with rage.

Publicly, the Panamanian press described the leaked remarks as evidence of a "filthy plot" to discredit and debilitate Panama. Privately, Torrijos used Noriega's counterintelligence about U.S. bugging to set a bilevel mousetrap to force the U.S. government into backing down. Panama's new ambassador to Washington, Gabriel Lewis Galindo, was instructed to carry out step one: Lewis informed the State Department that the Panamanian government was going to send a high-level mission to Washington to hold a press conference to denounce the "lies" that the U.S. side was spreading in the press and to accuse the United States of negotiating in bad faith.

A few minutes later, the international operator put through another call to Lewis from Panama. Torrijos was on the line. His words were angry, but his voice was light, Lewis recalled.

"I want you to know what's going on," Torrijos said. "I'm going to change the negotiating team. I'll send them to Washington to give a press conference to get lots of TV coverage. We're going to tell the world what has really been going on in this treaty business."

Strange, thought Lewis, Torrijos seldom called, and it was out of character for him to repeat matters already covered by the foreign minister. Torrijos went on: "I want you to know what we are going to say in that press conference. The Americans have been tapping my phone, lots of our phones, because they are trying to find out whom we are paying in the U.S. team. They are bugging our phones because they are concerned about this payoff business. But we found out what they are doing. We bought the tapes." Lewis wondered at the call but kept it to himself. It was late morning, Saturday, July 16.

Within hours, the Army Security Agency team monitoring the intercepts from Torrijos's house had prepared a transcript of the call and had sent what was later described as "an important intelligence report of the highest quality" to the National Security Council and the State Department. The report said that the Panamanian government would reveal highly secret U.S. intelligence operations (but disingenuously did not mention that the operation in question was the very bugging that allowed the Army Security Agency to obtain the information) and would charge that "high level members of the executive and legislative branch had asked for payoffs in return for arranging increases" in the payments to Panama under negotiation.

The report set off a firestorm of activity. Such accusations, even if untrue, would obliterate any prospect for gaining Senate approval of the Canal treaties even in the unlikely event the negotiators could put the imbroglio behind them and reach agreement. At the very least, administration officials knew, the wiretapping charge was true. And if it were ever shown that U.S. officials received bribes to make concessions to Panama, the scandal would be of Watergate proportions.

Torrijos's ploy got immediate results. NSC adviser Zbigniew Brzezinski issued a short press release repudiating as "incorrect in major details" the accounts of Linowitz's breakfast comments. In Panama, a quickly convened meeting of the Panamanian and American negotiators went further to put out the fire. Linowitz mollified the Panamanians by showing them the notes he used to brief the American journalists. He convinced them that the stories were inaccurate and that he had not used the dreaded word "intervention" to describe U.S. rights under any new treaties. He also convinced them that President Carter was willing to make compromises on the financial arrangements surrounding the treaties and that Panama should focus on economic benefits that would come into effect after the signing of the treaties and officially separate from them.

The crisis ended. No special delegation went to Washington. No press conference was held. But rumbling continued in the bowels of the U.S. government. The Senate Select Intelligence Committee and the attorney general's office conducted a massive investigation into the charges of payoffs. A full search of U.S. intelligence files was conducted. No substantiation for the charge was ever found.

Two months later, when Ambassador Lewis was in Panama, he asked Torrijos about the curious phone call. Torrijos laughed at his own cleverness. "It wasn't true at all," he said. "We didn't have anybody on the payroll. I was talking to you over a line I knew they had bugged. I was just feeding them information over their own intercept."

In August the negotiators announced that final agreement had been reached. Twin treaties, one governing the Canal and the Zone, the other the military aspects of U.S.-Panama relations, were signed on September 7, 1977, in a ceremony in Washington attended by virtually every Latin American head of state, democrats and dictators alike.

The first treaty declared all territories previously constituting the Canal Zone to be unequivocally Panamanian and established a timetable for the return of all properties and installations. The Canal itself and all operating control would change from U.S. to Panamanian hands at midnight December 31, 1999. During the transition, a U.S.-chartered corporation, the Panama Canal Commission, would run the Canal. Until 1990, its director and a majority of its governing board would be U.S. citizens; after that the director would be a Panamanian, nominated by the government of Panama and subject to confirmation by the U.S. Senate.

There was little ambiguity in the provisions about the operations of the Canal and the former Canal Zone, and it was in that area that the United States made its greatest concessions. Preferential treatment for U.S. citizens was phased out. Gone was the despised U.S. legal jurisdiction over a portion of Panamanian territory. Gone were the fences and guards prohibiting Panamanians from climbing Ancon Hill, the proud overlook on Panama City, the Canal and the Pacific Ocean.

Economically, Panama would reap immediate benefit. The minuscule $2.3 million annuity was raised to $10 million plus an annuity based on tonnage that was expected to generate at least $50 million.

In the provisions governing military matters, agreement was reached at the cost of certain logical incongruities. For the United States, the treaty preserved the U.S. right to defend the Canal unilaterally and indefinitely. Until the year 2000, the United States had the "primary responsibility to protect and defend the Panama Canal"; after that defense responsibilities were to be shared by U.S. and Panamanian forces. The language provided a thin veil for the hard fact that Panamanian territory, irrespective of the new treaties, remained subject to unilateral U.S. military action that required neither the invitation nor the approval of the Panamanian government.

A further incongruity lay in the treatment of the vast U.S. military establishment already ensconced in the former Canal Zone. The military bases had grown out of the clause in the 1903 treaty permitting U.S. "fortifications" to protect the Canal. It defied logic, however, to describe the array of harbors, airfields, training centers and electronic intelligence installations as having more than a remote connection to defense of the waterway. "The military bases have no sense, because the Canal is undefensible. They only are targeted at the heart of Panama," Torrijos had said. The new treaties left the contradiction intact: they spoke of the U.S. military presence exclusively in terms of defense of the Canal; then an appended agreement provided a complete list of U.S. installations, including those unrelated to Canal defense, whose presence in Panama was guaranteed until the year 2000.

Torrijos's fears that U.S. troops would be used against Panama itself, however, were seemingly allayed in a clarifying amendment, growing out of a personal meeting between Carter and Torrijos. The

U.S. right to defend the Canal "does not mean, nor shall it be interpreted as, a right of intervention of the United States in the internal affairs of Panama. Any United States action shall be directed at insuring that the Canal will remain open, secure, and accessible, and it shall never be directed against the territorial integrity or political independence of Panama." In other words, no big stick.

The U.S. bases would revert to Panama in 2000, and the legal ambiguity about their purpose until then did not—in 1977—appear to be a concern of either side. Unspoken in the treaty language, but understood by all parties at the time, was the possibility, even the likelihood, that Panama and the United States would negotiate leases, with a hefty price tag, for the continued presence of the main U.S. Southcom bases.

Noriega kept himself in the shadows during the treaty process. He traveled to Washington with Torrijos for the signing of the treaties. And when President Carter reciprocated with a triumphant visit to Panama in June 1978, Noriega personally coordinated the security arrangements. But Noriega's illegal activities of the early seventies and his dirty tricks during the negotiations rose to the surface in the most controversial stage of making the treaties a reality—the Senate ratification process.

A group of Republican senators, including conservative opponents, as well as moderates who ultimately voted for ratification, insisted on a full airing of the persistent charges that Panama was a haven for drug traffickers. The accusations originated with Representative John Murphy's Canal subcommittee and were based almost exclusively on the controversies surrounding the Him González and Moisés Torrijos cases six years earlier. Treaty supporters agreed to order an exhaustive report by the Senate Select Intelligence Committee, including a full review of classified CIA and DEA documents about Panama.

Senator Birch Bayh, chairman of the Intelligence Committee, presented the report in a two-day special plenary session. The investigation gave Torrijos essentially a clean bill. He had indeed known about the illicit drug-related activities of his brother, Moisés, and had helped him avoid arrest—but then, so had the United States. Nothing the investigation turned up would be sufficient for use in a U.S. court of law, Bayh said.

His conclusions on Noriega, however, were of a far higher order. Referring always elliptically to "the National Guard officer," Bayh's comments were prophetic:

> I think the best case there [regarding Panamanian officials involved in drug trafficking] would be the National Guard officer. Here, again, I do not think we have enough evidence, the kind of thing on which you could bring an indictment against him in this country.
>
> But you are asking me. And as one colleague to the other, from what I have read and sensed through all these documents, there is just a tremendous amount of smoke there, as far as the Guard official is concerned.
>
> If I might expand on that a bit: he is a very powerful figure in the Guard. Without trying to excuse the unwillingness of General Torrijos to really put the hammer on him, the general conception is that he is reluctant to do that because he needs his support to maintain the power base.

Why, then, had U.S. drug enforcement officials also kept their hands off Noriega? Bayh responded:

> [Noriega] . . . as our DEA people say, is now cooperating. They want him to continue to cooperate. [Classified material deleted.] There is evidence that when the Panamanians determine to do a good job, they can do a good job of enforcing and arresting people. We now have them in the record where they are cooperating, and they do not want anything like this to come along and destroy that cooperation.

The treaties were ratified on April 18, 1978, by a barebones two-thirds margin of 68 to 32. The politics of obtaining that slim victory required U.S. officials who were aware of Noriega's thuggery to play it down, to keep the focus of the debate on Torrijos, who could be exonerated. Once again, for greater reasons of state, potentially devastating revelations about Noriega's activities were swept aside.

For Noriega, the treaties ended the primary task Torrijos had set for him. Once again, he was free to seek out other opportunities. And no one, at least in the United States, seemed to be looking. Within a few months of the treaty ratification, Panama was eclipsed by a revolution exploding in Nicaragua.

CHAPTER 5

CENTRAL AMERICAN
CASABLANCA

On August 22, 1978, a group of guerrillas dressed as Nicaraguan soldiers walked into the National Palace in Managua and changed the course of Central American history. They fired their weapons over the heads of the assembled congressmen, who had just begun a session, and took fifteen hundred people hostage. The siege put the Sandinista National Liberation Front in headlines all over the world. The leader of the audacious operation called himself Comandante Zero and announced that the Sandinista Front would fight to the death to free Nicaragua from the U.S.-backed dictatorship of Anastasio Somoza. When the siege reached a triumphant, negotiated end two days later, Comandante Zero, his fighters and fifty freed political prisoners rode through cheering crowds to Managua's airport, where a plane sent by Omar Torrijos was waiting to fly them to Panama.

Edén Pastora was received as a hero and an ally when he arrived. The welcoming committee was led by two Torrijos loyalists, Lieutenant Colonel Manuel Noriega and Deputy Health Minister Hugo Spadafora. They came on board as soon as the plane landed to shake hands and to assure the jubilant Sandinistas of the revolutionary solidarity of the people and government of Panama. They said that Torrijos was anxious to meet them.

Pastora and a group of top Sandinistas who had just been released from a Somoza jail were taken to Farrallón, Torrijos's beloved sea-

side home. Torrijos spent several days with them, probing the Sandinista leaders' goals and political differences. At the third meeting,
he summoned only Pastora and other members of the Terceristas,
the most moderate of the three Sandinista factions. In them, he found
political soul mates who shared his vision of nationalist, nonideological revolution that avoided the ills of both U.S. capitalism and Cuban
communism.

Finally, Pastora was asked to come alone. He found Noriega and
most of the general staff waiting with Torrijos. Pastora told them of
the origin of his hatred for Somoza. One of Somoza's officers had
gotten into a land dispute with Pastora's father and had ordered him
killed. Pastora described how, as a seven-year-old boy, he did not
understand the word "assassinate" used in the telegram telling his
mother of her husband's death. Then Pastora broke down, sobbing;
when he gained control and looked up, he saw Torrijos wiping his
eyes. Noriega and some other officers were also hiding tears, Pastora
said. He started to apologize, but Torrijos interrupted, "Don't worry.
It's men like you who are needed by our people. I'm going to help
you go back at the head of an army."

To carry out his promise, Torrijos turned to the two men he had
assigned to welcome Pastora to Panama. Within days, Noriega had
conducted an inventory of the National Guard's meager surplus
stocks and skimmed enough rifles and other equipment to outfit
about five hundred Sandinista troops. Torrijos's generosity, and
Noriega's search, were so thorough that National Guard troops soon
were complaining about the lack of boots and replacement weapons.
Torrijos then ordered Noriega to fly to Cuba to arrange for Fidel
Castro to open an arms pipeline to the Sandinistas using Panama as
a cover.

Hugo Spadafora, a thirty-eight-year-old medical doctor, had a
more romantic task. He resigned his post in the Health Ministry and
announced that he was organizing an international brigade to fight
alongside the Sandinistas in Nicaragua. In an interview reflecting
Torrijos's thinking, Spadafora denounced the "forty-year dynastic
tyranny under which a brother country is suffering." He said that the
Somoza régime "represents a danger, a concrete threat for the progress of the Central American peoples." On September 28, only five

weeks after the palace takeover in Nicaragua, Spadafora and three hundred volunteers assembled at Don Bosco Church in downtown Panama City. The volunteers included Torrijos's son, Martín. After a patriotic ceremony invoking Simón Bolívar's vision of Latin American unity, the new Victoriano Lorenzo Brigade marched off to war.*

Torrijos's embrace of Pastora, Spadafora and Noriega as partners in a single covert enterprise demonstrated his knack for integrating antagonistic elements within his internationalist vision. Torrijos was a close friend of all three men. When in Panama, Pastora stayed at one of Torrijos's homes. Pastora and Noriega formed a friendship and alliance that would remain unbroken; for Noriega, however, Spadafora had only suspicion, rivalry and, finally, the fierce hatred from which tragedies are born.

It would be difficult to imagine two more different men than Hugo Spadafora and Manuel Noriega. In many ways, Spadafora was everything Noriega wasn't. Spadafora was extraordinarily tall by Panamanian standards, over six feet; he was light-skinned, light-haired and so good-looking he could have played himself in the movies he imagined being made of his life. He was gregarious and easygoing, a man his friends spoke of with natural affection and women treated as a demigod. His Italian immigrant parents gave him a good, comfortable life in the small city of Chitré. His father, Carmelo, owned a furniture factory, Mueblería Fino Fino. He wasn't rich, but was well off enough to send Hugo to medical school in Bologna, Italy.

Unlike Noriega's calculated maneuvering toward power, Hugo Spadafora careened from cause to cause, choosing sides with passion and abandon. Although never tempted by communism, he had embraced the agenda of leftist struggles in Latin America and Africa and had long inveighed against "imperialism," more often the European colonial than the U.S. variety. In the 1960s he volunteered unsuccessfully to fight in Cuba against the Americans and in Algeria against the French. Finally in 1966–1967, he spent a year as a guerrilla

*Victoriano Lorenzo was a hero in Panama's war of independence with Colombia.

doctor in the liberation movement led by Amilcar Cabral against Portuguese colonial rule in Guinea-Bissau.

After the 1968 coup in Panama, Spadafora joined an underground Arnulfista cell fighting against the National Guard in Chiriquí Province. "I thought it was just another 'cuartelazo' [barracks rebellion] intended to maintain the oligarchy in power," he wrote. He treated wounded rebels in safe houses and plotted new guerrilla offensives. But in July 1969 Torrijos's political police, DENI, raided his apartment and arrested him. He was surprised that he was not tortured or in any way mistreated; he was even more astonished when after about two weeks in jail he was brought to Torrijos himself for a long discussion of politics and the future of Panama. "I had the impression he was a leader who was taking great pains to be understood, that he was very concerned about the unpopularity of the *golpista* régime he was leading," Spadafora wrote. Torrijos listened with respect while Spadafora lectured him on the socioeconomic problems of Latin America, his revolutionary experiences in Africa and the kind of revolution that should be carried out in Panama.

Torrijos sent Spadafora off to the jungles of Darién Province to run a medical clinic—a combination of forced exile and Peace Corps–like mission in lieu of prison. He returned six months later a total convert to Torrijos's revolutionary vision. He worked as a government doctor in slum clinics and began to write newspaper columns advocating reform of the medical system. Torrijos was impressed and put him in charge of the medical system in Colón, which was perhaps the most poverty- and disease-ridden province in the country. When he met Pastora's plane that day in August 1978, Spadafora had been deputy minister—a health bureaucrat—for two years. His assignment by Torrijos to lead the Victoriano Lorenzo Brigade made him a revolutionary again.

The fight to rid Nicaragua of Somoza, personified by Comandante Zero, drew a symbolic line in the sand against the dictatorships that had displaced civilian governments in the majority of Latin American nations in the 1960s and 1970s. Venezuela, Costa Rica and Colombia were the only real democracies remaining, and their clear

identification with the anti-Somoza forces made support for the Sandinista rebellion internationally respectable.

Democratic respectability was something Torrijos still lacked and
very much desired. His success in obtaining an agreement on the
Canal treaties tended to mask the fact that he was himself a military
dictator in a country without elections or a free press. He very much
wanted Panama to be considered in the camp of moderate, progressive democracies. In October he announced a plan for a transition
to democratic government. A new president, Aristides Royo, was
named by the National Assembly, and Torrijos announced that he
was returning to the barracks, relinquishing his special Maximum
Leader status. While the National Guard remained very much in
control, Torrijos pointed the way to a future real democracy in 1984,
when the first national presidential elections would be held. Legislation legalizing political parties made, for the first time in a decade,
organized opposition to the régime possible. But in practice, the
reforms meant little immediate change and offered only a vaguely
defined political process drawn out over six years with no guarantees
except Torrijos's word.

Instead of quick democracy for his people, Torrijos offered democracy by association. He cloaked Panama in the democratic aura of
the Latin countries he was working with to get rid of the tyrant
Somoza. Vis-à-vis the United States, however, Torrijos had to play
a more delicate game. Despite the liberal administration of Democrat Jimmy Carter, Somoza appealed to deeply ingrained anticommunist attitudes that viewed any left-leaning revolution as a strategic
threat to the United States. Panama's treaties and the Sandinista
cause shared a common enemy in the emerging right wing of the
Republican party. And many of Somoza's staunchest allies held key
positions in the U.S. House of Representatives, which was drafting
enabling legislation that was indispensable to the implementation of
the Canal treaties. Panama's role in obtaining the guns for a Sandinista military victory had to be clandestine. Torrijos's idea, according to Pastora, was to arrange the arms network so that he and the
Latin American presidents, not Castro, would hold the key to the
weapons stock and they would make sure the favored Terceristas got
their fair share of the supplies and more.

And that, as usual, was where Noriega came in. His trip to Cuba was successful. Castro was anxious to help the Sandinistas in a way that would not provoke U.S. intervention on behalf of Somoza. Noriega's job was to set up a supply route for Cuban weapons that was discreet. The center of Noriega's arms network was familiar ground: The border province of Chiriquí and its capital, David, where nine years earlier Noriega had prevented the overthrow of Torrijos.

Planes loaded with crates of assault rifles began to arrive at David airport from Cuba. The weapons were stored and transshipped in smaller planes across the Costa Rican border. The ultimate destination was airstrips near Sandinista bases in Guanacaste Province in northern Costa Rica, and for that final leg Noriega recruited two young pilots he had known from his lieutenant days in Chiriquí.

Floyd Carlton and César Rodríguez were hustlers who had hung around airports and were always available for odd jobs. Carlton had once done Noriega a favor: Working as a clerk in the David courthouse, he waylaid the paperwork in a civil suit a farmer had brought against Noriega for shooting the farmer's horse. Rodríguez liked to have Noriega and Carlton over to his father's house to drink the sweet homemade wine his father concocted from mangos. Rodríguez and Carlton had worked their way through pilot's school in Panama City and had earned an uneven living flying the small Pipers and Cessnas owned by businessmen and National Guard officers; they had a reputation as bushwackers—pilots who could land and take off anywhere—and usually they were safe. They were always fearless. Neither had a plane or a steady job, and their clothes had a dusty look about them when Noriega found them in 1978 and asked them if they would like some dangerous work and some good money.

He sent them to Costa Rica, where they met former Costa Rican president Daniel Oduber, who was handling anti-Somoza arrangements for the Costa Rican government. They joined two other Panamanian pilots, Teófilo Watson and Alberto Audemar, and worked out of an airstrip owned by Manuel Enrique "Pillique" Guerra. It was an operation born of idealism and carried out with a spirit of adventure. The pilots were paid well.

Meanwhile, Pastora had an idea to keep the Sandinistas on the front pages: He wanted to create his own makeshift air force to launch bombing raids into the heart of Somoza's territory. On one of his trips to confer with Torrijos, Pastora flew into the National Guard's Paitilla Airport in Panama City. He asked about a twin-engine Beechcraft Baron he had seen in one of the military hangars. He was told it had recently been confiscated from a drug smuggler and might be available. Torrijos was intrigued by the notion of outfitting a *cazabombardero* [fighter-bomber], and he gave the plane to Pastora to take to Costa Rica.

There, Pillique Guerra and several mechanics mounted two 30-caliber machine guns on the plane's nose and cut a large hole in the belly of the fuselage. They installed a door and a magazine that would hold two 25-pound bombs. When the door was opened by hand and the magazine tilted, the bombs would slide out. Unfortunately, the Costa Rican officials keeping track of the Sandinista support operation refused to let Pastora launch his planned air raid from Costa Rican soil. Pastora and César Rodríguez flew the plane back to Panama, to the military base of Rio Hato, where it was hidden under camouflage. Pastora showed the plane to Torrijos, who examined what Pastora called the "Sandinista Air Force" with the glee of a schoolboy prankster.

"I said I needed authorization to take off," Pastora would later recall. "He didn't say yes or no. I took advantage of the neither yes nor no. I ran to César Rodríguez, said we have the order of the general. He took off that night at two A.M. By five he was bombing. He dropped about five bombs. Two fell near a school, two near the bunker, and another on the hill. He couldn't count on much accuracy—he let them go from an altitude of about three thousand feet. It didn't matter, the political effect was tremendous."

The Cuban arms shipped through Panama and Costa Rica provided most of the Sandinista weaponry and ammunition, but Noriega was working on a separate track to arrange direct arms purchases in Miami. The deal he set up would also make some extra money for himself and his partners. The main operators were Edgardo López Grimaldi and Carlos Whitgreen. López was one of Noriega's G2 associates and was assigned, under civilian cover, as Panamanian

consul to Miami. Whitgreen also did occasional G2 security work for
Noriega, but mainly he was a businessman and drinking crony. He
set up a front corporation, disingenuously called Caza y Pesca—
Hunting and Fishing Club, Inc. Whitgreen was president and
Noriega was one of the shareholders. López's assignment was to
place orders for one thousand weapons at gun stores in Miami and
ship them to Panama for transfer to the Sandinistas. In the late 1970s,
U.S. gun stores did not yet stock assault rifles, such as Chinese
AK47s and Israeli Uzis, so López had to settle for deer-hunting
rifles, such as the Remington Woodmaster 30.06, and Colt .45 pistols. He was also able to locate a few World War II vintage M1
carbines and some Vietnam era AR15s (the semiautomatic version of
the M16).

Many of the orders were placed at Garcia's National Gun Shop
in Miami's Little Havana, which unknown to the Panamanians was
under the close scrutiny of Donald Kimbler of the Bureau of Alcohol, Tobacco and Firearms, who was keeping track of possible terrorist groups forming among the anti-Castro Cubans. Checking
Garcia's logs of rifle sales in October 1978, Kimbler routinely followed up on a series of recent large transactions involving the same
buyer and stumbled on the Panama connection. The gun buyer led
Kimbler to López, who admitted his involvement and blurted out
that he was acting on the instructions of "an official of the
Panamanian G2." López then quickly got out of town, and the
Panamanian Foreign Ministry drew up papers for the State Department backdating his resignation from the consular post to make it
appear he was a private citizen at the time of the interview with
Kimbler.

Kimbler's investigation led to the discovery of purchases of more
than eight hundred rifles in twenty separate transactions. He also
interviewed gun dealers who said that the Panamanian buyers told
them the guns were destined for the Nicaraguan guerrillas and that
they intended to buy $2 million worth of arms.

While the Miami U.S. attorney's office was putting together the
case for an indictment, even more blatant evidence turned up showing Panama's role in shipping arms to the Sandinistas. On March 13
and 16, 1979, Somoza's National Guard intercepted two vans loaded

with arms at Peñas Blancas on the Costa Rican border. Among other munitions, the vans contained forty-nine Belgian-made FAL infantry weapons and ninety U.S.-made M1 carbines. The serial numbers of the FALs identified them as purchased by Cuba in 1959; seventy of the M1s had been bought from U.S. gun dealers and shipped to Noriega's Caza y Pesca in Panama.

The seizures and the investigation tying Noriega and his partners to arms shipments came at an embarrassing moment for the U.S. government. As the war in Nicaragua raged on in 1979 toward an increasingly inevitable Sandinista victory, the Carter administration at first distanced itself from Somoza, then began to pressure him to step down. While suspicious of the presence of Marxists among the Sandinistas, the administration hoped to promote moderate elements such as Pastora's Terceristas and bolster the position of non-Sandinista politicians and businessmen who had turned against Somoza. The U.S. strategy was not unlike the public position adopted by Torrijos, who took advantage of his personal relationship with President Carter to lobby Washington toward more resolute actions to speed Somoza's removal.

At the same time, opponents of the Panama Canal treaties were waging last-ditch efforts to defeat treaty-related legislation pending in the House of Representatives. The arms-supply issue was aired in hearings organized by Representative John Murphy, who was not only a close personal friend of Somoza's but had suffered humiliation at the hands of Torrijos during his 1972 visit to Panama. As the State Department and White House issued noncommittal statements that they were "watching closely" the reports of alleged arms shipments via Panama, Murphy marshaled the evidence to support his notion that Nicaragua's troubles were the result of a communist plot by the likes of Fidel Castro and the tinpot dictator Omar Torrijos. In June and July, ending only a few days before the victorious Sandinistas marched in victory into Managua on July 19, Murphy presented the evidence.

Murphy's Panama Canal subcommittee put on a full show, with captured M1s and rocket launchers laid out on cloth-covered tables. The administration easily stonewalled. State Department official Brian Atwood blandly stated that there was "no evidence of

Panamanian government approval of the gun smuggling" and suggested that the conservatives on the committee were just giving the Somoza government a "forum" to excoriate its Latin American enemies such as Torrijos. The real U.S. priority for Central America, Atwood said, was the smooth implementation of the Canal treaties:

> Let me . . . emphasiz[e] very strongly on behalf of the administration that nothing could diminish our influence in that crucial area of the world more than defeating the Panama Canal implementing legislation or encumbering it with amendments which violate the treaties. Nothing could strengthen the hand of our adversaries—Cuba and the Soviet Union—more than forcing the United States to go back on its treaty obligation to Panama.

The Murphy hearings achieved little more than a short delay in the treaty legislation, and the charges of Panama's gun running soon were mooted by the Sandinista victory. Panama's enemies had the right evidence at the wrong time. The evidence presented in the hearings in June and July was strong and confirmed by later unassailable reports. But a Sandinista victory was inevitable by the time the hearings ended, and except for the minority of conservatives in Congress the defeat of Somoza was welcomed in the United States. Indeed, Torrijos's goals, if not his methods, were well in line with U.S. interests.

Reluctant for political reasons to act against Torrijos, U.S. officials involved at the time used the familiar denial that there was any evidence against Panama that would hold up in a court of law. But even that dodge turned out to be untrue, particularly regarding Noriega's involvement. In January 1980, the U.S. attorney's office in Miami attempted to revive the Caza y Pesca case. Whitgreen and several others had been indicted the previous May for illegal purchase and transport of weapons, but the case was dismissed on a technicality. This time, the prosecutors notified their superiors in Washington that they intended to indict the two Panamanian officials involved, Noriega and the Panamanian consul López, in addition to Whitgreen. Customs agents had developed new evidence, including a letter from Noriega, linking him firmly to the arms transactions. Investigators had also turned up expense vouchers paid by G2.

But again, foreign policy considerations prevailed. Panama had just done an enormous favor for the Carter administration. Torrijos offered refuge to the deposed shah of Iran, whose presence in the United States after his overthrow by the Ayatollah Khomeini in 1979 had become increasing untenable.* Noriega handled the operation in Panama, and he had put Whitgreen in charge of the shah's personal security. On January 30, FBI Special Agent Frank Gibbons transmitted a message: Torrijos would be embarrassed if the two officials directly concerned with the shah's stay in Panama were to be indicted. The U.S. attorneys working on the case understood that the U.S. agency behind the cautionary message was actually the CIA, whose long relationship with the shah and concern for his welfare were well known. U.S. attorney J. V. Eskenazi wrote a perplexed letter to his boss in the criminal division of the Justice Department. He said his office wanted to proceed with the indictment:

> However, due to the information from the FBI, it was agreed by all present that the matters referred to herein should be brought to the attention of the Departments of Justice, State and Treasury for further guidance. Unfortunately, those of us in law enforcement in Miami find ourselves frequently attempting to enforce the laws of the United States, but simultaneously being caught between foreign policy considerations over which we have no control (and often, no knowledge).

Eskenazi said that he would wait for instructions before proceeding with the planned indictment. They never came. The case languished for two more years, during which two successive U.S. attorneys assigned to it resigned. Then it was dropped as "too old."

Panama was not of course the only country whose arms trafficking to the Sandinistas passed conveniently unnoticed. Venezuela and Costa Rica played indispensable roles in the same, well-coordinated pipeline that started in Cuba and ended in the battlefields of Nicaragua. The volume of arms reaching the Sandinistas at the height of

*According to Díaz Herrera and other reports, the shah paid Torrijos $12 million, deposited in a Swiss bank, for the privilege.

the conflict can only be estimated. A Costa Rican congressional investigation, whose report was made public in 1981, concluded that "approximately one million pounds of arms and munitions" passed through Costa Rica to the Sandinistas between December 1978 and July 1979. Panamanian planes and pilots made about half of the flights, the report said.

Under Pastora's command, Hugo Spadafora and the Victoriano Lorenzo Brigade were among the first columns to cross the Costa Rican border into southern Nicaragua in June 1979 to begin the final offensive against Somoza. The brigade, a force of almost two hundred men, was dispersed among regular Sandinista units, and its members fought under Nicaraguan commanders. But Spadafora had become one of Pastora's closest lieutenants and was given his own troop command.* With the opening of the southern front, his unit was engaged for weeks during the heaviest fighting in the war. Pastora had hoped to liberate the city of Rivas in order to install a provisional government that would maximize Pastora's role and that of the moderates, vis-à-vis the more radical Sandinista factions fighting in the north; instead, his offensive stalled as Somoza poured thousands of his best troops into the south, which allowed the northern Sandinista units to capture town after town and eventually occupy León, the second largest city, and to advance on Managua.

The Sandinista victory on July 19 brought a moment of rare Pan-American unity. Democrats and progressives, leftists and centrists, rich and poor, Cubans and Americans found a common theme of joy and optimism in Somoza's defeat. The U.S. administration for the first time looked on passively as a former anticommunist ally fell to an opposition led by leftist guerrillas, then extended a hand in friendship to the new régime. In Washington, one enthusiastic congressman, Tom Harkin of Iowa, echoed John F. Kennedy in declaring, "*Yo soy un Sandinista*—I am a Sandinista."

But the honeymoon was brief. Torrijos had been involved in futile last-minute efforts to preserve the Nicaraguan National Guard as a counterbalance to total Sandinista control. Only days after the vic-

*Spadafora's role was so prominent that Somoza once personally announced— erroneously—that Spadafora had been killed.

tory, he sent Lieutenant Colonel Rubén Darío Paredes—a graduate of Nicaragua's military school—to head a Panamanian mission to assist the new régime in organizing a police force. Torrijos also proposed an elaborate plan for Costa Rica and Venezuela to provide doctors, teachers and economic advisers. The plan called for a combination of Latin American manpower and U.S. money. Cuba's role, according to Torrijos's proposals, would not be greater than that of any of Nicaragua's other Latin American allies, and all Cuban and Panamanian military contacts with Nicaragua would end after a few months.

Two weeks after the victory, Torrijos again sent Noriega to Cuba to express concern about the "presence of a large number of Cuban advisors" in Nicaragua, according to a U.S. intelligence report. Little else in Nicaragua worked out as Torrijos envisioned. Pastora, the Sandinistas' most visible leader during the war, was excluded from the powerful Sandinista National Directorate and was given a ceremonial post as deputy minister of interior, subordinate to Interior Minister Tomás Borge. By the end of the year, all Panamanian military advisers had returned to Panama and had been replaced by Cubans, who showed no sign of leaving soon. For the Sandinistas, Torrijos's emissaries were too closely identified with the United States and with support for Pastora's faction. Financial aid arrived from Europe and even from the United States, but Torrijos's sweeping ideas for Latin American assistance did not materialize.

Torrijos's arms network and the international brigade were put to new uses. The Sandinista victory fueled smoldering revolutionary fires all over Central America. In El Salvador, laboring under two decades of corrupt military rule, a chant rose up: "*Nicaragua venció; El Salvador vencerá*—Nicaragua won; El Salvador will win." As the Salvadoran guerrillas prepared for battle, Noriega's arms pipeline was available to provide the weapons, this time for a price.

The pipeline was bursting with undelivered arms and ammunition from Cuba and Venezuela when the Nicaraguan war ended, and most of the surplus remained in warehouses in Costa Rica and Panama. Floyd Carlton and César Rodríguez formed their own air cargo company, Aviones de Panamá, but were still using planes provided by Noriega from those confiscated from drug traffickers. Noriega was a silent partner. The Panamanians had the weapons; the Salvadoran guerrillas had a $10 million war chest from kidnappings carried out in the 1970s. Rodríguez and Carlton charged them full price. The flights out of Pillique Guerra's airstrips continued almost uninterrupted in late 1979 and early 1980, only now they bypassed Nicaragua and went on to rural airstrips in El Salvador. The guerrilla groups' weapon of choice was the American M16, which used easily obtainable NATO-standard 7.62-mm ammunition. Noriega brought in another partner, Jorge Krupnick, who got the M16s in the European arms market. Krupnick expanded the new enterprise's offerings to include Chinese built RPG2 rocket launchers and other armaments that were superior to those left over from the Sandinista caches. The weapons arrived on small freighters and were stored in the Panama Free Zone—immune from Customs inspection on Noriega's orders.

César Rodríguez would often go to the Free Zone warehouse to select samples and smuggle them back to Panama City. There, the matériel was displayed in a clandestine arms showroom in a building housing a music recording studio off the Vía Argentina. Salvadoran and later Colombian guerrilla representatives were brought to look over the merchandise and make their purchases.

By June 1980, Rodríguez and Carlton had made at least sixteen flights to El Salvador, with payloads of three thousand pounds each flight. On Saturday June 14, they planned a double load. They flew two empty planes from Paitilla Airport to Tamarindo airstrip in Costa Rica, Rodríguez in an Aerocommander and Carlton in a two-engine Piper Seneca. Rodríguez took along a 55-gallon fuel tank so his plane could make it all the way back to Panama on the return trip without refueling in Costa Rica. Sunday was Father's Day in Panama and they had family plans.

At the airstrip, guerrilla agents were in a hurry to load the planes—they had had problems with the Costa Rican Rural Guard on their way to the airstrip with the trucks. When Carlton took off, he realized that his plane was overloaded. When he circled around he saw that Rodríguez, in the smaller Aerocommander, was having trouble too. He bumped along the dirt runway and barely made it airborne, clipping a fence at the end with his landing gear. After a two-hour flight out over the Pacific to skirt Nicaragua, they reached the landing zone at a farm cooperative called Miraflores outside the city of San Miguel in eastern El Salvador. It was dark and a group of peasant guerrilla supporters had marked the runway with torches and lanterns. When Rodríguez touched down, he realized the fence he hit on takeoff had sheared his hydraulic line; he had no brakes. Unable to stop, he crumpled the small plane against a tree at the end of the airstrip.

Carlton came down behind him and had the peasants quickly unload his plane while he tried to free Rodríguez from the wreckage. He used one of the assault rifles from his cargo to break out the windshield of the Aerocommander. Rodríguez had broken both legs and was in great pain as Carlton dragged him through the window. He didn't think to take the airplane documents with him. Carlton thought he heard helicopters approaching. He took off as soon as he got Rodríguez aboard and flew low and fast to escape the choppers.

The next day, El Salvador announced that it had captured a crashed Aerocommander 560A with the Panamanian registry HP776. The plane was loaded with 22,000 rounds of 7.62-mm ammunition in boxes with Venezuelan markings. The report noted that the seizure was the second time in recent months that Venezuelan ammunition had been captured. Papers found in the plane showed it was registered to the Panamanian Air Force. Within several days, César Rodríguez's name and Aviones de Panamá were also linked to the crash. Ricardo Bilonick, a former diplomat who had served as Gabriel Lewis's deputy during the treaty negotiations, was identified as one of Rodríguez's partners. The Panamanian Air Force put out a fairly flimsy story that the papers were forged, then that the plane had been stolen from a hangar at Paitilla Airport. Nevertheless, the Salvadoran military accepted Panama's explanations, and the incident was officially resolved with promises of investigations. The crash received almost no attention in the United States at the time or later when a fierce debate arose over U.S. charges that the Sandinista government was smuggling arms to the Salvadoran guerrillas.

There are some indications that Noriega may have been acting behind Torrijos's back in continuing the arms pipeline to aid the

Salvadoran rebels. Torrijos had studied at the Salvadoran military academy and was good friends with many in the Salvadoran high command, especially with junta member Colonel Adolfo Majano, who was seen in 1980 as a well-intentioned reformer who could be counted on to stop the military death squads that were killing more than one hundred people a month. Torrijos was deeply concerned about events in El Salvador and in recent months had been talking to U.S. representatives about carving out a role for himself as a peacemaker. According to Torrijos aide José Blandón, Torrijos harshly reprimanded Noriega about the arms sales and ordered an investigation. After that the arms traffic became sporadic but did not entirely stop.

In the last year of his life, Omar Torrijos seemed to look back rather than forward, at the historic advances he had brought to Panama rather than at the infighting and corruption that were growing out of the system he had created. He offered a dual legacy of lofty patriotism and social reform on one side and unspeakable venality on the other.

Torrijos had given his small, nondescript country an international identity, one of almost heroic proportions in the Third World. As if by accident, without the oratorical or ideological flourishes of a Fidel Castro, his military revolution had wrought enormous social, racial, even psychological changes in the lives of the vast majority of Panamanians. More than the reforms in land distribution, health care, education, the essence of "Torrijismo" was the inchoate national pride he instilled in a people who had been more servants than slaves, more bought-out than downtrodden. By peacefully settling Panama's historic score with the United States, he gave concrete reality to Panama as a country; by imposing a government that flaunted its middle-class, multiracial character, he had halted social polarization and short-circuited the appeal of Marxist radicalism.

The underside of the Torrijos legacy was a National Guard that was unchecked and unmonitored, that was run for the personal benefit of those who comprised its upper echelons. In sweeping away the old-style cronyism of the Union Club, Torrijos had left the country in political adolescence. By repression and exile, he had emasculated the political parties, rendering them incapable of governing or even of mounting an effective campaign for honest government. It may not have occurred to Torrijos to challenge Panama's ingrained tradition of influence-peddling and payoffs—the idea that a time of rule is a time of enrichment. Common parlance in Panama lacked even the terminology to express such concepts as conflict of interest and ethics in government.

Instead, Torrijos attempted to channel the fruits of corruption to promote his revolution, to serve both his selfish and his enlightened purposes. The system was disarmingly simple: Torrijos bought or gained control of businesses and arranged for them to have a monopoly or to receive other kinds of preferential treatment. The companies provided second salaries for National Guard officers and their profits were available for special projects not covered in the national budget.

"These are institutional companies, whose resources are available to whomever is commander in chief," said Ernesto Pérez Balladares, who as finance minister oversaw the operations of the system. "When the high command needs money that it cannot justify taking from the national budget, it obtains it from these companies."

Ironically, Torrijos wanted his officers to have a good living without having to take bribes that might compromise their dedication to the revolution. Official salaries were minimal. As a lieutenant colonel and head of G2, Noriega was listed on payroll records as receiving $484.50 a month in the mid-seventies. In 1980, his salary had risen to only $1,537.20. Torrijos's system allowed virtually every Panamanian National Guard officer who had reached the rank of major to receive off-the-book payments that doubled and tripled his salary. The higher the rank, the higher the multiple.

The system was perhaps even more insidious because it appeared to have no victims. No money was stolen from the taxpayers and certainly none from the poor. Those who paid the most to finance the system were foreign companies and Panamanian businessmen, who benefited and therefore seldom complained. Officers such as Noriega, Díaz Herrera and Paredes lived comfortably but not ostentatiously. Torrijos used much of the slush fund to help poor families and to provide stipends for students whose families could not afford to support them at the university.

Torrijos also used the money to buy friends abroad and to support his internationalist campaigns. Support for the Sandinistas was one such project, but there were others. Díaz Herrera claims that Torrijos made a $200,000 contribution to French Socialist leader François Mitterrand in the 1970s, when Mitterrand was merely an also-ran in French elections. When economist Nicolás Ardito Barletta became president of Panama in 1984, and got a look at the books, he discovered that Torrijos had contributed $5 million to the cause of the Polisario guerrillas in northern Africa and to other quixotic international causes.

Torrijos was also the architect of a special relationship with Castro's Cuba—a wary alliance based not on politics but on Latin solidarity and a desire to keep U.S. power at bay. For Cuba, Panama was a grand supermarket where it was able to purchase a multitude of U.S. goods forbidden to them by the U.S. trade embargo. Companies operating out of the Colón Free Zone, such as Transit, S.A., run by Noriega's friend and partner Carlos Duque, imported what the Cubans needed and sold it to Panamanian shell companies that acted as fronts for the Cuban government. A company called Reciclaje, S.A., was used by the Cubans to obtain computers—from IBM PCs to sophisticated mainframes. The high-technology goods were especially prized, but mundane items such as spare parts for Cuba's 1950s fleet of U.S. cars and trucks made up much of the trade.

The Cubans had virtual free run of the small port of Vacamonte, which was home away from home for a fleet of Cuban shrimp trawlers. The catch was processed and frozen in Vacamonte and sold with Panamanian labels to enthusiastic customers in the United States.

Panama City under Torrijos was wide open and international, an ideologically neutral haven that provided a place of operations close to the Central American conflicts, a place where allies could meet and plot, where enemies could make discreet contact. Panama became what Casablanca in Morocco had been during World War II, a hub of clandestine activity, a trading post for arms, money and intelligence. Most of the intrigues that were played out in bars, banks and hotels involved the wars in Central America. Torrijos encouraged the Cubans to use Panama in much the same way as the United States used it—as a forward base for political and espionage contacts with Latin America. Manuel "Barbaroja" Piniero, the red-bearded Cuban intelligence chief and head of Latin American operations, used Panama as his headquarters and played cat-and-mouse games with American intelligence. Salvadoran guerrillas used Panamanian banks and eventually used Panama City as headquarters for their chief political leader, Guillermo Ungo.

Factions involved in virtually every world conflict operated out of Panama. The Palestinians had an office. The Libyans began their operations after Noriega traveled to Tripoli in 1977 to talk to Muammar Qaddafi, bringing back what U.S. intelligence described as a "substantial" amount of money.

None of the operations compared to those of the Israelis, however. The Israelis' extraofficial representative for the operations, a former Mossad official named Mike Harari, was a Casablanca figure right out of central casting: Short, dark and well-muscled, with short-cropped, graying hair, Harari was a shadowy presence at Torrijos's—and later at Noriega's—side for almost fifteen years. Once the Mossad station chief in Mexico, he had led a Mossad hit squad hunting down Palestinian terrorists who had attacked the Munich Olympics in 1972, but ended up murdering an innocent Moroccan waiter in Norway instead. He arrived in Panama the following year, ostensibly retired from Mossad, and struck up a friendship with Torrijos and Noriega. He began a lucrative career as a broker for multimillion dollar business deals involving Israel and acted as a kind of visiting professor in espionage for Noriega's G2. U.S. military officials credit Harari with mediating Israeli assistance and training to equip G2 with sophisticated espionage and electronic surveillance techniques the United States would not provide. In Panama, the Israelis spied on the PLO and the Libyans and ran their own arms business. They sold first to Somoza, then to the Guatemalan military dictatorship to sop up the market left by the U.S. ban on military sales to those countries. Later, Harari would be the middleman for arms shipments to the Contras.

·   ·   ·

In 1981, Torrijos became increasingly remote. He seemed to lose interest in keeping track of the complex system he had created but now barely controlled. He still made a daily round of early morning calls to his general staff to grill them on their days' activities and to keep in touch, but he rarely showed up at general headquarters. He spent most of his time outside Panama City, often in his tranquil beachside compound at Farrallón, south of the capital. But his favorite spot was a modest villa in the small village of Coclecito, in the mountains marking the border between Coclé and Colón provinces. When he brought visitors he took them on jogging excursions with his soldiers that lasted hours.

Torrijos's withdrawal allowed Noriega's power to grow. G2 was expanded to encompass economic research and other activities. There was a department in G2 that mirrored practically every branch of government—the Canal, the banking sector, a geopolitical section. Noriega created the impression that he had his hand in everything. It was about that time that Torrijos joked with his cousin, Lieutenant Colonel Roberto Díaz Herrera, that Noriega had grown so powerful that "even I am afraid of him."

Hugo Spadafora, back in Panama City with a Mercedes-Benz 280 confiscated from Somoza's fleet, looked around for a new war to fight. He had shaved his beard and had gotten a divorce. He had a bodyguard with an Uzi, a monthly stipend from Torrijos to live on and an unencumbered life. "I know that I'm something of a romantic, but I'm also very pragmatic. Revolutions are coming to Latin America through historical imperative. Either you participate or you're a failed revolutionary. And I'm participating," he told a reporter who visited him at his apartment. He compared himself to Lafayette and Ché Guevara. "The time has come for the creation of a Bolivarian force—independent of superpowers and governments and capable of combating militarily anywhere in the continent where the armed struggle is the only avenue left for peoples seeking their liberation," he declared.

Spadafora deepened his friendship with Edén Pastora. Pastora made frequent trips to Panama, and Spadafora flew even more often to Nicaragua. They debated about where to go for their next revolution. Pastora was growing restive at his ineffectual role in Nicaragua; the Sandinista revolution going on around him, without him, was too Marxist for his taste. He thought the next fight should be against the dictatorship in Guatemala. Spadafora favored going to El Salvador, but Pastora considered the National Liberation Front, the FMLN, too new, too radical. The Guatemalans, by contrast, had been fighting off and on for thirty years and had formed a new group with a democratic socialist bent, along the lines of Pastora's Terceristas.

Spadafora followed up on the idea. He had a meeting with Floyd Carlton, his friend from the time of the Sandinista victory. Spadafora asked Carlton how much it would cost to set up an arms supply pipeline to Guatemala like the one they had used in Nicaragua. He told Carlton he was working on "something big." Spadafora then traveled to Libya and Israel in search of financial and arms support for revolution in Guatemala and El Salvador. He met with Qaddafi and, according to one account, received a promise of funds.

In May 1981, Spadafora offered to re-form the Victoriano Lorenzo Brigade to fight with the FMLN rebels. "The U.S. military, political and economic intervention in El Salvador must be answered by Latin America's youth," he said.

A few weeks later, Edén Pastora decided to make his move. He sent word to Torrijos that he was secretly going to leave Nicaragua and come to Panama. The revolution had gone too far left, he said, and he wanted nothing more to do with it. On July 7, 1981, Pastora and a group of close associates drove in caravan into Costa Rica, where they were met by Spadafora. Hours later, when the caravan reached Paso Canoas, the border with Panama, Noriega's G2 was waiting to escort them to Panama City.

Pastora and his lieutenants presented a "project" to Torrijos: to use Panama as a base for a liberation struggle in Guatemala. Pastora described for Torrijos his contacts with ORPA, the Guatemalan Organization of the People in Arms. They are like us, he argued, anti-imperialist, social democratic, noncommunist. The talking, plotting and partying went on for three weeks.

Torrijos projected on Pastora and Spadafora the lofty ideals for noncommunist revolution that he still hoped would solve the terrible ills of Central America and avoid the descent into venality and corruption that his own Panamanian revolution had taken. The meetings sparked Torrijos out of his deepening morosity. He was animated for the first time in months. Perhaps for that reason, because the Pastora-Spadafora project appealed so clearly to his idealistic side, Torrijos kept Noriega out of the meetings and away from any direct role in the planning.

Noriega fumed at being excluded from an international operation, one that clearly fell within the domain of his G2. He had an ally in Pastora, who wanted the benefit of Noriega's broad intelligence capability. But Spadafora wanted no part of Noriega, and his counsel prevailed with Torrijos.

There had been bad blood between Spadafora and Noriega from the first time they had met socially in the early 1970s. With their wives at an official reception, Noriega had cornered Spadafora and had grilled him about his experiences in Africa. When Spadafora had tried to lighten the conversation with a remark intended to bring the women in and change the subject, Noriega ordered another drink and hammered away with the same line of questioning. Finally, Spadafora stood up, turned his back and left Noriega sputtering drunkenly in midsentence.

They had avoided all but the most cursory contact until Torrijos forced them to work together in assisting Pastora and the Sandinistas. Spadafora's disdain for Noriega turned to disgust as he witnessed firsthand Noriega's attempts to turn a profit from the arms deals. Noriega considered Spadafora a sanctimonious lightweight and tried unsuccessfully to cut him off from access to Torrijos. Instead, Spadafora appeared to grow in Torrijos's eyes. In one particularly bitter incident, Spadafora told Torrijos, in Noriega's presence, that Noriega was disloyal and was plotting to overthrow him. Torrijos's decision to cut Noriega out of the planning for the Central American liberation project turned their mutual dislike into insoluble hostility.

Toward the end of the month, Torrijos said that he was going to fly to Coclecito and wanted to take Pastora along for one of his marches. The morning of the flight, July 30, Torrijos sent a car to pick up Pastora at his son, Martín's, house, where Pastora was staying. But Pastora had spent the night elsewhere with a woman he had met. He missed the trip.

Later it would be said that Torrijos had no sense of danger and forced his pilots to fly no matter what the weather. That day, he chose to fly despite the storm front shrouding the mountains around Coclecito, and heedless of the relative inexperience of the pilot. The plane struck the top of a hill while the pilot was maneuvering for a landing. All aboard were killed.

That Noriega took charge of the investigation of the crash gave cause for much speculation years later. Independent technical investigators sent by the airplane manufacturer, DeHavilland, ruled it was an accident. In any case, the man who had held Noriega in check for almost twenty years was gone.

CHAPTER 6

GUNS TO DRUGS

The year Omar Torrijos died was the year Ronald Reagan became president and four guerrilla armies went to war in countries only a short plane ride from Panama. Nineteen eighty-one was also the year the Colombian cocaine cartel was born.

The region around Panama was a war zone. Every country that was not itself at war was a staging area for someone else's war. El Salvador's FMLN, with Nicaragua's support, launched an all-out offensive in January. At midyear, the remnants of Somoza's National Guard were mustered into an organized force that would come to be called the Contras. The CIA provided money, Argentina the training, Honduras and Costa Rica the staging areas. Guatemalan rebels, some based in Mexico, began the fiercest fighting in decades. In Colombia, the M-19 guerrillas fought not only the government but the Colombian drug lords.

The wars opened spigots of foreign money and spawned an underworld whose currency was cash, weapons and information. A network of semilegal private airstrips and small air charter and air freight companies was transformed into the logistical grid for the clandestine armies.

Cocaine flowed in and around the war traffic, overlapping and duplicating the clandestine network. The rising curve of cocaine imports to the United States followed almost exactly the flow of U.S.

exports of arms and military advisers to Central America. Experts still debate whether there is any causal link—just as they debated the same question about the flow of heroin during the Vietnam war—but the factual coincidence of the cocaine explosion with the Central American political crisis was indisputable.*

Over a few short years the cottage industry of cocaine was transformed. By 1985 it would be at its peak, an industry with yearly profits in the billions of dollars, all of it produced in the coca fields and processing factories in Peru, Bolivia and Colombia and transshipped through Central America, Mexico and the Caribbean. Peru's president Alan García would call it "Latin America's only successful multinational."

Torrijos's death removed the tethers from Noriega at an opportune time. From a purely financial point of view, a venture capitalist could not have chosen a better moment than the cusp of the 1980s to get in on the ground floor of the exploding cocaine industry. Noriega had a lot to invest—an established and protected network for clandestine transport, supply and finance. With Torrijos dead, Noriega was an entrepreneur in search of an enterprise.

The cocaine trade has always been a uniquely Latin American industry; the coca bushes that provide its raw material grow only in the Andean mountains, primarily in Peru and Bolivia, and have never been successfully transplanted out of the region. In the 1960s and early 1970s cocaine was processed into paste in Peru and Bolivia and refined into the crystal cocaine hydrochloride in small laboratories in northern Chile, then smuggled north in small amounts and sold to an upscale crowd of movie stars and athletes. Because of its short supply and astronomical price, it had yet to enjoy the mass popularity of marijuana and other so-called soft drugs. Then, in the

*Bruce Bagley, in "Colombia and the War on Drugs," *Foreign Affairs,* Fall 1988, cites DEA estimates that 14 to 19 metric tons of cocaine were smuggled into the United States in 1976, 45 tons in 1982. Colombia's revenues from drugs were about $1.5 billion in 1980, and $2.5 to $3 billion in 1985. p. 76. A rough measure of arms flow during the same period, total arms transfers between the United States and Latin America, rose from $955 million in 1976 to $2.8 billion in 1982. Arms Control and Disarmament Agency figures.

mid-1970s, refining operations shifted to Colombia—also a major center of marijuana growing—and a group of young Colombian cocaine entrepreneurs had an idea that should have been the pride of the supply-side economists. Marijuana was being shipped to the States by planeload and yachtload; why not use the same bulk-shipping methods for cocaine to increase profits vastly?

The masterminds of the cocaine revolution grew up in the tradition of Latin American small farmers, shopkeepers and petty criminals rather than in the world of international crime syndicates. But Colombia added a special historical ingredient: It was the country that named an era of its history *La Violencia* for the hundreds of thousands of mostly political murders that were still occurring in the late 1940s, about the time when Pablo Escobar, Jorge Ochoa, Carlos Lehder and José Gonzalo Rodríguez were born.

Jorge Luis Ochoa Vásquez had perhaps the sharpest wits for business and organization. He was a unifier, a builder of coalitions. His family owned a restaurant on the outskirts of the picturesque Andean city of Medellín, his father trained horses, and his uncle Fabio dabbled in cocaine deals with the older generation of small-time drug dealers. By 1974, Jorge was pulling his family out of the lower middle class with his income from shipments of 40 or 50 kilos a month of cocaine to the United States.

He teamed up with his boyhood friend, Pablo Escobar Gaviria, the son of a schoolteacher and a small farmer, a town boy with roots in the *campo,* the countryside. Roly-poly and outgoing, Escobar began his criminal career stealing, grinding down and reselling grave stones, then graduated to car theft and kidnapping. As a teenager he worked for a while as a guard for an operation smuggling stereo equipment out of the Colón Free Zone. In 1976, he and his cousin, Gustavo Gaviria, were arrested in Medellín's largest cocaine bust that year—39 kilos.

That same year, a small-time Colombian hood named Carlos Lehder Rivas began shipping cocaine in his partner's girlfriend's suitcases from his auto dealership in Medellín to the U.S. East Coast. Lehder was born in a coffee town near Medellín but grew up to be a teenage car thief and petty dope dealer in New York and Detroit after his mother immigrated to the United States. He had the long hair of a hippie, and a smart mouth in both Spanish and English. The American counterculture exposed him to a smattering of Marxism and imbued him with a love for Beatles songs. He later showed an attraction for the politics and anti-Semitism of Adolf Hitler—perhaps an emulation of the imagined Germany of his father, who immigrated to Colombia at the end of World War II.

There was a host of other Colombians who were mainstays in the growing cocaine trade: José Gonzalo Rodríguez Gacha, known as "the Mexican"; Pablo Correa Arroyave, who was Jorge Ochoa's cousin and one of Escobar's top lieutenents; Gilberto José Rodríguez Orejuela, "the Chess Player," one of the leaders of the constellation of traffickers from Cali. In 1984 he would be arrested with an account book describing the year's sales of 4 metric tons of cocaine.

The total number of significant traffickers in the late 1970s was around two hundred, all operating more or less independently and trying to keep up with the rising demand from the United States. They fought and occasionally settled scores with murders and kidnappings, but were also ready to pool resources to make an attractive deal.

Carlos Lehder is usually credited with implementing the transshipment scheme that revolutionized the cocaine business. In August 1977, Lehder and a partner outfitted a twin-engine plane with a loran, a long-range navigation system, and gave the pilot the coordinates of Pablo Escobar's ranch outside Medellín. The pilot took off from Nassau, having masked his destination with a flight plan for one of the southernmost Bahama islands, and picked up 250 kilos of cocaine at Escobar's airstrip. He stopped at Nassau to refuel, then flew to a small strip in the Carolinas, where the merchandise was off-loaded and delivered to Colombian distributors in Fort Lauderdale, Florida. The flight did not attract attention in the busy private air lanes between the Bahamas and the United States. On flight records, Lehder's plane never left Bahamian airspace.

The load was five times larger than any previous smuggling venture Lehder was involved in, and he and his partner cleared $1 million for the two-day operation. He immediately invested his share to set up a transshipment network to repeat the profitable process. A year later, he virtually owned the island of Norman's Cay, an idyllic spot fifty miles south of Nassau. He improved the airstrip and built a large hangar to disguise the loading operations and to store the cocaine. In seven flights known to have been completed in 1978, Lehder's operation moved almost one and a half tons of cocaine.

Other traffickers quickly imitated the large-scale transshipments, and the new volume moved the Colombian traffickers to more cooperative ways of doing business. They created informal networks to pool enough cocaine to put together a shipment, usually around 300 to 500 kilos. Each trafficker, small or large, identified his packets of cocaine with individual markings resembling cattle brands of the old West.

The mass shipments escalated the need for a dependable supply of cocaine and created the problem of returning the illegal profits to the Colombian traffickers. In the United States, the plentiful supply of high-quality drug led to lowered street prices and increased demand. As business doubled and tripled, it overwhelmed the informal, decentralized distribution networks that had serviced the cocaine trade in the past, in which each cocaine importer marketed his few kilos to dealers he knew personally and trusted. Traffickers bought up automatic money counters and filled safe houses with log jams of cash. As the decade ended, the cocaine trade was moving headlong into vertical integration.

Jorge Ochoa made the first step toward forming an alliance of traffickers, with his and Pablo Escobar's organizations in leading roles. On April 18, 1981, he convened a meeting at his father's ranch, known as Hacienda Veracruz, near Barranquilla. Lehder attended, but Ochoa emerged in control of a greatly expanded air shipment operation. Eventually he would preside over a jungle airstrip capable of handling commercial jets and supported by a state-of-the-art communications and navigation system. Ochoa also began to assert control over the distribution network in the United States.

Pablo Escobar's people began to impose order on the chaotic production end of the cocaine trade. He specialized in importing raw coca paste from suppliers in Peru and Bolivia, constructing refining factories and security. Ochoa and Escobar also encouraged the planting of coca bushes in Colombia as an insurance policy against becoming too dependent on supplies from other countries.

Lehder's flights of several tons of cocaine had netted him $100 million, according to his own boast, but by this time he was being displaced by Ochoa's even bigger air operations, which logged almost 20 tons of cocaine shipments in the first months after the Hacienda Veracruz meeting. Profits returned to Colombia in 1981 were already approaching $1 billion a year and would double again and again in the coming years.

Manuel Noriega, after his foray into drug trafficking in 1971–72, had kept up an image of drug enforcer during the rest of the decade. His antinarcotics unit and Customs officials made frequent arrests of "mules," the men and women attempting to smuggle a kilo or two of cocaine from Colombia to the United States by hiding it on their bodies. The story of how Noriega maneuvered his way into a piece of the Colombian cocaine action begins, according to the best evidence, in 1981. That evidence, which U.S. investigators say they can corroborate, marks Noriega's trail from arms smuggling to drug deals that make his 1970s crimes seem penny-ante by comparison: Noriega, in his typical, well-organized way, appeared to have tried over a period of several years to become a major player in the multibillion-dollar trade in cocaine and money; then, as he had done before, he got out when things got too hot.

In 1981, Noriega was involved in smuggling weapons to a newly reactivated Colombian guerrilla group, M-19. Named after the date of an election that had been stolen from a progressive candidate, the April 19 Movement was only the latest of the many groups that since the 1960s had kept Colombia in constant warfare. Jaime Bateman, founder and leader of M-19, had been a personal friend of Omar Torrijos and had often visited him in Panama; just before his death, Torrijos met with Bateman to counsel him to give up the armed struggle and to take up peaceful means.

While Torrijos was counseling peace, Noriega was selling M-19 small allotments of European- and U.S.-made weapons from his Colón Free Zone warehouse. An April 1981 offensive had been launched with Panamanian support but had failed. With money raised from a series of kidnappings, M-19 had been able to buy a gigantic shipment of more than 100 tons of arms and ammunition for delivery in October and November 1981. The weapons had been purchased in Europe and stored in Panama, one batch in the Canal Free Zone warehouse of Explonsa, a Noriega-controlled company. Another, larger load was stashed at the fishing port of Vacamonte, where Torrijos had allowed the Cuban government to set up a large shrimping operation.

On October 20, an M-19 commando hijacked a Curtiss C46 owned by the Colombian Aeropesca air cargo company, on its way from Medellín to Barranquilla, Colombia. The plane was found the next day in the jungle region of Caquetá, abandoned half submerged in the Orteguaza River. All accounts agree that the hijackers used the plane to ship a load of arms to their bases in Caquetá, a sparsely populated Amazonian area in the far south of Colombia. The Colombian press reported that the hijacked plane picked up the arms from the far northern province of Guajira, on the Caribbean coast of Colombia. But a U.S. intelligence report, based on sources whose identities are blanked out, told a story of Panamanian involvement.

"Information they [the sources] had obtained indicated the hijacked aircraft had flown to Panama not [to] the Guajira to pick up weapons. [deletion] The weapons had been picked up near La Palma in Darién or on the Atlantic Coast, east of Colón," the report said. Boxes found on the plane were special impermeable shipping crates used to pack perfume or explosives, and they all bore markings identifying their destination as Colón, Panama. "The recent hijacking . . . by the M-19 is just the latest in a series of weapons, munitions, terrorist and guerrilla groups originating in/or transiting Panama for Colombia," the report said.

The activities had at least the indirect sanction of Panamanian authorities. "A small group of senior GOP [government of Panama] and Panama National Guard (GN) officers are involved in facilitating, if not outright assisting, the 19 April Movement (M-19) guerrillas operating in Colombia. This involvement may have some minor ideological basis but the predominant motivation is personal profit. The master hand behind this involvement, they [the sources] believe, is GN G2, LTC Manuel Noriega. [Among] others they suspect as being involved are GN G2 Maj Julean [sic] Melo. . . ."

A few weeks later, the second part of the shipment left Vacamonte port in a freighter, the *Karina,* with a Panamanian crew and several M-19 guerrillas on board. Part of the cargo was transferred to another ship, which completed the delivery at an M-19 pickup point in Colombia. But the *Karina* was intercepted by the Colombian Navy and sunk after a battle. Twenty people on the *Karina* died and three M-19 guerrillas were captured.

Undeterred by its naval defeat, M-19 got bolder and took on an even more dangerous target. On November 12, 1981, an M-19 commando kidnapped Marta Nieves Ochoa, the youngest sister of Jorge Ochoa, who was well on his way to becoming Colombia's richest drug lord. They demanded $1 million in ransom—some accounts put the demand as high as $15 million.

The kidnapping spurred Ochoa into action that ultimately resulted in the first formal organization of Colombian traffickers into what came to be called the Medellín cartel. In late November, Ochoa gathered the traffickers in an "assembly" that took place at Ochoa's restaurant, La Margarita, in Medellín. The meeting included at least twenty leading traffickers, and perhaps several times that many. They agreed to cooperate in order to stop M-19 and to get Marta Ochoa back. In violence-ridden Colombia, kidnapping was a fairly common tactic; the traffickers themselves used it in their gang wars. But the M-19 threat was of another order—a rival outlaw group that saw the traffickers as ideological enemies and their millions as fair prey—and had to be stopped. The traffickers assessed themselves at least $30,000 apiece—the total was over $7 million—to create an armed antiguerrilla force to fight M-19. They called the group MAS, *Muerte a Secuestradores,* Death to Kidnappers. It was the cartel's first official act.

MAS went into action against M-19 with the zeal of a religious crusade. The following weeks have been described as open warfare between two underground armies, each brandishing the latest in assault weaponry. MAS units acted as death squads, kidnapping and murdering suspected M-19 sympathizers, and as counterinsurgency patrols on search-and-destroy missions against M-19 installations. Some reports say that over one hundred M-19 militants were killed or abducted in six weeks in January and February.

M-19 sued for peace in early February and, according to several accounts, asked Noriega, who had been so helpful in arranging arms shipments, to mediate the dispute. The meeting was set up in Panama City and the talks lasted several weeks, with Noriega in the background. On February 17, Marta Ochoa was freed unharmed; the next day MAS released five M-19 hostages. How much money exchanged hands is not known. A police report said that the ransom was $535,000; the Ochoas claimed that they paid nothing. In any case, the existence of MAS and the negotiations were effective insurance against any more M-19 kidnappings of relatives of the newly organized cartel.

For Noriega, the episode was the opportunity he was seeking. The M-19 negotiations gave him and the cartel leaders a chance to get to know one another. The courtship was brief. Very soon after the meetings in Panama, Noriega and the cartel began to do business. First, the appropriate middlemen had to be found.

Floyd Carlton and César Rodríguez in 1982 were businessmen on the way up. Their charter company, Aviones de Panamá, operated out of a large hangar at Paitilla Airport on the bay in Panama City. Only ten minutes from the banking district on a straight shot up 50 Street, Paitilla was the airport of choice for the private flights of Panamanian and foreign businessmen. Carlton and Rodríguez had their own planes—twin-engine Beechcrafts that were capable of making the trip to Florida in six hours, with a fuel stop in the Cayman Islands.

Their customers were among the richest and most powerful men in Panama—Eric Arturo Delvalle, the sugar magnate; Fernando Manfredo, Panama's top man in the Panama Canal administration; and of course, Manuel Noriega, their silent partner in the gunrunning business they had on the side. Their association with Noriega had become closer and more visible. Since the Sandinista arms supply operation, it was common knowledge that they were "Noriega's pilots." They partied together. César, especially, reveled in the benefits of their association with Noriega. "Just let people see me carrying his briefcase, and the deals come pouring in," César once remarked to a friend.

The exclusive use of the Paitilla hangar, right next to the National

Guard hangar, was worth a hundred briefcases as a symbol of the two partners' access and privilege. They were prosperous for the first time in their lives. Floyd had gotten married and bought a ranch in Chiriquí; César, working hard to become a playboy, spent his money on nightlife. The stories of his gun-running exploits had earned him the nickname, Capitán Veneno—Captain Poison. The two pilots had come a long way from hustling jobs in Chiriquí. They had gotten to Beechcrafts; Learjets could not be far away.

Around the time of the negotiations that resulted in the release of Jorge Ochoa's sister, a well-dressed Colombian named Francisco Chávez Hill began to hang around Floyd and César at the Aviones hangar. He chartered planes from them to fly to Medellín; he threw his money around; he bragged to Carlton that he worked "for the most powerful people in Colombia." It didn't take much imagination for Carlton to figure out what kind of business Chávez was in.

Sometime in June, Chávez offered to take Carlton to meet his people. He said he had noticed that Carlton and Rodríguez "enjoyed a certain type of immunity." Chávez and Carlton flew together to Medellín. At the Intercontinental Hotel, against a magnificent mountain backdrop, Carlton was introduced to Pablo Escobar and Gustavo Gaviria. Chávez had given Carlton the impression that the business proposal would involve shipping money to be laundered in Panama. Now Escobar said he needed Carlton to fly cocaine.

Carlton balked.

"Go ahead and ask Noriega," Escobar said.

Carlton had carefully avoided any reference to the source of his immunity in Panama. Escobar made light of Carlton's discretion. He said he had dealt with Noriega before, that Noriega had confiscated a ship with a load of 800 kilos of cocaine. He said he had paid Noriega $1 million to return the ship and crew, and had never gotten the drugs back.

Carlton returned to Panama. Noriega was angry when he was told about the cartel's proposal, mostly because Carlton had not consulted with him before making the trip to Medellín. A few weeks later, at a party, Noriega brought up the subject again.

Carlton said he had understood from their first conversation that Noriega wanted him to drop the matter, and he had.

"Well, find out what the deal really consists of, and then you can talk to me about it and see if we can go ahead with it. But as usual, I don't know anything about it. Don't use Panamanian aircraft," Noriega said. In other words, don't get caught as Carlton and Rodríguez had in El Salvador the year before, with a plane traceable to the National Guard.

Carlton flew back to Medellín with a mandate to do business. Escobar and Gaviria told Carlton what the payoff would be— $30,000 per flight to Noriega, $400 per kilo to Carlton. The planned cargo was 300 kilos of pure cocaine. Then the traffickers arranged to send several men back to Panama with Carlton to inspect the airstrips Carlton planned to use. The airfields passed; the price didn't.

"Do they think I am starving?" Noriega asked as he and Carlton flew together on a short trip. "If they do, they're wrong. Tell them no less than $100,000 a trip. And in advance."

Carlton recalls that Escobar chuckled when he told him about his boss's increased price. Noriega's name was never mentioned by Carlton, who was beginning to feel like a bad actor in a transparent role.

The first flight took off sometime in November 1982, from Escobar's El Cafetal airstrip northwest of Medellín. Carlton piloted the Piper Cheyenne with a cartel copilot named David Rodrigo Ortiz. They landed at an abandoned World War II strip known as Calzada Larga, a few miles east of Panama City.

Noriega's man had begun to do business with the cartel, but the cartel still didn't trust Noriega. Carlton discovered later that there was no cocaine in the duffel bags loaded on the plane. Escobar told him that they had sent him on a trial run with a dummy load—just in case Noriega intended to set a trap.

There was no trap, and Escobar paid up—although not in advance as Noriega demanded. A few days after the plane deposited its cargo safely for transshipment to the United States, a cartel bagman arrived at Carlton's office with $220,000 in U.S. dollars. Carlton kept $120,000. Noriega's aide, Captain Luis del Cid, came over to pick up Noriega's $100,000.

The next flight took place less than a month later. Carlton flew 400 kilos—this time he checked to be sure it was cocaine—from Escobar's ranch, Hacienda Napoles, near Medellín, again to Calzada Larga in Panama. Noriega's payment—he had again raised the price, to $150,000—was delivered in advance to Explonsa, the company Noriega used in his arms deals. Carlton's pay remained the same.

The operations had gone off without a hitch. Carlton met again with his cartel contacts. They were enthusiastic, ready to branch out. They talked about shipping money from Miami, about buying better planes, about bringing César into the operation. For Floyd and César, the deals were their first chance to make really big money and they thought of almost nothing else.

For Noriega, the drug deals were a profitable sideline that occupied little of his time. They were only one area of opportunity opened up by Torrijos's death; Noriega was preoccupied with even larger game. He was on his way to taking total power in Panama. He anticipated few obstacles. The new commander of the National Guard, Colonel Florencio Florez, showed no ambition and had not even promoted himself to general. He made no attempt to interfere with Noriega's running of G2.

Noriega's first serious challenge came from outside the military.

After Torrijos's death, Hugo Spadafora spent the rest of 1981 with Edén Pastora, helping to build international support for the Guatemalan revolution. Pastora was out of public sight. He shuttled to Cuba, Panama and Nicaragua, assuring Castro and the Sandinistas that he was no longer a factor in Nicaragua, that he only wanted their support to carry the revolution to other oppressed peoples. But the internationalist project had lost its most important backer in Omar Torrijos. Castro gave the idea lip service, and the Sandinistas were openly mistrustful. They talked to the Guatemalan revolutionary groups that Pastora and Spadafora were seeking to help; the groups said "thanks but no thanks" to the internationalist brigade. To make matters worse, Noriega had withdrawn all the financial support Torrijos had provided to Spadafora, had taken back the airplane Spadafora had been using and had dismantled and disarmed the Victoriano Lorenzo Brigade.

By Christmas time 1981, Spadafora was back in Panama, redirecting his political energy and outrage, for the moment at least, at his old nemesis, Noriega. Spadafora, still remembered as a hero of the fight against Somoza, easily commanded press attention in Panama. In an interview with Channel 4 TV on December 19, Spadafora blandly called for a political agreement between the government party and the opposition parties, an idea that was the subject of broad discussion at the time. Then, seemingly out of the blue, Spadafora lashed out at Noriega's G2, charging that it was the "political arm" of the National Guard and "has retained its character of instrument of repression from the epoch of the military dictatorship." He charged that G2 was carrying out "arbitrary arrests, intimidation and attempting to manipulate political groups," but gave few specifics.

The charges had broken the unwritten opposition rule against directly attacking the National Guard on the issue of its handling of the transition to democratic rule. One journalist, Mayín Correa, reacted with surprise: "Really, no one has ever accused the G2, straight out, just like that, of repression, of arbitrary detentions, of intimidation, of manipulating political groups. Just like that against the G2. I've never even heard the opposition do that."

Noriega responded indirectly. Two days later, his G2 deputy, Lieutenant Colonel Julián Melo, called Spadafora's closest friend, Abdiel Juliao.

"Colonel Noriega is upset about this, but he is happy too. He's glad that everybody will know now that we are enemies. Tell Hugo to keep his nose out of the National Guard's business. When he attacks Noriega, he is attacking the Guard. The National Guard is a unity. Tell Hugo he has already been tried and sentenced," Melo said. He then put Noriega himself on the line.

It was evening, and there was noise of a Christmas party behind Noriega's voice, but Juliao heard him clearly: "You tell Hugo he had better watch his mouth. Anyone can die from a fishbone caught in his throat."

Spadafora was never one to shrink from a fight. He arranged for another interview, January 18, 1982 with Mayín Correa's morning talk show on Radio Continente. His voice tight with anger, he described the threats, then added to his arsenal of denunciations of Noriega:

"So I've had it with Lieutenant Colonel Noriega thinking that he can play cat and mouse games with me, because I am not a mouse nor do I have the calling to become one. So I have decided to let him know that I am on to him; I am on to him with the arm of truth. And I went to his friend, Señor Carlos Duque, to tell him that Noriega doesn't know it yet but I am on to him about drug trafficking, and I already have gathered certain elements. . . ."

Before Spadafora could finish the sentence, the station abruptly went off the air. The electricity from the government-owned electric company had been cut off.

Afterward, Mayin Correa asked Spadafora what he was talking about. He was mysterious about his information, saying only that he had been talking to his old buddies from the Victoriano Lorenzo Brigade who had fought in Nicaragua. Many of them had gotten jobs in Noriega's G2. He said he was investigating a house where drug traffickers were holding meetings.

CHAPTER 7

℈ⅿⅿⅿⅿⅿⅿⅿⅿⅿⅿⅿⅿⅿⅿⅿⅿⅿⅿⅿⅿⅿⅿⅿⅿℭ

OUR MAN
IN PANAMA

℈ⅼⅼⅼⅼⅼⅼⅼⅼⅼⅼⅼⅼⅼⅼⅼⅼⅼⅼⅼⅼⅼⅼⅼⅼⅼⅼⅼℭ

In March 1982, Noriega was still several steps from absolute power; he faced many rivals inside and outside the National Guard.

Panama was a country up for grabs. The National Guard and the government it controlled were reorganizing. The government was in charge of carrying out Torrijos's promised transition to democracy and independent civilian rule, which was to be completed by the presidential and parliamentary elections—the first free voting since 1968—scheduled for May 1984. Torrijos had set up a political party in 1978, the Democratic Revolutionary Party (PRD). Modeled on the Mexican PRI, which had successfully run Mexico as a one-party state for decades, the PRD was intended to institutionalize the Torrijos revolution in a broad-based party spanning peasants to businessmen, left to right. In fact, the party drew most of its base from the thousands of military families, teachers and government employees who had benefited most from the Torrijos years.

Now, with Torrijos gone, the legitimacy of National Guard rule was questioned as never before. The main opposition leaders, including the charismatic Arnulfo Arias, had returned from exile. Arias, at eighty and following bypass surgery, had slowed but kept himself at the center of political life. He installed himself in his unobtrusive house in Panama City or at his coffee plantation in Chiriquí and received a stream of visitors, progovernment and opposition, military

and civilian, all anxious to discuss the country's post-Torrijos era.
Although the newly legalized parties, including Arias's authentic
Panamanista party, were weakly organized congregations around
single leaders, politics had again become serious business, whose main
agenda was the orderly removal of the National Guard from power.
At stake was not only control of the government but control of a
potentially gigantic pool of patronage created by a half billion dollars
of former Canal Zone properties being gradually returned to Panama.

A group of businessmen, led by former exile Roberto Eisenmann,
was publishing the new *La Prensa,* a snappy-looking, tightly written
newspaper that was stealing readers and advertisers from ERSA, the
National Guard-controlled chain. Eisenmann had raised $1 million
to build a state-of-the-art, all-computerized newspaper plant. By
selling stock in shares no larger than $5,000, he assured that no
individual or party owned enough to control the paper's editorial
content. Starting from scratch in 1980, the paper hit hard and fast
with exposés of government corruption, naming names of National
Guard officials and the sources of their fat off-the-books incomes.
Dirt too salacious or too speculative to run as news appeared barely
disguised as witty anecdotes in the back-page column, *En Pocas
Palabras* ("*In Few Words*"). Politically, *La Prensa* reflected the
moderate right of center, free-enterprise values of the Panama City
business community and most of the opposition parties.

On the other side of the political divide, no one seemed capable
of exerting much direction for the nation. The president, Aristides
Royo, an aloof former education minister, made it clear to the National Guard's party that he owed his job to Torrijos rather than to
a crowd of cronies, and he quarreled incessantly with PRD leaders
over government jobs and perks. Florencio Florez, who had inherited Torrijos's post out of seniority, held nominal power over a troika
of powerful senior officers: Noriega, still the G2; Torrijos's cousin
Díaz Herrera, the executive secretary of the general staff; and Lieutenant Colonel Rubén Darío Paredes, the chief of staff, ranking
second to Florez. Each had created a solid base in the National
Guard; each had the clear ambition to become *numero uno.* Whether
that meant chief of the Guard or president of the country could be
worked out later.

Their first step was to remove Florez, and they took it on March 3, 1982. For several weeks, Paredes, Noriega and Díaz Herrera had been meeting secretly to plot the future of the National Guard. They had nothing personal against Florez. He was an affable sportsman, a racehorse aficionado, not a politician. But Florez was too passive, they told each other, too amenable to the civilian politicians who saw the transition to democracy as a contest for power with the National Guard. What bothered them most was that at this crucial moment in the National Guard's history, Florez declined to project himself as a national leader but seemed to epitomize the subordinate military officer.

The morning of the *golpe,* the three colonels rose at four-thirty to check with each other by phone, and by six-thirty they were in their offices in command headquarters. Their leader, by seniority, was Paredes, a proud-postured black whose training in Somoza's Nicaragua had made him the most pro-U.S., anticommunist member of the troika. They had planned to have control of the complex before Florez arrived at work, and they were shaken to learn that Florez had spent the night at his apartment in the building. They feared a leak, a hardly unlikely possibility since by this time they had brought a half dozen other top officers into their plans. Noriega was on the phone in his first-floor office coordinating last-minute arrangements with two captains who had agreed to move their combat units from bases across the city to surround the headquarters complex in case there was resistance.

At seven, Noriega joined Paredes, Díaz Herrera and another senior officer, Lieutenant Colonel Armando Contreras, in Paredes's office. Contreras was an important ally because as G3 he controlled troop operations and ranked just behind Paredes as deputy chief of staff. The group now seemed irresistible, consisting of four of the top seven officers. At Paredes's signal, they walked abreast down the long corridor from Paredes's office in the north wing and marched into the commander's office in the south wing. Paredes wore his service side arm; the others were unarmed. "We tried to look nonchalant," Díaz Herrera would recall. "But it wasn't exactly business as usual to see us four gorillas marching down the hall at seven in the morning."

Florez's startled secretary told them the commander had gone to the officers' mess for breakfast. The four men tramped down the stairs, across the parade grounds and into the building in the opposite corner of the complex. When they didn't find Florez there, Paredes became agitated. He was sure Florez had gotten word and had barricaded himself in a strong garrison to organize resistance to the putsch. The plotters knew how tenuous were the pledges of support they had gotten from other officers. Their success depended on their ability to give orders to the captains and majors actually in charge of the Guard's armed units. A prolonged show of resistance by Florez could turn the tables by rallying uncommitted officers and calling the plotters' bluff.

They were told that Florez had gone to a building across the street used by Noriega's G2 units to hold intelligence courses. Now rushing in a barely dignified trot, the four officers recrossed the parade grounds, exited the compound and crossed over to the unimposing G2 buildings. As they entered, Noriega hung back a few moments to give instructions by phone for combat units to surround the building. They found Colonel Florez conducting a routine inspection accompanied by only one assistant. He blanched when he saw the phalanx of officers, led by the fiercely excited Paredes, whose pistol was now stuck conspicuously in his waistband.

"Comandante, the general staff has decided it is time for you to retire," Paredes said. "Lieutenant Colonel Díaz has prepared your retirement papers. *Tranquilo,* don't get upset. Just sign the papers and you'll be accompanied to your home. We'll station a few guards for a while. Nothing will happen to you."

It was over. Not a shot had been fired. With Florez in custody and command headquarters secured, the rest of the *golpe* was carried out by phone. Díaz Herrera called all major military units outside Panama City to tell them that Lieutenant Colonel Paredes was their new commander. Contreras did the same for units inside Panama City.

Shortly after nine, Noriega called his contact, CIA station chief Tim Desmond, at the U.S. embassy to advise him of the changes. Noriega assured him that there was "no problem in the Guard" and that the Guard remained united.

Paredes himself called President Royo. Since, according to the constitution, only the president could mandate a commanding officer's retirement, Paredes instructed Royo to announce the changes. He said he would send over a prepared statement.

After a day filled with rumors of troop movements, President Royo convened the press in the presidential palace and read two presidential decrees announcing Florez's retirement and Paredes's promotion to commander in chief of the National Guard. The decision to retire Florez and two other senior officers was taken by the president, he said, "in coordination with the general staff of the National Guard as stated in Article 2 of the constitution, which states that there should be a harmonious collaboration and close relationship between the executive and other branches and the armed forces."

The following Monday the military leaders sat down in Paredes's new office to ensure harmony in their own ranks as they shared and passed on power in the coming years. By race, class and education, these sons of Torrijos's National Guard were self-consciously set apart from the civilian elite Torrijos had excluded from power since 1968. They would form alliances and talk about promises of restored civilian democracy, but the bottom line was power, and their meeting on March 8 was to keep it in the National Guard. They talked loftily about preserving the legacy of Torrijos, then worked on the details of satisfying each officer's personal ambitions. All still in their forties, they were young enough to envision an arrangement that would allow each to have a turn at the top. Paredes made an offer they could not appear to refuse. He wanted to be elected president in the May 1984 elections. By stepping down as chief of the National Guard to run, he would open the top spot to the next in line. Having agreed on the principal of rotation in power, the rest was a matter of setting a timetable.

They talked for hours. Noriega at some point gathered up his notes on the deal and went downstairs to his office to draft the finished pact for all to sign. He typed it in all-caps and gave it a grandiose title, SECRET, PLAN TORRIJOS, HISTORIC TIMETABLE—COMMITMENT OF THE NATIONAL GUARD.

Its centerpiece was point four:

Comandante Paredes, with the support and loyalty of the whole institution, particularly the entire general staff (including its recently retired members), commits himself to retire voluntarily in the first quarter (March) of 1983. From that moment on, the general staff as a whole commits itself to helping the by-then civilian Rubén Darío Paredes (retired) to become politically active in order that, in a normal and altruistic way and without the institution resorting to coercion or questionable or immoral actions, Paredes obtains the candidacy . . . for president of the republic.

Inspired in the desires of General Omar Torrijos Herrera (Q.E.P.D.), the officer corps and general staff of the institution will join together so that, with legal means but bringing to bear the prestige of all the members of our institution, the Torrijista process will be continued through the presidential candidacy of Paredes, obtaining a categorical triumph in the 1984 elections.

The document went on to set the timetable for the other participants. Upon Paredes's retirement, Colonel Contreras would become commander of the National Guard and would hold that title until March 1984. Noriega would be commander from March 1984 to July 31, 1987; he would be succeeded by Díaz Herrera, who would serve one year and "coordinate with the general staff and . . . President Rubén Darío Paredes" to arrange the future succession before the end of Paredes's term, in 1989. The self-interest of the exercise was made explicit in point eight (emphasis added).

It is agreed that today's comandante and tomorrow's president Paredes will remain committed, in close and determinant connection with the successive comandantes, *to preserve the rights, aspirations, feasible advantages and ethical and reasonable privileges of the general staff members who leave active service,* in a gesture of broad collegiality and fraternity.

By 1987, Noriega's scheduled retirement date, he would have served twenty-five years in the National Guard, be in his early fifties and be well positioned for a presidential run of his own in 1989. That part was unstated in the agreement, perhaps because almost exactly the same thing could be said about Díaz Herrera. The pact cemented a close working relationship for the present, but poised the two ambitious men in rivalry that could only sharpen in the coming years.

The home fires banked, Noriega turned his attention to his U.S. military and intelligence contacts. Through a few conversations over drinks, he was able to shape the U.S. perception of what had happened inside the National Guard. A March 19 U.S. Army Intelligence cable reported Noriega's spin on the recent events, placing himself as the key actor and main beneficiary. "In discussions with Noriega, source got the impression [ ] Noriega was the 'take charge person' in the group," the report said. Asked about the reasons for the abrupt takeover, Noriega is quoted as saying that Colonel Florez "did not have the capacity to be the commandant and was not listening to me." Noriega then corrected that to be the "GN [National Guard] staff" that Florez was ignoring.

In cables to Washington, Ambassador Ambler Moss reported that the changes should give no cause for alarm. He noted that "some of the hopes for a more apolitical GN which had arisen during Col. Florez' incumbency as Guard commander have been dulled." But he agreed with the "popular consensus" in Panama that the reshuffle was "another case of '*Quítate tú para que suba yo*' (You get out and let me in)." Moss speculated that the Noriega–Díaz Herrera relationship could develop into a rivalry and that Paredes would probably retire to run for president, leaving Noriega as commander of the Guard. None of this, however, was negative: "In the short run, U.S.–Panama relations should not rpt not be materially affected since both Paredes and Noriega have cooperated with the U.S. But Paredes will be more decisive than Florez was, and, overall, Panama will continue on, if not step up, its Third World, nonaligned course while cooperating with the U.S. on most basic issues."

Paredes as commandant was everything Moss expected. Outspoken, genial, self-confident, he moved rapidly through political and diplomatic circles to engrave his stamp on the incipient politicking for the 1984 elections. Torrijos had groomed him as a politician-soldier by giving him the post of agriculture minister in the mid-1970s. His manner was gruff but he was reassuring in a series of public speeches. At Torrijos's hometown of Santiago in Veraguas Province, he described the recent changes as the revival of Tor-rijismo, the vague, progressive tenets of their former leader. He sanctified the National Guard, comparing the general staff to "an altar where its members take communion daily" and set out his goal: "Once we are through with hunger, once we have reinforced the executive branch, once we have strengthened the morale of all our men, women, youth and peasants, only then will we be able to say that we have gotten rid of the danger threatening Latin America: Communism."

Paredes stated grandly that he did not intend to interfere with the government of President Royo, but within weeks Paredes had locked the civilian president firmly in his sights. Like Florez, Royo engen-dered no great animosity. But neither had he attracted any significant body of support, political or military, since the death of his mentor. Indifferent to economics, he had little remedy as the country slid into recession after 1980. Although known as left-leaning, he disparaged the military-backed Democratic Revolutionary Party and flirted politically with Arnulfo Arias, the military's archenemy. He had offended the United States with his friendliness toward Cuba and his harsh criticism of the United States for siding with Britain over Argentina in the Falklands war.

But all or none of those reasons was enough for Paredes. On July 30, 1982, as the country prepared to commemorate the first anniver-sary of Torrijos's death, Paredes put his pistol in his belt again, gathered his team of Noriega and Díaz Herrera and paid an early morning call on soon to be former president Royo. As before, Díaz Herrera brought along the resignation statement for Royo to sign. Paredes spoke softly, making no accusations and few criticisms. When the vigorous forty-two-year-old Royo, appearing on television that night, said he was resigning as president because of a severe sore throat, there were hoots heard around the country. The coup became known as the *gargantazo*—the blow to the throat.

At a ceremony to transfer the presidential sash to Vice President Ricardo de la Espriella, Paredes dropped any pretext about who was in charge. He read a long and detailed list of "recommendations," including the firing of the comptroller general and the attorney

general and the proforma resignations of all ministers, deputy ministers, provincial governors, mayors and ambassadors. The work of the
Electoral Tribunal, which was ruling on the eligibility of political
parties and other election issues, was to be set aside. Paredes also
asked for a host of new laws and a review of the labor code. Then,
after a mildly prurient comment that "democracy has a female name
and everyone wants to flirt with her, not to say something else," he
lashed out at the press for publishing "insult and slander" and at
radio talk shows for allowing "anyone to say what he pleases" on
telephone call-ins. Forgetting to frame it as a recommendation, he
decreed that effective immediately "all the newspapers, whether
those favoring the government or of the opposition, all, every single
one, will be out of circulation for seven days, seven days."

Such a raw example of diktat had not been experienced since the
very earliest days of the Torrijos régime. The papers remained closed
for six of the seven days decreed by Paredes. Worse, the opposition
La Prensa was occupied by troops for several days and viciously
vandalized. Corrosive acid was poured on machines, computer wir-
ing was ripped out and files were destroyed and stolen. Conspicuously missing were the files on the National Guard and on the
company, Transit, S.A., which a few weeks before had been the
subject of a *La Prensa* exposé. The article had said the company was
generating millions of dollars in kickbacks for National Guard officers, including General Paredes.

The U.S. State Department stayed out of the fight, saying "we
anticipate no change in our relations with Panama." But aside from
the newspaper closings, the coup was welcomed by the U.S. embassy,
whose cables said that Royo's "anti-U.S. rhetoric" would not be
missed—a reference to his public slaps at U.S. policy in El Salvador
and frequent complaints about implementing the Canal treaties. New
President de la Espriella was Stanford educated, a former Chase
Manhattan Bank employee and a free-enterprise economist whose
first appointments were nonideological technocrats who went to
work to cut the national budget deficit by 12 percent. Using the
across-the-board resignations "recommended" by Paredes, de la Espriella swept the government clean of the leftists brought in by
Torrijos and Royo. Paredes and de la Espriella, evaluated on the axis

of communism versus anticommunism, were seen as important new assets for U.S. policy in the region.

The remainder of 1982 and most of 1983 were times of peace and politics, if not prosperity, in Panama. The economic boom many had expected from the return of the Canal did not materialize, and Panama went into an economic slump that was a product partly of general hard times worldwide and partly of Panama's mounting foreign debt payments. Economic growth stayed just above zero, and as the country focused increasingly on possible candidates for the 1984 elections, it was clear that there were really only two issues: economic recovery and independence from the military.

Paredes made little effort to disguise his presidential ambitions. He promoted the idea that the president elected in the 1984 elections should be a candidate of "national unity," that is, one whose support spanned both the government and major opposition parties. In an interview in early 1983, he described a presidential mold only a former Guard commandant could fill: "We want the military out of power, but it can only be with a powerful president, someone who can not only win, but can lead. Only a strong president can keep the military out of power."

Paredes sent his smoothest political emissary, Díaz Herrera, to court the grand old man of Panamanian politics, three-time president Arnulfo Arias. If Arias gave even tacit approval, Paredes calculated, his party could be persuaded to join the government party, the PRD, in an unbeatable coalition. Arias was friendly and indicated his willingness to end his two-decade feud with the military, but he had fashioned a half-century political career by keeping his plans to himself. He was noncommittal. Paredes suffered from the political malady that often befalls reigning strongmen and is only diagnosed, too late, after they leave power. No one says no to a dictator, and Paredes's bluster was hardly conducive to political candor.

He got none from Noriega, who—to judge from later events—had a quite realistic sense of Paredes's low popularity. And Noriega had his own reasons to play a careful double game with his commandant's aspirations. If Paredes got discouraged about his presidential prospects, he might have second thoughts about stepping down from the National Guard. Noriega became anxious when Paredes begged off resigning in March 1983, as called for in the timetable of the secret Plan Torrijos. Noriega delicately negotiated the new date for Paredes's retirement—and his own promotion. They set the date for August 12, 1983. It would be the first-ever voluntary transfer of command since the 1968 coup, and they planned an appropriately grand ceremony.

Beneath the political and military maneuvering, Noriega was presiding over at least two levels of clandestine activity. Now a full colonel and occupying the number-two post of chief of staff, Noriega continued personal control of the intelligence apparatus and created a new center of independent power, an elite guard of commandos trained by advisers from the Israeli Defense Force. Known as UESAT (for Special Antiterrorist Units), the commandos had their own remote base and were under the command of a former Noriega G2 officer.

At one level, Noriega opened the doors to the United States to use Panama as a staging area for its expanding military activities in Nicaragua and El Salvador. The CIA was working furiously during all of 1983 to build up the Contras as a fighting force capable of overthrowing the Sandinista government. The Contras and their allies, with seemingly unlimited U.S. money and supplies, were optimistic. Managua by Christmas 1983 did not seem an unrealistic goal. It was barely an inconvenience that official U.S. policy limited support for the Contras to arms interdiction from Nicaragua to El Salvador. The CIA and the Contras were going all out, and Panama was to have a role.

U.S. Senator Patrick Leahy of Vermont learned the extent of that role in a visit to Panama on January 13, 1983. As a member of the Senate Intelligence Committee overseeing the CIA, he demanded, and received, a briefing on CIA operations in Panama. According to investigative reporter Bob Woodward, Dewey Clarridge, CIA chief of Latin American operations, came to Leahy's room at the Caesar Park Marriott and talked about Noriega. He said Noriega had been helping the CIA for some time, but also had a similarly close relationship with the Cubans. In Woodward's paraphrase, Clarridge said, "Of, course, there's no telling what he's providing the Cubans. In all, this is a deadly game. Nonetheless, Noriega is going to allow the CIA to set up a contra training facility here. The facility has to be kept secret at any cost. If it leaks, Noriega will have grounds to cancel and refuse to allow the training." The training was intended to prepare Contra troops operating in Costa Rica to invade Nicaragua from the south, Clarridge said.

Perhaps the most important Panamanian contribution was passive: not preventing the conversion of U.S. Southcom into the nerve center for U.S. operations in the region. Under the treaty, as Panama interpreted it, U.S. bases in Panama were limited to protecting the Canal. The United States accepted the concept but argued that the preservation of regional security was an indispensable part of Canal security. Fighting against communism in El Salvador and Nicaragua, according to the U.S. military doctrine, was as important to keeping the Canal safe as guarding the locks.

Southcom was rapidly being reconfigured. The once sleepy bases, airfields and schools whirled with activity. U.S. military advisers officially based in Panama shuttled back and forth to El Salvador to train the Salvadoran army—and to circumvent the Reagan administration's publicly declared ceiling of fifty-five advisers based in El Salvador. In addition, in 1983 so many Salvadoran officers were enrolled at the School of the Americas at Fort Gulick near Colón that they nearly outnumbered students from all other countries combined. U.S. facilities that collected and analyzed intelligence also greatly expanded. U.S. Navy vessels bristling with antennas left ports in Panama to station themselves off the coast of Nicaragua, close enough to eavesdrop on Sandinista military and government communications. The spy ships sent their raw intelligence tapes back to Southcom for analysis. Southcom intelligence units also manned electronic listening stations on Tiger Island, off El Salvador.

In early 1983, four AC130 air reconnaissance planes were brought to Howard Air Force Base, the largest U.S. airfield, just a few miles south of Panama City. The aircraft were specially outfitted with 40-mm cannon and electronic surveillance equipment. The planes made nightly low-altitude flights over guerrilla-controlled areas in El Salvador to provide tactical battlefield intelligence to Salvadoran army units on the ground. Also at Howard a small fleet of planes hauled weapons and ammunition to Honduras to supply the CIA's Contra forces, which had grown to over five thousand troops.

All this was done with the knowledge and permission of the Panamanians, according to several U.S. officials. Both sides understood, however, that publicly Panama would continue to oppose U.S. policy in Central America, despite its private acquiescence to U.S. bases being used to support that policy. When details of the training and spy ships were published in the United States, President de la Espriella protested, but the Panamanian objections never went beyond words.

At the same time, Noriega was involved in a still deeper level of clandestine activity, one that he presumably concealed even from his U.S. intelligence contacts. His contacts with the Colombian cartel, through Floyd Carlton, were expanding from drug flights to shipments of money for laundering in Panama, and Carlton was bringing his friend, César Rodríguez, in on the action.

In January 1983, Carlton received Noriega's permission to buy his first Learjet. Carlton flew to Miami and met with César Rodríguez, who had arrived earlier. They negotiated the purchase of a Learjet 25, tail number N281R. The purchase was straightforward, but the ownership and use of the plane were complex. Carlton and Rodríguez bought the plane (and registered it with one of their companies) as a front for cartel leader Pablo Escobar. An Escobar emissary, whom they knew only as "Blue Jeans," met with them in Miami and provided the money, $685,000, to buy the plane and refit it for its special purposes. Two secret compartments were built into the nose to carry shipments of money.

The arrangement, which Carlton said was cleared with Noriega, was for the cartel to pay for the plane but for Noriega to use it on official trips to establish the plane's "official cover." When Noriega was not using the plane, Carlton and his partners used it to fly money. Carlton, Rodríguez and three other pilots who had been part of the arms-smuggling operations—Eduardo Pardo, Teófilo Watson and Daniel Miranda—were trained to fly it. In early May, Miranda and Pardo flew a shipment of $800,000 in cash from cartel contacts in Miami to Panama for laundering.

César Rodríguez took the initiative in the money-laundering operation and made an undetermined number of flights in 1983. Always a loudmouth, he bragged to friends who noticed his increased wealth that his new business was "transporting suitcases." The Learjet 25 continued to do double duty as money shuttle and official business, and on one trip, Rodríguez flew Panamanian official José Blandón to Managua in the Learjet, then continued on to Miami. He picked up Blandón on the way back. During the final leg to Panama, Rodríguez showed Blandón suitcases he said were full of money and boasted that he was part of an operation with Noriega's permission that was bringing more than $2 billion into Panama. When they landed at Paitilla, the plane taxied into César's hangar and the suitcases were loaded into an armored car for delivery to a bank.

Carlton meanwhile had agreed to fly another load of cocaine. Noriega at first instructed him to delay the shipment because of upcoming joint military exercises with the United States. Finally, Carlton took off from El Cafetal airstrip near Medellín and flew 400 kilos of cocaine to Coronado airfield on the Pacific coast about fifty miles south of Panama City. Carlton delivered Noriega's payment, $150,000, to the offices of Explonsa, as he had on a shipment the previous December.

Noriega's attitude toward the drug trafficking, according to Carlton, was one of take the money and run, and he counseled Carlton to increase his prices for the flights. During one of their meetings, Noriega said, "You're making peanuts, that's why César is ahead of you. . . . This opportunity only comes once in a lifetime. You have to make enough money so that you can live a decent life. This isn't going to last forever."

The morning of August 12, 1983, brought sights and sounds that Latin Americans usually associate with an impending military coup. Since before dawn, military vehicles had crowded the grimy streets around command headquarters. There were howitzer rounds and rifle volleys as the cargo and reconnaissance planes of Panama's meager air force flew over Panama City. But the military activity was entirely peaceful, part of the spectacle Noriega had planned to celebrate his promotion to commander in chief of the National Guard.

The site of the ceremonial transfer of power from General Paredes to newly appointed General Noriega was chosen for maximum symbolic impact. For more than seventy-five years the peninsula known as Fort Amador had been U.S. territory. Its long western shore, extended by a causeway to offshore islands, traced the first miles of the Panama Canal, and its installations housed the coastal artillery units whose massive concrete emplacements once housed the heaviest caliber guns in the world. Now, in accordance with the Canal treaties, Fort Amador's military systems were jointly operated by Panamanian and U.S. forces, and hundreds of acres of grounds and buildings had been turned over to Panama. Noriega arrayed every unit he was to command—from the eleven military garrisons distributed around the country to policemen in bright green uniforms—on the oval parade grounds once trod only by American soldiers.

Noriega and the outgoing Paredes stood at the reviewing stand with only President de la Espriella between them. To their back was the Canal. Straight ahead, if they looked over the heads of the troops, they had a view of the trimmed fairways of the American golf course.

A unit of paratroopers in full packs stood at attention on the grounds. A squad of sky divers jumped out of planes barely visible overhead and made spectacular precision landings in front of the reviewing stand. The invited guests included Panama's poor as well as its elite—a tradition Torrijos had instilled in his protégés. The foreigners included dozens of diplomats and military officers, many of them representatives of U.S. Southcom.

Noriega's acceptance speech had elements of a chieftain's harangue to the troops and a preacher's exhortation to the faithful. "As dawn broke this morning, at the hour of the God of our hearts," he began, "I made Tony Noriega's confession to the Gods of Panama and the Gods of the universe. I laid bare my transgressions and asked for the moral laws so that I might try, as much as humanly possible, to uphold them."

He then elaborately praised his fellow officers—most effusively his second in command, Colonel Díaz Herrera, with whom he said he "shared bonds that go beyond this profession . . . that go beyond Torrijism . . . beyond the weapons we have shared and the destiny they will have." He promised a new era for the Panamanian military in preparation for the responsibilities of the year 2000. He called his fellow soldiers for the first time the Panama Defense Forces, which was soon to become their official name.

Then he launched into an oration on peace and war in Central America. "Today, as a Christian, I offer peace, peace, peace. [Applause.] However, peace is a two-way street. Peace will be maintained as long as everyone's rights are respected. [Applause.] All Panamanians, regardless of political differences, should understand clearly that we must all prevent the chaos and destruction that exist in neighboring countries. . . . This is a tragic condition of states and nations where dialogue and peaceful solutions were ignored, where the elements of poverty, illiteracy, and sickness were allowed to prosper. Panamanian society is fearful and apprehensive about the violence that prevails in the region to which we belong geographically, where we abide. Panamanian society, at all social levels, is afraid. We, the national defense forces, cannot be indifferent, geopolitically speaking, to the Central American tragedy. We cannot be mere spectators in this drama. We cannot deny that there is a spiral of violence with a ripple effect. Neither can we overlook the clashes that exist between the so-called hostile triangles and the security triangle."

He had a sober message for the politicians. "We will be in our barracks, as groups opposed to the régime demand with their outcries. However, it would be an unacceptable, hypocritical pretension to say that, having played an important role in our national life, this force would remain idle in the task of achieving reconciliation among Panamanians. The country's panorama is not at all bright. Future prospects are gloomy, but we must have faith and we do have faith in men and women who, throughout their public life, have shown genuine love for their fatherland and a sincere desire to serve it. . . ." He solemnly pledged the National Guard to assist in and guarantee the coming democratic elections.

The ambiguity of this embrace of the political process was preserved as he laid aside his text and turned to envelop General Paredes in a manly hug. "Rubén, today we give you over to your friends, the people, who have come to receive you. And here remaining behind is your family of olive green, who say to you as to the paratrooper: 'Good jump.' "

The good feelings lasted through the round of parties that weekend and for several weeks after. Having jumped, Paredes found neither the parachute promised by his National Guard cohorts nor the soft landing expected from the civilians whose flattery had been so lavish until August 12. The avalanche of endorsements he had been led to anticipate from political parties did not materialize. The crafty Arnulfo Arias postponed a decision on a candidate at his party's convention three days later. But when asked about Paredes's candidacy, he unleashed a withering one-liner: "Anyone who is thirty-five years old, even an illiterate, can be president of the republic." Of Noriega, he commented evenly, "He is one of the best among them. I hope he continues to gradually learn that he has to respect the rights of the citizens in every respect."

No party representatives accompanied Paredes when he formally announced his candidacy on August 20. Still clinging to the notion that he was a "unity candidate" above the partisan frays, he said only that he was holding "productive talks with the most important parties in the republic." The "majority" of the parties had pledged their support, he said, but he was not yet authorized to name them. Only the small right-wing Labor party (PALA) had officially nominated Paredes at the time of his announcement.

In quick succession, President de la Espriella and Noriega, who had become close friends and shared a delight for political intrigue, signaled they were backing away from Paredes. De la Espriella abruptly fired four government ministers closely identified with Paredes. The new foreign minister, Oydén Ortega, was a moderate leftist and an outspoken critic of U.S. Central American policy. Noriega and Díaz Herrera held a closed door, three-hour meeting with leaders of the main opposition parties, then made a public pledge of National Guard neutrality in the campaign.

Noriega invited Paredes to his beach house at Caleta, near Panama City, to administer the coup de grace. With Díaz Herrera and Colonel Marcos Justine, he informed Paredes that he was no longer considered the candidate of the National Guard or of the Democratic Revolutionary Party. The March 1982 agreement had not stood the test of political reality nor of Paredes's political blunders. To Paredes's protests, Díaz Herrera bluntly countered: "You know how it works, General: we put in the candidates; we take them out. It's that simple."

Within days, Paredes's political candidacy had disappeared unmourned. Without fanfare, Noriega cut off the former general's remaining military privileges. He was restricted from entering command headquarters unless invited. As a final indignity, Paredes was informed he could no longer fill up his cars at the National Guard station. Many reasons were offered for the abandonment of Paredes—but for Noriega one reason was sufficient: the need to sweep from the stage the only person strong enough to challenge Noriega's personal rule.

It would be several years before it dawned on the opposition—and the U.S. embassy—that Paredes had been the last best hope of stopping Noriega, but for the moment there was rejoicing, as in a front-page editorial in *La Prensa*: "Now that this obstacle has been removed—regardless of how the miracle took place—the gloomy national political panorama has cleared and we can now hope for elections that will genuinely express and respect the people's will. The republic has gained what Paredes has lost."

To the U.S. embassy, Noriega's arrival at the pinnacle of Panamanian power was hardly a surprise and only mildly disquieting. The United States had a new ambassador, a tough professional from the ranks of foreign service officers who still considered regional expertise, language ability and immersion in local politics to be a number-one responsibility. Everett "Ted" Briggs had been born in Havana, Cuba, of American parents and had grown up speaking Spanish; he had served in three Latin American countries and as deputy assistant secretary of state for Latin America. Briggs was also a conservative with a genuine enthusiasm for Ronald Reagan's Central America policy. His description of the events at his new posting, in a cable to Washington, alternated between skepticism and praise.

"It was clearly Noriega's day, with a presence and eloquence that

surprised even those who have closely followed Noriega's career,"
the cable began, referring to the ceremony marking the change of
command. Ambassador Briggs noted with approval Noriega's statement in a newspaper interview "in which he blamed 'Marxists' for
taking advantage of injustices in Central America to further their
political cause" and stressed the common interests and profound ties
between the United States and Panama.

Then Briggs heaped on a dose of caution:

> Did Noriega mean it? This is the question that has pervaded the
> political scene since Friday's ceremony. Many observers, who are
> accustomed to regarding Noriega as a sort of diminutive Darth Vader,
> scoff at his assurances about taking the Guard back to the barracks
> and assuring free and honest elections in 1984. . . . Other less cynical
> observers would agree that the outcome depends on how Noriega sees
> his own interests and those of the Guard. But allow themselves to hope
> that he sees a more professional and apolitical Guard subordinate to
> the constitutionally elected government as serving those interests. In
> any event Noriega's speech was an eloquent and very public commit-
> ment from which he might find it difficult (though not absolutely
> impossible) to extricate himself.

On September 22, Steven Michael Kalish arrived at Omar Torrijos
Airport (formerly Tocumen) in a chartered Learjet. A limousine sent
by César Rodríguez drove onto the tarmac to meet the plane and to
take its two passengers and their heavy suitcases downtown to Rodríguez's offices in the Bank of Boston building.

Kalish had started selling grass in the sixties at his high school in
Bellaire, Texas, a Houston suburb. By 1983 he had a Ferrari, a BMW,
a Chevy Blazer and more money than he could handle. That summer
he and his partners had organized the largest marijuana-smuggling
operation of their careers. An oceangoing tug named *The Bulldog*
pushed a refrigerated barge loaded with 280,000 pounds of marijuana
from Colombia on a circuitous route that ended in Louisiana. The
cargo was off-loaded into tractor trailers and driven to Ohio, where
it was divided and sent out through a distribution network and sold.
Kalish was in charge of the logistics of the operation, which involved

more than one hundred people. That operation netted $15 to
$20 million; other smaller deals that summer brought in another
$15 million. The money had been stacking up in Kalish's lakeside
house on St. Charlotte Drive in Tampa.

"The currency filled entire rooms. Although we were sending out
millions of dollars to our Colombian suppliers, at one point we had
in excess of $35 million in Tampa. We used money-counting ma-
chines, but had to stop any counting because we could not keep up
with the volume," Kalish would testify four years later. Banks in the
Cayman Islands that Kalish's organization had been using to launder
cash had told them they had reached the limit.

Kalish needed another outlet to launder his money. He also
needed a safer base of operations than Tampa. He was a fugitive from
a smuggling conviction in Texas. The connection to Panama was
typically informal: Over drinks one day in Fort Lauderdale, the
brother-in-law of his Colombian marijuana supplier introduced him
to a Cuban-American named George Martínez, who said he knew
a guy in Panama named César who was capable of handling large
amounts of cash. George and Steve flew down to Panama together
in the Learjet.

César Rodríguez leased three floors of the Bank of Boston building. In the twentieth-floor penthouse, he ran an exclusive restaurant,
the Tower Club, and below it a spa and members-only club for PDF
officers and politicians. He met Kalish and Martínez in his offices on
the seventeenth floor. Rodríguez offered him a complete package of
services: contacts with discreet bankers, shell corporations to hide
his paper trail, investment opportunities, even an armored-car service to pick up his money at the airport and deliver it to the banks.
Kalish had brought $2.4 million with him in cash. He said he was
interested in bringing $100 million more to Panama. Rodríguez im-
mediately arranged for Kalish to deposit his cash in two banks,
BANAICO and BCCI.

Kalish was impressed. On the tour of the clubs, he was introduced
to military people and government officials. One man introduced as
an official took him aside and warned him that Panamanian intelligence had been informed that the Drug Enforcement Administration

had Kalish's plane under surveillance. He advised Kalish to send the plane back empty as a precaution, which Kalish did.

Kalish also liked Rodríguez's relaxed manner. At dinner that night, Rodríguez brought his partner Enrique Pretelt. They talked about protection. They told Kalish that they would take him to meet their silent partner, General Tony Noriega. It was a name that meant nothing to Kalish, who got a quick explanation on the power of the military in Panama.

"They run the country, they control everything. That's the bottom line. That's what you need to know, Brown," Rodríguez said, using Kalish's false name. "This man is the boss. Anything we want to do in Panama we can do because we have his approval. He's our partner in the money-laundering operation you are currently involved in. And all our future business will involve him. You need to meet him, talk to him; you need to give him a feel for what kind of person you are. And you should give him a gift."

"What kind of gift?"

"You give him some money, and you make it an amount that you feel reflects the seriousness of your intentions to do business in Panama."

The next day, Rodríguez picked up Kalish and Martínez at their hotel and drove to Noriega's home. Pretelt was already there. They had a drink at the open-air bar next to an aviary that held Noriega's macaws and parrots. Then they were shown in to Noriega's office. Noriega was sitting behind a large wooden desk. Kalish noticed the display cases for Noriega's collections. There were antique guns in one, some of them gold plated. In another there were dozens of figurines of frogs and toads.

Noriega was affable. He asked Kalish what kind of business he had in mind while he was in Panama. Kalish answered in English, with Rodríguez translating. "I said I wanted to live in Panama. I wanted to bank and invest my monies in Panama. I wanted a place where I could feel comfortable without the U.S. authorities breathing down my neck. I wanted a place where I didn't have to worry about the Communists seizing control. And it seemed to me that Panama presented me with all these opportunities," Kalish said in describing the conversation later. There was no mention of drugs, just money.

Noriega said he would be happy to have Kalish do business in Panama. He said his friends Kiki and César would see to his needs, but if there were any problems to feel free to get in touch with him personally.

Kalish had brought his new silver Halliburton briefcase—elegantly thin and, made of light aircraft aluminum, virtually indestructible. Inside Kalish had placed $300,000 in cash. As they talked, he moved the briefcase from his lap to the floor beside his chair. When he got up to shake hands, he left the briefcase and began to walk out.

"Brown, you're leaving your briefcase," Noriega called after him.

"No, it's *para tí*; it's for you," Kalish said.

Noriega smiled.

A few hours later, Noriega sent word that Kalish and Martínez were invited to a party that night at the offices of the Panama Canal Commission. When they got there Noriega was already quite drunk and greeted them as if they were old friends.

"Brown, anything you want in Panama, you just ask," he said.

Kalish and Martínez spent much of the evening in an office that appeared to be used by Noriega. They drank and snorted cocaine and looked out the large plate-glass windows with a magnificent view of the Panama Canal. Kalish had a feeling he was going to enjoy being in Panama.

Nothing about Kalish or César Rodríguez's drug-related activity was known publicly, but in 1983 Panama's increasingly feisty opposition press had begun to raise new questions about alleged National Guard complicity with drug trafficking and money laundering. *La Prensa*'s column *En Pocas Palabras* hammered away at every congressional report and newspaper article generated in the United States that mentioned Panama. The column picked up a report, on money laundering, by the Senate Permanent Subcommittee on Investigations in February, quoting it as saying that "Witnesses in Panama consider it common knowledge that the Guard has links—and receives payments—from various traffickers of drugs, arms and other kinds of contraband." In May, a Cuban American named Ramón Milian Rodríguez had been arrested trying to take off from Fort Lauderdale, Florida, with boxes packed with more than $5.4 million in cash on board his Learjet bound for Panama. *En Pocas Palabras* reported that the man's operations accounted for more than $200 million in money shipments to Panama. Another column questioned why the remote, supposedly abandoned airstrip known as Calzada Larga was protected by National Guard troops.

The charges lacked specifics, and none of them mentioned Noriega, but Ambassador Briggs took the accounts seriously enough to look into them. Soon after Noriega took over as commander, Briggs convened the embassy "country team": deputy chief of mission William Price, political officer Ashley Hewitt, CIA chief of station Jerry Svat and military attaché Lieutenant Colonel Jerry Walker. "What do we really know about this man?" Briggs asked, looking from one official to another. "I want every one of you to scour your files and your sources and give me the bottom line. I want specifics, not vague charges, but I want everything, every bit of evidence there is to be found."

The investigation would take some time. Meanwhile, the CIA's Jerry Svat argued vehemently for giving Noriega the benefit of the doubt. "Let's give the guy a chance; he's not so bad," a participant remembers Svat saying. There was a long heated discussion, with political officer Ashley Hewitt making the case that Noriega was antidemocratic, repressive, and generally "bad news." But the general's unsavory reputation had to be weighed against his solid record of cooperation with U.S. policies in the region. In the end, it was decided that Noriega would be brought in, brought up, brought along. The first step in his metamorphosis was a red-carpet visit to the United States.

On Monday, November 14, Noriega's entourage took off for Miami and Washington in a Panamanian Air Force Falcon jet. The trip was festive, with champagne and delicate snacks available throughout the flight. Noriega's U.S. escorts were military attaché Jerry Walker and military group commander Lieutenant Colonel Charles "Chico" Stone. Another man on board was part of the festivities but not part of the official party; Enrique "Kiki" Pretelt, jewelry-store and nightclub owner, was known to the Americans on board only as Noriega's friend and business associate.

In Washington, the Panamanians were taken to suites overlooking the Potomac River at the Watergate Hotel, all expenses paid by the U.S. government. Ambassador Briggs had flown to Washington separately. At the State Department and the National Security Council, Noriega's meetings were at the secondary levels appropriate to a dignitary who was not head of state. Noriega discussed plans for the 1984 Panamanian elections with Briggs and Langhorne Motley, assistant secretary of state for inter-American affairs. At the NSC, Noriega met with Latin America adviser Roger Fontaine and General Robert Schweitzer. In the hallway, Noriega's party exchanged greetings with NSC aide Oliver North. In August, North had traveled to Panama to accompany Secretary of State Caspar Weinberger.

These meetings were intended, not for the discussion of substantive policy programs, but rather to raise Noriega's profile inside the Washington bureaucracy. The lavish suites and dinners and the friendly attention from senior U.S. officials were overt efforts to court a new friend, to establish the kind of access and personal rapport that would lay the groundwork for future cooperation.

Almost two whole days, however, were set aside for the institutions that did have long-standing working relations with Noriega. His two U.S. military escorts were miffed when they arrived with him at CIA headquarters in Langley, Virginia; chief of station Jerry Svat had arrived from Panama to handle the CIA portion of Noriega's visit and unceremoniously swept Noriega off down the hall for a meeting with CIA Director William Casey, leaving Colonels Walker and Stone to cool their heels until late afternoon. Nothing is known about the meetings at the CIA that day, but Noriega would later boast to the general staff back in Panama about his four-hour intimate lunch with Casey and hint at secret operations.

The next day at the Pentagon, Noriega and his group were honored at a lunch hosted by Richard Armitage, the assistant secretary of defense for inter-American affairs. He also met with Secretary of Defense Weinberger and with Defense Intelligence Agency and other Army intelligence officials. He had a particularly friendly encounter with Nestor Sanchez, whom Noriega had known for many years. Sanchez was Armitage's deputy and a veteran of thirty years of Latin American operations for the CIA.

Noriega and his entourage were in their element at the Pentagon, military men talking to military men. And Pentagon officials greeted Noriega's rise to power with great satisfaction. One of his first actions as commandant had been to set in motion an elaborate plan to restructure the National Guard into a more professional fighting force, renaming it the Panama Defense Forces. The restructuring had been urged on Panama for years. It was seen in Washington as an absolute necessity if Panama was to fulfill its treaty obligations to defend the Panama Canal. A barely hidden by-product of the changes was to make the Panamanian military financially and personally dependent on the United States.

The three days in Washington were not all work. Every evening the Americans and Panamanians got together for drinks in one of the Watergate suites. Noriega was most often in the company of a tall, impressively beautiful Panamanian woman who had flown in from Panama. One evening Svat took Noriega and his mistress out to dinner at a Washington restaurant.

Noriega's friend Kiki Pretelt attended none of the official meetings but always joined the group in the evening. He and Noriega were often engrossed in conversations about plans to buy new airplanes for the PDF.

On Tuesday, César Rodríguez showed up. Rodríguez had flown in from Panama on Steven Kalish's Learjet 35. The marijuana smuggler's plane was for Noriega's use for the rest of his travels in the United States. It was one of Kalish's favors.

Noriega was high-spirited and confident. He talked every day by phone with his wife, while lavishing gracious attention on his mistress in Washington. Noriega told Walker and Stone he was going on to Las Vegas for a few days of fun and asked if they would like to go along as his guest. Walker had a commitment he couldn't break, but Stone was eager to go. Noriega said his wife was going to meet him in Las Vegas, and she could bring Stone's wife along. Stone cleared the junket with Ambassador Briggs, who saw it as an opportunity not to be missed for Stone to establish a useful friendship with

Noriega. They departed in the two jets on Friday morning, leaving Noriega's mistress and César Rodríguez behind.

When they checked in at the Stardust Hotel, the manager met them and told them it was all on the house. Their host, Noriega later told Stone, was Jay Lerner, an American who held the concession for slot machines at Panama's many casinos. During the weekend of shows, gambling and shopping, Noriega was seldom without Felicidad, his wife, whom he called by her pet name "Muñeca," Spanish for doll. He showed her the kind of genuine interest and consideration indicative not only of a durable marriage but also of a strong partnership. They drank heavily as they played roulette and other games, laughing when they won but apparently indifferent to losses. On Sunday, the party loaded up their now mountainous luggage in the two planes and flew back to Panama via Florida.

In Panama, the U.S. embassy was gearing up for another high-level meeting with Noriega. Vice President George Bush planned to visit Panama in early December after attending the inauguration of Argentina's new democratic president, Raul Alfonsín. Ambassador Briggs and his team put together a thick set of briefing papers to prepare the vice president and his staff.

The priority item on Bush's agenda was not to be drugs, but rather America's proinsurgency campaign in Nicaragua and counterinsurgency efforts in El Salvador. Nevertheless, Bush held a variety of high-profile antidrug positions in the Reagan administration, and his chief antinarcotics staffer, former Admiral Daniel Murphy, was with him on the trip. And Panama had recently been in the spotlight as a money-laundering haven. A front-page *Wall Street Journal* article, which appeared about the time Noriega left for the United States, reported that cash was pouring in in cardboard boxes: "Panama, a tax haven with one of the Western Hemisphere's tightest bank secrecy laws, is fast becoming a favored spot to stash illicit drug profits." The article quoted from a videotape of a drug dealer bragging that "military guards" protected his money on arrival in Panama.

The article described the spectacular arrest of Ramón Milian Rodríguez the previous May. The Milian case was of particular personal interest to Bush; he had gone to Florida to appear at a press conference trumpeting Milian's arrest as the largest seizure of drug money so far.

Briggs had asked his team to come up with its best intelligence on drug and corruption allegations against Noriega, and he had their conclusions in front of him on December 11, when Bush arrived in Panama. State Department, DEA and Pentagon officials who participated in the investigative meetings convened by Briggs said that their files showed many unproven allegations against Noriega—but no hard evidence. "We met and had a couple of meetings in which we tried to lay on the table everything we knew about Noriega, the bad things. At the meetings I attended—and the ambassador met separately with the CIA people—there was no information in the embassy or at U.S. Southcom that could directly link Noriega to drugs. And that's what I presume the ambassador told Vice President Bush," one participant said.

Noriega and his antinarcotics unit, moreover, had assisted U.S. drug enforcement. Milian's arrest had been the direct result of a cable from Noriega's antinarcotics unit to U.S. Customs in Florida alerting them to his many flights with money into Panama. Noriega personally had met with the DEA officer in Panama, Jim Bramble, to facilitate quick boarding procedures by the U.S. Coast Guard of Panamanian-registry ships suspected of carrying drugs.

The meeting, at the Omar Torrijos Airport VIP lounge, was short and stiffly formal. Bush, on Briggs's recommendation, directed his attention to President de la Espriella rather than to Noriega, but his message was intended for the general, who he knew was the real power in Panama. Most of the time was spent talking about Central America, the dangers of Cuban influence in Nicaragua and U.S. needs for understanding and cooperation in the region.

Toward the end there was a brief exchange about drug enforcement. Bush inoffensively introduced the U.S. concern about reports of money laundering in Panama and said that the United States could help Panama crack down on it. He suggested that negotiations begin on a mutual legal assistance treaty, similar to the agreement the United States has with Switzerland, to restrict the laundering without unduly compromising bank secrecy, which he agreed was an important cornerstone of Panama's banking industry.

De la Espriella said his country would be happy to begin such conversations. He had another point to make. He wanted the vice president to know that the recent allegations linking Panamanian officials to the drug trade were untrue. Bush said politely that he was unaware of the charges. According to several accounts, Noriega gave an impeccably understated performance as the subordinate military chief, sitting alertly on the edge of his chair but saying almost nothing, deferring to President de la Espriella. He gave no indication that he and Bush had met before—as they had, in December 1976, when the topic was charges of Panamanian involvement in terrorist bombings.

Noriega's three months of contacts with his U.S. allies had been exquisitely orchestrated and had given him just what he needed: the image of a flexible team player. For someone in Noriega's subordinate position vis-à-vis the United States, establishing trust was not so important as establishing usefulness; he had learned that the locus of his own power was in the favors he was asked to perform. Over the next several months and years, he would find ways to be helpful in Central America. He would make the right noises about the war on drugs. He would pick a presidential candidate whose qualifications could have been written up in Washington (as some observers claim they were). Manuel Noriega had had a long relationship with the United States; he was confident he would do just enough, when the time came, to keep his North American friends happy—and looking the other way.

CHAPTER 8

MARGIN BY FRAUD

On February 13, 1984, Nicolás Ardito Barletta stepped off a private plane that had brought him from Washington, D.C., to become Noriega's annointed candidate for president. The Learjet Noriega sent to fetch him belonged to marijuana smuggler Steven Kalish and had been used to ferry drug money for laundering in Panamanian banks. The ownership of the plane was just one of the secrets Noriega kept from the future president.

Another was Noriega's decision that same afternoon to dispose of a sitting Panamanian president for the second time in less than two years. Ricardo de la Espriella had been a useful foot soldier for Noriega; he had helped in the maneuvering that pulled the rug out from under General Paredes and had been an enthusiastic participant in planning the strategy for the PDF and its civilian parties to win the elections scheduled for May 6. No reason was given for de la Espriella's resignation. He had returned on Sunday from the inauguration of Venezuela's president, Jaime Lusinchi, but by three-thirty P.M. Monday, de la Espriella was resting at a beach resort outside Panama City, and his vice president, Jorge Illueca, had taken the oath of office as the new president.

One of de la Espriella's mistakes was that he aspired to become a real president, democratically elected, and had lobbied Noriega to change the election laws to allow a sitting president to become the candidate. Another mistake was having a few too many drinks at a reception in the Caracas Hilton and saying out loud that Noriega's choice of Barletta was a mistake and would be a disaster for Panama.

That weekend was an ominous start to the presidential campaign that was intended to return Panama to democracy. An opposition spokesman charged that the change of government was a *golpe de estado,* a coup d'état, in response to the consolidation of the opposition slate and de la Espriella's reluctance to use government resources to finance the pro-PDF candidate.

The consolidation had been hard won. Just the previous Saturday, the two main opposition parties, the Panamanista of Arnulfo Arias and the Christian Democrat, had joined forces. The Christian Democrats agreed to support Arias for president and his closest adviser, Miami banker Carlos Rodríguez, for first vice president. That left only the second vice presidential slot for the Christian Democrats' own leader, Ricardo Arias Calderón, an acerbic former seminarian who combined intellectual strength with an almost total lack of mirth and charisma. Several other parties also swallowed the bitter pill and supported Arnulfo Arias. They considered Arias an old-fashioned populist whose antimilitary rhetoric would close off any possibility of entente with the PDF. Their misgivings were only partly eased by Arias's secret promise to step down in six months and allow Carlos Rodríguez to be president. The opposition slate took the name ADO—the Democratic Opposition Alliance.

On the progovernment side, the choice of a candidate was an even harder fight. The PRD, the official Torrijista party, had pretensions of becoming an independent civilian force that would run the country in a loose alliance with the military. The party had received recognition as a member of the Socialist International and carefully cultivated its relations with other Latin American social democratic parties. It wanted to name a moderate leftist from its own ranks, Ernesto Pérez Balladares, as presidential candidate.

Noriega and Díaz Herrera had other ideas about the nature of the party, and Díaz Herrera was given the job of pushing the party back into line. "We knew that Pérez Balladares controlled the party. He had managed a lot of money and done a lot of favors and bought some leaders. There was a strong lobby for him. But we also knew that the party was the first line of defense for the defense forces, and we weren't about to let go of it," Díaz Herrera said.

Noriega had outlined the formula for a successful candidate in an interview several months earlier: an administrator, an economist, a man with international connections "to know which doors to knock on" for development help; a serious man, a young man, a man without "traumas" from the past; and, of course, a Torrijista. In other words, a fresh new face untainted by PRD corruption. In their discussions, Noriega and Díaz Herrera agreed that to allow the PRD to have its way was to drive all other political forces into the arms of Arnulfo and the opposition. A PRD candidate could not win even a "Panamanian victory." An outsider would serve the dual purpose of building a coalition with other parties and keeping the PRD firmly under military control.

"Nicky" Barletta had a résumé that fit the bill. He was forty-five, the son of a prosperous but not oligarchical bus company owner. He earned his credentials as a Torrijista and a reputation as an economic whiz kid when he was planning minister in the first Torrijos cabinet in 1968. During the Canal negotiations he had crunched the numbers and prepared unassailable arguments showing the overwhelmingly one-sided profits the United States had garnered while in control of the Canal. Since 1978 he had been a vice president of the World Bank. Among his friends he counted Secretary of State George Shultz, who had been his teacher and mentor at the University of Chicago, where Barletta took his doctorate in economics.

Barletta's most important political asset, from Noriega's point of view, was that he had no political assets. He was relatively well known and respected in Panama but had never been a player, never joined the PRD, never controlled a budget or distributed patronage. He also had an attractive wife and three children. And he was hungry for the job—not the kind of man who would stray very far from Noriega's control.

Díaz Herrera had one, at least half-serious reservation: "You are just a little bit too honest," he told Barletta in one meeting before Noriega made the final choice. "You know that you can't be like that in the government. One has friends and they have to be helped."

Once decided on Barletta, Noriega shoved him down his party's throat. He summoned the PRD National Executive Committee to command headquarters on January 8. With Díaz Herrera at his side, he told them that Barletta was the best candidate to ensure social peace and, in effect, gave the assembled leaders a direct order. Immediately following the meeting, the PRD officially endorsed Barletta as the PRD's candidate.

Díaz Herrera then used the Barletta candidacy as a bargaining chip in negotiations with potential coalition partners. He offered the vice presidential slot to sugar magnate Eric Arturo Delvalle, of the small, business-oriented Republican party. The negotiations were easy, with few illusions about who would be in charge.

The second vice presidential slot was offered to physician and former health minister Roderick Esquivel, leader of the Liberals. Esquivel wanted the terms spelled out more explicitly. He wanted a clear commitment about the power relationship between the military and any new government headed by Barletta. Esquivel met with Noriega, Díaz Herrera and Barletta and reached agreement on a four-point but never written pact. Only the first point was a concession by the military, that the PDF would withdraw to the barracks and stay out of government entirely.

The other terms described the gradual weaning of the officer corps from the corruption that had become so integral to their way of life. Point two, as Esquivel tells it, provided for a transition period for officers "to rededicate themselves to real military duties." Point three provided "some plums" for the PDF to hand out. Noriega had pointed out that the people looked on the PDF as a Santa Claus expected to dispense favors and that it would hurt their prestige to stop abruptly.

Finally, point four called for a clean slate for the PDF: immunity from prosecution for past corruption and abuses of human rights. Panama had never had the egregious crimes of such countries as El Salvador, Chile and Argentina, and it seemed reasonable to phase out the traditional corrupt practices.

A fourth party, the rightist Labor party, led by Noriega's brother-in-law, Ramón Sieiro, became an enthusiastic partner in the new coalition, UNADE (National Democratic Union).

Barletta exchanged his banker's pinstripes for straw hat and *guayabera*—the loose tropical shirt—and ran an energetic, come-from-behind campaign. He projected a modern technocratic image and promised to use his expertise and connections to rejuvenate Panama as a booming service and export center like Singapore and Taiwan in the Far East.

His campaign was slick and well financed. Businessman Gabriel Lewis, the former ambassador, brought together a team of former Carter administration campaign experts to package Barletta. "We are using the most sophisticated and modern techniques. We have a good product in Nicky, and he [is being] sold professionally," Lewis told a reporter at the time. One of Barletta's most attractive features was that he brought his own war chest. He raised almost $5 million from donors, many of them representing corporations in Panama, the United States, Europe and Japan. That was only part of the funds available to government candidates. Millions more came out of Noriega's personal $25-million slush fund in the International Bank of Credit and Commerce (BCCI). The government electric company, IHRE, allowed its enormous cash flow to be skimmed to channel money to PRD candidates.

There was little penury in the Arnulfo Arias campaign either, which had the generous support of Panama's wealthiest citizens. Still, Arnulfo did not attempt to emulate the sumptuous style of the official candidate. He based his campaign on sixty years of political connections. He traveled from town to town in a decorated bus called the "Fufomobile," after his nickname. Appearing in his trademark dark glasses and bulky white, double-breasted suit, he did not so much ask for votes as hold audiences to receive the adulation of the people. His younger vice presidential candidates stayed in the background and were amazed at his uncanny memory as he greeted by name the minor local politicos in remote villages whose allegiance he had won in the campaigns in the 1940s, 1950s and 1960s. The frenetic Ricardo Arias Calderón, whose adult life had been dedicated to his own determination to become president, took notes as he watched the master politician at work. It was the campaign of the last of the Latin American caudillos, the vanished breed of civilian semidictators such as Perón of Argentina, Cárdenas of Mexico, Arosemena of Ecuador, whose message was secondary to their inexorable magnetism, the immediacy of their contact with the masses.

Arias did not offer a concrete program to counter the technocratic promises of Barletta. His message was a powerful indictment of the government's decades of corruption and a promise that his régime would sweep aside the evildoers. He reminded the crowds of his past battles with the military, of the five wounds he had received in coups and in assassination attempts. He promised there would be no more beggars and no more drugs in Panama. "Gentlemen, we will finish with the drugs that are sold on every corner of this city and the other cities of the republic, because this is the fault of the Guard, which brings them in to degenerate us completely," he said in Colón.

The excitement of the presidential campaign permeated as well the new life Steven Kalish was creating for himself in Panama. He was caught up in Noriega's enthusiasm for Barletta as a vehicle to prevent the unpredictable opposition from coming to power. Noriega, in Kalish's view, was an authentic nationalist maneuvering carefully to keep his country from again falling under U.S. domination, while keeping communist forces at bay. The Barletta strategy would guarantee security for Kalish's increasing investments in Panama, and Kalish was anxious to support it.

Kiki Pretelt arranged for Kalish to be invited to a small fundraising breakfast shortly after Barletta's arrival. Kalish sent a contribution of $75,000 in cash, but didn't show up. He thought it was inappropriate for a convicted drug smuggler and fugitive to meet personally with the candidate. "See, I believed in Nicolás Barletta," Kalish said. "He was Noriega's candidate, and he seemed very qualified to run Panama. You've got to understand, I've always been an idealist. I'm aware of the fact that Noriega would still run the military, and for my needs and my purposes, it's fine. But even though I'm a drug trafficker, I still didn't want to subvert the rights of the people of Panama. I wanted to believe, I'd like to believe that I'm supporting a democratic country."

Since arriving the previous September, Kalish had found a paradise in Panama. Kalish liked the Panamanian women. They were pretty, full of fun and sexually liberated—he and César Rodríguez shared a taste for partying hard and working hard. None of the Panamanians he knew questioned the source of his wealth.

César had arranged for Kalish to obtain three Panamanian passports, one of them diplomatic, in the name of Frank Brown. The price was $25,000 to $60,000 apiece. Kalish immediately began to ship cash from his Tampa home to Panama, $2 or $3 million at a time. The money was deposited in BCCI, the bank that handled both César Rodríguez's and Noriega's accounts.

Kalish took advantage of Panama's no-questions-asked laws to set up a front corporation he called Exclusive Services of Panama. He paid $400,000 for a 25 percent interest in Servicios Turísticos, S.A., a front company owned jointly by Pretelt, Rodríguez and Noriega. The company had no assets—so Kalish understood that his payment was a direct payoff to his three partners. But the arrangement also allowed him to use his money for lucrative "investments" to generate what amounted to kickbacks on purchases of equipment for the PDF.

The system was complex and depended on their connection to Noriega. Kalish would use one of his companies to buy aircraft parts, putting up the cash for the purchase. He would sell the items to Servicios Turísticos with a large markup. Servicios Turísticos would sell the parts to the Panamanian Air Force for a still higher price and be paid by the National Bank of Panama, which handled the government treasury accounts. The profits on the transactions, which only took a few days to complete, usually amounted to about 30 percent. The profits to Servicios Turísticos were divided equally among the four partners, including Noriega.

One of the largest deals involved the purchase of a Boeing 727–100 for $2.2 million—the plane Noriega outfitted for official trips as the government's equivalent to U.S. Air Force One. Kalish made the $500,000 down payment and arranged the financing. In a second large deal, he paid $1,650,000 for a Bell executive helicopter for Noriega's use. He billed the PDF $1,950,000 and received an irrevocable letter of credit for that amount as guarantee of monthly payments with interest. Four years later, in jail, Kalish was still receiving checks of $36,000 from the PDF.

By Christmas time, Kalish had bought a $500,000 house two blocks from Noriega's in the Altos del Golf/San Francisco neighborhood and was throwing lavish parties for his new friends. At one, Noriega and César Rodríguez drove up together in César's BMW. César was dressed in an outlandish green outfit from shirt to shoes. Noriega drank champagne from the bottle. Kalish had hired a band from the Dominican Republic.

Kalish had a girlfriend in the United States, whom he would later marry, but he was also surrounded by girls in Panama. Not only did he throw his money around, but he was young, tall and good-looking. Noriega, who was none of those things except rich, delighted in joking with Kalish and César about their women. He wanted every detail. Everyone agreed that César took the prize for the most beautiful girl. Terre Lind* had just dropped out of the University of Indiana, where she majored in public relations. She had long blond hair, a perfect body and an unaffected smile that was as friendly as it was sensual. César was so smitten with her that he was flying her back and forth to Indiana every other weekend.

César also knew who was boss. And when Noriega went beyond lascivious jokes and said he wanted César to fix him up with Terre, César grumbled but complied. He flew her down and got her a suite at the Caesar Park Marriott Hotel on the bay. Noriega spent the weekend with her. At the end, he left her a gift—$10,000 in cash.

Kalish also had his dues to pay with Noriega. Just before Christmas, he went to Pretelt's jewelry store and spent $20,000 on gifts for Noriega's wife. For Noriega, he bought a gold-plated 30-30 rifle on one of his trips to the United States. On December 23, he went to a Christmas party at PDF headquarters and presented the jewelry and gun, together with a gift of $100,000 in cash.

Floyd Carlton was seldom at the parties thrown by César and César's new friends. Carlton was a brooder, a worrier. He was self-conscious about his lack of education and country-boy ways, and he never felt comfortable in César's nouveau riche circles in Panama City. The complex business deals that so engaged César were a mystery to Carlton. When things were simpler, when they were

*Not her real name.

flying charters and shipping weapons, he had done his share of partying and womanizing with Noriega and his friends. But now he had a family—a wife he was close to and three small children to dote on. At thirty-five, he didn't think of himself as a criminal, as a drug trafficker. He was a pilot, providing a good living for his family.

But Carlton's simplicity was also his curse. Unlike César, whose eyes gleamed with avarice, Floyd projected honesty and reliability, traits that earned him the affection of both his bosses, Noriega and Escobar. Years later, as a prisoner, he would often talk of his attempts to separate himself from Noriega and the drug business, of his presentiments of tragedy. But as deals were offered, he always got back in.

By January 1984, Carlton had carried out three cocaine flights for cartel chief Pablo Escobar and was making plans for the fourth. But when he met with Noriega for approval he was told that things were changing. Noriega had returned from his tour of the upper echelons of power in Washington and had had a meeting with the American vice president. There had been public complaints about trafficking through Panama, and Noriega told Carlton that he had to be "more careful about his person." He was a general now and talked grandly of his role as mediator in the Central American conflicts.

This was going to be Carlton's last cocaine flight, Noriega said, but that didn't mean he shouldn't take full advantage of this final opportunity. In the past Noriega had lectured him about the economics of the cocaine trade. A kilo of cocaine sold for $65,000 in the United States, he said, and Carlton was only getting $400 a kilo. Noriega was raising his price for this last load to $200,000; he urged Carlton to do the same.

"Don't be dumb. Make some money. But don't tell them this is going to be your last trip," Noriega said.

Carlton didn't ask for more money, but he worried what Noriega's new attitude would mean for him. When Noriega's $200,000 was delivered, Carlton packed it in a cardboard box and drove to meet Captain Luis del Cid at the rear entrance to command headquarters. Del Cid, giddy at handling so much money, tried to make a joke: "I hope this isn't a bomb."

"Pray God it doesn't turn into a bomb," Carlton replied glumly.

A few days later, Carlton flew 400 kilos of cocaine from Hacienda Napoles to the Coronado beach airfield south of Panama City. Carlton was secretly relieved that Noriega had ordered him to stop trafficking through Panama. In his conversations with Pablo Escobar he realized that the Colombian traffickers were increasingly irritated at Noriega's arrogance. Escobar had cursed when he recounted how Noriega had allowed the cartel to pay for the Learjet, then had invented a pretext to confiscate it, daring the Colombians to do something about it. Carlton had also picked up a number of indications that he wasn't the only one the Colombians were dealing with in Panama. César was involved, he knew. And once, in Escobar's well-fortified offices in Medellín, Carlton had run into another Noriega intimate, Ricardo Bilonick. They had run guns together a few years back, and Bilonick had since bought his own air cargo company, INAIR. If Bilonick was involved, Noriega had to have a piece as well, for, as Carlton was fond of repeating, "Nothing goes on in Panama that this señor doesn't know about."

Noriega, despite his admonition to Carlton, was becoming immersed in even larger drug operations than those with Carlton. Shortly after the presidential campaign went into full swing in mid February, Noriega invited Steven Kalish to spend some time at one of his country homes, in Chiriquí. They were there to talk business, but also to have a good time. Noriega brought his mistress, a tall, strawberry blond named Marcella. Kalish had flown his girlfriend, Denise, in from Los Angeles. When she arrived at her guest room, she found a large bouquet of flowers and a handwritten note: "Miss Denis [sic], Welcome to Panama, Your Friend, General Noriega, 18 Feb. 1984, Panama."

Kalish was preparing to ship two gigantic loads of marijuana totaling 1.4 million pounds from Colombia to the United States. One of the loads was to originate in Medellín and be transported on a container ship via the Panama Canal to New York City. Noriega had agreed that his Customs officials would provide phony seals on the containers to mask their Colombian embarkation, which was sure to invite scrutiny on arrival in the United States. Noriega's fee for these services was to be $1 million, toward which Kalish had advanced $500,000.

Kalish also sensed that things were changing in his relationship with Noriega. While at the beach house, Noriega pressed Kalish to be extremely cautious and to shield him from any link to his operations—and he warned Kalish about getting too close to Kiki Pretelt and César Rodríguez. It was one of the rare occasions when Noriega spoke English.

"Deal directly with me on this," Noriega said, referring to the planned marijuana shipment. "Leave Kiki and César completely out of it. Call me directly. When two people have a secret, there's nothing to worry about. When someone else knows, the whole world knows."

At about the time that Kalish and Noriega were talking, Hugo Spadafora was making it his business to find out some of Noriega's secrets and was writing them down in a thick notebook he always carried.

Since making his first public attack on Noriega in early 1982, Spadafora had spent most of his time outside the country. He was now a Contra, a veteran of many months as a guerrilla inside Nicaragua. He was a man whose interests and energies were continually diverted from one project to another. Medicine, a family, politics had not been challenge enough to hold him for long. War alone, it seemed, enveloped and fixed his ego for long periods of concentrated effort, war and the burning certainty of righteous anger.

He had stood at Edén Pastora's side in April 1982 when Comandante Zero finally denounced what he began to call the "nine pseudo comandantes" ruling Nicaragua. Spadafora, in a mainly symbolic gesture, convoked the Victoriano Lorenzo Brigade to muster an international force to fight with Edén against the Sandinistas. By early 1983, Spadafora was in northern Costa Rica again, this time with a bare handful of followers—among them his bodyguard cum protégé Victoriano Morales, who used the nom de guerre "Risa." But they were ready and experienced fighters who were welcomed by Pastora, as he awaited the mass defections he expected his denunciations to provoke from the Sandinista army. Few defectors, but many other volunteers had responded to his promise to create an independent, democratic and authentically Sandinista movement that would soon march on Managua and reclaim the revolution.

Spadafora's first assignment under Pastora was to cross over into the vast but sparsely populated Zalaya Province, which makes up almost the entire Caribbean coast of Nicaragua. With a unit of twenty men, he penetrated more than fifty miles north of the border, to the confluence of two small rivers, the Punta Gorda and the Pijibaya. On Pastora's orders, the guerrillas worked the farms and small villages to build up a network of support for the rebellion. Although they carried rifles, they were under strict orders to avoid any intentional contact with the Sandinista army. The orders grated on Spadafora's action-oriented nature. In his daily radio calls to the base camp inside Costa Rica, Spadafora began a running dispute with Pastora over the no-combat restriction. Finally, Pastora told him that orders were orders and the debate was ended. He shouted over the scratchy connection that Spadafora's protests were bordering on insubordination and that he wouldn't listen to them anymore. Spadafora abruptly cut off the radio contact.

The next day he opened fire on a Sandinista patrol. The attack revealed his position and drew a full-scale counterinsurgency operation to the region. Spadafora had to flee, making the long journey by foot and evacuating more than one hundred peasant supporters who feared that they had been discovered as well.

Pastora respected Spadafora's courage but began to doubt his friend's perseverance in a war Pastora thought might last ten years. Spadafora came out anxious to go back inside, and more convinced than ever that Pastora's strategy of a safe border haven as a launching pad for attacks into Nicaragua was overly cautious.

By May 1983, Pastora had sent Spadafora even deeper into Zalaya Province, to an area inland from the town of Bluefields along the Escondito and Rama rivers. This time there were no restrictions on combat. Spadafora's fighters found themselves in a nearly ideal environment to carry out guerrilla warfare. The area was inhabited by Indians along the river and English-speaking blacks in the town of Bluefields and along the coast. Neither of the groups had ever identified strongly with the Spanish-speakers of the western half of Nicaragua. The Miskito Indians, at first supportive of the Sandinista revolution, had launched a fierce armed rebellion in early 1982 that was virtually independent of the emerging Contra movement.

Spadafora's unit soon joined with a group of Miskito guerrillas in operations to attack Nicaraguan ferries and barges carrying freight on the Escondito River, one of the few transportation links to the more populous western Nicaragua.

Spadafora developed great affection for his Miskito comrades, and his experiences with them deepened his quarrel with Pastora over the war's strategy. He became convinced that Zalaya Province and its Miskito population were the key to defeating the Sandinistas. And his conviction soon was formulated into military dogma. "The best, and until now the only, terrain on which to militarily defeat a communist régime is peasant war in rural areas," he wrote. "[In Nicaragua] the principal force in this struggle is the indigenous population of the . . . Atlantic Zone [Caribbean Coast]. The characteristics of this part of Nicaraguan territory and of its native inhabitants are almost all to the advantage of the antitotalitarian combatants and to the disadvantage of the neosomocista dictatorship."

The most important advantage for Spadafora, sensitive as he was to his and Pastora's de facto alliance with the United States in its fight to destroy the Sandinistas, was the Miskitos' relative immunity to the charge that their war was a "foreign invasion" of Nicaragua. He mentioned the protection of the jungle, the abundance of food and water and the ease of resupply via the long coastline. "In the five months that I was there in zone with military responsibility, I could observe how, almost spontaneously, the peasant population has adopted the guerrilla tactics of Augusto César Sandino. All that many of them want is a rifle with enough bullets, and they continue to live in their houses in their habitual work. They carry out various actions: they defend the zone, inform on enemy movements, act as couriers, transport military supplies, give food and teach the full-time *guerrilleros* the roads, short cuts, ravines, etc., that can be used for mounting ambushes or as attack and escape routes."

It was not that Pastora did not agree that the Miskito struggle was important. But Pastora controlled the supplies, and Spadafora could not accept Pastora's allocating an abundance of supplies to his border-based army, which rarely met the enemy, while the Miskitos, who were fighting almost daily, had almost nothing. Spadafora pleaded by radio for Pastora to send supplies not only to his unit but to the Miskito fighters as well. The arguments by radio began again. Spadafora wanted to move more quickly against the Sandinistas, but he saw Pastora hoarding the supplies to protect his border position. Spadafora became furious when one load of supplies consisted almost entirely of toilet paper.

He was also communicating by radio with the Miskito leader, Brooklyn Rivera, who led a faction of the Miskitos allied with Pastora and was based in Costa Rica. In Spadafora, Rivera found a rare "Ladino"—as the Indians called the Spanish-speakers—who understood their cause and did not see the Indians as simple adjuncts of the larger Contra cause. In September 1983, after almost five months fighting inside Nicaragua, Spadafora and some of Rivera's men made a dramatic gesture to bring the issue to a head inside ARDE, the umbrella alliance of several Contra groups including Rivera's Miskitos and Pastora's Revolutionary Sandinista Front. They announced by radio that they would make the long march south from the Escondito River to Pastora's base camp on the San Juan River, just inside Nicaragua from Costa Rica. He also radioed ahead his resignation from ARDE "because of disagreement with [Pastora's] conduct of the war." On September 30, Spadafora arrived at the river and was picked up in a motorboat by Pastora's aide, Carol Prado, who pleaded with Spadafora not to break publicly with Pastora. Spadafora agreed to keep his dissent out of the press.

Brooklyn Rivera arranged for the entire ARDE directorate to meet to hear Spadafora's arguments for a new strategy based on all-out support for the Miskito uprising in Zalaya. Going beyond strategy, however, Spadafora assailed Pastora as an "insecure, unstable" and divisive leader who was holding ARDE back from seizing the initiative inside Nicaragua. Pastora was furious that he was forced to submit to Spadafora's criticism of his leadership, but the other members of the directorate, Rivera, Alfonso Robelo, the anti-Somoza business leader recently turned Contra, and Fernando "El Negro" Chamorro, another former Sandinista, were receptive. Pastora defended his cautious approach to the war as part of a prolonged political as well as military strategy and also as the consequence of the undependable supply pipeline from the gringos who were supporting ARDE.

The dispute was for the moment successfully papered over. Spadafora agreed to continue fighting under the command of Brooklyn Rivera and did not make public his break with Pastora. But Spadafora's dissent was the beginning of a flood of disillusionment with Pastora among his allies. In the first year of his military opposition to the Sandinistas he had accomplished virtually nothing except the twenty-four-hour occupation of a small town a few miles from the border. He became erratic and autocratic, insisting on controlling all aspects of military strategy—insisting that his force of left-of-center social democrats were the inheritors of the true Sandinista revolution and would win the war independent of the other major Contra force, the CIA-directed FDN in Honduras, which he considered irretrievably tainted by its leaders' former ties to the Somoza National Guard.

Manuel Noriega was a factor in the dispute, at least as far as Spadafora and Pastora were concerned. Pastora traveled regularly to Panama and was cultivating his relationship with Noriega. He envisioned Noriega in a role similar to that played by Torrijos in the struggle against Somoza. The Panamanian leader could provide a channel for supplies and money to support Pastora as a moderate alternative to the Sandinistas—essentially the idea behind Torrijos's actions a few years earlier. The problem was Spadafora. Pastora unsuccessfully tried to get him to keep his criticisms of Noriega private as long as Spadafora was so closely identified with Pastora. Pastora became convinced that Spadafora cared more about fighting Noriega than fighting the Sandinistas and that Spadafora's quarrel was costing Pastora an important ally. When the break with Spadafora came, Pastora had no regrets. Planeloads of weapons supplied by the United States began to arrive via Panama in the coming months, and in July 1984 Noriega made a direct contribution of $100,000 to Pastora's forces.

Spadafora spent some time in Panama in October 1983. He took his new wife with him. Ari Bejarano was a twenty-year-old Costa Rican who was studying international politics at the University of Costa Rica. She was dark-eyed and intelligent, with an intense appetite for all-night discussions on politics and social change that matched Spadafora's. The trip to Panama revived Spadafora's interest in the upcoming elections—and his outrage that Manuel Noriega had promoted himself to general and was in command of the Defense Forces. Spadafora wanted to be a participant in his country's passage through the elections, but he was deeply skeptical that any transition presided over by Noriega would result in real democracy.

He returned to Costa Rica to begin his work with Brooklyn Rivera and the Miskitos, but in the coming months he shuttled back and forth to Panama. He was developing a new strategy to fight Noriega from afar, while continuing the war against the Sandinistas. He would fight Noriega with facts, the damning facts of corruption he had always known about from the Torrijos period and the sketchy reports of drug trafficking he had picked up two years before. Unlike the opposition activists, who were shut off from the military and most of the government, Spadafora was an insider, a famous and respected Torrijista with almost unlimited access. He also had the kind of pleasant personality that inclined people to trust and confide in him.

In the first months of 1984, as the country debated the choice of opposition and progovernment presidential candidates, Spadafora made the rounds of the veterans of the old Victoriano Lorenzo Brigade. They had been put on the government payroll as a reward for their participation in the fight against Somoza in 1979, and many had been hired by Noriega to work in G2. He talked to old friends, like leftist journalist Miguel Antonio Bernal, who filled Spadafora in on the grapevine and on what had appeared in the press. He recorded every fact, every lead in his loose-leaf datebook. Taking notes during private conversations was almost unheard of in Panama, especially when discussing such sensitive matters. The gesture was provocative and signaled the seriousness and potential threat of what Spadafora was doing.

Spadafora renewed his friendship with Floyd Carlton, César Rodríguez and Kiki Pretelt. Once, when they were all in Chitré, Spadafora's hometown, for a Mardi Gras celebration attended by Noriega, he invited the three men and several women to his house to continue the party. He brought out the notebook, as if to inform them rather than to interrogate. He ticked off examples of corruption

General Manuel Antonio Noriega Moreno, chief of intelligence 1970–1983, commander of the Panama Defense Forces 1983–1989, chief of state December 15–December 20, 1989.

General Omar Torrijos ruled Panama for thirteen years with a mixture of charisma, cronyism and moderate social reforms. He signed new treaties with the United States to return control of the Panama Canal to Panama.

General Rubén Darío Paredes, a politically inept but highly professional soldier, succeeded Torrijos, then resigned to run unsuccessfully for president.

Paredes's departure left a fierce rivalry between Noriega and Colonel Roberto Díaz Herrera, Torrijos's cousin and the sharpest political mind in the Panama Defense Forces.

Hugo Spadafora, romantic revolutionary, follower of Omar Torrijos and Noriega's most uncompromising adversary, was assassinated in 1985 after uncovering details about Noriega's drug trafficking.

Arnulfo Arias, an uncorruptible autocrat, was elected president and deposed by the military three times. In 1984 elections, Noriega's forces resorted to fraud to deny Arias his fourth presidency.

Despite its own studies establishing fraud, the United States recognized Nicolás Ardito Barletta as Panama's new president. He was overthrown in 1985.

Businessman Eric Arturo Delvalle, who was installed as president by Noriega in 1985 and then removed by Noriega in 1988, was recognized by the United States as the sole legitimate government March 1988–September 1989.

Banker and journalist Roberto Eisenmann founded the newspaper *La Prensa* as a crusade against the corruption of the military regime. The PDF ransacked the *La Prensa* plant shortly after it began publishing in 1980 and forced it to close several times.

Noriega's main value to the United States was his support for U.S. Central America operations run from U.S. bases in Panama. National Security Council aide Lieutenant Colonel Oliver North (second from left) was a frequent visitor to Panama. He accompanied U.S. ambassador Everett Briggs and Defense Secretary Caspar Weinberger on an inspection of U.S. Jungle Operations Center in Panama in September 1983.

Fidel Castro met secretly with a Panamanian delegation July 4–6, 1984, including (from left) Major Lorenzo Purcell, José Blandón, Captain Felipe Camargo, Enrique "Kiki" Pretelt (who was later indicted with Noriega on drug charges) and Lieutenant Colonel Elias Castillo. Blandón's charge that Fidel was a party to Noriega's dealings with the Colombian cocaine cartel, hurriedly incorporated in the Miami indictment, is uncorroborated and highly questionable.

Steven Michael Kalish, a convicted marijuana smuggler, testified before the Senate Permanent Subcommittee on Investigations that he gave Noriega $300,000 in cash before he began to run his drug-trafficking and money-laundering operations out of Panama.

Mass protests broke out in Panama City in June 1987 after Colonel Díaz Herrera denounced Noriega for corruption and murder. Noriega's riot-control troops used tear gas and clubs to break up protests whenever they were attempted.

Noriega struck a boxer's victory pose after defying the various U.S. attempts to force him to step down after he was indicted by Miami and Tampa grand juries in February 1988.

Noriega handed out weapons to civilians loosely organized in "Dignity Battalions" intended to defend against U.S. military action. Some of the battalions were composed of young boys, who marched through Panama City in a show of defiance.

The Noriega issue dogged Vice President George Bush during the 1988 campaign and resurfaced in late 1989 as Noriega's continuation in power became a source of embarrassment to the Bush presidency.

The December 20, 1989, invasion of Panama resulted in the installation of Guillermo Endara, a follower of the late Arnulfo Arias, as Panama's new president.

in the official party, the PRD—saying this person stole this, that person stole something else. He had the details of the arms transactions. He talked about the shady businesses that former General Paredes's two sons had gotten into—and about a payoff to Paredes involving a thoroughbred horse. It was all done in good humor as part of the drinking and camaraderie of old friends.

On another trip, Carlton went to Spadafora's apartment in Panama City. They began to talk about César Rodríguez, how he and Carlton had grown apart over the past year. They had been adventurers together, then partners. Now, it seemed, all César cared about was money. Carlton recalled that once after the victory against Somoza, César had talked unflinchingly about an offer to participate in a plot to assassinate Somoza in his sanctuary in Paraguay. César had wanted to charge $5 million—and those trying to hire him ended up finding another team of killers to do the job much cheaper.

"That's why I wanted to talk to you," Spadafora said, paging through his notebook. "You have a beautiful family; you haven't lost all the ideals we had in the old days. But drugs is a criminal business. Whoever is involved in drugs ends up paying for it sooner or later.

"I know all about you and César, about your drug trafficking for Noriega. I can easily believe it as far as César is concerned, but I don't want to believe it about you," Spadafora said.

Carlton was stunned and ashamed. Spadafora was one of the few people whose respect he craved. He didn't challenge Spadafora's accusation and was too chagrined to ask him how he had obtained the information. It seemed irrefutable; it was all written down in Spadafora's book.

"It's not too late to get yourself off that road," Spadafora admonished him. "I promise I won't use any information I have against you because you are my friend. But stop before it is too late."

Spadafora continued to read from his book and to take more notes on his conversation with Carlton. Carlton asked him why he cared so much about things that were just going to cause him big problems. Spadafora picked up the notebook, and hefted it. "This little book is going to make a revolution in the world some day," he said.

"I hope it will be for the best," Carlton said.

· · ·

On March 15, as the electoral battle between Nicky Barletta and Arnulfo Arias gathered steam, Spadafora drove to *La Prensa*'s boxy office in northern Panama City and dictated a statement that filled almost a page. In the first paragraph he fused his hatred for Noriega with his contempt for the Sandinista régime:

> First, I want to say that honestly, just as I do not recognize the title of Comandante for the nine traitors that badly govern Nicaragua, I don't recognize the rank of general for Manuel Antonio Noriega. We, the authentic Sandinistas, consider the nine Nicaraguan tyrants pseudo comandantes; and by the same token I consider Noriega a pseudo comandante, who has reached his position and his rank on the basis of treason and opportunism, as is public knowledge.

Spadafora did what no opposition candidate, not even Arnulfo Arias, had dared to do: attack Noriega directly, without euphemisms, without innuendo. The statement was a rambling, egocentric cry of a Cassandra warning of a disaster that awaited the country. "Noriega and his accomplices are closing off the way for a peaceful solution, and if things continue in the direction they are going, there will be no solution left except violence."

He reminded his readers of his previous published statements, calling for national unity as an antidote to partisan battling between the Torrijistas and the opposition. The current elections, he said, should be called the elections of "national disunity" because of Noriega's greed for power and riches:

> In this regard, I, who has been identified for a long time as a friend of the Guard, believe it is time to point out that it is a shame . . . that Noriega's activities for years now are soiling the uniform of the members of the Defense Forces, activities involving drug trafficking, arms trafficking and political manipulation. . . .
>
> It is time we say openly that it is a national disgrace that an international trafficker travels around the world representing us, talking of democracy, of peace in Central America, about the Contadora group, etc., when he is precisely the principal obstacle to democracy in Panama. It is a disgrace that has to be unmasked. *There are people in this country that know a lot about this, but they don't dare speak out*

publicly. But I will say it clearly: Noriega is the principal person responsible for the intrigues, deals and plots—in the end of all the corruption—against democracy.

It was as if Spadafora had reduced all of Panama's conflicts to a jousting match between the White Knight and the Black Prince. Almost half of the statement was devoted to recounting his personal disputes with Noriega—how Spadafora had denounced Noriega's plotting to Torrijos; how Torrijos, on Spadafora's advice, excluded Noriega from dealings with Edén Pastora in 1981; how Noriega took revenge against Spadafora after Torrijos's death by keeping him in a "virtual prison" at Torrijos's Farrallón beach compound. He claimed that Noriega had twice tried to buy him off with bribes.

The statement was strengthened by Spadafora's revolutionary and Torrijista credentials, but tarnished by personal invective and lack of concrete evidence. He made no reference to the information about drug trafficking he had discussed with Carlton. Then, once again, having broken his lance against Noriega's armor, Spadafora headed back to Costa Rica, to fight his other war.

On the emotional level, Floyd Carlton may have wanted to heed Spadafora's advice to get out of the drug business. He was a man who had always been moved around by his friends. But Carlton had other friends to whom it was difficult to say no, friends like Pablo Escobar.

In the first days of May, just before the country was to go to the polls, Carlton received a call at his Chiriquí ranch from Ricardo Bilonick—the INAIR owner whom Carlton had seen in Escobar's office in Medellín the previous year. He gave Carlton a telephone number and said "your father wants to see you urgently." "Your father" was a reference to Escobar.

"What are you doing here? You know how the situation is here," Carlton said when he reached Escobar.

"Just get here as soon as you can," Escobar said. He gave him an address in Panama City.

Carlton was troubled by Escobar's presence in Panama. Noriega had said that the time to make drug deals was over. He had made it clear that Carlton's January cocaine flight was to be his last—at

least the last for which he could count on Noriega's direct involvement and protection. Noriega was involved in bigger game, gaining
control of all of Panama by getting his candidate into office, and he
had had to put up with some savage charges of corruption and drug
dealing.

Not only was Noriega in the spotlight because of the election in
a few days, but the Colombian cocaine organization—Escobar and
Ochoa in particular—were white hot because of events in Colombia.
In early March, just before Spadafora's outburst in *La Prensa,*
Colombian police raided Tranquilandia, the largest cocaine laboratory in the world, and confiscated 14 tons of cocaine. In retaliation,
the traffickers gunned down the man who ordered the raid, Colombian Justice Minister Rodrigo Lara Bonilla. That crime, which was
apparently ordered by cartel security chief Escobar, had triggered a
mammoth dragnet in Colombia for the leaders of the traffickers, who
until that time had been allowed to operate almost untouched inside
Colombia. The assassination occurred on April 30. The press was full
of speculation about where the drug bosses had fled. Now, a few days
later, Escobar was in Panama in the middle of the country's most
important and sensitive political event in two decades.

"Don't worry about anything. We've paid for protection, $5 mil-
lion," Escobar said when Carlton arrived. The address Escobar had
given him was an office building on 50 Street in the middle of the city.
Carlton was awestruck by the scene. Besides Escobar, Carlton saw
Jorge Ochoa, his brother Fabio, Gustavo Gaviria, Carlos Lehder,
Gilberto Rodríguez Orejuela, José Gonzalo Rodríguez Gacha and
dozens of second-level Colombians. "The cream of the cream of the
drug world was there," Carlton would say later. They had set themselves up in a suite of offices that already had the bustling feel of a
large corporation. The cartel support staff consisted of dozens of
secretaries and aides and a contingent of bodyguards—at least one
hundred people by Carlton's estimate.

Carlton was not one to ask a lot of questions, but from conversations with Escobar and Gaviria, he gathered that the cartel was
moving its operations into Panama and Nicaragua. Carlton's assignment was to fly a suitcase of money to make a payoff in Nicaragua,
where the cartel was building a cocaine laboratory to replace its

operations at Tranquilandia. Later, he was asked to go to the United States to buy a C130 transport plane to carry cocaine base from plantations in South America. One of Escobar's pilots told him that another laboratory was being constructed in Panama, in Darién Province.

The raid on the Darién factory, approved by Noriega and claimed by him as his proudest trophy in the war against drugs, was only one incident in an array of bewildering events before and after May 1984.* The events were pivotal in Noriega's evolving relationships with the Colombian cartel, on the one hand, and the U.S. Drug Enforcement Administration, on the other: the $5 million bribe given to Lieutenant Colonel Melo to allow the Darién facility to be constructed and the precursor chemicals to be transshipped through Panama to the cartel's new factories; the alleged assassination plot by Melo against Noriega after the lab was seized and the efforts by cartel representatives, with marijuana smuggler Steven Kalish's assistance, to recover their money; the "trial" of Melo, his dismissal from the PDF and the return of at least $2 million of the bribe money to the cartel.

Steven Kalish flew his Learjet to the United States for the last time on July 23. Three days later he was arrested at Tampa airport as he was about to board the jet for a return flight to Panama. Also in July, Panama hosted the U.S. government's regional Interagency Conference on Narcotics—a meeting of all DEA and U.S. embassy personnel with drug enforcement responsibilities in Latin America. Noriega made a good impression. One official commented later: "I'm not sure, but I think Noriega's cooperation with the DEA in certain matters dated from conversations with American officials at that conference. From his perspective [it was] a way to keep us off his back while he dealt with the cartel."

Prior to May 1984, if the most reliable accounts can be believed, Noriega seemed intent on collecting as much money as possible from the various drug traffickers he was dealing with. After the Darién raid Noriega seemed to be closing up shop, paying off outstanding

*The events of May 1984 are described in Chapter One.

obligations and creating a new image for himself—that of the states-
man-soldier standing behind a democratically elected president.

Nicky Barletta and Arnulfo Arias wound up their campaigns with
back-to-back mass rallies, both filling the Vía España with tens of
thousands of supporters. Barletta had started out stiff and pedantic
but by the end had warmed to campaigning. He played with effect
to the contrast between his youth, energy and expertise and Arias's
negative, backward-looking denunciations of the Torrijos era.

"In my government, there might be mistakes but nobody will be
able to steal with impunity," Barletta thundered in his final speech.
"To this end I dedicate my honor and my life. . . . Vote for me and
you will know the most untiring worker in our history. Thank you,
friends. This has been the greatest and most emotional experience of
my life."

The final opinion poll showed a neck-and-neck race, with Barletta
enjoying a 46 to 38 percent edge. The ADO opposition alliance
claimed loudly that Arias would win by a landslide and that any
other result would be fraud. Sunday, May 6, election day, was un-
eventful. Two teams of U.S. observers roamed freely around the
polling places and noted only occasional, inconsequential irregula-
rites—nothing of a magnitude capable of changing the outcome.

The slow process of hand counting the ballots at the 3,902 polling
places began in early evening, in many places under the watchful eye
of opposition poll watchers. Again, there were few complaints. When
the counting was complete, all the ballots were burned in the presence of witnesses—a practice introduced to prevent the stuffing of
fraudulent ballots in stored boxes, which would then be included in
a recount. The next step was for the official documents of each voting
table to be certified with the signatures and fingerprints of each vote
counter, then forwarded to a regional vote-counting board, which
would compile totals for the region and transmit them to the National Vote Counting Board.

As the night progressed, however, the process ground to a virtual
halt. Almost no results had reached the National Board. By four
A.M., Monday, *La Prensa* had gathered figures from voting places it
said represented about 20 percent of the total, showing Arias with

a hefty lead of 10,266 votes. But *La Prensa*'s count was haphazard. The opposition had no systematic method to deliver the counts from the thousands of voting places in order to conduct its own parallel count. Between the polling place and the final national count, the opposition had to depend on the government's system.

Noriega, however, did not leave the results to chance. He assigned Major Alberto Purcell to set up a nationwide vote-monitoring system, using the PDF lieutenants stationed in every locality and an efficient military communications network. The system allowed Noriega to bypass the complicated regional and national vote-reporting procedures and have comprehensive and accurate results from most of the country within hours.

Colonel Roberto Díaz Herrera, analyzing the results as they came in, went from optimism to panic as the night wore on. He had hoped to win fairly. Failing that, his instructions were to arrange a win by whatever means. "I believed those polls carried out by those fancy American political consultants, and they showed us winning by six or seven points. So we were tranquil, confident that we would win without fraud. But when the results started coming in—we were losing in Chiriquí; we were losing in Colón. Sure, we had to do something, and I was pushing to do it," Díaz Herrera said. At midnight, the government suspended the count.

The next morning, the Arnulfo supporters were convinced that their worst fears were being realized. By late afternoon, hundreds of ADO partisans gathered in a shouting mob outside the Legislative Palace, where the National Vote Counting Board was convened. Suddenly, just after dark, automatic weapons were fired, and the crowd scattered in panic. When it was over, two ADO supporters were dead and forty were wounded. The gunmen wore PRD campaign hats and T-shirts, and some had "F7" written on their shirts. A television crew taped most of the violence, and stills from the tape were later used to identify the men as thugs employed by Noriega.

While the opposition shouted foul, Díaz Herrera calmly proceeded to organize the rigging of the vote count. Some of the tactics were crude: a PDF soldier broke into the circuit counting locale in a remote area of Chiriquí at five A.M. and simply stole the official tally. When it showed up in Panama City the tally sheet had 3,500 more votes for Barletta than it had when the counters last saw it in Chiriquí.

Other tactics were more sophisticated and took advantage of the complexities of the electoral law, which allowed any party to challenge the count of any voting table by alleging that fraud had occurred. Díaz Herrera convened an extraofficial meeting of the two electoral judges willing to participate in the fraud. They met in secret each evening at Díaz Herrera's house in Altos del Golf. There, they combed the vote count reports to choose which tables to nullify to shift just enough votes for Barletta to win. It was tedious work that lasted for almost a week, while the country waited in increasing frustration for official results.

Several evenings, Barletta himself came to the house to find out how the count was going. Díaz Herrera, who had no great affection for Barletta, pulled a practical joke on the nervous candidate. One night as they walked to Barletta's car, parked inside the walled courtyard, Díaz Herrera suddenly said, "How did those *La Prensa* reporters get in here?" Barletta was terrified until he realized it was a joke.

The count was finally announced ten days after the election by the judges who had met at Díaz Herrera's house. They declared Barletta the winner by the razor-thin margin of 1,713 votes out of a total of more than 600,000 cast. Barletta hailed the result as the "will of the people" and said he would lead a government of national reconciliation. A short time later he announced he had an invitation to travel to Washington to meet President Reagan.

The opposition attempted to mount mass demonstrations to protest what they were convinced was a fraud, but enthusiasm waned after a few weeks as public outrage gave way to the more traditional Panamanian spirit of accommodation. Whatever the actual count, it was agreed that the presidential election had been close. As vice presidential candidate Carlos Rodríguez commented wryly to an embassy political officer, Arnulfo had won the election, but not by a margin big enough for a "Panamanian victory"—one that the government couldn't steal.

To mollify the opposition, Barletta's forces conceded that there had been irregularities in the races for the National Assembly. A period of horse-trading ensued that amounted to Barletta insisting that politicians in his own coalition give up some of their seats in favor of opposition candidates. Six seats that had originally been in the government column were "reconsidered" and granted to the opposition parties, which nevertheless ended up with only sixteen of sixty-seven seats in the new one-house legislature.

The PDF also dealt with the matter of Silverio Brown—television stills had identified him as the leader of the gang who the day after the election had attacked the opposition demonstration and killed two people. Noriega had a personal relationship with Brown. For a year prior to the attack, he had been paid by Noriega to act as a bodyguard and gofer for one of his mistresses, Magdalena Kusmisik, who had borne him his only son. In late August, Brown called Kusmisik to plead for his life. He asked her to "tell the general he was not involved in the things that the general thought he was and there was no need to have him killed." A week later, DENI, Noriega's political and criminal investigative police, announced that Brown was dead. He had been arrested and shot in the act of "grabbing a gun from one of the officers" who had him in custody. An autopsy showed he had been shot three times in the back.

According to the police, Brown was one of a gang of fifteen men arrested for a series of robberies. Another member of the gang showed up seeking asylum in the Venezuelan embassy and told a far different story. Angelo Wassel Rock said that he had been hired by G2 as part of a paramilitary group under Brown's leadership that called itself "Seventh Force." Wassel said that the group's "special tasks" included the shootings at the National Assembly and the theft of ballot boxes. He said that after Brown's death he feared for his life because there was "an order to eliminate everyone from the Seventh Force."

A few days before the elections in Panama Hugo Spadafora had gone back into the jungle with the Miskito Indian fighters. He saw combat in the Pearl Lagoon area in the heart of Zalaya Province. Unlike any other part of the sputtering Contra war against the Sandinistas, the Miskitos' uprising was having steady success. There was none of the factional fighting that plagued the Contra forces

outside Nicaragua—even the distinctions between Contra units identified with Brooklyn Rivera and his rival Steadman Fagoth seemed
to disappear inside Nicaragua. There, unlike anywhere else the Contras were fighting, the Sandinistas were on the defensive, forced to
stay close to the protection of their garrisons.

Spadafora came out of the combat zone after three months more
convinced than ever that the main Contra bodies—ARDE and Pastora in the south and the U.S.-controlled FDN in the north—should
provide active support for the Miskito struggle that was the Nicaraguan régime's Achilles' heel. But during his stay inside Nicaragua,
Contra infighting had become more pronounced. Edén Pastora had
narrowly escaped an assassin's bomb during a press conference on
May 30. So bitter had been his disputes with his American sponsors
and the other Contra factions that he suspected his allies no less than
the Sandinista government of committing the crime. Spadafora made
public his criticisms of Pastora and the general Contra strategy in a
series of articles and interviews. He argued that the only thing standing between the Miskitos and victory was the lack of weapons and
supplies, which the "border war" strategists in the FDN and ARDE
refused to supply. He held the Reagan administration responsible for
what he called an "absurd" policy of supplying the border armies
while ignoring the Miskitos.

Having developed the strategic thesis that the war could only be
won by adopting the Indian cause, Spadafora conceived the corro-
lary that the "internationalist" role he played should no longer be
as fighter but as facilitator. "What we need to do is to get what aid
we can and offer it to whoever needs it inside Nicaragua. We'll get
it there, forget about the politics," he told Guy Gugliotta, a reporter
for *The Miami Herald.*

But the "we" Spadafora could count on was an ever-diminishing
group. With Brooklyn Rivera, as with Pastora before him, Spadafora
had bitter disputes over the leader's failure to provide supplies. When
he left the war zone, Spadafora and Rivera severed their relationship—amicably according to Rivera. On his return to Costa Rica,
Spadafora found an increasingly hostile environment. He was
greeted by a story in *La Nación* of San José, in which one of the

ARDE lieutenants, Comandante Colmillo, accused Spadafora of losing weapons and supplies entrusted to his units. Colmillo, echoing Pastora's old complaint that Spadafora cared more about fighting Noriega than the Sandinistas, said Spadafora waylaid the weapons "apparently [because] he is preparing for a personal war, but who knows why or against whom."

Another ARDE leader, Orion Pastora, called Spadafora an "opportunist" who was politically immature, mishandled funds and had "confused the militants" with his questioning of ARDE strategy. "We simply don't trust him anymore," Orion Pastora concluded.

Spadafora and his wife, Ari, would have brushed off the attacks as more of Pastora's recriminations. But a visit from a Nicaraguan friend convinced them to take the attacks more seriously. The Nicaraguan, a Contra activist, said that their house was under surveillance by a group of Nicaraguans who had been contracted by Noriega to assassinate him. According to the Nicaraguan, the man in charge of the plot was Sebastián González, a Contra *comandante* known as "Wachan," who had been in charge of logistics for ARDE until he too had split from Pastora earlier in the year.

The alleged plot made sense to Spadafora. Wachan was one of his most bitter rivals in ARDE, and, as logistics chief, Wachan had been the target of many of Spadafora's criticisms about the failure of ARDE to supply adequately the guerrillas fighting inside Nicaragua. In addition, Spadafora told Ari, he had recently received information that Wachan was involved in drug trafficking—carrying drugs to the United States on the same planes and from the same Costa Rican airstrips used to land supplies for ARDE. Most importantly, Spadafora knew that Wachan had been Pastora's go-between in his relations with Panama and Noriega. Wachan, a Nicaraguan national, had spent long periods of his life in Panama and was a good friend of Noriega's. A pilot, he was part of the flyboy crowd in Chiriquí in the 1960s, along with César Rodríguez, Enrique Pretelt and Floyd Carlton. He was rumored to have introduced Noriega to his wife, Felicidad.

Spadafora sought protection from his friends at the Costa Rican intelligence agency, DIS. They offered protection and recommended that he go into hiding. Spadafora spent a few days at the home of one of the agents, then decided he would confront the threat directly—in Panama.

In the first days of September 1984, Spadafora and Ari traveled to Panama using their customary semiclandestine route to stay out of unnecessary trouble with Costa Rican authorities. Although it was well known that Spadafora lived in Costa Rica and he had many friends in the government of President Luis Alberto Monge, Spadafora was officially an illegal alien, officially banned from living in Costa Rica as a known Contra fighter violating Costa Rica's neutrality statutes. The ban was honored in the breach. In his frequent trips to Panama, Spadafora used a simple subterfuge to avoid passing through Costa Rican border checkpoints. He and Ari traveled by bus to Paso Canoas, the village straddling the border. Ari would continue across the border in the bus, while Spadafora would disembark and cross over on foot. He would then get back on the bus after it had passed through Costa Rican authorities. There were several Panamanian checkpoints on the highway. Spadafora didn't anticipate trouble. Some of the Panamanian guards knew Spadafora and greeted him by name.

They arrived in Panama City without difficulty, but it was the first time the trip over the border had made him nervous. Spadafora took the alleged threat from Noriega seriously, but as an attempt at intimidation, not as an actual intent to kill him. Not that Noriega wasn't capable of murder, but his victims had always been petty criminals, never a public figure, much less a war hero and Torrijista like Spadafora. And Spadafora felt the aura of invincibility of a soldier who had survived three wars. His reaction to Noriega's threat was to strike back in kind.

He called his friend Alvin Weeden, a lawyer and opposition activist whose hatred of the military had begun with the 1968 coup and had grown only deeper. Spadafora told Weeden about his investigation of Noriega's crimes and said that he wanted Weeden to use the information to bring suit against Noriega in Panamanian court. Weeden laughed at the idea that any Panamanian court would take action against the dictatorship, but he was intrigued. He saw the potential of the suit as a propaganda weapon not only to expose Noriega but to destroy the illusion of an independent judiciary under Panama's new "democracy."

The idea was great, Weeden said, but Spadafora's notebook contained too few specifics to make a strong case. He needed more names, places and dates. Rather than filing the suit now, he recommended that Spadafora make the effort public and gather more damaging information.

A few days later, *La Prensa* gave Spadafora his forum. "Because of the political situation in Panama, which presages a grave crisis in the near future, I have decided to devote more time to political action in Panama," the interview began. Then he announced his new initiative:

> I am a member of a group of citizens who are studying the possibility of bringing formal charges against Manuel Antonio Noriega for abuse of power and full complicity in drug trafficking. We are aware that . . . it is illusory to expect a conviction of a dictator in power for his participation in such traffic. . . . Therefore, our objective is to collect all possible evidence and proof—to which anyone can contribute by contacting my lawyer, Alvin Weeden—and to present it not only to the courts of justice but to the supreme judge of our country, the people.

Then Spadafora responded to the threat he had received with a threat of his own, one that went far beyond the rhetorical brickbats of his past denunciations:

> If Noriega and his gang achieve their criminal attempt to install a full-fledged military dictatorship, mocking the popular aspirations for democracy, the people will have no other recourse but war. In that event, we will do our duty: participate actively on the ground in the organization and leadership of an armed movement.

Some of his friends had expressed surprise, he said, that he was still able to come and go in Panama because of his public denunciations of Noriega. "I want to end by saying publicly what Noriega already knows: the day that they don't allow me to enter and circulate freely in my country, that will be the day I enter at the head of a guerrilla force."

In a radio interview three weeks later, Spadafora commented on the upcoming inauguration of Nicolás Barletta as president. The new president had to choose, he said, between the "road of dignity and the road of shame." He could stand up to Noriega, end the military domination of the country and find in that endeavor the overwhelming support of the Panamanian people, including those who voted for Arnulfo Arias. "If, on the contrary, President Barletta follows the road of shame, subordinating himself and accepting Noriega's and his gang's domination . . . ," Spadafora said, "he will lead the country to disaster . . . and will make it inevitable that our people will respond with violence to such abuses, to such repression."

The hypothetical choice Spadafora presented to Barletta was not unlike the moral dilemma facing the U.S. government following the controversial elections. Should the United States recognize Barletta as the legitimate president or should it back opposition cries for a recount? President Reagan appeared to have resolved the question in favor of unquestioning recognition of Barletta's victory when he received "president-elect" Barletta in the Oval Office on July 26.

Even as Barletta's courtesy visit was taking place, however, a young U.S. embassy officer in Panama was methodically undermining the factual basis for U.S. recognition of the election's fairness. James Cason was the second ranked political officer; chief political officer Ashley Hewitt had assigned him the task of compiling a routine report on the fraud charges and an assessment of their veracity.

Cason buried himself in the task as if he were Woodward and Bernstein investigating the Watergate scandal. His small office on the top floor, with its single window on the bay, became a maze of paper. Election actas from most of the 3,902 voting tables were stacked on every horizontal surface. He obtained two nearly complete sets of the results, one from the opposition ADO and a second from UNADE, the Barletta coalition, and all available reports from the circuit and national counting boards. For two months, Cason had time for little else. He counted and compared the actas, checked voter registration lists against actual tallies, rearranged the data to test his own hypothesis and scrutinized each of the opposition charges of fraud against the actual results.

When he turned in his report to Hewitt in late July, it was half an inch thick. The conclusion was inescapable: Arnulfo Arias had been elected president by at least four thousand votes, perhaps by more than eight thousand. There had been ballot stuffing, falsification of documents, systematic rigging of the vote count and a pattern of rulings by the electoral tribunal that ensured a Barletta victory.

Cason's major finding was that 62,564 votes—about 9 percent of the total—were never counted in the final tally. That was the total of votes that were the target of "challenges" by either the opposition or the government. The electoral tribunal refused to rule on whether any fraud had occurred in any of the challenged tables—and decreed that none of the challenged votes would be counted. Cason, by analyzing each of the 372 challenged tables, reached "the inescapable conclusion . . . that almost all of the challenges were frivolous and designed to reduce the Arias vote totals, which in fact they did." Cason also found that, ironically, the opposition had "shot itself in the foot" by the actions of its own poorly trained poll watchers, whose indiscriminate challenges to voting results in some districts had facilitated the government's manipulation of the vote count. The ADO poll watchers in many cases challenged the results of tables showing a victory by Arias, alleging that Arias's vote total was less than it should have been. Through such "clumsiness," the opposition lost "enough [votes] in Chiriquí Province alone to have beaten [Barletta] for the presidency."

Cason's report was a devastating indictment of the official position that demonstrable irregularities had not been substantive enough to have altered the outcome of the election. The report was also potentially embarrassing to Ambassador Briggs, whose preelection cables to Washington stressed that tampering was unlikely. "Our conclusion is that the electoral system is a good one, with the chances for widespread fraud slim. That fraud which may occur should be isolated and should not statistically affect the outcome," Briggs said in an April 18 cable detailing the voting procedures. "This election appears to be shaping up to be one of the cleanest ever."

Among Briggs's main concerns about the "question of fraud" was its prominence in opposition rhetoric:

> The possibility of fraud continues to preoccupy many, and has become a virtual obsession with the opposition, which appears to believe so firmly in their candidate's preordained victory that any shortfall will, by definition, be due to hanky-panky on the part of the government. . . . There is also a disturbing tendency on the part of some opposition leaders to point the finger at us, asserting that we "promised them" a clean election and if it fails to occur (i.e., if Arias is not elected), the U.S. is somehow responsible either through sheer stupidity or actually being in league with the devil. While obviously fraud cannot be ruled out, it continues to be our judgment that fraud at a level likely significantly to affect the outcome would be extremely difficult to carry out. Fraud at a level necessary to assure a Barletta victory would be obvious to the world at large and would undo most of the positive effects of having an election to begin with.

Cason's investigation made that position untenable. The Barletta election was tainted, and in September 1984, with Barletta's inauguration fast approaching, the question of what to do was unavoidable. The options were clear cut: the United States could make its findings public and in effect divest the incoming Barletta government of legitimacy; it could keep its findings in the realm of silent diplomacy and signal its displeasure at the corruption of the democratic process by keeping a low profile at Barletta's inauguration ceremonies; or it could stay the course already begun and support Barletta on pragmatic geopolitical grounds.

In any event, the debate in the embassy over the illegitimacy of Barletta's election was barely a tempest in a teapot. There was never serious consideration given to anything other than full support of Barletta, even after Cason's report. To the extent there was any real soul searching, it took place in private conversations between political chief Ashley Hewitt and the ambassador. The matter was seldom mentioned at embassy staff meetings. Briggs's main concern again was perception: he admonished Hewitt to keep the more idealistic staffers—Cason and junior political officer Mark Wong, who helped Cason research and draft the report—from leaking their conclusions to the press.

Almost two months passed between the drafting of the report and its dispatch to Washington. When Briggs finally signed off on the report, he ordered it sent to the State Department via pouch, a so-called airgram. That method virtually guaranteed that it would go unnoticed in Washington. The pouch, in the age of instant telex, computer and telephone communications, had become the method for transmitting the least urgent documents, mainly on administrative and personnel matters. By not sending a cable on the report, at least summarizing its findings, its conclusions were not distributed to the White House and other agencies. Sending the report by airgram was the kiss-off of indifference.

Briggs's decision to minimize the impact of his political section's investigation was the result of a conscious pragmatic policy that met with no known dissent in the State Department, not even by Hewitt. As one officer described it, "We decided to cooperate with the inevitable, so that the next time around Panama would have a real election." Another officer involved said it was "not that agonizing a decision. . . . Given evidence available to us, any action other than willingness to work with the declared winner would put us in the position of court of last resort. We had been in that position too many times before."

The State Department officers insisted that the decision to accept Barletta's election was not based on any U.S. favoritism toward his candidacy. The embassy had bent over backward to project scrupulous neutrality during the campaign, to counteract the general perception that Barletta, because of his close ties to Washington and to Secretary of State Shultz, had the Reagan administration's blessing. All disclaimers aside, however, Briggs and his analysts clearly saw Barletta's victory as being in the best interests of stability in Panama as well as in the best interests of the United States. An Arias presidency, by contrast, had few if any defenders in the U.S. bureaucracy, and would have been seen as a virtual guarantee of instability that invited another military overthrow. No one in the U.S. decision-making loop argued to pressure Panama for a recount.

Far from signaling any displeasure, the State Department planned an all-out show of warm support for Barletta during his October 11 inauguration. Secretary of State Shultz was to lead the U.S. delegation. Briefing papers prepared for Shultz reflected high U.S. hopes that the new Panamanian president would be an important ally in the Reagan administration's Central America policy vis-à-vis Nicaragua. Barletta is "eager to cooperate," Assistant Secretary of State Tony Motley wrote. "We look to Barletta to perceive [deletion] the essential parallelism of Panama's national security interests with those of the U.S. in the region." In another memo to Shultz, Motley added: "When Barletta visited Washington in July, you agreed that we should jointly develop an action agenda of U.S.-Panama issues. His ability to start his term 'doing favors' for the U.S. is constrained by his fragile political situation, but there are clearly areas of coincident interest where early further movement is desirable and attainable. One such area involves regional security and Contadora. . . ." Motley was referring to the Central American peace negotiations, whose meetings were held on Panama's idyllic tropical island of Contadora.

When Shultz arrived in Panama the evening of October 10, his motorcade went directly from the airport to Barletta's home for a first, informal meeting. Barletta greeted Shultz as an old friend, but also with the deference of a student for his teacher. As a special show of respect, Barletta had ordered that Shultz would receive all of the perquisites of a visiting head of state—ranking him with the three Latin American presidents who were attending the ceremonies.

Shultz almost immediately turned the conversation to Contadora. For more than a year, Panama, Colombia, Mexico and Venezuela had been sponsoring talks intended to resolve the conflicts in El Salvador and Nicaragua. Panama had been a major force in initiating the negotiations, which explicitly excluded the United States. The diplomatic effort had reached a climax in the weeks preceding Barletta's inauguration. A draft treaty, known as the "Acta," had been drawn up, and on September 21, Nicaragua had suddenly announced it would sign the treaty without further changes. The abrupt action had put the United States in a bind since the draft treaty called not only for the end of foreign support of the various Contra forces but for a ban on foreign military maneuvers in the area—in effect, a ban on the rapidly expanding U.S. military "exercises" in Honduras.

Shultz laid out to Barletta the U.S. view that the Acta should not be signed without further concessions from Nicaragua. Barletta, according to the U.S. report on the meeting, "asked what the next moves regarding the Acta should be." Shultz replied that Panama and the other Contadora nations "should keep up friendly pressure on the Central American five [to continue negotiating] but not try to force the issue or risk aborting the chance of a settlement."

Shultz was asking for a small favor: for Panama to get on board with the other U.S. allies in the region in isolating Nicaragua in the Contadora negotiations. Within a month after Barletta's inauguration, the United States had gotten its way. With Panama's help, the Contadora treaty was pulled back from the brink of being signed. By the end of the year, the once-promising Contadora process had ground to a virtual halt.

The small quid pro quo of Shultz's visit and Barletta's favor was a seemingly insignificant example of the diplomatic transactions the United States needed to keep its Central American policy—and the Contras—afloat. It demonstrated, however, how completely U.S. goals in the rest of the region determined not only U.S. actions but U.S. perceptions of Panama. Already, a veneer of unreality had come to characterize the official U.S. image of Panama. It had taken some intellectual sleight of hand to recast Noriega from suspected thug who played both sides of the fence to friendly general presiding over the kind of transition to democracy the United States was prescribing for the rest of Central America. An even grander effort was required to give a benign interpretation to the mounting circumstantial evidence during 1984 of high-level complicity in cocaine trafficking— most of it public after the Darién raid, the Melo firing and the presence of the cartel leaders in Panama. With regard to Barletta, election fraud did not fit in the U.S. picture of the vigorous, forward-thinking, American-educated president, so it was air-brushed out.

After all, as U.S. officials would say many times looking back later, Panama seemed to be doing fine; it was the one country in Central America where the United States did not have a problem.

CHAPTER 9

REMEMBER ME WHEN
THE BOMB EXPLODES . . .

Two events captured the image of the "new Noriega" in 1985. In February Noriega appeared as invited speaker at the John F. Kennedy School of Government at Harvard University. The occasion was a conference on the role of the military in the crisis in Central America. He proudly contrasted the peaceful atmosphere and new democracy of Panama to the violence in the rest of the region, casting Panama—and, by association, himself—in the role of peacemaker. He insisted that the Contadora peace process continued to advance—"despite the fact that the egos of some politicians are more important to them than are the suffering of the people."

The speech was lavishly covered in the progovernment press. In case anyone missed the point, *El Matutino* noted the "honor" of Noriega's invitation to address "one of the highest democratic forums in North America, whose platform is reserved only for those world personalities whose participation in the lives of the modern public has been positive."

The U.S. press ignored Noriega's speech, but a Southcom "Weekly Intelligence Summary" described it in detail as "motivated by his desire to offset his and the PDF's dismal reputations and to create a personal image as: a peacemaker . . . a defender of democracy . . . and opponent of communism."

In Panama, Noriega unabashedly imitated the peripatetic, populist style of Omar Torrijos, visiting the most remote and disadvantaged villages of the country. In a visit to the town of San Antonio, on the Costa Rican border, he flew in with his helicopters to land on a baseball field in the middle of a game. The villagers and farmers from the surrounding hills had been waiting for hours for his arrival and had created a carnival atmosphere, with a country lunch and music on loudspeakers. When Noriega got out of the helicopter, the people lined up to shake his hand. They all assembled in the village's rundown school. A young boy recited a poem; another welcomed Noriega in the name of the school and said how wonderful it was that he had come. Then a village leader solemnly rose to say that their school was falling apart and that they would appreciate any help the PDF could give them, according to the list of needs he had drawn up for the *comandante*'s convenience. Afterward, Noriega installed himself in a private room at the back and received those who wanted to see him one by one. Each had a favor to ask, and all went away with something, if only the satisfaction that Noriega, in their presence, had turned to an aide and told him to take care of the matter. There were scholarships for worthy sons and nephews, grandmothers with letters spelling out their problems with Social Security payments.

The trip to San Antonio was only one of dozens of such excursions to bring the PDF to the people, just as the Harvard appearance was part of weeks of travel abroad. Noriega was constantly upstaging the new civilian government, keeping the initiative, projecting himself as the real center of power and perquisites in Panama.

He also took pains to cultivate the approval of the United States, especially to neutralize the opposition's barrage of allegations about PDF corruption and drug trafficking. The new Noriega was no longer seen with suspicious characters like César Rodríguez. Noriega had even forced Rodríguez to sell his $900,000 house, a block from Noriega's, and move away. Rumors flew that there was serious bad blood between Noriega and his old friend.

Noriega also made sure that the DEA got whatever cooperation it asked for to cement the impression that Panama was a leader in the war against cocaine. He allowed U.S. agents to install surveillance equipment at Omar Torrijos International Airport to monitor the coming and going of suspected traffickers. The agents also picked up ample evidence of the large money-laundering traffic into Panama. They watched as boxes and crates of money from private planes were unloaded into Brinks armored cars, which transported the money to Panamanian banks. Since there was nothing illegal about importing cash into Panama, the agents could do little except record the tail numbers of the airplanes and find out the identities of the suspects.

But Noriega worked the issue of money laundering masterfully. He had opened negotiations with the United States on a Mutual Legal Assistance Treaty, which would limit Panama's bank secrecy in criminal cases. The negotiations, and the publication of the draft treaty in early 1985, caused squeals of indignant protest from the opposition, many of whose most prominent members were bankers. *La Prensa,* in banner headlines, said that the proposed law put "at grave risk" the secrecy "that is considered the pillar on which the International Financial Center of Panama rests."

Having put the opposition on the defensive in an area of its special interest, Noriega then ordered his Special Narcotics Unit, under Inspector Luis Quiel, to move against one of the most notorious money launderers, the First Inter-Americas Bank, which was owned by cartel figures Gilberto Rodríguez Orejuela and Jorge Ochoa. Noriega's men claimed that in pursuing the case against the bank they turned over information to the DEA that led to the capture of Ochoa in Madrid in November 1984. Ochoa avoided extradition to the United States and was turned over to Colombia to face the farcical charge of falsifying a document in order to illegally import fighting bulls. But in Panama, the Inter-Americas Bank and all its assets were confiscated—a major blow to the cartel and a public relations coup for Noriega.

Noriega's actions in effect diverted suspicion from him as Panama came more into focus as a narcotics trouble spot. *La Prensa* reprinted a *Time* article recycling the Melo and INAIR cases and published long excerpts from U.S. congressional documents describing drug trafficking and money laundering in Panama. But to Noriega's main clientele, the U.S. officials, the charges didn't stick.

DEA officer Thomas Telles, who had arrived in mid 1984 in the midst of the Melo scandal, had been impressed by Melo's arrest and by a year of cooperation: "I felt pleased. Here were officers who were willing to do their own people. It gave me a feeling of relief—I had just transferred in from Mexico. It was nice to see I was dealing with people I could be comfortable with."

The State Department, having put to rest its prior skepticism that Noriega was a potential Darth Vader, was promoting good relations with Panama as a way to bolster the democratic transition represented by the Barletta presidency. When asked, embassy officials were most likely to call relations "excellent" and to praise Barletta's attempts to reform Panama's economy. U.S. economic assistance poured in, shooting to $75 million from $12 million in 1984. Barletta lived up to his promise to deliver new loans from the World Bank and other multinational lending institutions. With the firm vote of the United States in those quarters, Panama received $137 million in new loans, up from $83 million the year before.

Noriega's success was the cause of deep disillusionment for Hugo Spadafora. He saw Noriega, following the election of Barletta, in a de facto alliance with the United States. Worse, Spadafora learned that Noriega had become an important secret backer of the Contra cause, a man whose friendship was cultivated not only by Pastora but by other Contra leaders. Worse still, Spadafora began to realize that the drug trafficking he accused Noriega of was also rife among his Costa Rican–based Contra associates. Spadafora's two great causes—the struggles against the Sandinistas and against Noriega— had collided and then interpenetrated, blurring the clean lines of good and evil along which he had oriented his life.

In 1985, nothing seemed simple or clean. The Contra struggle was dragging on into its third year with little show of progress. Spadafora found himself making common cause and common activity with the U.S. agents whose government's support of Noriega he despised but whose covert supply and financial operations he promoted as essential to the anti-Sandinista war.

Back in San José, surrounded by intrigue, Spadafora became one of the intriguers. At odds with the Nicaraguans he most admired, Pastora and Brooklyn Rivera, he moved increasingly in the crowd of foreigners who had attached themselves to the Contra cause. One was John Hull, an Indiana farmer who owned a large ranch in northern Costa Rica and helped when he could to eliminate what he saw as the communist menace across the nearby border. A group of Miami Cubans had established themselves in San José, bringing money and supplies and offering to fight. Felipe Vidal, alias "Morgan," shared Spadafora's contempt for the do-nothing "border war" strategy of Pastora and the fixed-army strategy of the Honduras-based FDN. Spadafora and his young bride, Ari, were taken with Vidal's intellect and evident courage. Vidal had a record in Miami for marijuana dealing and a reputation among ARDE leaders as being a possible provocateur because of his penchant for suggesting bombings and other terrorist tactics. There was also an American who went by the phony name of John Cattle, whose main interest seemed to be the money he could make by helping the Contras.

Spadafora and his friends spent long hours at Ari's house discussing strategy, but Ari lost interest and no longer participated, preferring to immerse herself in her university studies. The group included Spadafora's faithful Panamanian sidekicks, Risa and Johnny, who had spent long months fighting inside Nicaragua the previous year but also had broken with Pastora. They were idle and restless. Disconnected, as was Spadafora, from any official Contra organization, they had lost the monthly stipends they had been receiving from ARDE. They talked of ways to "go back inside," of strategies to get the war moving again and of putting themselves back in the thick of it. Spadafora revived his international brigade, this time called the Brigada Bolivariana after Latin America's hero, Simón Bolívar. Their objective was to solve the hitherto intractable problem of getting supplies to the Miskitos and to other fighting units inside Nicaragua.

Resupply was the preoccupation of the various U.S. government operatives working with the Contras. The Boland amendment, passed the previous October, had put the CIA arms pipeline out of business. The Reagan administration's man in charge of circumventing the congressional restrictions was Lieutenant Colonel Oliver North, and his man in Costa Rica was tall, smooth-cheeked Rob Owen, whose zeal, earnest manner and well-starched clothes gave him the appearance more of a Mormon missionary than a covert arms broker. Owen worked with the CIA's well-known station chief, Joe Fernandez, who affected the alias Tomás Castillo but couldn't get anyone outside of Washington to use it. They had two problems: keeping supplies coming from the United States without Congress finding out about North's role and neutralizing Edén Pastora's leadership so that his several thousand fighters would join the unified (and CIA-dominated) Contra command under FDN chief Adolfo Calero.

Spadafora met Owen through rancher John Hull and quickly won Owen's admiration as a true believer and honest broker. Owen saw Spadafora and his small brigade as having an important role and began to promote them in memos to Oliver North:

> As for getting some military operations started, my recommendation is you supply enough arms and ammunition to equip 50 men to go inside and make contact with the fighters, Pastora's and the Indians'. They will come out with the necessary contacts and coordinates to start resupplying directly inside either by air or boat. Also good intelligence. The people are there as are the leaders. The three leaders would be Hugo Spatafora [sic], Felipe Vidal and Risa, who [referring only to Risa] came out about 3 months ago and had 680 men under him. Granted, none of the 3 are Nicaraguan, but they are respected by the people inside and have been in before for extended periods of time. They don't want to see a border war fought as they know it will accomplish nothing.

Owen listed the weapons and other supplies needed for Spadafora's mission. The planning continued through the summer— Owen and North supplying money and hardware from the "private aid network" organized by North, Spadafora providing men and contacts among the units fighting in Nicaragua. Spadafora was reluctant to admit to his wife the ultimate goal of the mission: to cut Pastora off from his troop commanders by removing their dependency on him for the supply lifeline. Spadafora and his new American sponsor were plotting to deliver the coup de grace to the struggling Pastora.

. . .

North's Contra support operations aroused no such reservations of conscience from Noriega. As a Southcom intelligence analyst put it in one report, Noriega knew "which side his bread was buttered on." Leaving relations with the U.S. embassy and the international money men to President Barletta, Noriega solidified his relationship with the CIA, which had always been his main line of access to the U.S. government. By early 1985, Noriega also had developed a working relationship with NSC's Oliver North. He let it be known that the U.S. agenda was his agenda: the U.S. game in Central America was the Nicaraguan war, not Panama, and Noriega recognized a real priority when he saw it.

North was a regular visitor to Panama in 1985. On January 17 he accompanied NSC chief Robert McFarlane to discuss "options for support to the armed/unarmed opposition" to the Nicaraguan government. The idea was to push Central Americans toward providing "lethal assistance" to the Contras—which the United States was forbidden to do under the Boland amendment. What agreements were reached in Panama are still secret. But in March, according to another North memo, Noriega provided a Panamanian explosives expert for a bold act of sabotage inside Nicaragua. A commando raid organized by North and led by a British soldier of fortune bombed a military complex, ammunition dump and hospital in Managua. Miraculously, no one was killed, and the embarrassed Sandinista government covered up the incident as an accidental explosion of natural gas.

In June, Noriega allegedly met with North on a yacht in Balboa harbor and agreed to train Contra troops in Panama for an invasion of Nicaragua planned for early 1986, according to the unconfirmed testimony of former Panamanian official José Blandón. Apparently, no training took place, however.

Panama also began to play an ancillary but important role in the operation's dealing with both Iran and the Contras known as North's "enterprise." North's representatives, Albert Hakim and Richard Secord, set up several secret Panamanian corporations: among others, Lake Resources, Stanford Technology, Udall Research Co. and NRAF Inc. The first two companies were used as fronts to hide

North's funneling of money from Iranian arms sales to the Nicaraguan Contras; Udall and NRAF were fronts for the Contra arms supply operation. In addition, money to the FDN was transferred to Contra accounts in Panamanian banks.

Publicly, Noriega signaled that, despite Panama's officially neutral role in the Contadora peace process, his country was strongly tilting against Nicaragua. In August, Noriega proclaimed during a visit to Costa Rica that "the border between Panama and Costa Rica does not end at Paso Canoas [in the south with Panama] but at Peñas Blancas"—a reference to the northern Costa Rican crossing with Nicaragua, where a serious border clash between the two countries had occurred the month before. Noriega began shuttling to Honduras, Nicaragua, Costa Rica, Guatemala and El Salvador to float the idea of an international peacekeeping force, made up of Latin military units, to keep the fighting in Nicaragua from spreading throughout the region. In Nicaragua, he met with President Daniel Ortega and offered Panama as a go-between and center for peace "dialogue." Noriega's proposals seemed to be an attempt to get beyond the stalled Contadora formula. He justified Panama's special ability to achieve a breakthrough because "Panama is the only country that has maintained good relations with other countries by fostering dialogue, questioning when it has been necessary, and praising everything worth merit. . . . At present, Panama is the point through which all the region's conflicting positions can be reconciled."

Noriega's peace initiative was grandiose but lacked the grounding in careful diplomacy needed for its success. It was, as diplomats like to say, a dive into an empty pool. Nevertheless, Noriega seemed intent on making his debut on the world stage. His travels—now well orchestrated and amply covered at home—included trips to the United States, Japan, Taiwan, France, England and Peru, in addition to his peregrinations in Central America.

Noriega, the backstage operator, was finally a performer at the height of his power and wealth. His uniform had four stars and the insignia of a paratrooper. At PDF headquarters, he commissioned a mural for the conference room across from his office depicting the Battle of One Thousand Days, an epic moment in Panama's struggle for independence. The painting featured prominently a General

Noriega from the nineteenth century, a war hero who may or may not have been related by blood to Noriega. Whenever he was asked about it, Noriega just smiled.

Hugo Spadafora divided his time between his Contra support activities and travel to Panama to plan new attacks on Noriega. During his visits to Panama, he arranged for the first time to meet U.S. Commander Paul Mahlstedt, special assistant and sometime executive officer to Southcom Commander General Paul Gorman. The sessions were long, informal drink-and-dinner affairs at the house of a mutual friend. Spadafora attempted to enlist Southcom help in his supply network in Costa Rica and to warn against the U.S. military's cozy relationship with Noriega. He was told that supplying the Contras was not within Southcom's area of activity, but that he could be put in touch with "the people who do that." Spadafora said he didn't want anything to do with the CIA.

Mahlstedt reported his conversations to his Southcom chief, General Paul Gorman, and checked Spadafora out with the CIA station. Unreliable, station chief Jerry Svat said. "He's been with the left, he's been with the right, nobody knows where he really is." Svat, however, was one of Noriega's greatest backers in the U.S. mission in Panama, and his opinion may have been influenced by Spadafora's agenda against Noriega.

During some of the conversations with Mahlstedt, Spadafora discussed the feasibility of mounting a guerrilla war to challenge Noriega. He talked about basing a guerrilla force in Darién Province, which he knew well from his days in Torrijos's health service. He had also made contacts in Chiriquí Province, which lacked Darién's remoteness but whose population of prosperous farmers could be counted on to support any antimilitary movement. Spadafora stressed that at this stage it was all talk. Guerrilla war would be the last resort, he said.

Spadafora's investigation of Noriega's drug trafficking was still Spadafora's top priority, and in mid-1985 he thought he was making progress. Almost exactly one year after the scandal over Colonel Julián Melo had brought accusations of drug trafficking uncomfortably close to Noriega, another Noriega crony was in the news in a spectacular drug case. This time it was Floyd Carlton. Panamanian insiders knew Carlton as Noriega's pilot whose business at the Paitilla airport hangar had PDF protection. Spadafora knew more, and he decided the new scandal provided the ideal moment to pull together his evidence—and to act.*

Over the past year, Floyd Carlton's reservations about the cocaine business had dissipated under an explosion of profits from his deals with the Colombian cartel. Panama could no longer be used as a transshipment point—Noriega had made that clear—but Carlton had shifted to airstrips he was familiar with in Costa Rica. He knew some of the strips from his flights of guns during the Sandinista war against Somoza and some of the strips were still being used to channel weapons to the Contras.

Carlton no longer flew the shipments himself; he hired his own pilots. He had come a long way from the time when Noriega had lectured him about the price of cocaine. Now he was charging the cartel $3,000 a kilo to transport cocaine from Colombia all the way to southern Florida. In Florida, Carlton had his own distributors to market the cocaine wholesale and a money-laundering operation to deal with the profits.

Never ostentatious, Carlton was now extremely rich. Besides his Chiriquí ranch, La Ponderosa, he had a home in David, two in Panama City, a beachside villa and two condominiums in Miami. He had the usual boats and planes, but his real love was sports cars—which he cared for lovingly, hiring a full-time mechanic to keep them at top performance.

By mid-1985, Carlton's operation had carried out a half-dozen flights of 500 kilograms each. After paying his pilots and ground crews and bribes to Costa Rican officials, Carlton netted about $1 million per load. Then, in May, a routine cocaine flight went wrong.

Teófilo Watson was one of the Chiriquí pilots who had worked

---

*Melo was free and prospering, the charges against him having been quietly dropped in December 1984. He later opened Financiero Facilito, a money brokerage in Panama City.

with Noriega since they were teenagers in the 1960s. He, Carlton and César Rodríguez had been the mainstays of Noriega's arms pipeline to the Sandinistas in 1978. In 1985, Watson was Carlton's partner and main cocaine pilot. One day in May, Watson took off from Tamarindo airstrip in Costa Rica to fly to Colombia. He picked up a load of 538 kilos of cocaine at a strip south of Medellín and began the trip back to Tamarindo, where another Carlton pilot, Miguel Alemany Soto, was waiting to refuel and fly the plane the final leg to the United States.

Watson never arrived, the plane and drugs were never found and Carlton was left trying to explain to his Colombian suppliers how a $3 million cocaine shipment had vanished into thin air. Carlton and Alemany Soto investigated and concluded that the Costa Ricans they had hired to handle ground operations had lured Watson to land at another strip, then murdered him and stole the cocaine. They suspected that one of the murderers was a Contra activist named Carlos Eduardo Zapporoli, who had the drugs flown to a strip on the farm owned by John Hull, the American Contra supporter. The Costa Rican officer who was Carlton's source said Zapporoli used the money from the drugs to buy weapons for the Contras.

Carlton, Alemany Soto and several others—with an invitation they couldn't refuse—flew to Medellín to make things right with the owners of the cocaine, Luis José Ospina and Leopoldo Rodríguez, who operated out of the city of Pereira south of Medellín. The Colombians accused Carlton of stealing the drugs, and Carlton knew the penalty for theft. But the Pereira traffickers were lesser figures in the cartel, and Carlton was able to appeal to his old friend, Pablo Escobar, who intervened and allowed Carlton and his associates to leave Colombia safely.

The next day Carlton flew to Miami. The Pereira group, convinced of Carlton's guilt, hired a Panamanian named Alberto Audemar to shake down Carlton's people in Panama and to find the drugs. Audemar knew Carlton well—he also had flown guns to the Sandinistas and had briefly been Carlton's partner in 1984 in a drug-smuggling operation. Audemar's tactics included the kidnapping and torture of Carlton's cousin and Watson's wife. With a small gang, Audemar set an ambush for Carlton at his La Ponderosa ranch in Chiriquí, then, when Carlton didn't show, used power shovels to dig up the newly landscaped yard, where he thought the dope was buried. But Carlton called his friends in the PDF from Miami and Audemar's gang was arrested in late July; the case was turned over to the courts—and the whole sordid mess hit the Panamanian papers, with, as the Panamanians say, "a luxury of details," including the exact number of kilos of cocaine that Carlton and Watson were missing.

As soon as Hugo Spadafora learned of the trouble his old friend was in, he began an intense effort to contact him. Through one of Carlton's relatives, Spadafora located Carlton in Miami. Carlton's base of operations was an airplane sales agency known as DIACSA, just south of Miami International Airport on Northwest Twelfth Street. DIACSA's owner was a Cuban, Alfredo Caballero, well known in Costa Rican Contra circles. Caballero had flown one of the B26 bombers against Castro in the 1961 Bay of Pigs invasion, then lived many years in Nicaragua during Somoza. He was a friend of Mario Calero, the FDN's supply chief, and was an important supplier of airplanes and equipment to the Contras.

Many of Carlton's drug-smuggling flights had been planned at the Formica-topped conference table in Caballero's second-floor office at DIACSA. Later, after Caballero was indicted for his drug activities with Carlton, he would receive two Contra-assistance contracts totaling $41,130 from the State Department's Nicaraguan Humanitarian Assistance Office.

Spadafora reached Carlton at a vulnerable moment. His name was in the papers as a major trafficker. His operation was blown, and he was hiding out from what he feared might be a Colombian hit team, like the Audemar gang in Panama. At first he refused to talk to Spadafora, but Spadafora was friendly and consoling. He said he was very sorry for what had happened, especially the embarrassment it caused Carlton's family. He advised Carlton to consider carefully what to do next, "Never to take one step without seeing where I was going to give the other step," Carlton recounted later.

Spadafora was nudging Carlton gently toward cooperation—a possibility that had already occurred to Carlton as he saw his business crumble around him. Spadafora said that he was going to move against Noriega, that he had "something firsthand, [and] was going to take care of Noriega."

As Carlton recalled it, the conversation went along these lines:

> He only asked one favor of me, to please confirm for him the dates of the flights I had done.

> So I told him, "Are you crazy? Why are you asking me that crap on the phone," and then he told me, "No, no, we're not saying anything bad. . . ." He realized that I didn't want to talk about that. I didn't want to talk about things that would incriminate me on the phone.

> And then he told me, "No, don't worry. We're not saying that you have done any bad flights. We're just talking about the flights you did with your family."

> Then I told him, "Hugo, why me? If you have some affection for me why do you have to involve me in this thing?"

> So he tells me, "Because I know you're not in agreement with certain things that are going on, because what you did, I know that you're sorry for it, because César didn't want to help me."

> So I told him, "Well, okay." I spoke to him about some of the dates that I have already mentioned to the [DEA] agents, and he wrote them down.

> And he tells me, "I'm going to write down an A for you. I'm going to give you an A in your homework."

> That means in our language that he was very happy. And he just told me to remember and to think of him when the bomb exploded in Panama.

At the time of his conversation with Carlton, Hugo Spadafora was moving his narcotics investigation into high gear. His American friends, Rob Owen and John Cattle, had broken down his resistance to dealing with U.S. officials, and Cattle, especially, urged him to take his information about Noriega to the DEA. Cattle set up a meeting with Robert Nieves, the DEA's new resident agent in Costa Rica.

They met in a room in the Amstel Hotel in San José in late July

1985. Nieves, a Puerto Rican who spoke perfect Spanish, had never heard of Spadafora or his reputation. He listened to a ten-minute monologue by Spadafora: that General Manuel Noriega and Contra operative Sebastián "Wachan" González were major drug dealers in Central America, that others involved in the Contra movement were assisting in drug shipments, that Wachan and Noriega had schemed to kill Spadafora because of Spadafora's agitation against them.

Nieves, who had only been in Central America for a month, found the story a fascinating introduction to the intrigues of Central America, but too vague to make a case out of.

"I'm a cop," Nieves said. "You're not giving me any facts. I need a person who saw this stuff, documents, telephone receipts. Right now these are just vague representations. It's not helpful; we can't get anything moving on this."

Spadafora said that was no problem. He jotted down in his notebook the kinds of evidence Nieves requested. He took Nieves to meet a Nicaraguan, who Nieves presumed to be a Contra. The Nicaraguan didn't have much to say, but Spadafora promised that the man would get back in touch soon with Nieves with more information. The man never did, and Nieves didn't follow up. Spadafora also gave him Risa's name as a source on the drug running.

Nieves was impressed with Spadafora, especially after he reported on his meeting to the embassy's political officer, who filled him in on Spadafora's history. Nieves saw in Spadafora the charisma that was ascribed to him, but also discounted the importance of the meeting as the ego trip of an out-of-power agitator. The main thrust of Spadafora's denunciations was Noriega, but the sources he referred Nieves to were best equipped to report on drug involvement by the Contras. Digging up dirt on the Contras did not win many points in the U.S. embassy in Costa Rica, which in 1985 was one of the nerve centers of the U.S. war effort against Nicaragua. The ambassador, Lewis Tambs, was a political appointee and ideologue, a man with a fierce temper and little tolerance for those who picked nits with his anticommunist protégés. Nieves did not open an investigative file on the material provided by Spadafora; his sketchy notes of the meeting remained in his desk.

Weeks later, Spadafora called Nieves. It was now early September

1985. They met again, this time at Spadafora's house in San José. Spadafora asked, as if quizzing about how well Nieves had carried out his assignment, what had happened with the information. Nieves said it had gone nowhere.

They went over the same material. By this time, Spadafora had spoken to Carlton and had gotten the specific dates of the drug flights for which the cartel had paid protection money to Noriega. But Spadafora, perhaps in keeping with his promise not to involve Carlton personally, did not mention Carlton or the flight dates. He insisted that he "had sources" for his charges, but did not name them.

Nieves liked the tall Panamanian but was getting frustrated. He lectured Spadafora on the difference between political denunciation and police fact. Spadafora's sources weren't enough, unless one of them was willing to come forward and provide eyewitness, firsthand testimony.

"Don't worry, I know what you need," Spadafora said. "I'll get it for you." He said he'd be able to move on it right away. In a few days, he said, he would be traveling to Panama.

Back in Panama, the civilian government under President Barletta was lurching from crisis to crisis. Always opinionated, Barletta reacted to adversity with increasing arrogance and self-righteousness. Whatever his debts to Noriega for coming to power, he played the part of the independent civilian ruler. But his indifference to building a base in Panama's nascent civilian political culture deprived him of his only potential counterbalance to Noriega's domination. Never popular with the PRD establishment, Barletta alienated it almost completely with austerity measures attacking its sacred cows—attempting to dismantle the protective labor code and cut back government employment. Then, also in the name of reforms requested by the International Monetary Fund, he tried to raise taxes and drove a stake into the heart of whatever remained of his big business support. The opposition started the nickname "Fraudito"—playing on one of his last names, Ardito—and the name stuck.

August 1985 was a troubled month. There was hardly a day without a strike or a protest of some sort—labor unions, students, truck-ers, government employees, and a march by the opposition to protest the three-hour kidnapping and beating—presumably by Noriega's thugs—of a prominent opposition leader, Dr. Mauro Zuñiga.

Noriega, who usually met with Barletta for breakfast each Tuesday, had backed his man and the democratic symbols he represented for ten months, but now he seemed to lose patience. He chose the celebration of his second anniversary as chief of the PDF to deliver a scolding to the quarreling civilians both in and out of the government. Barletta looked on from the speaker's platform at Fort Cimarron, the base of the new elite Battalion 2000. "A simple look at the panorama of our country shows us that discontent, not satisfaction, is steadily growing," Noriega said. In an unmistakable reference to Barletta's controversial labor code reforms intended to make it easier to fire workers, he proclaimed, "The solid links prevailing between the workers and the Defense Forces of Panama since the years of our General Torrijos will gather more strength and importance during these periods of crisis, under the sacred principles of a right to a job, respect for people's achievement, and economic security for Panamanian families." He then bitterly denounced the "fanatics" who had fomented the recent opposition strikes and student riots. "They struggle to divide us, but they cannot achieve their goal. They raise the banner of an antimilitaristic ghost in order for their political career to be launched and to thrive under its shadow through the shedding of other people's blood."

During the first days of September, Noriega was hardly in Panama at all. Returning from another shuttle to Nicaragua and Costa Rica, he took off on a low-profile five-day trip to Peru for a reunion of his class at the military academy. He flew again to Costa Rica to discuss his peace initiative. Then, with no public notice, on September 11 or 12 he slipped away to France. It was a personal trip, with no political or military agenda. He was going to spend some time at his French villa—and check into a clinic for special allergy treatments.

On Saturday morning, September 14, a young Costa Rican peasant, Franklin Vargas, walked across a small wooden bridge near his home just a few hundred yards north of the Panamanian border. He was going after some chickens that had strayed. The locale was known as Laurel de Corredores—a few farmhouses along a dirt road that crossed unrestricted into Panama. Glancing over the side of the bridge, Vargas saw two legs sticking out of the shallow water. The rest of the body was submerged and hidden inside an olive green canvas bag.

The rural police arrived about an hour later and pulled out the body of a tall white man. The man's head had been hacked off. They slogged through the weeds and water and searched the road. Two freshly broken teeth were found, but no head. The bag tied around the body bore the legend "Domestic: U.S. Mail, J 460 1." In the middle of the victim's back, someone had scratched "F–8."

Hugo Spadafora should have arrived by bus in Panama City on Friday night, and when he didn't his father, Carmelo, began to look for him. Ari Spadafora arrived by plane from Costa Rica the next morning. She said that Hugo had left home at eight A.M. on Friday, on his normal route to Panama: commuter plane to a town near the border, taxi to the border, walk across the border to avoid Costa Rican authorities, catch a bus to David and then to Panama City. On Sunday, Ari got some chilling news. Three friends of Hugo's, Panamanian *brigadistas* who had fought with Spadafora against Somoza and had recently rejoined him to fight with the Miskitos, said they were in a bus going from Panama to Costa Rica and had seen Spadafora taken off a bus at a PDF border post several miles inside Panama on Friday just after noon. Ari and Carmelo quickly obtained a writ of habeas corpus to determine where he was being held.

On Monday, Spadafora's friend Risa Morales went to the San José morgue and identified the headless body found near the border as that of Hugo Spadafora. He recognized an old scar on Spadafora's leg. About the same time, Costa Rican police investigators received a copy of Spadafora's fingerprints from Panama and verified that the body was Spadafora's.

Tuesday's *La Prensa* carried the headline THEY EXECUTED SPADAFORA. Carmelo Spadafora, in a statement, said, "For me and for all our relatives and friends, the macabre murder of Dr. Hugo Spadafora Franco was planned and coldly executed by the chief of G2, Colonel Julio Ow Young, carrying out the orders of the Comandante of the National Guard, General Manuel A. Noriega." He charged that witnesses had seen Spadafora stopped and released twice at PDF checkpoints during the bus ride from Paso Canoas on the Costa Rican border. When the bus reached the town of Concepción, he said, Spadafora was taken off the bus a third time and led away to a PDF garrison. "We have complete and authentic proof of these facts," Spadafora said, noting that his son had been careful to identify himself by name and by waving his identity card to the bus driver and passengers as he was being taken prisoner.

The grieving face of Spadafora's septuagenarian father on television and in the newspapers had special impact. Carmelo was a well-known Torrijista and PRD activist. He had served in the assembly in the 1970s and as mayor of his home city, Chitré. This was not merely hysterical opposition rhetoric. Spadafora's murder was a blow that at once destroyed the already tattered myth of political reconciliation in the tradition of Torrijos and destroyed Panama's unique status as an exception to the violence convulsing Central America.

Thousands of people crowded the runway of Paitilla Airport to receive Spadafora's body when it arrived by small plane from Costa Rica. Although no soldiers were in evidence, the atmosphere was angry. Groups representing the PRD—Spadafora's original political base—and the opposition pushed and shoved each other for the right to escort the coffin across the tarmac. A PRD representative, Humberto López Tironi, nervously fingering a large cigar, denounced the opposition for using Spadafora's death to fan a "seditious campaign to discredit the Defense Forces." There would be a full investigation to find the killer, he said. Ascetic Ricardo Arias of the Christian Democrats reminded reporters of Hugo's denunciations of Noriega.

But neither group had the credentials to claim Spadafora as a comrade, and Spadafora's family—including most of his twelve brothers and sisters present—didn't try to take sides. The chants were simple demands for *"justicia"* and emotional proclamations of *"presente"* whenever someone intoned Hugo's name. The signs scattered throughout the crowd were homemade, with no unified message. In fact, there was little indication of any formal organization, much less orchestration, of the event. Panama was unpracticed in the

morbid politics of death that had become second nature to her neighbors—El Salvador, Nicaragua and Honduras—where murder and
disappearance were more regular than elections and funerals were a
political ritual. In Panama, the last suspected political assassination
had occurred more than ten years before.* Now, when some in the
crowd shouted "Noriega, *Asesino*" it was as if they were borrowing
some other country's vocabulary.

A decapitation; a missing head; a victim so visible, so protected by
reputation and past political ties; an atrocity so black it defied even
the logic of terrorism: This must be someplace else, people in the
crowd said. This can't be happening in Panama.

With Noriega out of the country, the acting commander in chief
was Colonel Roberto Díaz Herrera. His first thought when he heard
the news reports about the discovery of Spadafora's body was that
once again Noriega had left him holding the bag. Only this time the
mess was much more serious than having to fire a colonel involved
in drug trafficking, as he had done in the Melo case a year earlier.

Díaz Herrera immediately called Major Luis Córdoba, commander of the military zone covering Chiriquí and the Costa Rican
border. Chiriquí, as always, was a key post, and Noriega had placed
Córdoba there because of his unconditional loyalty. "Papo" Córdoba, fat, tough and hard-drinking, was a member of a group of
younger officers with a line to Noriega that bypassed the older colonels, like Díaz Herrera, who might have agendas independent of
Noriega's. The colonels called them the "Volvo" group, to distin-
guish them from the less-prosperous members of their rank who
drove Toyotas. Or they were known simply as the *pandilla*—the
gang.

"What's going on up there?" Díaz Herrera asked. "When I'm in
charge I want to be kept informed."

"No, my Colonel, here we don't know anything about that matter.
As far as we know, it happened in Costa Rica," Córdoba said.

Díaz Herrera called Colonel Ow Young, the head of G2, and

*In 1971, when the agrarian reform priest, Father Hector Gallegos, was abducted
and never seen again. See p. 50.

Major Nivaldo Madriñan, who was in charge of DENI, the political and investigative police. He got the same answer but was told there had been a new development. A German citizen living in Costa Rica had showed up at a border checkpoint claiming to have information about who killed Spadafora, information that exonerated the PDF from any connection. The new witness was Manfred Hoffman, a free-lance covert operator who had done work for the CIA—although Díaz Herrera was not told about that. He ordered Hoffman brought to Panama City and went with him on national television on Friday, September 20—as Spadafora's body was taken in caravan to Chitré for a mass funeral.

The appearance was a howling disaster that left Díaz Herrera red-faced with anger and humiliation. Hoffman rambled on about sophisticated electronic surveillance equipment he had once operated—although he was not now employed. He said he knew for a fact that a "faction" of the Salvadoran guerrilla group, the FMLN, had kidnapped Spadafora and killed him because of a dispute over weapons. But Hoffman was unable to explain how he knew that or to offer any corroborating facts.

The Hoffman episode left the impression that Díaz Herrera was firmly in charge of the cover-up of the crime and contributed to the theory—reflected in U.S. embassy dispatches—that Díaz Herrera himself may have ordered the murder in order to discredit Noriega. No evidence has ever appeared to indicate Díaz Herrera's involvement, but he almost immediately seized the opportunity to turn the uproar in the country to his own advantage—and against Noriega.

By the weekend, there was irrefutable circumstantial evidence that Spadafora had died in Panama and was last seen alive in PDF custody. The Costa Rican Office of Judicial Investigations (OIJ) carried out some quick detective work and released its preliminary report on September 20, based on interviews with eyewitnesses: The taxi driver who took Spadafora from the airplane said that he dropped Spadafora off a few yards from the Panamanian border; the three *brigadistas* gave their account and corroborated it with a detailed and accurate description of Spadafora's clothing; at Laurel, where the body had been found, two peasants said that they were awakened about midnight by vehicles passing by their houses, vehicles described as olive green, Japanese-made, four-wheel-drive jeeps such as those used by the PDF. One unidentified witness, who said he had known Spadafora for a long time, said that in November 1984 Major Luis Córdoba and his aide Mario del Cid had offered $5,000 to kill Spadafora in Costa Rican territory.

The report concluded: "As can be seen from this report, all indications lead to the supposition that Dr. Hugo Spadafora Franco was killed in Panamanian territory and his body dumped in Costa Rican territory."

In contrast, in David, Chiriquí, the main thrust of the Panamanian investigation, led by Attorney General José Calvo, was to obtain retractions from two witnesses, the bus driver and his assistant, who had said they had seen Spadafora detained.* Convinced now that Chiriquí's commander, Major Córdoba, was withholding information and was most likely directly involved in the crime, Díaz Herrera called a meeting of the general staff. He was careful to say nothing in direct criticism of General Noriega. Instead, he argued that the entire PDF was soiled by such a horrible crime and that they should act decisively against "certain undisciplined majors who have not been reporting to their colonels." In addition, he said, the situation in the country was in danger of getting out of control. Two or three colonels murmured supporting comments.

President Barletta was also measuring his options. He had quickly announced that the murder would be investigated through regular channels in the Justice Ministry—a proposal that drew hoots of skepticism. The Spadafora family demanded that Barletta name a special independent investigating team made up of prominent Panamanians. To dramatize their case, several Spadafora brothers and sisters, joined by leaders of COCINA, the organization of businessmen that had spearheaded the opposition to Barletta's economic policies, staged a sit-in at the U.N. office in Panama City. COCINA also called for the "immediate removal and trial" of Noriega and proclaimed a "civil disobedience campaign," which included a boycott on paying taxes and utility bills.

The Spadafora murder, one more crisis that Barletta didn't need,

---

*The two men reinstated their original testimony several weeks later.

occurred just as he thought he was getting his embattled economic program under control. Since Noriega's criticism a month earlier, Barletta knew he was in trouble and had been working hard to save his presidency. He had met with Noriega on September 6 and had won his support by promising to backpedal somewhat on the planned austerity measures. He had given a speech to American businessmen in Miami that was an appeal to the international banks to ease up on countries like Panama or risk destroying their fragile democracies. Barletta had also been given assurances that a high-ranking U.S. military leader had met with Noriega and had delivered the message that the United States would not put up with a military coup. Barletta's next step would be a speech at the U.N. General Assembly appealing for debt relief in the name of preserving democracy. He was scheduled to leave for New York just as the U.N. sit-in and COCINA campaign were launched.

As the opposition campaign gathered momentum, strengthened by middle-class outrage at the murder, the government and military seemed rudderless. General Noriega had been out of the country since several days before the murder and had not set a return date. On September 21—one week after the body was found—Barletta stated, somewhat ambiguously, that "if a commission to collaborate with the attorney general and the justice system is needed, we will have to put that into practice for the good of the whole country."

That statement brought Noriega's first reaction: a phone call from Paris to Barletta, waking him up at six-fifteen A.M. to warn him: "Stay close to the Defense Forces, be very careful. Don't do anything that will separate you from the Defense Forces." The following Monday, having failed to take decisive action to head off the opposition barrage, Barletta now removed himself further from the fray. He flew to New York with his most trusted advisers, leaving behind a politely worded "suggestion" for the attorney general to name a special commission to work alongside him in investigating the murder. Barletta's choices to serve on the commission included two former ambassadors to the United States, Carlos López Guevara and Roberto Alamán, and a prominent Torrijista legislator, Jorge Fábrega. The commission did not meet the Spadafora family's demand for total independence from the government, but Barletta calculated it would be sufficient to give legitimacy to the investigation while keeping him out of trouble with Noriega and the PDF. By leaving the plan an orphan in Panama as he went off to New York, however, Barletta achieved neither.

Ambassador Briggs was not impressed with Barletta's performance. In a September 24 cable, he wrote: "Aside from its other repercussions, the Spadafora affair has given President Barletta a clear opportunity to exert leadership. His half-step in responding to the demand that he appoint an independent investigating body illustrates the fact that he has failed to do so."

With both the president and Noriega out of the country, Díaz Herrera decided to make the move he had been secretly contemplating since Noriega took over as *comandante*. He took the first steps toward overthrowing Noriega. "I saw a great crisis coming. . . . I thought the opposition was going to take great advantage of that death. So, with Noriega away, I tried to see if I could orchestrate something against Noriega himself, something inside the barracks and with the politicians at my side. I went out on a limb, with the PRD and the armed forces, to see if I could pull off a putsch against Noriega," Díaz Herrera recounted.

On Wednesday, September 25, Díaz Herrera summoned the major leaders of the PRD to an urgent meeting at headquarters. The topic: Nicky Barletta's disloyalty to the PRD and the Defense Forces. Almost twenty politicians appeared, led by party president Rómulo Escobar Bethancourt and former vice president Gerardo González. The meeting began at eight P.M. and continued until long after midnight—with Díaz Herrera ordering in enough food and drink to keep the conversation going. The politicians, invited to speak against the man the military had imposed on their party, vented their spleens with gusto.

But for Díaz Herrera, the politicians gathering under the PDF roof was a sideshow to the main event. As they met, two combat units of five hundred men each were moving toward Panama City under Díaz Herrera's orders. They were members of Battalion 2000—the elite combat unit formed as part of the PDF reorganization—whose commander, Major Armando Palacios Góndola, was a friend of Díaz Herrera's. He ordered Palacios to move the troops from their base at Fort Cimarron, near the town of Chepó, about thirty-five miles east of Panama City. He justified the troop movement as needed to head off massive opposition demonstrations he said were forming in the city. To allay suspicion—and to cover himself in case the coup did not work—Díaz Herrera ordered Palacios to dispatch half of the troops to headquarters and half to the station of the Panama Transit Police, where they would report to Noriega's trusted brother-in-law, Major Aquilino Sieiro.

With the troops outside and the principal PRD leaders inside, Díaz Herrera technically had carried out a *cuartelazo*—a barracks uprising. Díaz Herrera's next move was to line up the support of the other major military units around the country. At one fell swoop, in unity with the PRD, they would get rid of both Noriega and Barletta and restructure the military and the government with Díaz Herrera at the helm.

But at the last possible moment, Díaz Herrera lost his nerve and didn't declare himself in rebellion. Within minutes of his order to Palacios, he received a call from Noriega in New York.

"What in the hell are you doing? What are you doing mobilizing troops?" Noriega demanded.

Díaz Herrera tried to go on the offensive. "I'm in charge of keeping a lid on things here and I'm about to have a hundred thousand people in the streets. This is your mess. How is it possible that you are out of the country with all this going on back here. I've been trying to get you on the phone for two days. And you tell me about your clinic and the treatments. You've got to get back here right away before things get out of control."

A while later, Díaz Herrera got another call, from Southcom commander John Galvin. It was the first time Galvin had ever called Díaz Herrera. Is Noriega coming back, Galvin wanted to know. Is there some trouble? What are these troop movements about?

Díaz Herrera assured him that everything was absolutely normal and that he was expecting General Noriega's return imminently.

If those two expressions of knowledge and concern were not enough to discourage Díaz Herrera, he went to the office of one of the colonels he had been counting on for support. He saw him engrossed in a telephone conversation, which Díaz Herrera assumed must be with Noriega. Others he thought might support him called and expressed their concern, signaling that he should back out while he still could. Díaz Herrera had lost the game to Noriega without either player turning over his cards.

Early that morning, Noriega had arrived in New York and had ensconced himself in his usual $850-a-night suite in the Helmsley Palace Hotel. He kept in touch with developments in Panama through phone calls from his group of loyalist majors—members of the *pandilla*—who were operating a parallel command headquarters out of a small office in the Vía Argentina district. In midafternoon, sensing trouble, Noriega ordered his limousine and rushed to La Guardia Airport to fly back to Panama. While the Learjet refueled in Miami, Noriega went to a public phone and called his home in Panama. For over an hour, as his staff patched his calls through, he talked to one officer after another, until he was satisfied that the situation was under control.

Noriega arrived near midnight and was greeted at Omar Torrijos Airport by Madriñan and other majors. They took a helicopter to PDF headquarters, where Díaz Herrera awaited him. Some troops in combat gear were still stationed in Barraza Plaza just outside the walls. Díaz Herrera saluted crisply and gave Noriega a firm *abrazo*. Then turning to point toward the soldiers in battle gear standing at attention, he said, "Your troops, my General, await your orders."

From that point, it was a matter of redirecting the coup fever against the one target he and Noriega could agree on.

President Nicolás Barletta, making the rounds of think tanks, international banks and diplomatic receptions in New York that same day, was also hearing the rumblings of trouble back home. He called to find out why the attorney general had not announced the formation of the investigative commission. Vice President Eric Delvalle, still in Panama and participating in the political maneuvering initiated that day against Barletta, gave him a half-warning. "I don't know why, but the military is worried about your action in the Spadafora case," he said. Late that night, a PRD leader, Fito Duque, called and told Barletta that Díaz Herrera had summoned the PRD leaders and was haranguing them about the need to get rid of the president.

The next day, Thursday, September 26, Barletta was picking up some intelligence about the coup attempt from the Americans—and mixed signals from his own advisers. He met with Secretary of State Shultz, Assistant Secretary Elliott Abrams and Ambassador Briggs in the morning for the signing of a joint pact between Panama, Japan and the United States to develop the Canal. During the day, Barletta and his advisers debated whether or not to cut short the trip and return to Panama. His foreign minister, Jorge Abadía, urged him to leave as soon as he had given his speech to the Assembly. Noriega had called and wanted Barletta to return. But Gabriel Lewis, the former ambassador who was acting as an adviser on the trip, told him he was safer in New York. He argued that Barletta was the president and that it was wrong in principle for him to respond to orders from the military.

Barletta was still not sure the upheaval in Panama was directed at him, and he reasoned that he could act as a mediator in whatever dispute was going on between Díaz Herrera and Noriega. Briggs advised him to stay in New York. "It's their fight," Briggs said. "Let them settle it back there. If you go back you'll get swept up in it."

The White House was also closely following the developments. In the afternoon, one of President Reagan's staff sent a message in the name of the president, urging Barletta not to go back.

Barletta had an excuse not to make the flight that night—a Caribbean hurricane was in the area. On Thursday evening, he made more calls to Panama, to Delvalle again and to Second Vice President Roderick Esquivel. Both said they thought it would be best for him to return. Barletta tried unsuccessfully to get through directly to Noriega. He was told Noriega had already gone to bed.

Finally, at midnight, Barletta abruptly ordered his entourage to the airport to board the Air Panama jet chartered for the trip. A journalist on Barletta's staff, Migdalia Fuentes, happened to glance along the side of the plane as she was climbing the gangway—and saw that someone had scrawled "F–8" in large figures.

It took Barletta more than fourteen hours after he arrived in Panama to accept the inevitable. After a rough flight through the night, he stopped off at his home only briefly to shower before reporting to Noriega's headquarters. Noriega was the soft cop appealing to Barletta's loyalty to the military and the party of Torrijos; Díaz Herrera was the hard cop, shouting and berating the president, making implied threats against Barletta's wife and children through pointed references to their health. They sat Barletta on a large chair in Noriega's office. Noriega sat on the sofa across from him. Díaz Herrera paced nervously, angrily, walking in and out of the office, returning with new accusers. He brought PRD politicians, Escobar Bethancourt and González and others, who two nights before had had a dress rehearsal for the event.

"You choose," Díaz Herrera said. "Either you resign or we have the Assembly put you on trial. They're ours, you know. Or we'll just appoint a junta and end this whole democratic process."

Barletta refused. He stalled for time. When after a few hours he said he was leaving, they said he could go when he signed the resignation. Barletta put up a tough defense, hoping he could convince Noriega, if not Díaz Herrera, that it would be political suicide to carry out a coup against him. He told them about his successful meetings with bankers in New York to renegotiate Panama's $4 billion debt, about the $60-million World Bank loan that was pending and for which his presence provided the bona fides.

The Spadafora murder and Barletta's mild attempt to name a commission caused some of the most heated exchanges. Barletta had failed to defend the honor of the PDF, they said. With his commission, he was leaving the opposition an open field to make a case that the military was involved.

"If you don't support the independent investigation, all Panama will believe you committed the crime," Barletta responded.

Barletta called his secretary at the presidential palace and instructed her to quietly remove all compromising papers from his desk. She told him he had received a call from Washington, from Elliott Abrams. Barletta took the number and immediately dialed it direct from one of Noriega's phones.

"How are you doing?" Abrams asked.

"I'm okay," Barletta said.

"Hang tough. Don't resign. We are supporting you in every way we can."

"I can't take much more of this. Please get moving and do something about it. I'm hanging tight."

Abrams also tried to get through directly to General Noriega, but Noriega didn't take his call. The next call that came from Washington was from Nestor Sanchez, who had known Noriega since his days at the CIA in the 1970s. Noriega took that call. Sanchez was now working at the Pentagon, as deputy assistant secretary for inter-American affairs. Sanchez's version of the call was that he had been designated by the Pentagon to pass on the message that the U.S. government "would be very concerned if constitutionality would be broken in Panama." Barletta heard only Noriega's end: *"Sí,* Nestor; *No,* Nestor."

But whatever Barletta thought the U.S. government could do to save him did not happen. He had hoped, not for the Marines, but at least for a call from the secretary of state, or better yet from the secretary of defense. At midnight, Barletta drafted his resignation in longhand and signed it. Then Noriega let him go home.

CHAPTER 10

WASHINGTON V. MIAMI

The U.S. response to Barletta's overthrow was a textbook case of silent diplomacy and mixed signals. The statement from the State Department resorted to a diplomatic sophism: "Our relations are between governments, not individuals." Ambassador Briggs, furious at the removal of a promising ally, boycotted the diplomatic corps's reception in honor of his successor, Eric Arturo Delvalle. In addition, a small amount of U.S. aid—$5 million—was suspended. The snub was barely noticed.

Nor was there any Panamanian demonstration of disapproval. The opposition greeted the new president with cynicism and jokes. With five presidents in office since Torrijos's death in 1981, and four of them thrown out by the military, the government had a "Kleenex presidency," the joke went—"Use once and discard." Delvalle's nickname "Tuturo" (for Arturo) almost immediately became "Tuturno" ("Your Turn").

Delvalle appeared side by side with Noriega, and both men did a lot of smiling. Delvalle quickly made it clear that the investigation of Spadafora's murder would follow Justice Ministry routine.

But the impact of the crime could not be covered up, no matter how embellished with official stamps and quasi-scientific procedures. Spadafora in life had been considered a gadfly, admired for his Quixotic crusades and guerrilla exploits, but hardly taken seriously as a force for political change. In death he came to symbolize the struggle for justice of a people grown so used to deals and compromise that they had to rediscover their own sense of moral outrage. The demand to find and punish those responsible for the murder created a new kind of opposition in Panama, an opposition that was pure and personal, targeted on Manuel Antonio Noriega and untainted by the pettiness of *rabiblanco* nostalgia for the old days of unchallenged rule by the elite.

It was of unmistakable significance that the first formidable challenge to Noriega's rule developed around a dead hero of Torrijismo, not out of the traditional opposition. When Spadafora was buried, eighty thousand people overwhelmed the streets of provincial Chitré to attend the funeral. While no one rallied to protest the overthrow of Barletta, hundreds and sometimes thousands gathered regularly to keep alive the demand for an honest investigation of Spadafora's death.

The leader of the new movement was Spadafora's younger brother, Winston, a lawyer. In October he went on a nineteen-day hunger strike; he organized a human chain of seven thousand people stretching four miles from Punta Paitilla on the north end of the bay to the presidential palace on the south—although Noriega's troops kept the demonstrators away from the building.

The National Guard–controlled ERSA tabloids went to extreme lengths to steer public opinion away from the conclusion that the Defense Forces, and Noriega, were responsible for Spadafora's death. The papers pointed to all of Spadafora's enemies, in particular to Pastora and the Colombian drug dealers. Accusations against the PDF were branded as "seditious," and one paper, *Crítica,* in an overflow of venom, charged that protesters forming the human chain had participated in "Satanic rites" at the Catholic Church's papal nunciature to prepare for the protest.

The horrible manner of Spadafora's murder gave rise to another exaggeration—that his death was preceded by the most sadistic tortures and sexual abuses. A recitation of that charge became a fixture in *La Prensa.* The autopsy performed in Costa Rica, however, showed evidence of a severe beating but none of sexual torture.

The U.S. embassy was not interested in the details of Spadafora's death, but in who did it; and within days, enough intelligence had been gathered to allow Ambassador Briggs to conclude, and to report to Washington, that PDF personnel killed Spadafora. The question of whether Noriega had ordered the killing could not be answered. The intelligence reports pointed to at least two possibilities: that Noriega ordered the killing or that the murder was committed by soldiers who mistakenly assumed that they were carrying out his orders. A third possibility, never fully discarded, was that Díaz Herrera had ordered the killing to discredit Noriega. Regardless of what happened, once Noriega found out about the killing, he actively participated in covering it up.

The Reagan administration, however, was not concerned primarily with the Spadafora murder. Most of the United State's allies in Central America—El Salvador, Honduras, the FDN Contras—had been linked by solid evidence to the use of death squads in their anticommunist crusades. More serious was the resulting destabilization of Panama and the ouster of Barletta. Central America's one spot of calm, Panama, had been "Add[ed] to the Critical List," as a *Washington Post* editorial put it. For the first time, a real, albeit low-key, debate about Noriega began in Washington.

At the State Department, there was talk of continuing to recognize Barletta and refusing to confer legitimacy on his replacement. Some of Barletta's supporters, including Second Vice President Roderick Esquivel, urged him to rescind his resignation, saying it was forced on him by Noriega, and to take asylum in a Latin American embassy. Such moves would force a constitutional crisis and invite U.S. pressure and sanctions. Barletta refused to seek asylum but argued that he had laid the groundwork for his eventual reinstatement by using the word "separate," rather than "resign," when he left office. A clause in the Panamanian constitution stipulated that a president could "separate himself" from his presidential functions for up to three months, then resume office.

Ambassador Briggs was said to have favored such a strategy of supporting Barletta, but he was overruled by the new assistant secretary of state, Elliott Abrams. Such a move would have been tantamount to breaking relations with Panama. It would almost certainly have resulted in a coup by Noriega and the probable imposition of direct military rule at a time when the United States was prescribing civilian governments as a solution to insurgency and instability in the region.

Noriega's greatest critic was Briggs, who had never had much use for him, but Briggs's advocacy of a hard line was muted by his dedication to Reagan administration policy in the region. Briggs was a team player, a Republican in his personal politics and a professional who aspired to greater responsibilities in the administration. Thus, the administration's Central America policy was "absolutely dominant" in the consideration of a course of action in Panama, one of Briggs's staff confided. In lieu of confrontation, the State Department recommended a mild, two-track strategy.

On the first track, the United States would do its best to shore up Delvalle, who had assured the U.S. ambassador that he could "handle" the military more adeptly than Barletta had. Delvalle would be treated as the primary interlocutor with the United States and as the embodiment of the promised transition to real democracy via the scheduled elections in 1989.

Noriega, on the second track, would be cut off from contact with the United States except on strictly military matters.

In the White House, two officials and a former official continued to promote a hard line on Panama aimed at Barletta's reinstatement. The officials were Constantine Menges, a foreign policy adviser at the National Security Council, and Carlton Turner, the president's special adviser on narcotics control. At the urging of Norman Bailey, a friend of Barletta's and a former NSC official, Menges and Turner composed a decision memo on Panama, intended to raise with President Reagan the issue of reinstating Barletta. The paper never made it past the desk of NSC chief Robert McFarlane, who in late 1985 was in the process of turning over his job to his deputy, Admiral John Poindexter. Menges had a reputation as a right-wing hothead and a leaker—a cannon too loose even for an NSC then in the throes of the first Iran-Contra transactions. Turner was an ineffective bureaucrat in a job with no clout. Neither of Barletta's defenders had responsibilities for Panama or Central America, and their counsel was easily ignored.

Menges and Turner's paper had the distinction of reviving the notion that Noriega was a national security danger because of his contacts with Cuba. Perhaps too predictably, given his reputation as an ideologue, Menges argued that Noriega was part of the Cuban-communist conspiracy to destroy democracy in Central America and to undermine U.S. society by promoting the flow of drugs.

Those in the U.S. government who knew—or thought they knew—Noriega were able to dismiss that notion as absurd. Noriega's contacts with Cuba were well known but accepted because it was thought that Noriega's access to and reporting on Cuba to U.S. intelligence outweighed the intelligence Noriega might be providing Cuba about the United States. The characterization of Noriega as a communist or communist tool—an argument at times put forward by Panama's conservative opposition—played to the weakest suit of Noriega's enemies. It was a hard case to make as long as Noriega's greatest defender was the top anticommunist fighter of them all, CIA Director William Casey.

In early November, Noriega flew to Washington to see Casey. The meeting has been portrayed in some accounts as part of an administration effort to deliver a stern message of disapproval to Noriega. But whatever ulterior motives may have been present elsewhere in the administration, Casey himself delivered as much of a pat on the back as a scolding. The only recorded account of that meeting was given by State Department official Frank McNeil:

> Casey's memcon [memorandum of conversation] made clear that he let Noriega off the hook. He scolded Noriega only for letting the Cubans use Panama to evade the trade embargo, but never mentioned narcotics nor, if I recall correctly, democracy. Mr. Casey's memcon noted that Noriega had been nervous when he came to [the] meeting but departed reassured, or words to that effect.

A month later, another high-level meeting with Noriega, also portrayed as sending a tough message, was similarly ineffective. This time the messenger was the new NSC chief, Admiral John Poindexter. He met with Noriega in Panama on December 12. If Poindexter's mission was to "read the riot act" to Noriega about drugs and democracy, as Poindexter later described it to Norman Bailey, he was making a bizarre detour from the main NSC agenda.

Poindexter had moved into McFarlane's job as national security adviser only a week before. Fall 1985 was a time of furious clandestine activity at the NSC: The arms deals with Iran were under way in an attempt to obtain the release of U.S. hostages in Lebanon; an ostensibly private fund-raising network managed out of the NSC was financing the Contras and a secret operation had begun to funnel weapons from U.S.-controlled stockpiles in El Salvador to Contra camps in Costa Rica and Honduras. Both projects would coalesce less than a month later with an arrangement to sell arms to Iran and to use the profits to finance the Contras. The central manager of the Iran-Contra agendas was Lieutenant Colonel Oliver North, the NSC's "political-military" aide.

Poindexter's trip to Panama was the shortest leg of a two-day tour that included El Salvador, Costa Rica, Honduras and Guatemala— the Central American countries most deeply involved in the U.S. effort to remove the Sandinista government from Nicaragua. The purpose of the tour was "to urge those countries to provide continued support for the armed Resistance." The meeting with Noriega took place at Howard Air Force Base and lasted only about fifteen minutes. Poindexter was accompanied by Elliott Abrams, Ambassador Briggs and Abrams's deputy, William Walker. Noriega brought his translator, Captain Moisés Cortizo, a West Point graduate, and several other officers. Those are the only facts about the meeting that have not been disputed.

The official U.S. version, from Ambassador Briggs in an interview with the author, has it that the meeting was "long and painful," during which Poindexter upbraided Noriega for his ouster of Barletta, his suspected drug trafficking and his assistance to Cuba in evading U.S. trade restrictions. Noriega was "humiliated" in front of his subordinates as Poindexter told him he had to "clean up his act." According to Briggs, the meeting had nothing to do with Nicaragua, which was not mentioned.

When the first version of the meeting was leaked to *The Miami*

Herald in mid-1986, it was portrayed as the beginning of a get-tough campaign designed to oust Noriega from power. According to that version, which describes the meeting as Briggs did, Poindexter was angry that Noriega had ignored his request to stop his objectionable activities and on his return to Washington "began raising the possibility of finding an alternative to Noriega."

A year later, in May 1987, the same *Miami Herald* reporter, Alfonso Chardy, wrote that "well-placed Panamanian sources" described the meeting as an effort to "persuad[e] Noriega to authorize the use of Panamanian territory and facilities to resupply the contras." When Noriega turned him down, Poindexter concluded that he was a "thug" and began a campaign to discredit Noriega and, "if possible, remove him."

Chardy had asked Noriega about the Poindexter meeting in an interview. According to a transcript of that interview, Noriega described Poindexter as "rushed" and "arrogant," a man who treated those he was talking to "as if they were the papers he had in his hand, as if they had no substance." Noriega denied that Poindexter had specifically asked for Panama to help the Contras because "he already felt our resistance." But he said that Poindexter complained that Panama's diplomatic activity regarding Contadora damaged U.S. interests, particularly since the PDF had gotten rid of Barletta, who was, Noriega noted, more amenable to the U.S. posture.

"He came to Panama, and put pressure, and his literal words were that Panama was a bad example for Central America because they [the United States] had a specific strategy against Nicaragua and they couldn't implement it because Panama was not aligned," Noriega said. "We rejected his proposal, and we considered it an insult, a lack of respect for all of us." He added that as a nonsmoker he was also irritated by Poindexter's pipe, which smelled like "burned wood."

Noriega offered still another version of the meeting during the heat of crisis in early 1988. In a February 7 interview on CBS's *60 Minutes*, he said, "They were going to hit Nicaragua. . . . They were going to invade Nicaragua and the only reason they hadn't done it was because Panama was in the way." He then had Captain Cortizo describe Poindexter's alleged request at the December 1985 meeting. "They wanted Panama forces to go in with American forces, but we'd go in first. Then we'd get the support from American troops that would be taking part in the invasion," Cortizo said.

The bottom line on what happened at that meeting, seen as a key event by all concerned, may not be known until the relevant documents are declassified. Whatever happened, however, the meeting and the confusion surrounding it exemplify the ambiguity of U.S. relations with Panama. Frank McNeil, who was reading the cable traffic from his post at the State Department's intelligence and research section, gave this assessment of the various U.S. contacts with Noriega following the Spadafora murder and Barletta ouster.

> The United States government . . . was giving thoroughly mixed signals . . . to Panama. The stated policy, backed by Ambassador Briggs and Assistant Secretary Motley, was to try to avoid a new Somoza and to support real civilian rule. The body language that Noriega saw from CIA, military intelligence, and some in DOD [Department of Defense] suggested otherwise, that if he could consolidate his hold, his friends in Washington would take care of things. The State Department could be safely ignored.

In December, Winston Spadafora took his crusade for justice to Washington. The Panamanian Justice Ministry, as expected, had closed his brother's murder investigation without filing charges. In Washington, Spadafora discovered that coverage of Panama had evaporated. Even in political circles, hardly anyone had heard of Hugo Spadafora. On a long shot, he asked for an interview with Senator Jesse Helms of North Carolina. Spadafora was reluctant to appeal to a man whose right-wing politics and years of campaigning against Panama's right to the Canal were so antithetical to his own thinking. But he was desperate, and Helms agreed to see him. Spadafora showed Helms the gory pictures of his brother's body—himself leaving the room because he had never looked at the pictures and did not want to. Helms was horrified.

"I'm going to promise you something," Helms said at the end of the meeting. "I'm going to promise to work my hardest to get justice for your brother and to raise the issue to the level of President Reagan's agenda." He said he would start by convening investigative hearings on Panama. Helms also introduced a resolution in the Senate calling attention to the crisis in Panama; it got only a handful of votes.

In Senator Jesse Helms, Noriega had acquired a tenacious adversary. Helms was the ranking Republican on the Senate Foreign Relations Committee as it came under Republican control in the 1980 elections, but a campaign promise had forced him to take the chairmanship of the Agriculture Committee. On the Foreign Relations Committee, Helms settled for the chairmanship of the subcommittee on Western Hemisphere affairs.

Helms was the pit bull of the Republican right, an undaunted opponent of any policy or personality—whether or not espoused by the Reagan administration—that did not meet ideological muster. Helms had defended anticommunist dictators all over the world and was a particular fan of President Pinochet of Chile and of military strongmen in El Salvador such as Major Roberto d'Aubuisson. His adoption of a human rights cause in a country that the Reagan administration counted among its allies in Central America was surprising, however, only to those unfamiliar with Helms's long battle against the Panama Canal treaties and against General Omar Torrijos. The treaties had passed, but Helms had never lowered his banner proclaiming U.S. rights to the Canal. It was no secret that he wanted the treaties rescinded.

Helms scheduled the hearings on Panama for March 10 and April 21, 1986. He wanted to give a forum for Panamanian opposition viewpoints and to get the State Department and other agencies on record about relations with Panama. A week prior to the hearings, Elliott Abrams contacted Helms's office.

The hearings are a bad idea, he said. The timing was wrong for public statements by American officials. "Come on, Noriega's really not that big a problem," he said. "He's really being helpful to us in something. It hasn't happened yet, but the Panamanians have promised they are going to help us with the Contras."

Abrams said that the promise had been made recently and that "training Contras" and other activities would begin soon. "If you have the hearings, it'll alienate them. It will provoke them and they won't help us with the Contras," he said. Abrams was told that

Helms was interested in helping the Contras in almost any way but not in help from someone like Noriega, and that the hearings would be going on as scheduled, with Abrams as the first government witness.

During his testimony on April 21, Abrams gave a critical but largely favorable assessment of the Panamanian régime, which he said was in the "middle" between dictatorship and democracy. He omitted any mention of Panamanian favors regarding the Contras but made it clear that Panama's actions with regard to Central America were what counted. Panama's positions on the region's conflicts are "compatible" with the views of the United States, he said:

> The people of Panama do not want a foreign dominated antidemo-cratic state, such as Nicaragua, fomenting armed conflict in the region. We have our tactical differences and differences in perception from the Government of Panama, but we have never lacked a sympathetic hearing for our views from Panama's Government. Also, and impor-tantly . . . there has been no dispute concerning U.S. military forces in Panama. In a region where we have too many problems, the virtual absence of difficulty about our most significant military bases is nota-ble and beneficial to us.

Abrams noted that Panama's close relationship with Cuba was a problem, especially Cuba's use of Panama "to purchase goods it cannot legally get directly from the United States." On the question of drugs, he praised Panama's "excellent cooperation" with the DEA, but added a caveat:

> Having acknowledged Panamanian official cooperation, I am com-pelled also to state that we are aware of and deeply troubled by persistent rumors of corrupt, official involvement of Panamanians in drug trafficking. A colonel in the defense forces was cashiered in 1984 for such involvement. We remain alert for evidence of other, similar activities.

Abrams's statement was well researched, reflecting an understand-ing of the PDF's extramilitary business ventures and of its domination of other Panamanian institutions. There were no easy answers to Panama's problems, he said, but he expressed confidence in the ability of Panamanians to resolve them.

When asked during the public hearings, none of the witnesses could provide specific evidence of drug trafficking by any official of the Panamanian government. But a day of closed hearings was also scheduled, and Helms and his staff expected to hear more.

The government witnesses called to testify considered the hearings so sensitive that they requested they be classified "code word"—a level above top secret. Even so, CIA and Defense Intelligence Agency representatives were reluctant to criticize Noriega. "He's not the kind of guy I'd want my daughter to go on a date with," the CIA representative allowed.

Helms's staff had prepared detailed questions, gleaned from conversations with Panamanian opposition sources, about Noriega's suspected drug-trafficking cronies. He ticked off a long list of names—César Rodríguez, Enrique Pretelt, Colonel Melo, Sebastián "Wachan" González and others. To each, the witnesses, there to provide the best of U.S. intelligence on Panama, replied that they had never heard the names.

Helms brought up the subject of Hugo Spadafora. The witnesses at the table exchanged glances and asked Helms to clear the room of all congressional staff members—even though all those present had "code word" security clearances. Helms complied, and the secret session within the secret hearing went on for forty minutes.

Only one detail of that briefing could be learned: At the time of Spadafora's death, the U.S. National Security Agency was intercepting Noriega's calls to Panama from France. One of the calls, between Noriega and Chiriquí commander, Major Luis Córdoba, was thought to refer to Spadafora. It took place on the afternoon of September 13, 1985, the day Spadafora was killed.

"We have the rabid dog," Córdoba said, according to the intercept.

"What do you do with a rabid dog?" Noriega was said to have replied.

· · ·

The Helms hearings produced few public revelations and no spectacular headlines in the United States but, as often happens in Washington, marked the beginning of that unique process by which policies are created in spite of the official position. In that symbiotic world occupied by the top Washington journalists and their sources, a current of interest and information began to flow. The presence of Roberto Eisenmann, owner of *La Prensa,* as a Nieman fellow in the United States facilitated the process. Eisenmann was intelligent, articulate and not only spoke flawless English but grasped the needs of American journalists for hard leads and verifiable facts.

On Wednesday, June 11, General Noriega flew to Washington, D.C. He planned to attend a ceremony the next day honoring an old friend, General Robert Schweitzer, to whom he intended to present a Panamanian decoration. He spent part of the afternoon on a pleasant cruise on the Potomac with NSC aides Raymond Burghardt and Oliver North. He met with his banker, Amjad Awan of BCCI. Panama's new ambassador, Kaisar Bazán, offered to host a reception, but Noriega declined. Bazán later learned that Noriega had met with CIA Director Bill Casey instead.

Noriega had reason to be upbeat. The fallout from the previous year's events had abated in Washington, and the Reagan administration seemed willing to give the new president, Eric Arturo Delvalle, a chance. Noriega and Delvalle had hired the high-priced but impeccably connected lobbying firm of Bill Hecht and Stuart Spencer to run interference in Washington, and their $360,000 fee was paying off. Delvalle had successfully negotiated almost $100 million in new international loans for Panama. The firm was taking the image of Delvalle as Panama's best hope for democracy to the highest seat of power. Spencer had been a Reagan insider since the 1960s and had worked on both his 1980 and 1984 campaigns. At Spencer's urging, according to Bazán, Reagan had agreed to meet with Delvalle in mid-June—the promise of a crowning touch of U.S. legitimacy.

(Hecht was given the job of persuading Helms to call off his attacks. He had worked closely with Helms as a lobbyist for the tobacco industry—Helms's main North Carolina constituency. They had a meeting that lasted only a few minutes. "No chance, my friend," Helms told him.)

The Delvalle-Reagan meeting was not to be. The June 12 edition of *The New York Times* had Noriega's picture on the front page next to an article by Seymour M. Hersh, headlined PANAMA STRONGMAN SAID TO TRADE IN DRUGS, ARMS AND ILLICIT MONEY. The article tied Noriega to the Spadafora killing, to the Melo affair, to the INAIR cocaine shipment and to the sale of arms to Colombian M-19 guerrillas. It said Noriega had been providing intelligence "simultaneously to Cuba and the United States" for the past fifteen years. Within twenty-four hours, three other major news organizations, *The Washington Post,* NBC News and *The Miami Herald* ran independently reported stories with some of the same information. It became what Washington likes to call a "feeding frenzy" on Noriega.

What was new about Hersh's article was not its litany of crimes and clandestine activities attributed to Noriega and the PDF—all that was familiar territory, at least to readers of *En Pocas Palabras* in Panama. But for the first time, the charges were made on the front page of *The New York Times.* They were backed up not by the self-interested rhetoric of the Panamanian opposition but by authoritative U.S. sources, described by Hersh as "American intelligence agencies," "senior State Department, White House, Pentagon and intelligence officials," "NSA intercepts," "a recent classified report by the Defense Intelligence Agency" and "reconnaissance film."

Coming from another reporter, the reliance on such anonymous sources, no matter how authoritative they were purported to be, might have had less impact. But Seymour Hersh was the reporter who had uncovered the My Lai massacre by U.S. soldiers in Vietnam, had broken many of the CIA scandals of the 1970s, had been on the front lines of the Watergate reporting. Hersh did not get things wrong. No one in Washington had intelligence sources like Sy Hersh's.

No one, perhaps, except Bob Woodward of *The Washington Post,* and Woodward and fellow investigative reporter Charles Babcock wrote the *Post*'s June 13 story on Noriega. It went beyond Hersh's account in detailing Noriega's status as an intelligence asset to the

United States and cited a "secret new intelligence study" by the CIA on Noriega's trafficking in drugs, arms and intelligence to Cuba.*

Noriega, who had refused to be interviewed by Hersh, stoically continued his round of appointments in Washington on the day *The New York Times* article appeared. He gave a speech at the biennial meeting of the Inter-American Defense Board, held at Fort McNair. The speech was a scathing attack on the Sandinista government, according to a U.S. officer present. "He said the peace negotiation effort has ended and the war has begun. We should all be on the right side to meet the serious communist threat."

It was an impressive performance of a professional military man, clearly intended to convince his U.S. military colleagues that Panama was an ally. But for Noriega's longtime associates in the U.S. military, the charges in that day's paper were deeply disturbing. Retired General Schweitzer, worried about possible embarrassment if he went through with the ceremony that afternoon, made a series of inquiries, to the State Department's Jim Michel and to Nestor Sanchez at the Pentagon, and was assured that there was "no truth" to the charges in the Hersh article.

The process set in motion by the Helms hearings showed a U.S. government deeply divided over what to think—and do—about Noriega. Official policy remained to prop up Delvalle and to do nothing to harm or to help Noriega. Those in the agencies dealing

---

*Attempts to obtain the DIA and CIA reports cited by Hersh and by Woodward and Babcock through the FOIA produced nothing. The DIA responded that no such document, as described in the Hersh article, could be found. The CIA has responded substantively to only one of many requests regarding Noriega. It released a single sheet entitled DRUG CORRUPTION, which was blacked out except for the first three sentences:

> Drug-related corruption, which can be found in virtually all major producing countries and key transshipment points, is impinging increasingly on US policy interests. The drug trade's huge profit margins allow traffickers to offer hefty bribes that are crippling antinarcotics efforts in many Latin American and Caribbean countries:
> • General Noriega has long participated in drug smuggling in Panama. [Rest of page deleted.]

The document bears no date, but it was released in response to a request for documents prepared in 1988 or 1989.

with Panama who disagreed with that policy apparently felt strongly enough to go outside channels to try to change it—by leaking intelligence information about Noriega to the press. The tactic was well-worn in Washington, and it had no immediate effect inside the government. The existing policy was reviewed and reaffirmed at several high-level meetings held just after the press barrage against Noriega. According to Frank McNeil, who was present, "the statement was made that Panama—that Noriega should be put on the shelf until Nicaragua was taken care of."

On the record, the new U.S. ambassador, Arthur Davis, delivered a note to the Panamanian Foreign Ministry saying that the United States "does not wish to speculate about the allegations" and stating that the U.S. government respects Panama's sovereignty and "has the intention to continue working together with its duly elected officials and representatives."

The idea that he might develop a drug-trafficking case against Manuel Antonio Noriega had been working around DEA agent Dan Moritz's mind since early in 1985, when he had talked to a young, scared informant named Carlos.* Carlos managed money and property for Floyd Carlton in Miami. He knew that the money flowing through Carlton's condo in Fontainebleau was drug money. He knew that Carlton had a connection to Noriega, and he knew César Rodríguez. One thing led to another, and to keep out of jail Carlos told his story to Dan Moritz and agreed to cooperate with the DEA.

Moritz had no special knowledge about Noriega, no preconceived notions about him being a valuable asset in Central America or the key to Panama's special brand of cooperation with the DEA. It wasn't that he started off to get Noriega. Noriega was a big fish, a corrupt official of a foreign government, and in Moritz's mind the higher up you worked a case the better. It was almost that simple. He mentioned the "Noriega connection" in some of his reports, and he discussed it with Richard Gregorie, the chief assistant U.S. attorney in Miami. It became a joke between them.

*Not his real name.

"When are you going to get me Noriega?" Gregorie would ask.

"It's going to happen. I think I can do it," Moritz would say. It was a joke for a year before they both realized it was serious.

The targets of the operation that grew out of Carlos's debriefing were Floyd Carlton and Alfredo Caballero, the airplane broker. Moritz went undercover, and Carlos took him over to DIACSA, Caballero's business on Northwest Twelfth Street, south of Miami International Airport. He was introduced as Daniel Martelli, someone able to turn cash into large denomination cashier's checks and international wire transfers without filing any reports that would allow the U.S. government to detect the transactions.

As Martelli the money launderer, Moritz charged a 3 percent commission and delivered foolproof service. He first met Floyd Carlton in March 1985; Caballero introduced them and they sat at the second-floor conference table at DIACSA for an hour and talked business. They discussed the banks Martelli would use and how to avoid filing CPRs—the Internal Revenue Service forms required for any cash transaction over $10,000. Moritz liked Carlton. He was low key, unassuming. He came on as a regular guy without the gold chains and other gaudy trappings of a South American drug dealer. Moritz left with $200,000 to launder. Eventually, he handled $3.8 million for Caballero and Carlton.

But the money wasn't the target. Moritz wanted to break the smuggling operation that was flying in the cocaine. In September he got the chance. Carlton had never let slip any details about the cocaine flights, but his chief pilot, Miguel Alemany Soto, told Carlos about a big flight coming up from Colombia through Mexico. Carlos was able to get the tail number of the plane and an approximate date. The pilot's name was Tony Aizprua, a Panamanian said to have occasionally worked for Noriega. Moritz put out a border lookout notice through EPIC, the El Paso drug intelligence central.

On September 23 the chase was on. Aizprua's plane had crossed the border from Mexico and had landed at Brownsville airport, in the southern tip of Texas. He refueled and took off after midnight, heading for Florida. Moritz ordered U.S. Air Force surveillance planes out of Homestead base south of Miami. Aizprua tried to shake the tail by faking landings at several airstrips in southern Florida. By eight-thirty A.M. he was running out of fuel.

Moritz's supervisor, Ken Kennedy, was listening to the chase on the police radio in his car as he drove to work on I-75 north of Miami. "He's coming down. He's landing on the highway, on I-75," he heard someone say. The radio described a stretch of I-75 that was closed off for construction, only a few miles from Kennedy's location. He slapped his red light on the roof of his car and speeded up to ninety miles per hour as he reached the empty section of highway. When he reached the Cessna Turbo Prop 441 stopped in the middle of the highway, its propellers were still turning and the cockpit door was open. The pilot had fled into a dense swamp that lay a few yards from the road. Kennedy, a round, red-faced former cop from New Jersey, waded in with his gun drawn and lost one of his shoes in the muck. He ran back, puffing, to inspect the plane as other police units arrived. The plane was loaded with twelve suitcases and four duffel bags. The total take: over 400 kilos of pure cocaine, worth at least $2 million wholesale, and three or four times that had it reached the distributors in Miami. The airplane alone was worth $1 million.

For Floyd Carlton, the plane's capture was the third major disaster in the last few months. He had been hiding out in Miami since July because of the disappearance of his pilot Teófilo Watson and the 538 kilos of cocaine in May. A few weeks ago his friend Hugo Spadafora had been murdered in Panama. Now his operation had lost a second plane and another multimillion-dollar cocaine load. Worse, from the capture of Aizprua's plane he had to assume that his operation had been detected by U.S. authorities, and it was no longer safe for him to remain in the United States.

In October Carlton returned to Panama and a few days later was picked up by DENI, the investigative police commanded by one of Noriega's closest associates, Major Nivaldo Madriñan. The detention was to protect both Carlton and Noriega: Carlton was out of reach of the Colombians who might still be looking for him, and his interrogation at the prison allowed Madriñan to clean up the traces of Carlton's connections to Noriega. Madriñan confiscated Carlton's DENI identification card, got rid of incriminating telephone records and even destroyed a picture showing Carlton as the pilot for the shah of Iran during his stay in Panama in 1979—evidence of his close association with Noriega because Noriega was in charge of security for the shah.

In January Carlton was released for lack of evidence—the Panamanian investigating judge said that no cocaine was found to substantiate the suspicions that Carlton was dealing in drugs. But Carlton felt trapped, and he decided to try the course recommended to him in his last conversation with Hugo Spadafora. He called the DEA's resident agent, Thomas Telles, and set up a meeting. Telles and another agent picked Carlton up at the Holiday Inn; for security they talked as they rode around Panama City.

Carlton explained the situation and said he wanted to cooperate with U.S. authorities in exchange for protection for himself and his family. Later he would give this account of that conversation:

> When they talked to me they asked me exactly what I wanted to speak about to them. And I asked, "Have you not heard my name?" And they said, "Yes, we have."
>
> And so I said, "On different occasions I have sent people to speak to you so that you interview me. But you have always told them that you have nothing to talk to me about." And the fact is that I believe that I can go before the American judicial system and speak of a lot of things that are happening in this country, and I can even prove them.
>
> So they asked, "Such as what?" So, I said, "Money laundering, drugs, weapons, corruption, assassinations." When I mentioned the name of General Noriega, they immediately became upset. And I noticed that. And of course I became nervous at that point. They did not try to contact me again.

The meeting seriously spooked Carlton. He was well aware of the close relations between Noriega and the DEA. He was afraid there might be a leak. He had already been told by a PDF officer in Chiriquí that Noriega's G2 considered him a problem and that "they were apparently looking for a way to do away with me." Carlton and his wife began to talk about getting out of Panama.

In Miami the DEA and the U.S. attorney's office decided it was time to "take down" Moritz's undercover operation. On January 23—only a few days after Carlton approached the DEA's Panama office—a Miami federal grand jury returned a secret indictment against Carlton; Caballero; Caballero's son, Luis; Tony Aizprua; and three other Carlton associates, Miguel Alemany Soto, Cecilio Sáenz Barria and Alejandro Benítez. They were charged with smuggling the 400 kilos of cocaine on the Aizprua flight and with twelve counts of conspiracy and money laundering.

The DEA agents moved in on Caballero's DIACSA office and arrested him and his son, then picked up Miguel Alemany Soto and Cecilio Sáenz Barria. They brought the prisoners into a room where Dan Moritz was waiting. It didn't take them long, after they discovered that their money launderer "Danny Martelli" was a DEA agent, to decide to cooperate. Two weeks later, Tony Aizprua was arrested in Los Angeles as he got off a plane from Panama. Aizprua was tougher, but eventually he cooperated, too.

Soon after the arrests of his entire circle of associates, Carlton had some more bad news: César Rodríguez was missing. César and Floyd had gone through good times and bad times together. They had been partners, broken up, become competitors. But in early 1986 they had gone back to being just friends again—talking about old times in Chiriquí, talking about Noriega, the man who had taken them as penniless kids, given them adventure and made them wealthy.

Now, their conversations about Noriega brought only bitterness. César was not doing so well either since Noriega had forced him to sell his house. He was still rich, living in a large suite on the sixteenth floor of the Holiday Inn overlooking the bay. But he had lost some of his businesses, including the Paitilla hangar franchise that was his badge of protection. Word was getting around that he was on the outs with Noriega. César's cocaine habit had also gotten out of control. Always a lithe, vigorous man, he had acquired the unhealthy, bloated look of dissipation.

César was furious because Noriega was sending intermediaries to him, always with the same message: Clean up your act. To retaliate, César began having his secretary, Sandra, tape his conversations with Noriega. Once, César had played a tape for Carlton. On it, César was screaming at Noriega: "Listen, don't send me any more messengers;

don't send me that little fag again [referring to an officer in the antinarcotics unit who had come to see César]. I have my balls very well secured for you to come and tell me this to my face. So stop sending me messages like I was a kid, because I'm no kid."

Noriega had threatened him, César told Carlton. The tapes were to make sure Noriega would pay if anything happened to César. They were his insurance policy.

César had tried to interest Carlton in one last cocaine deal—a 300-kilo-plus shipment he was putting together with Ahmet and Rubén Darío Paredes, the two sons of Noriega's rival, retired General Paredes. They had bought a boat, the *Krill,* and had arranged two pickup points in Colombia where the cocaine would be waiting.

"Don't do anything without Noriega's permission," Carlton warned.

"Don't worry; we're working with Cleto Hernández," Rodríguez said, referring to a captain who was one of Noriega's *pandilla* and the second in command of G2. César and his cohorts, who included an American, had also arranged to display an autographed picture of Noriega in the cabin of the *Krill* in the hope the picture would give their voyage the stamp of Noriega's protection.

On March 11 César and Rubén Darío flew to Medellín and checked into the Nutibara Hotel. They were seen with a Colombian woman, Nubia Pino de Bravo, the widow of a cocaine trafficker. On March 13, they went out and never came back. One week later, Colombian police boarded the *Krill* while it was anchored at the port of San Andrés, a Colombian island in the Caribbean north of Panama. They found 305 kilos of cocaine.

César Rodríguez's body was found in the small village of Itaguí, near Medellín. He had been bound and gagged and shot once in the head. Rubén Darío Paredes and Nubia Pino, who had been executed the same way, were found elsewhere in the town. Paredes still had a gold chain around his neck. The bodies had been discovered by Colombian police on March 13, but had not been identified until twelve days later.

The murders were typical of hundreds in Medellín, where the plenitude of hired assassins had bid down the price to under $1,000. The killers were never found, much less who paid them. It was presumed that Rodríguez and Paredes had a bad debt with one of the cartel groups and had paid with their lives. General Paredes personally had contacted the Ochoa family and was given assurances in the name of Jorge Ochoa that the family knew nothing about the murders.

Floyd Carlton had no proof, but he also had no doubt who had set the trap for César. To his mind, General Noriega had finally gotten rid of his most embarrassing former partner; Carlton didn't need much imagination to guess who might be next.

The information that Dan Moritz gleaned from his new prisoners convinced him more than ever that he should be looking beyond even Floyd Carlton to Manuel Noriega in Panama. Once Tony Aizprua decided to talk, he directly implicated Noriega in drug operations. Aizprua admitted participating in the 1984 ether smuggling, for which Colonel Melo—and presumably Noriega—had taken million-dollar protection payoffs. He claimed to have been one of Noriega's pilots and to have had conversations with Noriega about smuggling transactions. Aizprua also knew about Carlton's connections with Noriega and described Carlton as someone who would be susceptible to being rolled—to becoming a witness against Noriega—if they could get him in custody.

Moritz turned to the problem of luring Carlton out of Panama to a country where he could be arrested and extradited. The opportunity came in June. Word came to Alfredo Caballero, who was out on bail, that Floyd wanted to talk to him. Caballero called Floyd in Panama, and Floyd said that he had been unable to get any reliable information about the indictment and the evidence the U.S. authorities had against him. Caballero said that he was going to Costa Rica on business and would be willing to bring copies of the indictment and other documents his lawyers had managed to pry out of the U.S. attorney's office. He said he would call Floyd when he got to San José.

Caballero didn't relish the thought of acting as bait to trap a business associate he considered a friend. But he was facing the possibility of spending a decade or more in prison. More important, he had a family and a proud reputation in the Miami community as a freedom fighter against Castro. He had never been in jail before and even the short time in the Miami Correctional Center awaiting bail had been all he wanted to experience of criminal culture. Fellow prisoners taught him the golden rule: Once you're caught, bargain; the more you have to offer, the less time you'll spend in jail.

Caballero called Dan Moritz and offered Floyd Carlton.

Moritz and Caballero flew to San José, Costa Rica in late July and registered at the Cariari Hotel. Moritz took a room across the hall from Caballero's. Caballero called Carlton at his ranch in Chiriquí, and Carlton said he would drive to San José to meet him. He and several associates arrived at the Cariari on July 30 and went up to Caballero's room. Within minutes, Moritz, Robert Nieves, the DEA's resident agent, and a team of Costa Rican police swarmed into Caballero's room. Carlton didn't resist.

CHAPTER 11

SHOOTING THE KING

General Noriega exalted in a good fight. His enemies had landed some solid body blows in their attacks against him in the U.S. press, but Noriega remained confident. Well-placed friends in Washington still owed him favors. And he still had within him that spit-in-their-eye attitude of a street kid toward the rich and powerful, who made the rules and then expected the rest of the world to follow them. Noriega made his own rules, and as the fight got tougher, neither the North American superpower nor the blue-blood Panamanian *rabiblancos* seemed a match for the fierce tactics of a man who owed his survival to no one.

He was guided by two maxims. One was the motto of Omar Torrijos, who had often said, "The first duty of a man in power is to stay in power." The second was to "fool the enemy with astuteness and dexterity." Noriega had written a short but strikingly erudite book, *Psychological Operations.* In it he summarized thinkers from Socrates to Jung, but proclaimed a revealing admiration for Genghis Khan, "the father of psychological warfare," for his masterful use of rumor—spreading tales of his own invincibility and terrible cruelty to induce his adversaries to give up without a fight. He credited Genghis Khan with inventing the double agent—"taking control of the spies and agents of the enemies, seducing or terrorizing them to convert them to one's own cause, and using them as instruments. . . ."

Those were the lessons Noriega seemed to be applying as he counterattacked. He dismissed charges by *The New York Times* as "imbecilic" because they were based on anonymous sources or were the unsubstantiated accusations of Panama's enemies, such as Senator Jesse Helms, who wanted the United States to take back the Panama Canal. "It is not the United States as constituted governmental organization that is behind these maneuvers," he said. A U.S. embassy cable noted the distinction, with the comment, "It continues to appear that the FDP/GOP [Defense Forces/Government of Panama] wishes to avoid any public posture that might escalate into a full-blown diplomatic incident with the U.S."

Noriega had a lobbyist's appreciation for the fault lines inside the U.S. government and took his case to those he hoped would help him neutralize his attackers. In August 1986—two months after the Hersh articles—Noriega sent an emissary to Oliver North, the NSC official most directly involved in U.S. clandestine operations against Nicaragua. Noriega had an offer, North told his boss, Admiral John Poindexter: "Noriega's representative proposed that, in exchange for a promise from the USG [U.S. government] to help clean up Noriega's image and a commitment to lift the USG ban on military sales to the Panamanian defense forces, Noriega would assassinate the Sandinista leadership for the U.S. government."

The representative reminded North that Noriega had helped the United States before, with the bombing of the Sandinista military complex in March 1985, and still had "numerous assets in place in Nicaragua and could accomplish many essential things." North and Poindexter both noted in writing that U.S. law prohibited any U.S. government involvement in assassinations. But as Poindexter told North, "Panamanian assistance with sabotage would be another story." North said that the cost of the operations could be borne by his secret off-the-books fund, Project Democracy.

After consulting with Secretary of State Shultz and Elliott Abrams, North took Noriega up on his offer to meet personally in London to discuss the operations. At that meeting, in mid-September, Noriega said that he "would try to take immediate actions against the Sandinistas and offered a list of priorities including an oil refinery, an airport, and the Puerto Sandino off-load facility."

It could not be learned which, if any, of those actions Noriega carried out. North, however, did fulfill several things on his part of the bargain. Around the time of his meeting with Noriega's representative, North gave the go-ahead to the public relations firm, International Business Communications (IBC), which was handling a major portion of North's fund-raising for the Contras, to sign on to a campaign to improve Panama's image. According to the contract, a pro-Noriega businessman paid IBC $35,000 a month for the PR work, which continued on and off through the spring of 1987.

On October 14 North approached DEA chief Jack Lawn on Noriega's behalf because he had heard that the DEA was investigating the drug allegations against Noriega. Stephen Engelberg of *The New York Times* reported that Lawn rejected North's offer to intercede.

CIA Director William Casey also went out of his way to counter the attacks on Noriega. In September, Senator Helms marshaled an unusual coalition of liberal and conservative senators behind an amendment to the Intelligence Authorization Bill. The amendment required the CIA to report to the House and Senate Intelligence committees on the charges of PDF involvement in drug and arms trafficking, money laundering and the death of Hugo Spadafora.

Casey personally lobbied to have the amendment quashed, calling senators and getting the help of allies such as Senator Paul Laxalt to delay the vote. Helms received two angry calls from Casey, demanding that he pull back the amendment.

"You don't understand. You are destroying our policy. There are some things you don't know about, things Noriega is doing for the United States," Casey said.

"Fine, come up and tell me about them," Helms replied, but said he wouldn't withdraw the amendment. Casey got angrier, shouting that it was "demeaning" to the CIA to have to answer such inquiries. Then he hung up.

The Helms amendment, fighting the tide of administration opposition, passed by the slim margin of 53–46, thanks to the support of liberals such as Senator John Kerry, a cosponsor, and Edward

Kennedy. The amendment received little attention at the time, and the CIA "report," one and a half pages long submitted the following March, yielded nothing of substance. The Helms initiative, however, marked the beginning of what in the coming year became a phalanx of nearly unanimous congressional opposition to Noriega's rule.

During the fall of 1986, as Noriega was enlisting help from Oliver North, the Justice Department was acting on new, important developments that pushed knowledge about the drug-trafficking charges against Noriega high up into the DEA, the FBI and the attorney general's office.

Marijuana smuggler Steven Kalish had been in jail since his arrest in July 1984, but had not yet gone to trial. Following César Rodríguez's death, Kalish had sent a secret letter to Noriega, promising to keep their relationship out of his case and warning Noriega about incriminating documents he knew to exist in César Rodríguez's files. But in the spring of 1986, Kalish learned that he was about to be indicted in three states on drug smuggling and tough criminal conspiracy counts. With his past convictions and bail violations, Kalish realized that he would most likely spend the rest of his life in jail. He began to undergo the moral transformation not uncommon to criminal suspects on the eve of conviction. He hired a new, savvy Washington lawyer and instructed him to get a plea bargain. Kalish's part of the bargain, he said, was to provide information on his lucrative partnerships with and payments to Manuel Noriega.

Attorney Sam Buffone outlined what Kalish had to say about Noriega in a letter to Associate Attorney General Steven Trott of the Justice Department. Trott was also in charge of the administration's interagency task force on money laundering. Buffone's letter reminded Trott of a new antidrug law requiring Justice Department action on cases involving possible charges against foreign officials. On Friday, September 19, 1986, Kalish was brought to a remote and heavily guarded compound at Camp LeJeune, a Marine base in North Carolina. He spent three hours undergoing questioning by agents of the DEA, the FBI and Customs and by an assistant U.S. attorney from a district where Kalish faced charges.

The following Tuesday, Kalish was brought to Washington to

meet with Trott. He expected the offer of a reduced sentence. Instead, after spending the day across the street from the main Justice Department building, he was finally told that there would be no meeting, and no deal in exchange for his cooperation on Noriega. "Sorry, we're your friends; others in the government are not. We want to go forward on this, but you'll have to let us work it out," one of the U.S. attorneys said apologetically. Whether the "others" in the government blocking Kalish's cooperation had anything to do with the actions by North and Casey could not be learned.

Meanwhile, Floyd Carlton was sitting in a dirty San José jail as extradition papers moved slowly through the Costa Rican court system. He also was in touch with Noriega, who sent him messages to sit tight, "not to say anything, to keep quiet." Noriega promised Carlton that the most he would have to spend in prison in the United States was five years and that he would use his influence to get him out. But Carlton's letters back were increasingly harsh. After César's death, there could be no more trusting. Later he summed up his feelings about Noriega: "You're near him and you feel death near to you. That person inspires you with terror."

So in January 1987, when Carlton was finally put on a plane to the United States, his reaction was "Thank God." He smoked menthol cigarettes and talked to DEA agents Dan Moritz and Ken Kennedy, who had come to pick him up, as if they were old friends. He worried about getting his wife and kids safely to Miami. The idea of standing up in court and talking about Noriega in public filled him with terror. But he told Moritz and Kennedy he would consider it.

In Panama, Noriega was applying another lesson learned from Torrijos. He fine-tuned his repression of the opposition, keeping them off balance and taking advantage of their infighting, faintheartedness and lack of grass-roots organizations. He targeted three articulate newspapermen—La Prensa owner Roberto Eisenmann, En Pocas Palabras columnist Guillermo Sánchez Borbón and leftist writer Miguel Antonio Bernal—who were attempting to convert the U.S. attacks into an anti-Noriega movement. He maneuvered them into voluntary exile through a combination of anonymous threats and legal action, using tough libel laws skewed to protect the military.

Nevertheless, the volley of attacks and the U.S. decision to minimize its contacts with him took their toll on Noriega's relations with
his civilian allies in the PRD—the Torrijista party—and the conservative business sector represented by President Delvalle. Delvalle had
never had a close relationship with Noriega, and his elite bearing put
him on the far side of that invisible divide in Panama's class and
racial politics. It was perhaps inevitable that, during a period of such
strain, Noriega would suspect that he was being undermined by his
seemingly compliant president. Delvalle had given the key post of
ambassador to the United States to his closest associate, Kaisar
Bazán, a man with presidential ambitions. Bazán had patched things
up for Delvalle in Washington—replacing the aborted interview with
President Reagan with a friendly meeting in October with Secretary
of State Shultz. Delvalle seemed to be gaining at Noriega's expense.
In November, Noriega attempted to tighten the reins on Delvalle. He
forced a cabinet shake-up to bring in more dependable, promilitary
ministers. He served notice that he wanted his own man as ambassador to the United States. And Noriega fired one of Delvalle's most
astute political advisers, a Torrijista stalwart and PRD insider
named José Blandón.

As 1987 began, Panama on the surface betrayed barely a ripple of
unrest. Delvalle had managed to pull together a package of economic
reforms that satisfied Panama's international creditors and passed
the assembly without major opposition. The economy had turned
upward, with modest but firm growth in 1985 and 1986. Exports were
up; unemployment was inching down. Successful renegotiations had
led to an IMF agreement that had brought foreign debt payments
under control. Prospects for 1987 were even better.

Noriega's strained relations with the United States began to ease.
The Southcom chief, General John Galvin, set up a series of meetings
with Noriega and top officers on Central America. The meetings
took place in the most secure part of Southcom headquarters, the
underground bunker known as the "tunnel" at Quarry Heights.
Ambassador Arthur Davis, optimistic that a transition to democracy
was again on track, initiated regular breakfast meetings with
Noriega.

Noriega's relations with the DEA had never been better. His

antinarcotics unit was an integral part of an operation described as "nothing less than the largest and most successful undercover investigation in federal drug law enforcement history." Operation Pisces was concluded that spring with the arrests of 115 traffickers and the seizure of 10,000 pounds of cocaine and $49 million in assets. Among those indicted were Pablo Escobar and Fabio Ochoa, Jorge Ochoa's father.

Panama was credited with forty of the arrests and the freezing of fifty-two suspected money-laundering accounts in eighteen Panamanian banks. Attorney General Edwin Meese, with Panamanian Attorney General Carlos Villalaz standing beside him, announced the success at a May 6 press conference that heaped praise on Panama's cooperation. "Operation Pisces could not have achieved the great success it has without the assistance of the government of Panama. Officials from Mr. Villalaz's government met with individuals from our government during the past six months to develop a joint strategy. Panama merits the highest commendation for its exceptional initiative and performance during Operation Pisces," Meese said.

For the DEA's officer in Panama, Fred Duncan, the operation was solid evidence that Noriega's cooperation was genuine. Starting in 1984, at U.S. request Noriega's men had turned over dozens of traffickers. The U.S. Coast Guard was allowed virtually instantaneous clearance, resulting in the boarding of more than two hundred ships of Panamanian registry and the confiscation of 1,000 tons of marijuana and 31 tons of cocaine.

Operation Pisces required the DEA to trust completely that Noriega's antinarcotics unit, led by Captain Luis Quiel and DENI chief Nivaldo Madriñan, would not compromise secret information. Quiel and his men were told the names of DEA undercover agents and had helped them set up secret meetings in Panama. Eleven days before the arrests were made and bank accounts seized, the DEA turned over a three-inch-thick brief on the entire case, detailing the names of suspects and the evidence against them. The Panamanians carried out the arrests and seizures without a hitch. The DEA concluded that none of the information given to the Panamanians had been leaked or otherwise compromised.

DEA administrator Jack Lawn rewarded Noriega with a glowing letter of commendation—known as an "attaboy" in international law enforcement circles. And more important, the annual report of the State Department's International Narcotics Matters Division certified that Panama "fully cooperated" with U.S. antinarcotics efforts.

Organized opposition to Noriega and the Delvalle government was at a low ebb in the spring of 1987. The political parties had sunk into immobility. Arnulfo Arias, holding tightly to his party despite his waning health, spoke out bombastically but infrequently against Noriega. His former vice presidential candidate, Carlos Rodríguez, had moved back to Miami to run his business, Dadeland Bank, in partnership with newly exiled Roberto Eisenmann. The most active leader was Christian Democrat Ricardo Arias Calderón, who kept up a steady stream of denunciations, reports and meetings with the basic theme of forcing the government and the PDF to recognize Arnulfo Arias as president. But the Christian Democrats had little organization outside of Panama City, and Arias Calderón's shrill attacks were easily brushed aside with ERSA press jibes playing on his nickname, *La Monja Loca*—the crazy nun.

A new opposition began to take shape, a group of mostly young businessmen and professionals in such organizations as the Chamber of Commerce, the Panamanian Association of Business Executives (APEDE) and the Confederation of Business Executives (CONEP), even the Lions and Rotary clubs. They saw no point in continuing to go head to head with the military over the 1984 fraud. They began to seek a new, longer range strategy to wrest power from the PDF. There seemed to be little chance of changing the government, much less affect the PDF's domination over it, until the next presidential elections, scheduled for 1989.

"We had come to the conclusion we could not overthrow the government," said Eduardo Vallarino, then president of APEDE. "Our long-term goals [of restoring democracy] meant we needed more personal contact with the military officers. At the same time we intended to bring into the open the increasing militarization, to make an issue of military control of civilian institutions."

An annual APEDE-sponsored conference on April 25 took as its theme "the role of the military in the defense and recovery of the Canal" and gave the young leaders an opportunity to try out their new, less confrontational tactics. To their satisfaction, Noriega accepted their invitation to address the conference and brought several of his top officers with him. He gave a speech designed to offend nobody, then took the entire board of APEDE to a reception he had prepared on the second floor of the hotel, the Riande, where the conference was taking place.

Noriega was affable, dispensing effusive *abrazos* and handshakes to the business leaders. He retired to a private room with three of them, "Eddie" Vallarino, Chamber of Commerce president Aurelio "Yeyo" Barria and Chinchoro Cárdenas. They talked frankly about the elections, still three years away.

"We'll be neutral. But we don't want the game played like it was in Argentina if the other team wins," Noriega said, referring to Argentina's civilian government's attempts to prosecute that country's military for corruption and abuses of human rights.

"Don't worry," Vallarino replied, keeping the metaphor. "Our goals are limited. We'll play the Panamanian game. We won't put the referee on trial."

The only discordant note in the atmosphere of good feeling at the APEDE conference was an outburst by Colonel Roberto Díaz Herrera, who took the floor to denounce the businessmen for joining the Yankee campaign against Panama. "This meeting doesn't have anything to do with the defense of the Canal. It should be called 'How to overthrow General Noriega.'" He passed up the drinking and back-slapping with Noriega and the opposition businessmen. Some of those who knew him noted how thin Díaz Herrera looked, and the uncommon intensity of his eyes.

Díaz Herrera had faded from public view since his unsuccessful attempt to ignite a military coup against Noriega after Spadafora's death. He remained the number-two officer in the PDF, as chief of the general staff. But rumors were rampant that he had been pushed out of any channels of real power. Noriega himself was the source of some of the rumors, confiding to several U.S. officers in the fall of 1986 that Díaz Herrera was about to be retired. By early 1987, Díaz

Herrera had become the butt of jokes and had all but ceased attending the daily general staff meetings.

Díaz Herrera's eclipse was viewed with relief in U.S. government circles. He had always been seen as a dangerous leftist, even as procommunist—a perception Noriega had helped shape. He was the PDF's most politically active officer, and any short list of future presidential candidates included him. He was consistently more strident than Noriega in his criticisms of the displaced *rabiblancos,* and Díaz Herrera's political base was seen as firmly established in the left-of-center wing of the PRD, whose meetings he seldom missed.

His relative silence was taken in civilian quarters as evidence of undercover efforts to position himself for the presidency in 1989. In fact, Díaz Herrera was undergoing a profound physical and psychological transformation that had its roots in his losing rivalry with Noriega.

"I was feeling more and more isolated," he said. "You start to notice when the ministers don't return your calls like they used to, when they start to go around you. They sensed that I no longer had power. It got harder and harder for me to pretend. I had been very active; I had my own group, my own following. And suddenly I found myself thrust aside, unable to do anything. I fell into a crisis of depression—it was a normal reaction. Every man has his emotional curve, and that was my moment to be depressed."

His physician suggested that he see a psychiatrist, Dr. Jaime Arroyo, who had served in one of Torrijos's cabinets. Arroyo prescribed an antidepressant, which Díaz Herrera found helped immensely. He gathered new energy and began to reflect on what had become of his life and his ideals. He had become rich by using his power for such corrupt deals as a scam to sell Panamanian visas to thousands of Cubans seeking to enter the United States. He was getting fat from too much drinking and eating, and he was in danger of losing his beautiful Venezuelan wife and three small children because of his barely disguised womanizing. Jolted out of this path by failure, he began what he described as a "search for myself."

His wife, Maigualida, had met a California woman in one of her trips to Buenos Aires and was introduced to yoga and the life and teachings of a famous Indian guru, Sai Baba. Díaz Herrera had at first laughed at her esoteric interests, then was attracted to the stories of the guru's power. Sai Baba, still in his fifties, was renowned for his ability to manipulate matter—to bend bars, to materialize coins and chocolates from his bare hands and to be in two places at once. Special power was imputed to his pictures, which hung in the houses and offices of millions of his followers and were said to exude a fine sacred ash.

Díaz Herrera invited Indira Devi, an eighty-six-year-old disciple of Sai Baba's, to come to Panama and sent an Air Force plane to get her. He also brought Californian Shama Calhoun, an attractive woman of thirty-six who was reputed to be a psychic. Díaz Herrera learned yoga exercises, deep breathing and meditation. He and his wife went on a strict vegetarian diet. He spent most of his time at home, a born-again family man.

By May, Díaz Herrera had lost thirty-six pounds and had gained the special faraway look of the recently enlightened. His military colleagues were intrigued, and some inquired about his *brujo*, his shaman or witchdoctor, and compared notes with their own. But most of those who knew him thought he had gone off the deep end: A wealthy colonel who stopped drinking, ate tofu and was faithful to his wife—he must be crazy.

When Noriega summoned him to headquarters on May 25, a Monday, Díaz Herrera knew what was coming, and he was ready. "People asked me if I was ill, but I had never felt so well in my life. My blood pressure was one-ten over seventy. I had a feeling of great vitality, as if I were a boxer at his best weight. I had incredible endurance. I didn't have an ounce of fat on me," he said.

Noriega had gathered almost the entire general staff in his office on the second floor—among them Colonels Marcos Justine, who had been a close friend, Elías Castillo, the tough professional with little appetite for politics, G2 chief Bernardo Barrera, and Leonidas Macias, the chief of police. Noriega was brief. Díaz Herrera had to go. He was a bad example and was sowing dissension among the young officers. The new chief of staff would be Justine.

"Work out the details with the boys here. I have an overseas call to attend to," he said and walked out.

The "details" included orchestrating a graceful, and profitable, exit for Díaz Herrera so that he would follow in the tradition of discarded Panamanian leaders who went out quietly. The negotiations went on for a week, with Díaz Herrera enlisting as mediator an influential friend from the Dominican Republic, José Francisco Peña Gómez, a vice president of the Socialist International. The package Peña Gómez worked out included a promotion to general before retirement in thirty days, a full-scale, public ceremony honoring his departure and an appointment as consul in Okinawa, Japan—a post said to offer the opportunity of earning hundreds of thousands in "fees."

Díaz Herrera was told that Noriega had agreed. On June 1 the PDF Order of the Day carried the announcement of Díaz Herrera's retirement. Díaz Herrera made a last peaceful visit to clean out his office at headquarters and said good-bye to his staff.

The next day, Friday, June 5, a friend called Díaz Herrera from PDF headquarters. "Be careful," he said. "Noriega has backed out of the agreement. He is preparing an announcement of your dishonorable discharge from the PDF for publication on Monday." No promotion, no ceremony, and Noriega's people were already putting out the story that Díaz Herrera's retirement was necessary because he was mentally ill.

That was all Díaz Herrera needed. He called Channel 13 and asked if they would be interested in interviewing him. His first statements that night were relatively mild. He referred to Noriega's rule as "incidental, momentary" in Panama's history and called for a revival of the ideals of Torrijismo. "We want a PDF that will not meddle in partisan politics and will not remove or install presidents, something that has indeed been done," he said, in the closest approximation to an accusation.

The next day, spurred by a Noriega rejoinder that he planned to stay on as commander for five more years, Díaz Herrera gathered a small group of local journalists at his house and talked for hours on tape. Unlike his predecessors in disgrace—presidents Royo, de la Espriella and Barletta, Colonel Florez and General Paredes, Díaz Herrera struck back at Noriega. He used the only weapon left to an officer stripped of command: his knowledge of the secrets of the PDF and Noriega.

His confession came with great difficulty, as he sipped coffee with the reporters in his study. After so many years of half truths and outright lies, he seemed to have lost the ability to make a direct statement. He rambled and circled around his subject, never raising his voice. He began without waiting for a question, making an ironic aside about Sai Baba as his "secret weapon" that had the superstitious Noriega worried. He touched on the death of Omar Torrijos, saying that his friend Francisco Peña Gómez had spoken with Torrijos twice from beyond the grave and that Torrijos had said he had been the victim of an assassination. "But I don't want to talk about that. I am not going to talk in depth about any of these things, unless it is before the attorney general of the Republic and with witnesses present.

"But there are things that could be ventilated," he said, then, in response to the insinuations that had already appeared in the ERSA press, looped into a defense of his mental health. Finally, when he got down to it, he accused himself first:

"Look at this millionaire's house. It's half stolen. Sure, I got this house with money from people who came from Cuba, with visas, and since I was on the general staff, I could sign for that, and they gave me part of the money. But that was just my share. There were two other shares in the deal. *Hombre,* around here if you get too honest, you get in trouble. Torrijos used to tell me, Roberto, don't be silly. Nobody is chemically pure. If you're too pure, you'll catch every cold that comes by.

"So that's why I say that this house is half stolen. Maybe they'll have to take it away. But if they do, we're going to take away a lot of things in this country."

Purged of his own sin, his quiet anger rose and he became righteous. "I'm ready to talk about things. Things like the death of Spadafora, about the death of Torrijos and other things." Once started, he didn't stop talking for days in a marathon of interviews and press conferences. Among his charges: The 1984 electoral fraud was planned at his house with the participation of Nicolás Barletta and members of the electoral tribunal; Spadafora's murder was carried out by officers of the PDF Chiriquí garrison, Luis Córdoba and Mario del Cid, and supervised from Europe by General Noriega;

Torrijos's assassination was the result of a plot in which Noriega was directly involved, along with the CIA, General Wallace Nutting, who was chief of Southcom at the time, and Ricardo Arias Calderón; Torrijos received $12 million from the shah of Iran after giving him asylum in Panama, and the money remained in a secret Swiss bank account.

About the suspicions that Noriega was a drug trafficker, Díaz Herrera said he knew nothing. "I can't give any evidence [on that], and I hope and I don't believe there is any," he said.

Noriega called Díaz Herrera's statements "high treason . . . assassination because it comes from the bosom of the institution. We could forgive any sniper or enemy, but we cannot forgive a man who was fed, protected, and overfed by the institution, paternally taken care of by that man Torrijos, who . . . tried to make him one of his disciples."

Díaz Herrera was ordered to report to headquarters. Instead, he surrounded himself with a half dozen loyal soldiers armed with automatic rifles, brought an electricity generator into his house, filled the swimming pool with water and made his house the center of a rebellion against Noriega.

The reaction to Díaz Herrera's charges rose from some forgotten reservoir of outrage in the Panamanian people. Without anyone in the opposition parties or otherwise calling for public demonstrations, Panamanians by the thousands took to the streets. Every day for a week, they marched, chanted, barricaded the streets of Panama City and finally broke out in rioting as Noriega's special police units, with pictures of bare-fanged Doberman pinschers painted on their trucks, moved in with truncheons and tear gas.

By midweek, Panama was on the front pages and television screens of the world. Díaz Herrera's luxurious home in Altos del Golf—not far from Noriega's—became a mecca for priests, opposition leaders, diplomats, journalists and hundreds of young people sensing that the gaunt former colonel was doing something to change their country's destiny. Díaz Herrera began to dress in white and carried a Bible during all of his press appearances. He invited dozens of young people to spread out their sleeping bags on his front patio, behind the high stucco walls and iron gate that now, topped with sentinels and

barbed wire, made the house a fortress. He held prayer and meditation sessions and taught his new followers breathing techniques.

The archbishop of Panama, Marcos McGrath, arranged for several priests to stay at the house to provide a measure of protection—
asking in exchange that Díaz Herrera's men turn over their weapons.
Winston Spadafora, Hugo's brother, moved in and stayed for four
days. Noriega's troops at first surrounded the house, then pulled
back.

The opposition parties were taken by surprise. None had lamented
Díaz Herrera's departure. A Christian Democratic legislator, Arrel-
lano Lenox, praised his ouster as furthering the democratization of
the country because Díaz Herrera was a hard-liner who symbolized
PDF interference in politics. Now predictably the opposition parties
stuttered that he was saying what they had been saying all along.

Arnulfo Arias was one of the few party leaders who did not hang
back. With characteristic machismo he rode into the middle of a
battle between protesters and police outside an opposition radio
station, then announced he was going to march on the presidential
palace. Ricardo Arias Calderón also faced the police charges in the
streets and was beaten and briefly arrested.

But the people's outrage could not be contained or channeled by
the parties' narrow agendas. Through an accident of circumstances,
the initiative passed to the young businessmen and professionals who
so recently had clinked glasses with Noriega at the APEDE conference.

Chamber of Commerce President Aurelio Barria, a thirty-year-old
owner of a cigar factory and a small import-export firm, had just
returned from a trip to the Philippines sponsored by the U.S. National Endowment for Democracy (NED). He and several other
Panamanians had joined a Chilean delegation in an effort to learn
from and emulate the Philippines electoral monitoring organization,
Namfrel, which had played such an important role in the movement
against the government of Ferdinand Marcos.

A Panamanian Namfrel, combining a broad, nonpartisan citizens'
movement with technical methods to prevent fraud, was seen as key
to ensuring that the 1989 elections would finally bring democracy to
Panama. The Philippines parallel was encouraged by the energetic

new deputy chief of mission at the U.S. embassy, John Maisto, who had served in the Philippines prior to his transfer to Panama in late 1986 and had helped organize Panamanian participation in the tour.

Returning a few days before Díaz Herrera was forced into retirement, Barria had already convened meetings of numerous civic organizations and representatives of the Catholic Church to form the new organization, which was to be called MODELO. On Monday, June 8, the first day of the riots against Noriega, Barria and a few friends moved decisively to seize the opportunity. They met with the same organizations—twenty-six in all. They hammered out a plan of action and a name change and the next day announced the formation of the Civic Crusade for Justice and Democracy, with headquarters in Barria's Chamber of Commerce building in central Panama City.

The Civic Crusade's first statement demanded that all government officials implicated in Díaz Herrera's denunciations, including Noriega, step down pending a full investigation. To enforce their demand, the Civic Crusade called for an immediate campaign of civil disobedience, including refusal to pay taxes and public utility bills. Then they called on all citizens and businesses to take part in a nationwide sit-down strike beginning Thursday.

Smoke from tear gas and burning barricades hung over the city that day as rioting spread from the boarded-up commercial district to the working-class residential district of San Miguelito, which was considered a Torrijista bastion. President Delvalle declared a "state of urgency" and suspended civil liberties. More than one hundred people were arrested and herded into a makeshift "prison" in the bankrupt Panama Hilton Hotel.

The protesters, now responding to general guidance of the Civic Crusade, waved white handerchiefs as the symbol of their movement and banged pots and pans as its chorus. As the demonstrations became less spontaneous, they took on a noticeable stratification, with few people of color and few poor people among protesters clad now in gleaming white blouses and designer jeans. Crusade propaganda also fell into ridiculing Noriega's physical appearance, which could easily be interpreted—by those Panamanians who didn't count themselves among the country's beautiful people—as racist or at best as vicious insensitivity. Posters and pamphlets exaggerated Noriega's lips and nose and acne scars. A favorite picture in Crusade propaganda leaflets showed a white woman leaning out a window of a whizzing new Land-Rover waving a white handkerchief in one hand and holding a pineapple in the other.

For a brief moment, it looked as if Noriega might be tottering. He had been unable to follow through on his order that Díaz Herrera be arrested, and a formidable new opposition organization had for the first time mobilized mass protests of the kind that had not been seen since the anti-American riots of 1964. But whatever sympathy Díaz Herrera and his rebellion may have awakened among those who considered themselves followers of Torrijos, there was no evidence of it inside the PDF and the PRD, which rallied in support of Noriega. That weekend, Noriega flamboyantly convened a press conference in faraway David—a secure venue fraught with the memories of his one heroic moment, when he saved Torrijos from a coup in 1969. His press people summoned fifty journalists to Paitilla Airport, where they were loaded on planes chartered by Noriega and flown 250 miles to Chiriquí.

There, he declared that the country was "tending to return to normality" and spoke vaguely of the need for "reconciliation" and "dialogue." He then gave an ideological spin to the week's events. The crisis was caused by "the same ones who lost power in 1968" working together with U.S. "conservative groups" upset with Panama because of its failure to support a widening of the war in Central America. Theirs was a dangerous game intended to keep Panama from removing "the last stake of colonialism," but it could backfire: "We have been trying to prevent this from turning into a class struggle. But we see already that it is degenerating into a struggle between black and white, between rich and poor. But [they should keep in mind that] here there are more blacks than whites, more poor people than rich people."

Noriega also assured the American reporters present that there was no "confrontation" with the United States because of the crisis. And he praised Ambassador Davis's "tact" in resisting opposition efforts "to portray him as waving the flag of their movement."

The U.S. government had indeed reacted mildly to the Díaz Herrera affair. An embassy statement said, "The United States strongly supports the efforts of Panamanians to get all the facts out in the open in a manner that is fair to all." But Noriega's barely veiled appeal to the United States to at least remain neutral fell on fewer and fewer sympathetic ears in Washington. His strongest supporter, William Casey, had been hospitalized since December and had died of cancer the same weekend that Díaz Herrera began to speak out. Oliver North had been dismissed from the National Security Council, and the Iran-Contra scandal was being aired in congressional hearings that summer.

Other forces against Noriega were gaining strength in Washington. On June 13, Gabriel Lewis, the former ambassador who had been instrumental in the treaty negotiations and perhaps the military government's most important business ally, fled into exile and vowed to fight for Noriega's removal "with every penny at my disposal." One of Panama's richest men, Lewis had made a fortune with land deals, a bank and a container manufacturing company. He was the developer of Panama's best-known tourist spot, Contadora Island. He had backed Nicolás Barletta with advice and cash, and he was related by marriage to President Delvalle. A round, smiling man in his fifties, Lewis took pride in having few enemies and in his ability to bridge the hostile gulf between the military and the oligarchy, of which he was a prominent member.

True to form, when the crisis exploded in Panama, Lewis had tried to mediate, convening a meeting of two of Noriega's colonels and prominent pro- and antigovernment businessmen. But the negotiations degenerated into threats and recriminations when Lewis made it clear that Noriega's retirement from the PDF was the main item on the agenda. The PDF mouthpiece, *La República,* denounced Lewis's effort as a "plot to destabilize the present government and come to power with his gang of *rabiblancos.*"

Lewis was on the phone to his old friend Senator Ted Kennedy even before he boarded the plane to go into exile. Once he landed in Washington, he was tireless, making the rounds of senators' offices, lobbying for a strong U.S. stand against Noriega. It was characteristic of his flexibility and pragmatism that he slipped easily into a working relationship with Senator Helms and his staff—his archenemies during the 1970s treaty debate. Lewis's presence removed the last vestiges of reluctance by most liberal senators to attack the Panamanian régime.

As a result, on June 26 Senate Resolution 239 was passed calling for the immediate removal of General Noriega and other Panamanian officials pending an independent investigation of the charges of murder, election fraud and corruption. Only two senators voted no. One, Chris Dodd, the Connecticut Democrat, had just returned from a fact-finding trip to Panama and argued that such a naked attack would play into Noriega's hands. Dodd was defeated in an attempt to amend the resolution so that it reaffirmed Senate support for the Canal treaties.

The Senate action ignited an explosion of anti-American feeling in Panama, where press censorship and police repression had sapped the protest movement of its momentum. The following Tuesday, five thousand progovernment demonstrators led by three cabinet ministers and several PRD legislators rallied at the Foreign Ministry, then marched to the American embassy on Balboa Avenue. After shouting slogans such as "Davis out now" and "No to Gringo intervention," a group of about twenty young men began to throw stones at windows and at cars in the embassy parking lot. They moved down the street and attacked the office of the U.S. Information Service, whose windows, unlike those at the embassy, were not protected by metal grates. U.S. officials later charged that the stone-throwers had been paid $20 each for their participation in the attack. Ambassador Davis, in a diplomatic note, blamed the government for "dereliction of responsibility" and suspended payments of all grant aid to the PDF.

Three days later, another mob torched the upscale department store, Maison Dante, owned by exiled newspaperman Roberto Eisenmann. The new violence rekindled the somnolent protest movement—a general strike was declared and several weeks of demonstrations followed. But most important, the attacks identified the United States, or at least the U.S. embassy, with the crusade to remove Noriega. *La Prensa* and opposition groups cheered the Senate action as a sign that the United States was finally severing its ties with Noriega. An embassy cable noted that for the first time in memory a group of students—traditionally the most ardent nationalists—had marched down Balboa Avenue tearing down anti-American banners.

In Washington, where the Senate resolution had passed over objections of the administration, U.S. officials began incorporating a new anti-Noriega line in press briefings. They gave a stiffer spin to a semitough speech by Assistant Secretary Elliott Abrams that happened to be scheduled for the night of the attack on the embassy.

"The old complacency inside and outside of Panama over the inevitable dominance of the Panamanian Defense Forces in the nation's politics is gone. . . . Military leaders must remove their institution from politics, end any appearance of corruption and modernize their forces to carry out their large and important military tasks in defense of the Canal," Abrams told the Washington Foreign Affairs Council. He did not mention Noriega by name, but the briefers called the speech the "strongest" and "harshest" signal to date of Washington's growing "impatience."

Panama had suddenly leaped to a top spot on the U.S. foreign policy agenda. A RIG—restricted interagency group composed of senior officials from State, CIA, NSC and Defense—began to meet regularly on Panama, and officials were instructed to prepare contingency plans in the event of Noriega's removal. And a new aspect—seen as a complication by some officials—became known at the senior levels of the administration: the possibility that criminal charges for drug trafficking might soon be brought against Noriega in a U.S. court.

Steven Kalish had finally persuaded the U.S. attorney's office in Tampa, Florida, to allow him to plead guilty to lesser charges in exchange for his testimony on Noriega. It wasn't a great deal—Kalish's maximum sentence still stood at twenty years.

Kalish wasn't complaining. Gilchrist County Jail in the flatlands of northern Florida was a laid-back place, as jails go. The prisoners, most of them state witnesses under protection like himself, could cook their own meals and spend time alone with their wives and girlfriends. The exercise yard had a fence around it, but the fence was broken. Nobody worried much that these men would run away.

But what Kalish couldn't understand was why the prosecutors had made the deal and then had done nothing about it. He hadn't talked about Noriega to anyone from the prosecutor's office since March, when he agreed to testify. He had records and documents, but no one had asked to see them.

Suddenly, in late June, two assistant U.S. attorneys from Tampa and three other federal agents from the FBI and Customs showed up at the jail. They had their orders, and they were in a hurry. They spent all day with Kalish and part of the next, going over everything about Noriega. It was the most intense questioning he had undergone since he first offered to talk about Noriega almost a year before. Kalish had to be ready to go before a grand jury, they said. Then they left to write up their reports and have them ready for a meeting at the Justice Department on Monday morning.

Floyd Carlton's processing as a witness had also taken its good time, although he was never long without the company of his DEA interrogators. At first, Carlton insisted that he would be glad to tell them all he knew about Noriega, but he refused to go before a grand jury, much less appear in open court.

As soon as Carlton was brought in, the senior assistant U.S. attorney, Dick Gregorie, took over the case and briefed his boss, Leon Kellner, about the international politics involved. Sensitive cases were daily fare in Miami, and Kellner was a veteran of the internecine warfare in the U.S. government between national security/intelligence interests and law enforcement. In a city that was home to anti-Castro Cubans, former CIA assets, Nicaraguan Contras and covert operations both sanctioned and unsanctioned by Washington, the U.S. attorney in Miami needed a politician's instincts as much as a prosecutor's.

Both Kellner and Gregorie came from the North; Kellner was a New York corporate lawyer, Gregorie a veteran prosecutor who had specialized in organized crime in Boston and New Jersey. Kellner's office had handled the largest narcotics cases ever brought in the United States, including two indictments against cartel leaders Jorge Ochoa and Pablo Escobar, and Kellner was not shy about talking on the evening news. That earned him a bit of a reputation as a silk-suit showboat—"Neon Leon" they called him in Miami.

In 1986, one of Kellner's assistant U.S. attorneys had attempted to assemble a criminal case against Oliver North's arms resupply network. Kellner, with Gregorie's concurrence, reversed the junior prosecutor's recommendation to bring the gun-running allegations to the grand jury, and the case was delayed until it was splashed on the front pages along with the other revelations of the Iran-Contra scandal. The accounts of the aborted prosecution portrayed Kellner as complying with the request of his superiors in the Meese Justice Department, who purportedly were protecting a pet administration project. Kellner and Gregorie defended the decision to delay the case on its merits—that the junior prosecutor had built a jumbled case on unprovable supposition. But the suspicion stuck to Kellner's otherwise stellar record as the front-line U.S. prosecutor in the war against drugs.

And once burned, Kellner and Gregorie were twice shy. The Noriega case could have been handled in one of two ways: flashing a signal immediately to the Justice Department that a key Central American general was under investigation for drug running, or keeping a low profile until it was so firmly developed that it would be invulnerable to pressure from Washington. Gregorie and Kellner went with the latter approach.

"Nobody in Washington told Dick Gregorie to stop," Gregorie said. "Nobody said it was okay to go forward either. I just went ahead. I figured the more people up there that knew about it, the more heat that was put on, the more likely somebody high up in the administration was going to say, 'Hey, you can't do this.' "

So Gregorie didn't send up any flags when Floyd Carlton finally agreed, under some stiff threats of spending a lot of time in jail, to testify against Noriega. Just about the time when Díaz Herrera was throwing Panama into a crisis, Carlton was spending ten hours a day telling his story to two DEA agents in a windowless interrogation room called the Submarine. Dan Moritz had been transferred to Cleveland shortly after bringing Carlton back from Costa Rica, and he had been replaced by another young agent, Steven Grilli, who conducted the questioning with the help of a Spanish-speaking agent, Alberto Hernández. Gregorie attended the sessions for several hours each day. The three weeks in the Submarine left them all pasty faced from lack of daylight.

Carlton had all the signs of a strong witness. With remarkable detail, he led them through the many years of his relationship with Noriega, from the time Noriega had shot a farmer's horse in Chiriquí and Carlton, then a young court clerk, had helped him by destroying the records on the case. Carlton had a straightforward way of talking and an extraordinary memory for detail. Dates of trips he had taken years before were checked against his passport, and he was seldom more than a day or two off. His interrogators lectured him on the meaning of "hearsay" and its uselessness in court, and Carlton learned the lesson so well he would apologize when he provided details he didn't know firsthand.

For Carlton, the long sessions were a cathartic reprise of his life. Unlike many turncoat criminals who recite their stories with moral detachment, Carlton fell into episodes of bitter self-accusation followed by spells of sobbing. His breakdowns were most intense when the questioning involved his relationship with Hugo Spadafora. He begged to be spared having to testify on that subject and was told that it was of little direct relevance to the drug charges against Noriega and most likely would not come up in a trial. Grilli and Gregorie had the impression that the Spadafora murder was the one area in which Carlton seemed to have a lot of information he was holding back.

For all Carlton's promise of being a credible witness, Gregorie knew he was still only at the beginning of building a case to indict Noriega. Besides Carlton, he had only one other witness who claimed to have had firsthand drug dealings with Noriega. That witness was Tony Aizprua, whose spectacular landing of a planeload of cocaine on Miami's I-75 had been a decisive element in building the case against Carlton's smuggling group. But Aizprua had what was delicately referred to as a "polygraph problem"—a lie detector indicated he might be lying on the key allegations about his contacts with Noriega. And Carlton, for all his credibility, was still a felon with an incentive to make it easier on himself by implicating a bigger fish.

Gregorie knew he had a strong case, but he also knew he needed more than that; he needed an invulnerable case. He wanted to indict a man who was in effect a sitting head of state, one of the most powerful men in Central America. "If you're going to shoot the king," Gregorie liked to say, "you'd better have a very big gun."

CHAPTER 12

BULLETS
ARE KISSES

Noriega had caught the attention of another U.S. official investigation about the time Díaz Herrera began to speak out. Since early 1986, Senator John Kerry of Massachusetts had waged a lonely and much derided campaign to document allegations of drug trafficking and other forms of corruption by the U.S.-backed Contras. His small team of investigators, working out of Kerry's Senate office and lacking subpoena power, was among those who first pointed to the possibility that the activities of Oliver North were in violation of the Boland amendment ban on aiding the Contras.

When the Senate again came under Democratic control, in January 1987, Kerry moved his investigation to the Foreign Relations Subcommittee on Terrorism, Narcotics and International Communications, which Kerry chaired. By February, a new staff—still only two people, but bolstered by the subcommittee's subpoena power— was working under a new, no-holds-barred investigator.

Jack Blum had the deceptively easygoing demeanor of a tavern keeper combined with the rumpled savvy of a police reporter. He had grown up in New Jersey with an ornery disrespect for the pomposities of big business and secret government, which he suspected would cheat and rob freely if not watched closely. Since the 1960s he had been ferreting out scandals and exposing international corruption for Senate committees. He had investigated ITT covert operations in

Chile, overseas bribes by Lockheed Aircraft and the banking scams of Robert Vesco.

Blum moved the subcommittee investigation away from the narrowly defined Contra-related corruption to broader issues of drug trafficking in Central America and the Caribbean. Working his way through interviews with imprisoned drug pilots willing to talk about their exploits, he soon started hearing about Panama. In March, Blum had interviewed a young Cuban-American accountant named Ramón Milian Rodríguez, who claimed to have laundered hundreds of millions of dollars of cartel drug money through Panama. Milian, serving a forty-four-year sentence in a North Carolina prison, had been arrested in 1983 as he attempted to fly out of the country with a suitcase containing $5.4 million. In his interview with Blum, Milian said he personally had negotiated an agreement with Noriega to pay a commission ranging from 1½ to 3 percent in exchange for Noriega's protection and other services in Panama. According to Milian, Noriega was skimming up to $10 million from the monthly flow of $200 million of cartel cash through Panama.

The allegations that Blum was hearing about Noriega made the Contra-related drug transactions seem penny ante—a few pilots double dipping by flying guns in to the Contras then using the same planes and the same airfields to fly drugs out. But he found no pattern that major Contra leaders were colluding in the drug trafficking or evidence that the CIA was turning a blind eye to the trafficking going on around them. Milian was brought to Washington in late June for two days of closed-door testimony before Kerry's subcommittee. With Panama on the front pages every day, it took little to convince Kerry to make Panama and Noriega the main target of Blum's investigation.

There was another, more political side to the shift from Contras and drugs to Noriega and drugs. From Kerry's perspective, the fight against drugs was overshadowing the political struggle to block the Reagan administration's Contra policy. The past year had seen a dramatic focus of attention on cocaine addiction and the new menace, crack. Kerry was one of the first senators to look critically at the foreign policy and national security aspects of the misnamed war on drugs, and the Noriega issue seemed ideal to bring those issues to the fore. Unlike the fight to defund the Contras, Kerry knew that opposition to drugs and Noriega crossed party lines. An alliance between the Massachusetts liberal and Jesse Helms was not only incongruous, but it promised to be a juggernaut no other Washington power center could withstand.

If Kerry and Helms made strange political bedfellows, Helms's aide Deborah DeMoss and Jack Blum were the odd couple. DeMoss was Helms's Central America staff person on the Foreign Affairs Committee. A petite, twenty-seven-year-old former conservatory pianist with the determination of a jackhammer operator, DeMoss showed her dedication to Helms's ideological agenda by paying for her frequent trips to Central America out of her own pocket. She had learned fluent Spanish as a girl on trips to Mexico with her father, a wealthy Pennsylvania insurance executive, on evangelical preaching tours. By 1987, her Spanish had taken on the rough accents and barracks idiom of the Contra, Honduran and Salvadoran military officers she visited. On her desk, she kept photos of herself at a Contra training camp shooting an AK47.

With DeMoss's Central American contacts and Blum's access to the law enforcement network, they teamed up to keep tabs on the Florida investigations against Noriega and developed their own witnesses for public hearings. A tense competition ensued between the Miami investigators and the Kerry team. They shared the same goal, but their methods and standards were vastly different. Unlike the prosecutors, Blum and DeMoss were not limited to investigating particular crimes they could prove in court, nor were they bound by rules of evidence or by the need to establish facts beyond a reasonable doubt. Their rules were set by politics, and their interest was public exposure with or without bringing Noriega to trial.

In early August, it became known that federal prosecutors were investigating Noriega. "The probe by a federal grand jury in Miami is being pursued despite a split within the Reagan administration about whether to press for Noriega's ouster, with CIA and Pentagon officials reportedly maintaining that the fall of the Panamanian defense chief would endanger U.S. military bases in Panama," a *Los Angeles Times* story said. The bulk of the story, however, described the allegations made by Ramón Milian in his testimony before the

Kerry subcommittee in closed session and left the erroneous impression that Milian was the key witness against Noriega.

Another story a few days later reported on the second investigation going on in Tampa. The story said that the Miami and Tampa probes had only recently become full-scale investigations, after a meeting on July 16 at the Justice Department to "pull together all we had on him to see if it was prosecutable." All three stories said an indictment of Noriega was not imminent.

The Miami investigators assumed the leaks were coming from their new congressional friends. But no vital information was compromised, and the confusion over Milian was seen as a boon. As long as Noriega thought Milian was the witness, they could breathe easier about Floyd Carlton's safety. They were familiar with Milian's many stories about Noriega and major cartel figures. Since being sentenced to thirty-five years in prison for drug, money-laundering and tax fraud charges in 1985, he had offered to cooperate a number of times. The offers were rejected for several reasons, among them that he had testified at his own trial and was thought to have committed perjury. In addition, his offers tended to coincide with newspaper stories about cases he then claimed to know from the inside.

Milian's claims that he laundered up to $200 million a month as the Medellín cartel's "chief financial officer" and that he worked personally with Noriega were seen as fanciful. He had made neither claim in his first substantive interviews with investigators and his voluminous notebooks and computer records did not substantiate the Noriega contacts or such enormous sums of money.

In Panama, President Delvalle had sunk from public view. He had become the man in an empty suit, a name on government decrees and statements but a face and voice absent from public events. Increasingly reviled by the opposition as a traitor to his business peers and a spineless PDF lackey, he was heading toward the kind of messy confrontation he had patterned his life to avoid. It was not by acute intelligence, but by good humor and gentility that Delvalle occupied the precarious perch of a conservative in a traditionally left-of-center régime, a Jew in a country where anti-Semitism was an issue in presidential elections going back to the 1940s and a Union Club aristocrat immersed in the middle-class and nouveau-riche ethos of the PRD and PDF cadres. He kept the family fortune healthy and his personal life pleasant by adhering to the thoroughly Panamanian philosophy of one hand washes the other. His family sugar business depended on the government's allocation of a near monopoly portion of Panama's sugar export quota to the United States. He had no problem with returning the favor by allocating a number of well-paid sinecures to PDF officers and other Noriega cronies. In the 1970s he had employed César Rodríguez as a pilot—before Rodríguez was involved in arms and drug trafficking. Another questionable associate was Sebastián "Wachan" González, a close friend of Noriega's who was involved in shipping arms to Edén Pastora's forces through Panama to Costa Rica in the early 1980s. Delvalle hired González, a veterinarian, to care for his thoroughbred horses after González fled Costa Rica in 1984 to avoid arrest on cocaine-smuggling charges.

The increasing violence in Panama was causing Delvalle profound embarrassment. After promilitary thugs burned the department store, Maison Dante, Delvalle was subjected to whistles and catcalls in the normally sedate bar of the Union Club. The arson was especially galling to Delvalle because his daughter was married to David Eisenmann, brother of Roberto Eisenmann, Maison Dante's owner. When he finally spoke on television July 6, Delvalle offered to open a dialogue with the opposition and ordered the attorney general to investigate the charges by Díaz Herrera, still barricaded in his Altos del Golf house. But the opposition ridiculed the idea of an investigation by the same government office that had so superficially probed the murder of Hugo Spadafora. Dialogue was out of the question until Noriega stepped down, Civic Crusade spokesmen said.

By late July, Díaz Herrera's house had ceased to attract the opposition as a point of convergence. The crowds of young people in their sleeping bags kept coming. But the Civic Crusade and opposition party leaders, who never quite overcame their disgust at pretending that their old enemy, Díaz Herrera, was an ally, made little attempt to ensure the house's defense. When a group of armed men and helicopters attacked in the early morning of July 27, Díaz Herrera's six loyal bodyguards held them off for almost two hours. Then helicopter-borne troops slid down ropes commando-style to take control of the inner courtyard and capture Díaz Herrera and his family in an upstairs bedroom. In all, forty-five people were arrested. The PDF said that nobody was killed or wounded in the attack, and Díaz Herrera supported that claim after he was released from jail five months later, to go into exile in Venezuela. But one of Díaz Herrera's bodyguards said he saw at least one person wounded and then shot point-blank by a PDF soldier during the attack. Other eyewitness reports of several deaths in the attack were mentioned in U.S. embassy cables.

Díaz Herrera, like a spent bullet, had already ceased to figure in the opposition's battle with Noriega. Four general strikes had effectively shut down economic activity, but had not appreciably weakened Noriega's resolve to remain in power. Attempts to organize mass demonstrations were met by thousands of Noriega's troops in the streets. Anti-Noriega marches were scattered by soldiers using shotguns, tear gas and clubs. Many were wounded—most by bird shot—and two people were killed by gunfire. By mid-October, the main leaders of the Civic Crusade, Aurelio Barria, Gilberto Mallol and Eduardo Vallarino, had fled into exile in the United States. When a call for a mass demonstration on October 22 drew more troops than marchers, the opposition was clearly exhausted, locked in an impasse with Noriega.

Congress kept the pressure on in Washington. Military and economic aid—only $26 million—was cut off, and the possibility of future aid was all but eliminated by a series of congressional resolutions, all passing by lopsided votes. Additional sanctions, such as cutting off Panama's sugar quota, were threatened. The crisis was causing far greater damage elsewhere, however. The country's vital banking sector had begun to hemorrhage. Assets in international banks, which had been around $41 billion in June, had dropped below $33 billion by September and to $31.4 billion by year end—a loss of 23 percent in just six months. A debt renegotiation with the Paris Club was scuttled in July, and Panama went into default on its foreign payments. The default triggered the decision in November by the World Bank and the Inter-American Development Bank to halt all disbursement of existing loans. The country's modest economic upswing of early 1987 collapsed into negative growth.

. . .

Noriega was wounded, but not down. The opposition had delivered its best shot, and it wasn't good enough to dislodge him. He seemed unfazed by U.S. displeasure and economic pressures, opposition activity seemed to make him more defiant and the prospect of his removal in a coup was remote. Clearly, it was time to think about cutting a deal.

The idea seems to have occurred almost simultaneously to two veteran Panamanian politicians and—according to one of the participants in the clandestine maneuvering that ensued—to General Noriega himself.

Sometime in mid-August, Gabriel Lewis called together a group of old friends and Panama hands he had known since his stint in Washington as Panama's ambassador in the treaty negotiation days. The group included former ambassador William Jorden, former assistant secretary of state William D. Rogers, former Carter chief of staff Hamilton Jordan, and political consultant Joel McCleary, who had been enlisted by Lewis in 1984 to give campaign advice to Nicolás Barletta.

As they sat at a finely appointed luncheon at Lewis's house on Foxhall Road, Lewis asked them to act as a "think tank" on the Panama crisis. Noriega cannot be cornered because he will just fight all the harder, Lewis argued. We have to show him an exit he can walk through honorably. After several hours of batting around options for action, the group designated Joel McCleary to coalesce their ideas into a strategic plan.

A few days later, McCleary received a call from José Blandón, the Panamanian consul in New York. They met for breakfast at the Plaza Hotel. Blandón had just returned from a trip to Panama to consult with Noriega about the crisis. Noriega had authorized him, he said, to put out feelers with U.S. officials about a possible solution to the crisis. Perhaps it was serendipity; perhaps it was something else. But with Blandón's approach, a major piece in the deal-making seemed to be in place—the confidential liaison to Noriega himself. McCleary said that the first step was to talk to Gabriel Lewis.

That meeting was held in a suite at the Westin Hotel in Washington in strictest secrecy as befitted first contacts by warring parties.

So far the initiative involved only Americans and Lewis. The Civic Crusade and opposition party leaders knew nothing about it, and probably would have opposed the contact. Lewis, like Díaz Herrera, was viewed with some suspicion by traditional opposition sectors because of his long association with the Torrijos government and with Barletta. He intended to inform the opposition only after the basics of an arrangement had received the approval of the U.S. government. He wanted to put the pie on the opposition leaders' plates after it was baked.

Lewis knew José Blandón well, and they had in common their long association with and admiration for Torrijos. Still, it would be hard to imagine two more different people as political allies: Lewis had been born to privilege and was a millionaire several times over; Blandón's father was a woodworker who raised seven children on $40 a week in a furniture factory. His father's boss was Carmelo Spadafora, owner of Mueblería Fino-Fino in Chitré, and Blandón grew up with Hugo Spadafora. He had worked his way through university with jobs and scholarships, graduating from the University of Puerto Rico with a bachelor of science in agriculture.

Like Spadafora, Blandón came under suspicion as a dangerous radical after Torrijos took power in 1968, then went to work for Torrijos with devotion as the military government became an instrument of social change in Panama. After Torrijos's death, Blandón wore three hats as a loyal and influential worker at the second tier of the PRD leadership: He was a member of the PRD's broad-based political commission; he was a member of a small group of analysts at the party's Office of Political Intelligence, with access to intelligence produced by Noriega's G2; and he was in charge of the government-controlled electric company, IHRE.

Ideologically, Blandón was a Torrijista, a nationalist and a leftist, in that order. As a party worker, he had never run for office, although he was considered far more intelligent and competent than most of those who did. He rose to influence by attaching himself to men of power—first Torrijos, then Noriega, and then, apparently, President Delvalle.

When Gabriel Lewis renewed his acquaintance with Blandón in late August 1987, Blandón, as consul in New York, was thought to be in "golden exile." He had been one of the losers in the 1986 shake-up in Panama when Noriega forced President Delvalle to fire most of his cabinet and name Noriega loyalists. Blandón was not in the cabinet, but was one of Delvalle's closest advisers. He had fallen into *desgracia*—not disgraced, but out of favor with the ruling circle around Noriega, for which the penalty was a comfortable, lucrative job far from Panama.

Blandón's ultimate loyalties would not be questioned until much later. Certainly, Lewis saw no grounds for hairsplitting about Blandón's recent disputes with Noriega. In their meeting, Blandón represented himself as an envoy from Noriega and said he was also keeping President Delvalle informed about everything he was doing.

Noriega was willing to set the date for his own retirement for some time in the not too distant future, Blandón said, as long as the United States would give assurances that there would be no indictments. That was the heart of the plan, the quid pro quo. The political infrastructure that had to be put in place for such a transaction was more complex. The opposition groups, the government and the Defense Forces had to reach consensus on a political transition. Blandón said that Noriega had mentioned the first week of April 1988 as a convenient possible date for his retirement.

Blandón had no qualms about explaining to Lewis, a fellow Torrijista, the rationale he said was behind Noriega's approval of the plan: Both pillars of the Torrijos system, the Defense Forces and the PRD, would be saved from crumbling. An orderly, honorable retirement by Noriega, with a subsequent, limited housecleaning of the Defense Forces, would pave the way for the PRD to continue as a strong, if no longer dominant political force in Panama, while the Defense Forces would finally be able to make the long-promised transition back to the barracks with the assured professional status to which the institution had always aspired.

Blandón later described his conversation with Noriega:

"I told Noriega, I think the moment has come to negotiate. We have to look for a solution to the crisis. I tell you, Noriega was serene. I was talking to the real Noriega, the guy who thinks things through, the guy who knows that he is in trouble. I said, General, this is the best moment to resolve the problem with the United States. There are no indictments—we had information that they were coming. The United States is at a loss as to how to resolve this crisis. The administration has its own problems, with Iran-Contra.

"So we have to make a proposal of our own. It has to come from us, and it starts with your willingness to realize that the time has come to make your exit. I'm not saying that it's your fault. Politically, the top man pays the price for the errors of his subordinates.

"He said, I agree with you. But I'm not going to leave because the gringos are pushing me or because of the opposition.

"I said, now is the time, when the opposition is at its lowest level, when the gringos are without a plan, a proposal from us will yield the maximum that we will be able to get. It is when we will have to make the fewest concessions. The opposition cannot stop this plan, but we will have to sell it to them. The important thing is that you agree with it, the Defense Forces agree to it, the opposition and the U.S. government agree to it."

Plan Blandón, as it came to be called, set off three months of furious behind-the-scenes activity at the State Department and among the exiles in Miami. Blandón presented his proposal to the State Department in a meeting several weeks later with William Walker, Elliott Abrams's deputy. Walker was noncommittal, just listening.

In October, Blandón met with opposition leaders Ricardo Arias Calderón, Carlos Rodríguez and Roberto Eisenmann. He met with Elliott Abrams in the first week of November, then with a large group of Civic Crusade leaders two weeks later. An even higher level meeting at the State Department was promised. All parties expressed interest. He presented the plan to the Latin American leaders who had been closest to Panama's interests in years past, former presidents Carlos Andrés Pérez, Alfonso López Michelsen and Daniel Oduber. He wrote a letter about the plan to Spanish Prime Minister Felipe González.

Nothing in the plan met with strong objections. In all the meetings, Blandón stressed that he was keeping Noriega and Delvalle fully informed. What he didn't tell them was that Noriega did not know about Blandón's close coordination with Delvalle. He had insisted from the beginning that he was negotiating on Noriega's behalf and was loyal to Noriega. But sometime in the process, it was clear to those working with Blandón that his "loyalty" had become a façade.

Whatever Blandón's original sentiments, by November he was playing a dangerous game of triple alliances: to Noriega, to Delvalle and to the U.S.-backed opposition. As one participant described him, he was "someone who was trying to defect without saying he was a defector."

When Blandón's plan was finally drafted, by Joel McCleary in English, its genuine—or acquired—purpose was blatant: to force Noriega into accepting his own retirement and a series of reforms that amounted to a short-term Delvalle-opposition coalition followed by an elected government under total civilian control. It is impossible to read the document, however, as something to which Noriega had given prior approval.

Step #1: Through secret negotiations get leaders of key groups to sign off on specifics of the plan, as outlined below.

#2: Communicate the plan to Noriega and at the same time begin well orchestrated plan to pressure him into a timely acceptance. [He will try to buy time at first, but with sustained pressure, he will agree.] . . .

One of the major pressures that might force Noriega to accept the above reforms is the fact the government is drifting into a worse and worse financial crisis. . . .

Once agreement is reached on the major points above, then the hard part begins. It must be sold to Noriega. If this explanation to Noriega is timed with a series of events which remind him of his tentative hold on Panama, we will be successful. Sustained pressure must be put on Noriega. The pressure must come from every direction. . . . We must move fast because I fear that events could still get out of anyone's control.

The idea that Plan Blandón had Noriega's authorization seemed to exist only in Blandón's later descriptions of his actions and in hope. The plan concludes:

"To move this aggressively requires much confidence, but what is there to lose? What is the option? Even if Noriega does not accept the plan today, it's [sic] existence will moderate his behavior tomorrow. And, when he has time to think about the plan, he will accept it. I am sure of that."

Rather than an initiative by Noriega for his own peaceful retirement, the plan was more likely Blandón's own elaborate scheme to sandbag Noriega, or as the document puts it at one point: "Through conspiracy get consensus."

Blandón got his high-level meeting, with Undersecretary of State Richard Armacost on November 7, and according to Blandón, Armacost apparently acquiesced to the key U.S. concession demanded for the plan to work.

"The only problem for the plan," Blandón said, "is for the United States to look for a legal mechanism to stop the indictments."

"If that is the problem, we will take care of it," Armacost said, according to Blandón.

But soon after that meeting, Plan Blandón was dead. Someone sent Noriega the English draft. Blandón concluded that it must have been someone at the Department of Defense, where he thought Noriega retained a group of strong supporters. On December 21, Noriega called Blandón. Shouting obscenities, he said he had never authorized any negotiations. Whether or not he had was moot.

Blandón's was not the only attempt of uncertain authorization to work out a deal with Noriega. Retired Admiral Daniel Murphy traveled to Panama in August and in November and met with Noriega. Murphy had served as Vice President Bush's chief of staff and had primary responsibility for Bush's antinarcotics activities. Before each trip he met with senior officials at the Defense and State departments, the CIA, the NSC and the vice president's office. In Panama, he discussed with Noriega a plan similar to Blandón's for guaranteeing free elections, with one important difference. Murphy's proposal did not set a retirement date, saying only that Noriega had to step down "before the election in May 1989." Noriega said that he intended to resign at the time of the elections, but he agreed to consider an earlier date. "I am not inflexible," Murphy quoted him as saying.

Murphy and the Reagan administration insisted that Murphy's

trip was strictly private, with no official function or message regarding Noriega. In any case, the distinction between private and public was undoubtedly lost on Noriega, who reportedly took the visit as proof that there were still hard lines and soft lines in the U.S. government and that he could hold out for a better deal.

An admittedly official trip took place on the last day of the year. Assistant Secretary of Defense Richard Armitage had a long meeting with Noriega that press briefings in Washington described as a message that U.S. policy was unequivocal: The United States wanted him to resign. The Armitage trip was promoted as particularly effective because it delivered a strong message from the very Pentagon quarters so often described as harboring supporters of Noriega. The toughness of the message was blurred, however, when word spread in Panama that Armitage and Noriega appeared before other PDF officers laughing and drinking scotch.

Noriega also had begun to play up his supposed relationship with Vice President Bush, telling U.S. ambassador Davis that Bush had called him in the middle of the night in October 1983 with a special request. The U.S. invasion of Grenada was about to occur, he said, and Bush asked Noriega to contact Fidel Castro immediately to warn him to stay out of the fight because it was not directed at Cuba. The vice president's office denied that any call was ever made. In an interview in October 1987, Noriega commented on the vice president's ambitions: "Bush is my friend. I hope he becomes president."

There was a surreal quality to the events and statements in Panama and Washington as January moved into February. Noriega had signaled that he was willing to retire, as if setting the date were the only problem. The 1989 elections did not seem that far away—only a year and a half—and U.S. embassy officers in Panama were already working on the premise that a solution would have to wait until then. The opposition had once again been easily maneuvered into relative inaction as the secret negotiations went on. Publicly they proclaimed that Noriega's immediate removal was the only solution; behind the scenes they debated the difference between Noriega stepping down in April (Plan Blandón) or July (as some opposition leaders had indicated to Admiral Murphy would be acceptable).

The civilian government was in tatters, divided all but openly from Noriega but also divided against itself. Noriega had sent Aquilino Boyd, the former foreign minister, to Washington to try to prevent a Delvalle man, businessman Juan Sosa, from becoming the new ambassador; Boyd was unsuccessful. In secret, Delvalle was party to Blandón's conspiracy against Noriega; in public, he made veiled criticisms of Noriega. At the same time, however, Delvalle struck out viciously at his vice president, Roderick Esquivel, who since the June crisis had ceased to come to his office at the presidential palace and made open displays of his disdain for the government and Noriega. Delvalle had ordered Esquivel's staff evicted.

Noriega's side was already scrambling to find the cash to cover the traditional Christmas bonuses for government workers. The antinarcotics unit, led by Inspector Luis Quiel, continued to carry out joint operations and to share information with the DEA agents stationed in Panama. To the surprise of the DEA officers, Quiel's unit diligently pursued a DEA request in January to arrest Reinaldo Ruiz, a Cuban-American trafficker operating out of Panama. The arrest several weeks later and his deportation to the United States were major breakthroughs in the U.S. investigation of a drug ring operating high up in the Cuban government.

Such apparently unstinting cooperation by Panama with DEA requests had led to another breakthrough—in the DEA's investigation of Noriega himself. In an attempt to locate additional witnesses who might corroborate Floyd Carlton's testimony, a DEA intelligence analyst had turned up the file on a Colombian trafficker in an Oklahoma prison. The prisoner had begun to cooperate in an unrelated case and had mentioned Noriega. Miami DEA agent Steven Grilli interviewed him and found what was needed in the case against Noriega. The prisoner, Boris Olarte, said that he was the bagman making payoffs of $4 million to Noriega on behalf of the cartel in 1984—the same period Carlton had claimed that Noriega was receiving cartel protection payments. Olarte described meetings and meeting places that corroborated Carlton's testimony. The irony, pointed out by DEA agents in Washington who viewed the evidence against Noriega with skepticism, was that Noriega's antinarcotics unit had arrested Olarte in November 1986 and turned him over to the United States.

In Miami the DEA and the U.S. attorney's office shared little of that skepticism. They were putting the last touches on the Noriega investigation and were preparing to ask the grand jury to return an indictment. Leon Kellner, the U.S. attorney, was mildly surprised that the impending action against Noriega, which his people had reported in detail to Steven Trott, the associate attorney general, and to DEA administrator Jack Lawn, had not produced more bureaucratic flak. Now they were close, very close. In all, with Olarte, senior prosecutor Dick Gregorie had lined up nine witnesses in addition to Carlton. All but three were convicted felons.

In early January, Kellner found another potential witness against Noriega. Since mid-December, José Blandón had been giving hours of interviews to major news organizations. He was talking openly about corruption and criminal activity inside the Noriega régime, but he had imposed the condition that none of the journalists publish the material until he gave the go-ahead.

Kellner got a call from a producer for CBS's *60 Minutes*. They arranged an exchange: The CBS producer gave Kellner Blandón's name, promoting him as someone who had pictures of a Noriega drug-related meeting involving Fidel Castro in Havana. In return, Kellner allowed the program an interview with his main witness, Floyd Carlton.

Blandón's master plan had been stillborn, but he continued to hold out hope that Noriega could be persuaded to come to terms with the United States and the opposition before it was too late, before the indictments came down. Meeting frequently with State Department officials and U.S. senators, courted by the opposition and pursued by some of America's best-known journalists, including Watergate investigator Bob Woodward of *The Washington Post,* Blandón was undergoing a heady experience. His plan and the dizzying confusion of double and triple loyalties it encompassed became something like the famous palindrome: A Man, a Plan, a Canal—Panama. It could be read backward and forward, with Noriega as the initiator or as the target; it was intriguing and full of intellectual promise; in the end, no matter how it was construed it didn't quite make sense.

When he was notified that Kellner wanted him to testify before the grand jury, Blandón put him off. The pressure was building for him to go public and denounce Noriega from the inside, as Colonel Díaz Herrera had six months before. Senator Helms's staffer Deborah DeMoss wanted him to appear as the star witness in public hearings on Panama that Senators Kerry and Helms had scheduled for early February. But before he crossed that line, Blandón wanted to give his plan one last chance. On January 9, he met in Miami with two of his closest political friends, PRD leaders Rigoberto Paredes and Gerardo González, two men who represented—if anyone did—the truest defenders of the ideals of Torrijismo. He pleaded with them to convince Noriega that if he did not compromise now the result would be the destruction of the Torrijista party and perhaps of the Defense Forces as an institution. He said that he had to decide within three days whether to accept the grand jury subpoena to testify against Noriega. Noriega had three days, he said, to make up his mind.

Noriega's response, almost on cue, was to denounce Blandón as a traitor and to fire him from his post as New York consul. A week later Blandón announced that he was going to honor the grand jury subpoena.

Blandón was the last witness to appear before the grand jury, which had been hearing evidence against General Manuel Antonio Noriega of Panama for the past six months. Blandón's testimony added no new details about Noriega's alleged drug trafficking, but he knew Floyd Carlton, Ricardo Bilonick, César Rodríguez and many of the other major participants in the alleged drug deals. Most importantly, Blandón testified out of moral and political outrage, not as a man trying to reduce a sentence for his crimes. Blandón was able to fill in the gaps, and he seemed to give a broad and credible picture of how the Panamanian system worked and a detailed personal portrait of Noriega and his closest associates.

Blandón told the grand jury one story that did make its way into the indictment: He said that he personally met with Fidel Castro in late June 1984 to discuss a dispute between Noriega and the Colombian cartel as a result of the PDF raid on the Darién cocaine factory. He said that Castro mediated a settlement that resulted in the release of twenty-three prisoners and the return of $5 million in protection money.

The prosecutors decided to name Castro, but did not indict him. There was no independent corroboration for the story, but apparently it was too good for the prosecution to pass up—not only Noriega, but the archenemy of all good Miamians, Fidel Castro, involved in the drug business! No other witness, including Carlton, had any knowledge of the Cuban meeting. If the investigators had checked flight records and even press clips in Panama, they might have discovered that Blandón had gotten some basic facts of the Darién incident wrong: the dates for the trip to Cuba were wrong, and the prisoners supposedly released at Castro's urging had been freed more than one month before Blandón and Noriega went to Cuba.

There wasn't time for fact checking. Three days after Blandón's testimony, on Super Bowl Sunday, the investigative team gathered in Kellner's office. With the game between the New York Giants and the Denver Broncos crackling from an office television set, Kellner, Gregorie, Grilli and his supervisor Ken Kennedy pulled together their entire year's work and boiled it down to a seventy-eight page "Prosecution Memo" outlining the case for indicting Manuel Antonio Noriega and his associates. The memo required twenty-seven pages to recite Carlton's main allegations, another four for Blandón's. The memo also had the summary testimonies of drug pilot Tony Aizprua; of cartel operative Boris Olarte; of Carlos, who first brought Carlton to the DEA's attention; of a Panamanian who had been wounded twice in run-ins with the cartel. The gun, the memo argued in effect, was big enough to shoot the king.

One more step remained. The decision to indict required the go-ahead of the attorney general, representing the Reagan administration. And on Monday, February 1, the two prosecution teams, from Miami and Tampa, with their respective prosecutors and investigators, converged on Washington. Kellner and Gregorie were prepared for a fight. Having brought the investigation to the door of indictment, having decided in their best judgment that Noriega should be indicted, the two U.S. attorneys could be overruled by only the president or the attorney general. Kellner was prepared to go public if those higher in government attempted to obstruct the case. He and Gregorie were met by reporters when they got off the plane from Miami; more reporters and television cameras were waiting on the steps of the Justice Department.

The indictments could be stopped on two grounds: if the merits of the case were flawed or if the administration judged that the action against Noriega would so damage national security that the costs would outweigh the benefits.

They presented the prosecution memos to Associate Attorney General Steve Trott. The discussion on the merits of the evidence was thorough but brief. There was little second guessing of the standards of evidence brought by two of the top U.S. attorneys in the United States. Then they reached the last page in the Miami document, labeled "Problems." The final paragraph read:

> The second problem with the prosecution is the unknown evidence of Manuel Antonio Noriega's activities with United States intelligence agencies. It is not clear at this time whether Noriega may choose to make some claim of being an agent of the United States in some or all of his activities. Sensitive materials may be sought on discovery from U.S. intelligence agencies, and potentially embarrassing testimony may be brought out at trial, which are unknown to the prosecutors.

"What do you see as the difficulty?" Trott asked.

"The problem we see," Gregorie said, quoting himself later, "is that the defendant is going to be able to say 'I was an agent of the U.S. government. I was working for foreign intelligence. I was meeting with the drug dealers only because I was getting intelligence information, and I passed it along to the CIA, to the DIA, and to whatever intelligence unit I was working for. I demand to see my payment file, all the informant files and every file the CIA has about me."

Noriega would be able to use what had come to be known as the

graymail defense—or more recently the "Ollie North defense" because of its use in his 1988 trial. Because it was known that he had
worked in some capacity for a U.S. intelligence agency, his lawyers
had a right to bring out in trial any information that would prove
that relationship. In the past, former CIA employees had threatened
to expose highly classified—and potentially embarrassing—information as leverage to induce the U.S. government to drop charges or
grant lenient sentences in order to protect CIA secrets. Gregorie had
tried to find out about Noriega from the CIA. He received a file he
described as "a packet of newspaper clippings."

"Nobody has ever let us see that material," Gregorie said, "and
I don't know that they ever will."

"Indeed, that seems to be the case," Trott said. "So be it. You'll
have to live with it."

Attorney General Edwin Meese also gave his approval at a brief
early afternoon meeting. The next hurdle was the White House.
Kellner and Trott went first to National Security Adviser John Negroponte's office. Negroponte's deputy, Nicholas Rostow, made one
of the few overtly hostile comments of the day: "I find it peculiar that
a U.S. attorney is making foreign policy for the United States."

"I'm not making foreign policy. I'm indicting a crook," Kellner
replied.

At four P.M. Negroponte took Kellner to the White House Situation Room. There in solemn assembly were representatives of the
national security establishment of the United States: the CIA, the
several branches of the armed forces in full uniform, Deputy Secretary of State John C. Whitehead, Assistant Secretary of State
Abrams. Negroponte chaired the meeting and had Kellner sit next
to him at the large conference table.

Kellner laid out his case and his timetable for indictment. Then
Negroponte went around the room with the question: "Does anyone
have any objection to this?" No objections were raised. A military
officer wanted to know how to handle contacts with Noriega after
the indictment.

"Go ahead and meet him," Kellner said. "Just be sure and read
him his Miranda rights." Nobody laughed.

There was some discussion about the timing, about the secrecy of the indictment, about what might happen next. State asked Kellner to release a copy of the indictment to Ambassador Davis with authorization for him to show it to President Delvalle. But no one questioned the basic premise of the meeting: Noriega was about to be indicted.

No one discussed alternatives. Kellner had the impression that the group had already decided not to oppose the indictment. Indeed, it would have been nearly impossible to make a political argument for reversing the judicial process so near its completion. It was an election year; Congress was united and ready to pounce on any signs of softness toward Noriega; and finally, there was the Kellner factor. Who would go on record to recommend that Leon Kellner drop the indictment of Manuel Noriega? Who would ask Leon Kellner—the man some in Congress were convinced had obeyed orders to slow down the investigation of Oliver North—to go easy on another actor with CIA connections and with a documented role in North's activities?

Kellner was aware that the previous accusations gave him a card that could not be trumped. "With the notoriety and criticism and stories floating about, that I was asked to go slow on one case—which wasn't true—they weren't about to ask me to do it really," Kellner said.

Kellner and Tampa U.S. attorney Robert Merkle announced the indictments of Manuel Antonio Noriega the following Friday, February 5, at a crowded press conference in Miami. Customs and the FBI sent proud agents to take their place in the limelight for their agencies' roles in the investigation. Two chairs, saved for DEA agents Steve Grilli and Ken Kennedy, were vacant. They represented the DEA investigation that had begun back in early 1985 and that had progressed from Alfredo Caballero to Tony Aizprua to Floyd Carlton, and finally to Manuel Noriega. It wasn't that they weren't proud. The Noriega case had meant more to Grilli and Kennedy, and Dan Moritz in Cleveland, than perhaps any other case they had worked on. But they were ordered by their superiors not to attend the press conference. Even at that final hour, the DEA was divided between those who investigated Noriega as a criminal and those who swore by the authenticity of his cooperation.

The Miami indictment charged Noriega with twelve counts under the broad conspiracy statute known as RICO, the Racketeer Influenced and Corrupt Organizations Act. An earlier version of the indictment named as the "organization" the Panama Defense Forces, but Kellner had dropped that designation following the meetings at the White House. Noriega's fifteen codefendants included cartel leaders, Gustavo Gaviria and Pablo Escobar; PDF Captain Luis del Cid; businessman and former diplomat Ricardo Bilonick; Ahmet Paredes, son of retired General Rubén Darío Paredes; an American, Brian Alden Davidow; seven other Colombians; and two other Panamanians.

Their conspiracy involved shipping acetone ether and cocaine, shipping and laundering drug money and paying and accepting millions of dollars of protection money. The cumulative sentences possible, if Noriega were convicted, amounted to 145 years in prison and $1,145,000 in fines. The Tampa indictment, based on Kalish's testimony, named only Noriega and Enrique Pretelt. They were charged with conspiracy to smuggle marijuana and to launder drug money.

Noriega, as head of the Panamanian military, was the most powerful foreign official ever indicted by the United States. The only comparable case was the indictment of an obscure prime minister of the small islands of Turks and Caicos, a British dependency in the West Indies. That case had also been brought by Kellner's office.

In Panama, Noriega was quoted as saying that the indictment was "a joke and an absurd political maneuver." The Panamanian Foreign Ministry issued a more ominous statement: "The government warns that it is extremely dangerous to tax the patience, tolerance and good faith of the Panamanian people with campaigns that could spark unforeseen reactions."

In the days following the indictment, however, the streets were quiet; as if out of fear, awe or sheer incredulity, the Panamanian people were at a loss to react.

In Washington, the agencies that had acquiesced, even if by default or out of political inevitability, lost no time in sniping at the indictment. An unnamed DEA official was quoted as calling it a "publicity stunt" with no conceivable chance of bringing Noriega to trial, since Panama's constitution does not require extradition of Panamanian citizens. State Department, White House and Pentagon officials, also unnamed, told *The New York Times* that they feared the indictment would be counterproductive, causing Noriega to dig in deeper and perhaps retaliate against U.S. installations and citizens in Panama.

The indictment, finally a reality, was transformed almost immediately into a bargaining chip, and the two-year process of engineering Noriega's removal began. The first attempt was made by President Eric Delvalle, whose contacts with Blandón and U.S. officials had made his severance from Noriega an all-but-public fact. In late February, Delvalle offered Noriega a new version of Plan Blandón: He had been given assurances by Elliott Abrams that the State Department would ask the Justice Department to drop the charges if Noriega would step down and go into exile.

Noriega refused. A few days later, on February 25, Delvalle recorded a videotape that was broadcast on national television announcing that he had dismissed Noriega as commander of the PDF. Within hours, the White House gave its full backing to Delvalle's action. But Delvalle was already preparing to go into hiding. By dawn, Delvalle was a former president, dismissed by the Noriega-controlled National Assembly and abandoned by his entire cabinet. He was the fourth Panamanian president to be deposed in six years, and perhaps the least popular. Reviled by the opposition for his pro-Noriega role, his legitimacy had been doubly questionable: he had been elected vice president in the fraudulent 1984 elections, then elevated to president by the military coup against President Barletta.

Delvalle might have been expected to go quietly after his noble gesture of trying to fire Noriega. But Washington had other plans. The administration announced, as if words could change the facts, that Delvalle was still president of Panama and that he was the sole object of the United States's "unqualified support for civilian constitutional rule in Panama." And Vice President Bush, already campaigning hard for president, said that the United States should be prepared to do "whatever is necessary, including military force," to protect "sacred" U.S. interests in Panama.

Delvalle, the Noriega puppet who had cut his strings, was transformed by fiat into a courageous defender of democracy—then into a pawn in a gambit devised by Panamanian opposition leaders and their U.S. advisers for the quick and easy removal of Noriega.

The gambit was put into action the following Monday, February 29. From hiding, Delvalle issued a proclamation through the U.S. embassy in Panama ordering that all money owed to the government of Panama should be paid to an escrow account in the United States and that Delvalle's "lawful government" would not recognize any payments made to the Noriega-controlled government. The ousted president, in effect, was attempting to freeze all Panamanian assets and to lay personal claim to all taxes and fees, including the millions of dollars in monthly payments from the Panama Canal Commission, owed to the Panamanian government. It was a bonanza any deposed ruler might wish without the slightest hope of fulfillment. But the Panamanian group concocting the scheme had the cooperation of the U.S. government. Armed with Delvalle's proclamation and a State Department document backing his claim to be Panama's president, Delvalle's U.S. lawyers gained control over $35 to $40 million of Panamanian funds on deposit in four New York banks. The administration then announced that all Canal Commission payments, about $7 million a month, would be paid into Delvalle's escrow accounts. Other sanctions forbidding U.S. firms from conducting a variety of transactions with the Noriega government soon followed.

Cut off from a major part of its already depleted reserves of U.S. dollars, the Panamanian government ordered all banks to close temporarily. The Civic Crusade began a business strike to increase the pressure. That strike and several protests called by the opposition fizzled within a few days but in Washington, officials were already congratulating themselves for putting the skids under yet another unsavory dictator whose demise seemed to be following the script of Ferdinand Marcos and Jean-Claude Duvalier.

To complement the Delvalle gambit, Secretary of State George

Shultz made a thinly disguised appeal to the officers of the Panama Defense Forces to rise up against Noriega, calling the PDF "a strong and honorable force that has a significant and proper role to play" in a post-Noriega Panama. He secretly ordered U.S. embassies in several Latin American countries to "inform Panamanian military attachés of U.S. desire to work with PDF, but inability to do so while Noriega remains. Message includes support for PDF's important role in Panama as a professional military subordinate to civilian authority and expresses desire to resume close cooperation once PDF puts its house in order."

As if one cue, on March 16, a few air force officers and the head of the PDF's police division, Colonel Leonidas Macias, tried to overthrow Noriega. A few shots were fired, and the poorly coordinated coup attempt was easily put down by the small infantry company in charge of security at Noriega's command headquarters. By early afternoon, Noriega was posing for photographers and chatting with reporters from the steps outside his office.

"The bullets are kisses," he said, brushing aside questions about the gunfire during the attack. Noriega's movements were loose and he smiled broadly as he raised his fists in a boxer's salute. It was the United States versus Tony Noriega, and he had won the first round. He was enjoying not only the victory but the fight itself, glorying in the sheer outrageousness of the image he projected: the dark, ugly man from Panama laughing in Uncle Sam's face.

SNATCHING DEFEAT . . . AN EPILOGUE

Omar Torrijos had a maxim to guide his followers in their relations with the United States. The United States is like a monkey on a chain, he used to say. You can play with the monkey—but don't pull the chain too hard.

Manuel Noriega liked to repeat Torrijos's saying to illustrate that he knew how far he could go in goading the United States. His continued presence in Panama was an increasingly humiliating taunt to the U.S. government. He managed to survive the combined offensive of the United States executive, the judicial system and Congress operating in unprecedented unity to drive him from office. He played out the game with glee, confident he could outmaneuver his opponent, secure in the realization that he had almost nothing to lose.

Even after the abortive coup of March 16, 1988, U.S. officials continued to tell reporters that Noriega could not survive more than a few days longer. How could he hang on, they argued, facing a divided military, a determined opposition and the U.S. stranglehold on his economy's lifeblood, the U.S. dollar? With Noriega on the ropes—a favorite phrase of official briefers—the State Department dispatched negotiators to work out the terms of his resignation and exile. Noriega sent messages implying that he was ready to go quietly. The timing of his resignation, the place and length of his exile, and the status of the Miami indictment seemed to be details that were within reach of resolution. The designated negotiators—Romulo Escobar Bethancourt on the Panamanian side and Michael Kozak for the State Department—had worked successfully together in the treaty negotiations eleven years earlier.

Only after the talks had dragged on for two months, and after at least three false leaks by the administration that agreement had been reached, did the U.S. side realize that it had been hoodwinked. The U.S. humiliation was sealed on May 25, when Secretary of State George Shultz, acting on assurances that the deal was ready for him to announce, postponed his departure for Moscow to attend the summit meeting between President Reagan and Soviet leader Mikhail Gorbachev. But at the last minute, Noriega asked for more time, claiming that a special military advisory council had insisted that he remain as commander of the PDF. The negotiations collapsed.

Whether Noriega ever seriously intended to resign in response to the U.S. demands is doubtful. In hindsight, the talks appeared to be a tactic designed to gain the time he needed to repair divisions among his military supporters, to find ways around the U.S. economic sanctions and to outlast opposition strikes and protests.

By summer Noriega's ouster no longer seemed imminent. With his internal opposition increasingly inconsequential and his putative military opponents driven underground, Noriega settled in against the only enemy that counted, the United States. The price of the stalemate was the progressive deterioration of the Panamanian economy and the international banking complex at its center. The sanctions soon proved a blunt instrument that barely touched Noriega's military and civilian power base. The main sufferers were the U.S.-owned companies, the pro-U.S. Panamanian businessmen who were the backbone of the opposition to Noriega, and the Panamanian middle class. A congressional Government Accounting Office (GAO) report on the sanctions noted that "in Panama, the United States is in a unique situation in that it has never imposed sanctions in a country where a substantial number of U.S. citizens continued to reside and where the sanctions' objectives did not include encouraging U.S. business interests to leave the country."

By the end of 1988 Panama had absorbed the main force of the economic blow and had stabilized, albeit in an economic depression.

The country's economy declined 20 percent compared to 1987, and one fourth of the labor force was unemployed. The combined effect of reduced business activity and the U.S. ban on any payments to the Noriega government resulted in a loss of $480 million in revenues to the country. A government with a budget of over $1 billion was forced in the space of a few months to cut spending in half. No matter how drastic the cuts, however, military personnel and government workers got their paychecks.

Unable to back down despite the political ineffectiveness of the sanctions, the United States clung to the hollow Delvalle presidency, which had become a bad joke. Delvalle was shuttled from apartment to apartment, always under de facto U.S. protection in areas secured by treaty arrangements. His wife lived in the guarded residence of U.S. ambassador Davis and Davis's daughter, Susan, who had gained a reputation as a scrappy anti-Noriega activist. On the rare occasions he spoke out, Delvalle's press contacts were arranged through the U.S. embassy staff. He flew to Miami more and more often, and the visits there stretched from weeks to months. Returning to Panama in December 1988 when his mother died, Delvalle turned down U.S. embassy suggestions that he make a public appearance at her funeral.

The Delvalle "government" consisted of Juan Sosa, ambassador to the United States, and a handful of loyalists operating out of the premises of the Panamanian embassy in Washington and five consulates elsewhere in the United States. Delvalle also worked closely with former ambassador Gabriel Lewis and Jose Blandón. While his staff was skimpy, Delvalle's budget was fulsome: As "president" of Panama, he held nominal control over $375 million in escrow accounts set up to receive U.S. government and private business payments and other assets withheld from the Noriega regime. In fact, Delvalle's withdrawals of the Panamanian funds were contingent on the approval of the U.S. Treasury and State Department. The main expense was $750,000 allocated monthly for the operation of the embassy and consulates in the United States. No official U.S. government accounting was performed, however, to verify how the money was spent, according to the GAO report on Panamanian sanctions.

The Delvalle accounts provided the financial underpinning for a variety of plots to foment military coups against Noriega or otherwise arrange his removal. The plots were notable mainly for the public nature of their supposedly covert planning and for their almost total lack of success. Delvalle's "consulate" money was used to pay the salary and office expenses of Eduardo Herrera Hassan, a Panamanian colonel who was fired from his post as ambassador to Israel in early 1988 and who began to work with the CIA to plot Noriega's overthrow. An additional $1 million from Delvalle's account was withdrawn for an unspecified purpose "based on assurances by the then Assistant Secretary of State for Inter-American Affairs [Elliott Abrams] that the Department of State would assume responsibility for the decision," the GAO report noted.

In the twenty-one months after the failed coup attempt, the CIA was involved in at least five covert-action plans to get rid of Noriega, according to published reports, although how far these progressed was never really clear. An early plan, calling for the installation of the Delvalle government on U.S. military bases, was vetoed by the Pentagon. Another plan, in July 1988, called "Panama 3," was designed by Colonel Herrera Hassan but was opposed by the Senate Intelligence Committee on the grounds that it might violate the ban on U.S. government participation in political assassination.

"Panama 4" called for "nonlethal" assistance to the Panamanian opposition campaigning against Noriega's candidate in presidential elections scheduled for May 1989. Under the plan, for which $10 million was allocated to the CIA and approved by the Senate Intelligence Committee, radio equipment for secret opposition broadcasts was smuggled into Panama through a CIA unit, the Program Development Group, located at Fort Corozal in the former Canal Zone. But the clandestine station's broadcasts turned out to be almost inaudible, and the CIA funding was leaked to the press just a week before the elections. Opposition candidates denied receiving any covert money, but the stories caused them deep embarrassment.

The existence of still another covert-action plan, "Panama 5," was leaked to the U.S. press even before it got final consideration from the Senate Intelligence Committee in October 1989. The nature of this plan was unknown, except that administration sources stressed that it was not subject to the assassination ban as long as any killing involved in the plot was "accidental."

Noriega used the U.S. machinations against him to maximum effect, portraying himself as a beleaguered nationalist fighting Panama's century-long battle against U.S. domination. He had never been personally popular in Panama, never approaching the charisma of Torrijos, but his defiance of the "Yanquis" to the north reinforced his macho reputation and he had some success in galvanizing support for the PDF as the country's bulwark of national identity. There were moments in late 1988 when he actually seemed to gain in personal popularity. Had he stepped down then, as many observers in Panama expected, Manuel Noriega could have declared a victory against the United States and been assured of a modest and not entirely negative place in Latin American history. With his accumulated riches, he could have lived out his life in opulence.

But a meek retirement in his early fifties would not have been the style of the kid from Terraplén. As the May 1989 elections approached, Noriega's game grew increasingly nasty. He had long encouraged rumors that he would run for president in 1989. The election of a PDF president would have been the final realization of Plan Torrijos—the divvying up of power among Torrijos's successors in 1982. The Torrijista party, the PRD, proclaimed Noriega its preferred candidate at its convention in December 1988. But running would have meant retirement as PDF commander in January 1989. It was at that juncture, when Noriega refused to measure himself in an election against his despised opponents—even in a contest in which he controlled the rules and the referees—that the Panamanian melodrama passed irretrievably into the realm of national tragedy.

The opposition chose a ticket headed by Guillermo Endara, the easygoing Panamanista who had spent his political life in Arnulfo Arias's shadow. Ricardo Arias Calderón, the Christian Democrat, and businessman Guillermo "Billy" Ford were his running mates. Government supporters ran Noriega crony Carlos Duque—the owner of Transit, S.A., which had long been a major avenue for channeling private money to the PDF. The opposition, whose street campaigns to get rid of Noriega had so often faltered, finally was in its element. Despite the obstacles thrown up by Noriega—principal among them the continued lack of a free press—Endara and his running mates ran hard and effectively on a platform of returning the country to real democracy. Their strategy was to win decisively—a "Panamanian victory"—and to ensure that the results were closely monitored by outside observers.

As in 1984, both sides ended their campaigns with massive demonstrations. Noriega's supporters had become a clear minority. Panamanians, given an alternative to Noriega's rule, voted overwhelmingly for Endara. When a Catholic Church–sponsored independent straw count showed Endara winning easily, Noriega's electoral tribunal simply stopped the count and annulled the election. And when Noriega's goons beat the the opposition candidates bloody during a street protest—in full view of U.S. television cameras—all pretense of constitutional rule was discarded. Noriega arranged the appointment of a caretaker president, Francisco Rodríguez, the barely known former comptroller general.

Endara replaced the discredited Delvalle as the focal point of the opposition. The United States was finally able to abandon the fiction that Delvalle, by then living permanently in Miami, was the government of Panama. The summer and fall were rife with nasty confrontations between U.S. troops asserting their rights to move freely in Panama and PDF troops harassing them. U.S. ambassador Davis and most of the embassy staff were withdrawn as the United States sent in several thousand additional troops to bolster the U.S. bases.

The next major confrontation came on October 3, when the Urraca security company at Command Headquarters, led by Major Moisés Giroldi, tried to ambush Noriega as he arrived for work. The fighting lasted most of the morning, with Noriega barricaded in his office inside the headquarters and loyalist troops outside surrounding the complex to rescue him. By early afternoon, Noriega's forces had prevailed, despite some half-hearted maneuvers by U.S. Southcom troops to show support for the coup plotters. The attempt to overthrow Noriega departed radically from the bloodless scripts of past coup attempts. The combat was real, not vicariously conducted by telephone. After he had won, Noriega had the coup leader, Major Giroldi, and ten other coup participants executed.

The episode demonstrated a distinct erosion of Noriega's hold on his own military—Giroldi had been a Torrijista "hero," decorated by Noriega for his decisive role in putting down the previous coup on March 16, 1988. But for the United States, the October attempt offered little to cheer about. Giroldi had established contact with U.S. military officials and the CIA before the coup, but the Bush administration passed up the chance to step in decisively in his support. The coup plotters were considered politically unreliable, proclaiming their opposition to Noriega in the name of Torrijos and calling for new elections rather than backing the Endara victory, as the United States advocated. Later, Panamanian sources said Giroldi and his supporters had ties to the anti-U.S. "Tendencia" inside the Torrijista party. Finally, to the profound dismay of U.S. military men, the unit that came to Noriega's rescue was the crack U.S.-trained Batallion 2000, a model of the kind of professional force the United States had always held up as the antidote to military strong-men like Noriega.

In retrospect, it is clear that the October coup attempt was the last chance of using a Panamanian instrument to achieve the U.S. policy goal of removing Noriega. Ironically, perhaps, the leaked "Panama 5" CIA covert-action plan was the public portion of the administration's response—a declaration of continued U.S. action against Noriega in concert with the Panamanian opposition.

A far deeper secret, one that never leaked, was the Bush administration's decision to reactivate plans for a massive military intervention to smash not only Noriega but the entire PDF as an institution. During the weeks following the October coup attempt, the United States began to slip heavy offensive military equipment into Panama under cover of regular supply shipments to U.S. bases. The equipment included at least four tanks and Apache attack helicopters equipped with rapid-fire machineguns capable of saturating a football field with bullets.

·   ·   ·

It was, as one official confided to a reporter later, "a decision in search of an excuse." On Friday, December 15, Noriega began to pull the monkey's chain. He convened a new, handpicked National Assembly of Representatives he had created following the October coup attempt. The Assembly's main order of business was to pass a resolution stating, "The Republic of Panama is declared to be in a state of war while the aggression [by the United States] lasts. . . . To confront this aggression, the job of chief of government of Panama is hereby created, and Manuel Antonio Noriega is designated to carry out these responsibilities as Maximum Leader for national liberation."

Seen from the Panamanian perspective, the action was Noriega's attempt to cloak himself in the mantle of Torrijos. He had created a compliant, populist legislature and emulated the title, Maximum Leader, that Torrijos had bestowed on himself in the old constitution. The description of U.S. sanctions and other actions against the government as "war" had been a staple of the regime's rhetoric for months. But the day after the Assembly meeting the declaration became much more than bombast. Four unarmed U.S. servicemen made a wrong turn on their way to a Saturday night party and found themselves at a roadblock in front of PDF headquarters. The driver of the car apparently panicked and tried to speed away; the PDF soldiers opened fire and killed one serviceman and wounded a second. The incident was witnessed by a U.S. Navy officer and his wife who had been stopped at the same roadblock a half hour before and forcibly detained and roughed up.

There were other incidents on Sunday and Monday. In one, a U.S. soldier coming out of a laundromat drew his service pistol and shot a PDF policeman who demanded his identification. Southcom went on a state of alert just short of a war footing; the White House described the actions as the result of "lawlessness" and charged that Noriega had "created an atmosphere in which Panamanian Defense Forces feel free to fire on unarmed Americans." The State Department read out ominously worded statements of U.S. "concern that a climate of aggression has been developing that puts American lives at risk," and pointedly refused to rule out U.S. military action in response.

As the White House and State Department officials were briefing, President Bush had already given the go ahead, on Sunday, for what was called Operation Just Cause. Bush chose the "maximum" option, a full-scale air and ground invasion of Panama from U.S. bases on the mainland and in Panama. The first planeloads of troops, sent to double the U.S. military force in Panama from the 13,000 at Southcom to more than 26,000, landed during the day on Tuesday, December 19. Just after midnight, the U.S. forces opened an artillery barrage from the headquarters of the 193rd Brigade in Fort Amador across the small bay separating Fort Amador from PDF Command Headquarters. Five U.S. task forces carried out nearly simultaneous attacks against Noriega's installations in another part of Fort Amador, where he had his second most frequented office, and against PDF garrisons in Colón, Omar Torrijos Airport and Rio Hato.

By morning, the slum neighborhood of Chorrillo surrounding PDF Headquarters was in flames and the headquarters building destroyed. Fierce fighting was still under way at Fort Amador under the leadership of Panamanian West Point graduate Captain Moisés Cortizo. The vast firepower of the invading forces overwhelmed the inferior Panamanian forces, but there was unexpected resistance from almost every military target. And General Noriega remained free and apparently able to direct his troops in retreat.

The United States justified the invasion as self-defense in response to a "pattern of aggression" that included the declaration of war and the killing of the U.S. officer the previous weekend. The action's primary objective was to capture General Noriega and to bring him to trial in the United States. White House spokesman Marlin Fitzwater said that the "elected civilian leadership," Guillermo Endara and his running mates in the May elections, had been sworn in by a private attorney just minutes before the invasion. The Canal was also raised as a justification: A "climate of tension" in Panama threatened the Canal, and the invasion was needed to ensure its security and to guarantee the fulfillment of the Panama Canal Treaties. Then, in an unintended irony, U.S. military officials closed the Canal for two days, the first time in its history the Canal had ceased to operate for any reason other than landslides.

Fighting in Panama City continued through the weekend, with

Noriega's troops, operating in hit-and-run guerrilla bands, launching a spectacular but ineffective barrage of mortar fire near Quarry Heights—Southcom headquarters—on Friday. The anticipated celebrations by Panamanian citizens at their "liberation" failed to materialize. Instead, Colón and Panama City imploded in a frenzy of looting, as the PDF police force dissolved with nothing to take its place to keep order. Bands of well-armed young men who called themselves the "Dignity Battalions" roamed the streets and seemed to egg on the looters. The looting ended only when the stores were empty or came under the protection of civilian vigilantes.

By Sunday, Christmas Eve, the Panama Defense Forces had ceased to exist, and U.S. forces rounded up its members into prisoner of war camps. A few units surrendered intact and swore loyalty to the new Endara government, but even they were suspect and many were imprisoned despite their professed change of heart. The nearly 5,000 prisoners actually exceeded the number of combat troops in Noriega's army.

The Bush administration, frustrated at its failure to locate Noriega, had put a $1 million bounty on his head. U.S. troops had raided all the houses of his known friends and mistresses but come up with nothing. Then, just as Pope John Paul II was beginning his midnight Christmas mass in Rome, it was announced in Panama City that Manuel Noriega had turned up at the Papal Nunciature—the Vatican Embassy in Panama—and been given temporary refuge.

Only then did the Panamanians begin their first celebrations.

The U.S. invasion of Panama on December 20, 1989, was the largest American combat operation since the Vietnam War. It dwarfed the U.S. actions in Grenada in 1983 and the air attack on Libya in 1986. The only comparable antecedent was the 1965 invasion of the Dominican Republic, in which 22,000 U.S. troops prevented Juan Bosch, an elected but unacceptably leftist president, from coming to power.

Hundreds of Panamanian civilians died in the U.S. attacks, many of them in the bombardment of working-class neighborhoods in Chorrillo and San Miguelito—both strongholds of Noriega support. The true number may never be known, because many of the dead were buried in mass graves without identification. The official U.S.

estimate was 220. PDF casualties totaled around 300 dead and over 125 wounded; about two dozen United States soldiers and at least two U.S. civilians lost their lives.

In a news conference soon after the invasion, President Bush said he was saddened by the loss of life but "yes, it has been worth it." To those who repeated the criticism of world leaders, including that of Soviet leader Mikhail Gorbachev, Bush said, "If they kill an American Marine, that's real bad. And if they threaten and brutalize the wife of an American citizen, sexually threatening the lieutenant's wife while kicking him in the groin over and over again—then, Mr. Gorbachev, please understand, this president is going to do something about it."

With Noriega in the Vatican embassy, virtually all armed PDF resistance ceased. U.S. troops surrounded the embassy, but the Vatican, recalling its millennium-old tradition of granting sanctuary to the persecuted, refused U.S. demands to turn over Noriega, with a spokesman in Rome describing the U.S. troops as an "occupying army." Noriega's fate was in the hands of the diminutive Spanish cleric, Archbishop José Sebastián Laboa, who had been the Vatican's nuncio, or ambassador, in Panama, for many years and was considered one of Panama's best informed and most astute political observers. Laboa had been a participant in much of the intrigues and deal making, following the indictment, aimed at persuading Noriega to resign. Now, Laboa had no illusions about Noriega nor about Noriega's long friendship with the U.S. agencies so bent on destroying him. In his previous positions at the Vatican's Congregation of the Faith (the office that had once been called the Inquisition) Archbishop Laboa had spent many years as the devil's advocate—the lawyer whose function it was to detect the sinful traits in candidates for sainthood. In 1985, Laboa had reported to Rome that Noriega had amassed incontrovertible derogatory information about then vice president George Bush, information he later described as "dirty laundry" and "atomic bombs."

Laboa believed the drug charges against Noriega, but nevertheless retained a certain respect for Noriega's cunning—"more astuteness than intelligence," he would say. As he fended off the U.S. pressure tactics—including the playing of rock music at a deafening volume—

Laboa adopted the role of confessor counselor, spending hours in Noriega's spartan rooms persuading him that he had to face the consequences of his situation. Finally, on the tenth day, Noriega chose among the few options he had left. Just before nine P.M. on January 3, he donned a clean, pressed uniform with his four general's stars, walked out through the embassy's iron gates and surrendered to his U.S. counterpart, General Maxwell Thurman, commander of Southcom and of the invasion force.

The next day he was arraigned in Miami on multiple counts of drug trafficking and conspiracy, the charges listed in the indictment handed down twenty-three months before. His lawyers immediately launched a broad challenge to the U.S. case, asserting that his arrest was illegal, that his status as chief of state made him immune to prosecution, that he was a political prisoner captured illegally in an invasion that violated international law. The legal team announced it would seek release of classified intelligence documents on Noriega's work for the CIA, including files from the 1976 period when Noriega and President Bush, then the head of the CIA, had met for the first time. In defeat, Noriega positioned himself to fight on, mapping out, as this book goes to press, a strategy for what promised to be one of the most spectacular trials and media events of recent history.

Noriega was finally beaten, but only after he demonstrated remarkable endurance. In evaluating that tenacity, it is revealing to recall the lessons Noriega claims to have learned from "the father of psychological warfare," Genghis Khan. In his book on psychological operations, Noriega wrote: "You can just imagine the terrible effect on the morale of the princes and kings who were Genghis Khan's enemies when their own [spies] returned and gave them that distorted information portraying Genghis Khan and his men as invincible forces before which they must either surrender unconditionally or die."

For more than two decades, Noriega had taken great care to shape the perception his U.S. counterparts formed about him. He did not discourage portrayals of himself as Panama's Darth Vader. When he was described as the feared intelligence chief who had something on everybody in Panama, it was assumed he must also have a smoking gun to use against American officials to keep himself in power. When U.S. officials insisted that "not a sparrow falls" in Panama without Noriega making money from it, or that he was a "rent-a-colonel" with double and triple agendas even while appearing so compliant to U.S. interests, they may actually have been promoting the image Noriega created for himself. When Panamanian opposition leaders spread stories that he was a sexual pervert, a psychopath, a sadist, a rapist, a practitioner of dark cults, they may have fallen into Genghis Khan's trap. "Put down whatever you want [about Noriega] and it will be true," the congressional staffer had said to the Panamanian journalist. Noriega might have approved; he certainly would have smiled.

Seeing Noriega in terms of Genghis Khan's psychological operations helps us to understand how he could be perceived in such radically contradictory ways within the U.S. government: as the apprentice spy of his student years; as the narcotics trafficker of 1971–1972 who provoked a U.S. assassination plot; as the crafty nationalist backing up Torrijos's treaty negotiations with good intelligence and dirty tricks; as the real power in Panama, the man the U.S. military knew it had to cultivate to get free rein in Central America; as the Cuban ally who simultaneously helped Oliver North pull off sabotage operations inside Nicaragua; and finally as the DEA's trusted collaborator, while the investigation leading to his indictment plodded through other offices of the DEA and the Justice Department.

These shifting perceptions of Noriega, in the administration, in Congress, and in the press, bear much of the responsibility for the policy confusion about Panama. At the end, Noriega was reviled as if the United States had never had a greater enemy, communist, fascist or criminal. The U.S. invasion of Panama was unique in American history. Its rationale was not ideological but personal— the removal of a man portrayed as so black of heart, so evil of soul, that any means necessary, even an invasion, was justified to consummate his exorcism.

This book has attempted to draw a bottom line of fact—as distinct from the plethora of myths—about Noriega. To put Noriega's activities into perspective is not to defend them; it is to expose the consequences of basing monumental foreign policy decisions on hysteria and exaggeration. True, Noriega was an international criminal who, according to the most reliable evidence developed by U.S. investigative agencies, profited greatly from narcotics trafficking. The evidence shows he progressed from $150,000 bribes to $4 million protection payoffs. Estimates of his wealth vary widely—in 1986, when he was still a U.S. friend, U.S. officials estimated his wealth at about $16 million; by 1989, when he was an official enemy, the State Department estimate had escalated to $300 million. The vast bulk of Noriega's wealth, whatever the final figure, was most likely derived from the system of official corruption he inherited from Torrijos—in other words, the same kind of graft and systemic corruption that has allowed corrupt rulers in many other countries of the world, many still in office, to prosper at the expense of those who do business in their countries. The top estimates of his profits derived from drugs are $10 to $15 million—substantial sums, but leaving him a mid-level player in the billion-dollar league of the Latin American drug entrepreneurs. Moreover, the evidence suggests that Noriega participated in major drug activity for only a two-to-three-year period in the early 1980s and then became a trusted and overtly zealous DEA collaborator.

Noriega was certainly a cruel man who bears responsibility for a number of murders—the beheading of Hugo Spadafora is only the most egregious. But the scale of murder and repression in Panama under Noriega was far from the killing, torture and disappearances carried out during much of the same period in Chile, Argentina, El Salvador and Guatemala with considerably less U.S. official condemnation. The crimes and cruelty of Noriega cannot be minimized. Yet, compared with other international violators of human rights, the U.S. response seems disproportionate.

A third major charge was that Noriega maintained an intelligence relationship with Fidel Castro and allowed Panama to circumvent the U.S. embargo against Cuba. This was an old complaint, something U.S. officials objected to in the 1970s and early 1980s but, the record indicates, had long since decided they could live with.

Considering all these factors, why was U.S. hostility to Noriega so extreme when the Panamanian situation finally came to a crisis? My judgment is that the decision to force Noriega from power was not the result of any considered policy drafted by experts measuring the costs, benefits and alternatives. In fact, the Reagan and Bush administrations seemed to improvise as they went along, reacting to events in Panama and adapting to a building furor of antidrug sentiment in the United States. That incoherence of strategy is why they failed for so long to neutralize the Panamanian leader. The reconstruction of events for this book indicates that even after the accusations in *The New York Times* in June 1986 of Noriega's drug trafficking and intelligence contacts with Cuba, toleration of Noriega continued for another year. Clear opposition to Noriega emerged in the Reagan administration only after June 1987, as the inexorable response to events it did not control: the mass protest following Colonel Díaz Herrera's defiance of Noriega, the impending indictment of Noriega on drug charges and the unanimous Congressional outrage against Noriega. The administration remained deeply divided until well into 1988 over what to do about Noriega. Until Bush authorized the invasion, the administration was never a leader, never a shaper of events.

Once it finally began to act, the administration lurched into whatever options were presented, no matter how ill considered or contradictory. From a tactical point of view, many U.S. officials, even at the time, conceded that the criminal indictment of Noriega would make his departure from power much more difficult. Exposing Noriega to arrest and extradition in most Western countries was clearly not a policy likely to hasten his acceptance of exile. The U.S. prosecutors who brought the case realized that, under normal circumstances, the indictment of a sitting dictator far out of reach of U.S. law enforcement had virtually no prospect of culminating in a trial. The case was further complicated by Noriega's contacts with the CIA and the likelihood of a graymail, or the "Ollie North" defense—threatening the disclosure of U.S. intelligence secrets at trial. The indictment of Noriega was not only clumsy but clearly counterproductive.

Yet according to the U.S. attorney in Miami, Leon Kellner, no U.S. official ever raised the possibility of developing alternatives to indictment—such as taking the evidence against Noriega to an international forum as part of a multilateral effort to force Noriega out. When President Delvalle, in February 1988, wanted to channel his denunciation and attempted firing of Noriega through the Organization of American States, he was reportedly talked out of it by Elliott Abrams on behalf of the State Department. The United States belatedly took its case to the OAS in August 1989 and was able to muster considerable Latin American sympathy (which the invasion subsequently reversed).

The indictment and unilateral U.S. sanctions tended to personalize the crisis, rendering it a jingoistic vendetta of one U.S. president and then another against Noriega. The U.S. presidents appeared too often to be reacting viscerally to Noriega's calculated taunts. The sanctions and administration saber rattling made it impossible for the United States to forge a united front with Latin American countries to urge Noriega's removal. In those crucial moments in March 1988 when Noriega was at his weakest and world outrage against him was at its peak—a time for tactical subtlety—Abrams and his administration colleagues chose the unilateral course, expecting another quick victory for democracy such as those already achieved in Grenada, the Philippines and Haiti. The U.S. strategy enabled Noriega to hold on to a thread of Latin American legitimacy, portraying himself as a beleaguered nationalist withstanding U.S. intervention.

The high profile consistently adopted by the United States also fed the passive tendencies of the Panamanian opposition. Its leaders showed no stomach for the long-haul popular movement, such as that developed in the Philippines and elsewhere, to confront the dictatorship. Instead, the opposition fell into a pattern of launching a few sporadic demonstrations and then retreating into Miami exile and pleading for U.S. intervention. Even though popular sentiment to get rid of Noriega had spread to every social, racial and geographical sector of the country, the traditional opposition parties made little attempt to expand their organizations beyond their traditional strongholds among white businessmen and in the comfortable neighborhoods of Panama City.

In the end, the overwhelming U.S. role emasculated any possible "Panamanian solution" to which the United States so often rendered lip service. With a civilian opposition too weak to accomplish the task and Noriega's military adversaries too undemocratic and too few, the crisis boiled down to a contest of will between Manuel Noriega and George Bush. Neither had left himself a graceful retreat: Noriega was forced to live up to a lifelong reputation for macho; George Bush was hoping to dispel once and for all the "wimp factor" that had dogged his presidency. The result was an exercise of a superpower's military might to crush one of the smallest armies in the hemisphere, an inglorious invasion that was the final admission of U.S. failure in Panama.

The roots of that failure, of course, go far deeper than misconceived strategy and bungled tactics. The U.S. relationship with Noriega in intelligence and military matters was so close in the early years of the decade—in years we now know Noriega was involved in drug trafficking—that questions have been raised about a possible cover-up. If Noriega was providing crucial assistance for the U.S. war against Nicaragua or elsewhere in Central America, Reagan administration officials may well have been motivated to tolerate his illegal activities, perhaps even the drug trafficking. Another suspicion is that the administration turned against Noriega in retaliation for his refusal to continue cooperating with U.S. Central America policy.

The possibility that the Reagan administration acquiesced to Noriega's drug trafficking as a quid pro quo for his support of the U.S. anticommunist campaign in Central America is at the core of criticism of the U.S. handling of the Noriega affair.

The available evidence on this issue has been presented in these pages, but no definitive answers can be given so long as the relevant official documents remain secret. There is also room for speculation about Noriega's long relationship with the CIA in areas that may have nothing to do with Central America. But certain conclusions can be drawn about Our Man in Panama based on what we know now—conclusions not likely to be significantly changed by further revelations:

1. Whatever Noriega's role, U.S. goals elsewhere in Central America determined its actions and policies in Panama. During the crucial period Noriega was most involved in drug trafficking, 1982–1984, U.S. officials—at the embassy, in Southcom and in the various intelligence

agencies—were focused not on Panama itself but on Nicaragua, El Salvador and Honduras. Panama was merely a staging area for activities in other countries.

Noriega's greatest service to the United States may have been his willingness to allow the use of U.S. bases for military purposes in clear violation of the Panama Canal Treaties. Those activities involving bases in Panama, described in Chapter 7, were a prized contribution to the U.S. war effort, certainly one that earned Noriega a debt of gratitude from U.S. leaders.

There is also evidence that Panama was used to transship arms to Contra forces fighting under Edén Pastora, who also received a $100,000 payment from Noriega. Noriega's participation in the dirty tricks operations organized by Oliver North against Nicaragua in the spring of 1985 may have been more significant than now known. But there is no corroboration for José Blandón's claim that Noriega arranged to train Contras in Panama in 1985 in preparation for an invasion of Nicaragua in 1986 that never occurred. Doubts about Blandón's credibility have been noted previously; it seems significant, moreover, that North's notebooks and computer notes provide ample detail about Contra support activities by other countries but do not substantiate any of Blandón's claims. Indeed, they say very little at all about Panama between early 1985 and late 1986.

2. Panamanian opposition leaders have charged that Noriega's drug trafficking was common knowledge in Panama and that there was no excuse for official U. S. ignorance. In fact, in the early 1980s accusations of Panamanian official complicity in drug activity did not contain specific information about Noriega's involvement. There was certainly nothing even approaching the concrete evidence later provided by Floyd Carlton and Steven Kalish.

Ample evidence of Noriega's past drug activities, however, was developed by the Bureau of Narcotics and Dangerous Drugs in 1971–1972 and had been presented before the Senate during the debate over the Canal treaties. But that information seems to have been erased from the collective memories of U.S. officials making decisions about Panama during the 1980s. Had that evidence been recalled, the suspicions of Noriega's drug activities would not have been dismissed when they arose in 1984 as a result of the Julián Melo affair. U.S. officials dealing with Noriega then may not have had indictable evidence, but for too long they were willing to take a see-no-evil approach because confronting Noriega would put U.S. goals in Central America at risk.

3. A key event in the still murky connection between U.S. Central America policy and U.S. attitudes toward Noriega was a December 1985 meeting between NSC chief John Poindexter and Noriega. Noriega has used the meeting to bolster his case, belatedly, that the United States turned against him because he refused to go along with a U.S. invasion of Nicaragua. But some U.S. officials, notably Elliott Abrams and former U.S. ambassador Briggs, insist that Poindexter dressed down Noriega for his drug trafficking and other actions. Some press accounts, based on U.S. government sources, went further to depict the 1985 meeting as the beginning of an internal campaign by Poindexter to "get rid" of Noriega.

Both versions may be distorted. The Poindexter meeting with Noriega is one of the most closely guarded secrets of the Reagan administration. The idea that Poindexter began a campaign against Noriega is contradicted by most reliable evidence. There was no action taken against Noriega, certainly not by Poindexter or Abrams, during all of 1986. In fact connections between North, Poindexter's aide, and Noriega suggest that Noriega saw the National Security Council as a source of support, not criticism.

As described in Chapter 11, Noriega approached North with an offer of assassination and sabotage in Nicaragua and a request to "help clean up Noriega's image." Soon after, North contacted DEA chief Jack Lawn to discuss Noriega—just at a time the DEA investigation of Noriega was making headway. The episode is still shielded by many layers of U.S. government secrecy. Elliott Abrams was a party to the deliberations inside the administration about Noriega's offers. Two years later Abrams began to portray himself as the foremost advocate of a military solution to remove Noriega, but he has refused to discuss the 1986 contacts between North and Noriega. In my judgment, if there really was a cover-up attempted in the Noriega affair, the Poindexter-North-Abrams relationship should be the first place to look.

·   ·   ·

Panama was the sideshow in Central America, the one country that had most successfully avoided the region's ideological polarization and social conflicts. Panama, even as Noriega rose to power, was the last country the United States expected to produce trouble. It ended as it began in 1903, barely a country at all, and one whose destiny was determined not by its citizens but by the power reflexes of the United States. As Panama entered 1990 under indefinite U.S. military occupation its shattered institutions stood as a monument to conflicting U.S. motives. Noriega had been our ally in what counted most: the U.S. war against perceived communist influence in our backyard. He served our interest by recognizing our real first priority, the defense against challenges to U.S. influence in the area. When the war on communism conflicted with other U.S. goals—the war on drugs and the promotion of real democracy—the U.S. policy makers could not hold the several policies before them at one time. One was given our near exclusive attention, the others lip service. Manuel Noriega, despite rigged elections and a long history of corruption and drug activities, remained our man.

When he was finally removed at the cost of hundreds of human lives, the U.S. invasion was condemned around the world, but almost no one came to the defense of Manuel Noriega, who had treated his leadership of a country as a game, finally overplaying, finally pulling the monkey's chain once too often.

ACKNOWLEDGMENTS

My interest in writing a book about Panama and Manuel Noriega grew out of a trip to Panama in September 1985 to lecture on investigative reporting. I arrived the day Hugo Spadafora's decapitated body was identified in Costa Rica, thus confirming the political assassination that ended the climate of nonviolence that had made Panama such an exception in Central America.

I owe a debt of special gratitude to my friends Carlos López Guevara and José Barbero, who from opposite sides of the Panamanian conflict showed me that combination of political flexibility, middle-class common sense, and unfailing humor that is at the heart of Panamanian society.

Many people helped in the preparation of this book. Deborah Charles, my research assistant, gave me her hard work, sharp wit and enthusiasm. Scott Armstrong and the staff of the National Security Archive provided not only a place to work but an environment for journalistic investigation second to none in Washington. The Archive's support in my Freedom of Information Act searches was invaluable. The Fund for Investigative Journalism provided partial financial support. My employer, National Public Radio, supported my project in many ways and by allowing me that most precious commodity, time. My appreciation goes particularly to former foreign editor John McChesney, who saw my book project as part of the top quality journalism he was trying to build at NPR, and to Cadi Simon.

I am particularly grateful to the journalists who helped me think through the complexities and unanswered questions of the Panama story and who showed unstinting generosity in many other ways. My thanks to Andres Oppenheimer, Sam Dillon, and Alfonso Chardy of *The Miami Herald,* whose reporting on Panama outshone all others; and to Katherine King; Dimetrio Olaciregui and Lucia Newman; Martha Honey and Tony Avirgan; Guillermo Sánchez Borbón; Tom Gjelten; Howard Kohn and Vicky Monks; Stephen Engelberg; Murray Wass; John Kelly; Jay Horning; Brian Barger; Cheryl Arvidson; Jefferson Morley; and Steven Emerson.

Saul Landau, John Zindar, Lee Fleming, Jeff Stein and Frank Browning read early drafts, and my writing was immensely improved by their observations and insights. Peter Osnos of Random House saw a book in the Noriega story long before it was on the front pages, and Mark Riebling's editing made a crucial contribution to the book's final shape.

Charlotte Sheedy, Gabriel Lewis Galindo, Roberto Díaz Herrera, Judith de León, Cynthia Farrell, Eddie Becker, Peter Kornbluh, Malcolm Byrne, Ari de Spadafora, Gwenda Blair, Jerry Loeb, Martha Ann Overland, Lynda Davis, Linda Bunch, Andrea Eagan and Jim Gordon helped in many other ways. Carolina Kenrick and my children, Tomás, Sebastián and Camila, gave love and encouragement when it counted. Thanks to all of you.

NOTES

CHAPTER I: THE RAID

p. 6   Cocaine processing: Bramble and Quiel were looking at the final stage
in a refining process that would have begun in rudimentary sites in the
mountains of Peru or Bolivia. There, the shiny coca leaves are har-
vested by hand, dumped into huge vats (often just holes dug in the
ground and lined with black plastic sheets) and covered with kerosene
and dilute sulfuric acid. After days of mixing and stomping by workers
who wade in the vats up to their thighs, the resulting mush is strained.
The liquid is combined with a succession of other chemicals—ammo-
nia, potassium permanganate, gasoline, citric acid—and eventually
yields a lumpy white coagulate that is cocaine base. About 250 kilos
of leaves make 1 kilo of base, or paste, 75 percent pure.

For many years, when cocaine was little used and immensely expensive on the illegal market, hundreds of primitive basement laboratories
scattered throughout Latin America and the United States carried out
the final processing, from paste to powder, each lab producing only a
few kilos at a time. The genius of the Colombian drug entrepreneurs
was to impose vertical integration on the previously decentralized
cocaine-processing industry. They bought cocaine base by the ton, not
by the kilo, and captured a nearly total monopoly of supply. The
cocaine base was shipped by plane or truck to factories in Colombia.

p. 8   The DEA and the cartel: In early 1984, DEA agents like Bramble
were cautiously optimistic that their combined efforts with govern-

ments of such countries as Colombia and Panama were having some effect. The Colombians discovered the Tranquilandia complex in Caquetá Province, because of Operation Chemcon, perhaps the DEA's most successful undercover operation ever. The DEA tracked down the U.S. suppliers of chemicals they knew were being shipped to Colombia for use in cocaine processing. They planted two barrels of their own among a shipment of seventy-six drums; the special barrels were equipped with radio tracking devices and battery packs embedded in a false bottom. Military satellites followed the beeping barrels to their final destination, then the DEA passed the map coordinates to the Colombian police.

After the raid, mayhem broke out in Colombia. The Colombian attorney general, Rodrigo Lara Bonilla, launched the most intense drive against drug traffickers seen in Colombia until then. In late April, a man riding a small motorcycle darted through traffic and machine-gunned Lara Bonilla while he was driving to work. Police raided the homes of known cartel leaders, at least one of them a member of the Colombian parliament. The DEA developed intelligence that the cartel might be restarting some of its operations across the border inside Panama. Bramble had passed that information on to Inspector Quiel and asked him to have his men keep their eyes open in Darién. With that factory destroyed, the cartel had moved quickly to replace it and keep production going. Darién was only one of the sites where the cartel was thought to be building new factories. Others were later discovered in Ecuador and Brazil. Informants also said that the cartel was planning to build a cocaine factory in Nicaragua in 1984, but the plan was aborted, according to the informants, after the Reagan administration made some of that information public.

p. 8   Cocaine prices: I have used the low estimate of $5,000 per kilo of cocaine for all wholesale transactions involving production and shipping to the United States. Once in the United States, the value increases enormously.

p. 8   Tranquilandia figures: *The Miami Herald,* December 2, 1987. For the best description of the raid, see Guy Gugliotta and Jeff Leen, *Kings of Cocaine* (New York: Simon and Schuster, 1989), ch. 13.

p. 8   The names of the twenty-three prisoners are listed in the 1986 booklet, *16 Años de Lucha Contra el Narcotráfico,* published and distributed by the government of Panama, p. 246. Several other camp residents, presumably those with the most direct connection to the cartel, are known to have escaped in the second camp helicopter when PDF reconnaissance flyovers began prior to the attack. They have not been identified. Otalvaro Cabrera Medina was indicted by a Miami grand jury in February 1988 on trafficking charges.

p. 8   My account of the Darién raid is based on interviews with Bramble and Villalaz. The Panamanian government account, presumably based on Quiel's report, is contained in the booklet, *16 Años*. The most complete version of Alvarez's press conference is in *Crítica*, May 24, 1984.

p. 9   Turner meeting: *Matutino*, June 5, 1984. Carlton Turner, in an interview, said he did not recall the specifics of any of his several meetings with Noriega. He visited Panama in 1984 and 1985. Turner has since claimed to be one of the few U.S. officials to raise questions about Noriega's possible drug connections in this period, but his contemporary reports about his trips to Panama and contacts with Noriega have remained classified, and other officials are skeptical about his claims.

p. 9   Ether raids: Several shiploads of ethyl ether bound for Colombia were tracked from West Germany and Holland. An earlier raid netted 1,348 drums. Panama also claimed credit for another smaller seizure off Colombia because the tracking devices had been installed while the ship carrying the ether was docked in Colón's Coco Solo harbor. See *16 Años*, p. 60. DEA officials have not confirmed Panama's assistance in placing tracking devices.

p. 11   Spadafora statement: *La Prensa*, March 15, 1984.

p. 11   Penthouse meeting: This account is based on interviews with Steven Kalish, a federal prisoner serving a twenty-year sentence for drug smuggling. Kalish also testified publicly on his relationship with Noriega. See "Drugs and Money Laundering in Panama," Hearing before the Senate Permanent Subcommittee on Investigations, January 28, 1988 (Washington, D.C.: U.S. Government Printing Office, 1988). Conversations recounted in this chapter, in which he was a party, are based on his recollections.

p. 15   Mendez brothers: According to *16 Años*, the Panamanian government report, the Mendez brothers had been under investigation for several months in connection with ether shipments. The report adds some intriguing details about their role: "On April 11, 1984, DENI's antinarcotics office in Colón, an Atlantic port city that includes the Colón Free Zone, reported the existence of a big quantity of ethyl ether tanks, that had just arrived in the Free Zone from Germany in transit to Colombian ports. The investigation showed that the merchandise was handled by Gabriel Mendez, Olmedo Mendez and Ricardo Tribaldos. Jaime Castillo, Ricardo Tribaldos's partner, was in charge of the dirty work of receiving and dispatching the ethyl ether. Castillo and Tribaldos were old friends; they went to a military college in Lima. Castillo did not finish his studies as he could not pass the final exams. He joined DENI [Departmento Nacional de Investigaciones, the PDF's criminal investigation unit], but was expelled for immoral behavior. Castillo could act as informer for the mafia because he knew the authorities in charge of drug trafficking repression. . . .

"On June 5, 1984, Panama's Defense Forces were informed of the illegal activities of Gabriel Mendez, Olmedo Mendez and Ricardo Tribaldos, who had offered to pay $2 million so that the ethyl ether detected and captured in Panama, could be sent to Colombia. To achieve their sinister purpose, the delinquents threatened a massive withdrawal of Colombian funds from three banks operating in Panama, so as to damage the national economy by creating a climate of instability and insecurity."

p. 18   Noriega's travel: Exact dates are difficult to pinpoint in this account, and recollections of those participants who have provided information do not always agree. Angel's and Zambrano's arrests are mentioned in *16 Años* as occurring on June 22, while Noriega was in Paris. The call, according to Kalish, was the next day. Noriega then flew to Israel. Noriega's itinerary has been reconstructed from FBIS (Foreign Broadcast Information Service) references, Panamanian newspaper items and two U.S. military intelligence reports.

p. 18   Assassination scheme: The Panamanian government publication, *16 Años* (p. 62), has this account of the alleged assassination plot: "When the ether was confiscated and destroyed and the laboratory was found and its workers arrested, the drug-trafficking group questioned the protection they had paid for and did not get. The then Lieutenant Colonel Melo, Gabriel Mendez and Ricardo Tribaldos had a last meeting at Melo's mother's home, where the situation was analyzed. The then Lieutenant Colonel Melo said that considering the uncontrollable coercive actions under the irrevocable command of General Noriega, it was necessary to eliminate him and Colonel Roberto Díaz Herrera and he suggested that the Colombians should organize and carry out a criminal attempt to assassinate General Noriega, who was then in Europe."

Kalish claims that Noriega later credited him with bringing Melo's assassination scheme to light and with smoothing things over with cartel representatives. He said he was told by another PDF officer, Major Pérez, that Noriega said in a meeting with officers that he was grateful to "Brown" (Kalish's alias) for acting as intermediary.

p. 20   Call to Melo: Quiel related the conversation to a DEA official, emphasizing that the tape recording is available as proof of Noriega's innocence.

p. 20   Noriega call from Tel Aviv: Interview with Díaz Herrera, who mentions the exchange in his book, *Panamá: Mucho Más Que Noriega* (Caracas: Self-published, 1988), p. 89.

p. 21   Others present, according to Díaz Herrera, were Lieutenant Colonels Armijo, Garibaldo, Mina, Ow Young, Cal, and Alba.

p. 21   The account of the meeting in the officers' mess is based on the author's interviews with Díaz Herrera and on an unpublished interview with Melo by Andres Oppenheimer of *The Miami Herald.* Additional details were provided by two DEA officials, based on their sources in the PDF. Díaz Herrera said in an interview he was able to confirm that the money was indeed delivered, according to Noriega's orders. In his book, Díaz Herrera says that the Colombians complained that the entire amount paid to Melo was not returned to them. The missing money may have been as much as $1 million, but I was unable to find a firsthand source willing to clarify this point. Melo denies any was missing.

p. 24   Cartel offer: The cartel offered to stop their own drug trafficking and to help the Colombian authorities dismantle other trafficking operations. They said they were responsible for 70–80 percent of cocaine trafficking originating in Colombia, which was netting them about $2 billion a year. They denied that their organization was responsible for the murder of Lara Bonilla or that they were linked in any way to leftist guerrilla groups fighting the government. Colombia, in exchange, was asked only to allow them to liquidate and repatriate their assets—up to $5 billion—and resume life as "full citizens." The bottom-line demand was the suspension of all extradition proceedings pending against them with the United States. See *La Prensa,* July 5, 6, 10, 1984.

p. 24   Editorials and ADO statement, *La Prensa,* July 4, 5, 1984.

p. 24   Blandón's linking of Castro, Noriega and the cartel received wide publicity after February 11, 1988, when he testified before the Senate Subcommittee on Terrorism, Narcotics and International Communication, chaired by Senator John Kerry of Massachusetts. See *Drugs, Law Enforcement and Foreign Policy* (Parts I, II, III, IV), Hearings Before the Senate Subcommittee on Terrorism, Narcotics and International Communications (Washington, D.C.: U.S. Government Printing Office, 1988), hereinafter Kerry Hearings. The Castro link was included in the Miami indictment of Noriega, also based on Blandón's testimony. Castro, in a February 28, 1988, interview with NBC News, said that Blandón's statements were "lies and slanders." A Cuban government source told me that the Darién incident did come up in Noriega's conversation with Castro, but only as an example of Panama's success in cracking down on drug traffickers.

My account of the settlement is based primarily on the independent accounts of Díaz Herrera and Kalish. Neither knew what the other had to say about the episode at the time they discussed it with me; they have never met. Basic elements of their story are backed by documentary evidence.

This is Blandón's story, as told to the Kerry subcommittee (Kerry Hearings II, 100ff): Blandón says Noriega called him from London and ordered him to go to Havana to seek Castro's help with the conflict with the cartel. Noriega was on his way back from Israel, Blandón said, and feared returning to Panama until the cartel-Melo situation was cleared up. Blandón says he flew to Cuba, arriving before Noriega, and met with Castro. He says Castro demonstrated detailed knowledge about the Melo imbroglio. In the presence of Blandón and PDF Captain Felipe Camargo, Castro outlined the way Melo had divided the $5 million among Noriega and his partners, according to Blandón. He said Castro also exhibited knowledge of large amounts of cocaine, ether, equipment and prisoners captured at the factory. The solution suggested by Castro was for Noriega to return to the cartel the payoff money, the cocaine and the helicopter confiscated at the plant and to release the twenty-three prisoners arrested in the raid, Blandón said. When Noriega arrived, he talked alone with Castro until 3 A.M., and subsequently the settlement was carried out as suggested by Castro.

I am skeptical about Blandón's account for several reasons. First of all, a very high standard of evidence should be required to make a case that a sitting head of state would personally immerse himself in a dispute involving international criminals. Even assuming criminal intent on Castro's part, it is difficult to imagine him discussing protection payoffs, cocaine stockpiles and drug-processing machinery with a low-ranking civilian, Blandón, and a PDF captain, Camargo. Blandón and his defenders place great stock in the photographs that show Blandón, Noriega, Pretelt and others with Castro. But the photographs, while clearly establishing that a high-level, fully staffed meeting occurred, shed no light on the content of the talks.

More important, the dates and other facts do not gibe with what can be established independently of Blandón's version. Blandón says that the prisoners were released and that the money and equipment returned to the cartel after Noriega returned to Panama—that is, after July 6, 1984. In fact, the twenty-three prisoners were released more than a month earlier, in late May, according to Major Villalaz, who flew them to Colombia, and to Panamanian press accounts (*La Prensa,* May 27, 1984). According to Díaz Herrera and Kalish, the matter of the money and equipment also had been resolved before Noriega even arrived in Cuba. Blandón gives several dates for the Noriega-Castro meeting: June 22 or 28 (Kerry subcommittee) or June 29 (Miami grand jury). In an interview with the author, Blandón corrected that recollection by associating it with the visit of U.S. presidential candidate Jesse Jackson to Cuba a few days before his own visit. Jackson had left Cuba on June 28, and Blandón said his own arrival was the following Tuesday. He said that the Jackson visit—which resulted in the release of a number of Cuban political prisoners—was a topic of discussion in his meeting with Castro. That would place Blandón's arrival as July 3 and Noriega's July 5. Blandón also said that Noriega returned directly to Panama after spending two days in Cuba.

By that time, the PDF meeting dismissing Melo and returning the money had already occurred. The latest date for that meeting is Friday, June 29, since Melo's discharge was published the next day in the official Order of the Day.

Other circumstantial contradictions also cast doubt on the story. Castro's purported knowledge about the Darién raid and the inner workings of Melo's deal with the cartel was erroneous to the extent other facts are available. For example, Blandón has Castro saying that cocaine and ether were seized at the Darién plant. Yet other sources with firsthand knowledge of the raid, Major Villalaz and DEA agent Bramble, say that none was found and that the plant had not begun processing.

Blandón contends that Noriega was so fearful of the cartel's wrath or of Melo's planned coup that he delayed his return to Panama, going to Cuba instead. Blandón says that Castro provided Noriega with a bodyguard of twenty-five elite troops to accompany him in the plane back to Panama in case there was trouble (Kerry Hearings II, 105–6). As I point out in the text, Melo was already in custody in Panama and the danger of a coup had passed. If Noriega had thought there was a danger of Melo fomenting a coup in Panama, it is hard to believe that Noriega would have sent him there. Díaz Herrera, who greeted Noriega on his arrival in Panama, says he saw no Cuban troops.

In short, everyone else would have to be lying or seriously deceived—Kalish, Díaz Herrera, Villalaz and Bramble—for Blandón's story to hold up.

CHAPTER 2: THE KID FROM TERRAPLÉN

p. 29   Name that strikes terror: *The Washington Post,* March 8, 1978.

p. 29   Satanic sign question: The interviewer was T. D. Allman, whose entertaining, but rumor-ridden profile of Noriega appeared in *Vanity Fair,* June 1988.

p. 29   *Ego sum:* Cf. Exodus 3: 13–15: " 'But if they ask me what his name is, what am I to tell them?' And God said to Moses, 'I Am who I Am. . . . This is my name for all time.' " Noriega's use of the quotation reflects an understanding of modern biblical interpretation. *The Jerusalem Bible* (New York: Doubleday, 1966), p. 81, provides the following note: "It may be that Yahweh [the third person Hebrew form of 'I am'], is used here to imply the impossibility of giving an adequate definition of God. In Semitic thought, knowledge of a name gave power over the thing named; to know a god's name was to be able to call on him and to be certain of a hearing. The true God does not make himself man's slave in this way by revealing a name expressive of his essence. . . . Understood in this fashion, the name does not define God; nevertheless, for Israel it will always call to mind God's great deliverance of his chosen people and the divine generosity, fidelity and power that prompted it."

p. 30   Torrijos a prisoner: The story made its way into an op-ed piece by investigative reporter Seymour Hersh, citing American intelligence officials (*The New York Times,* May 4, 1988). An early and perhaps original version of the story was given wide circulation in the United States by a Panamanian named Alexis Watson, who claimed to be one of Noriega's G2 agents in the early 1970s. The claim that Noriega had held Torrijos prisoner in 1976 was only one of a litany of murders, dope deals and sexual deviations Watson attributed to Torrijos and Noriega. His deposition, circulated by opponents of the Panama Canal treaties, was discredited by investigators for the Senate Intelligence Committee, whose chairman, Senator Birch Bayh, reported on the matter to a closed session of the Senate, February 21–22, 1978, examining allegations of Panamanian corruption. Bayh said Watson was at one time considered a fabricator and possible intelligence plant by the FBI (see *Congressional Record,* Senate, 4125, February 23, 1975). Nevertheless, the story of Torrijos's detention was picked up from the transcript of the closed Senate session and reported without qualification in a March 4, 1978, UPI story. My interviews with U.S. military and diplomats in a position to know, including the U.S. and Panamanian ambassadors at the time, failed to produce any confirmatory evidence. Roberto Díaz Herrera, who was a top aide to Torrijos at the time, also denies flatly that any such thing occurred.

p. 31   Details of Noriega's early life are difficult to verify and sources are seldom willing to be named. In one case, a high school classmate of Noriega's shook visibly with fear and would only repeat one sentence, that as a youngster Noriega was "nothing out of the ordinary." The identity of Noriega's parents is a matter of public record. Some sources claim Noriega was actually born in 1934 and changed his birthdate to make himself four years younger in order to meet the age requirement for military school. I have used his birthdate as reported in U.S. Army Intelligence files, as released under the Freedom of Information Act (FOIA). The most complete portrait of Noriega is by Arturo G. Esparza, 470th Military Intelligence Unit, U.S. Southern Command, Biographic Report, Form 1396i, October 26, 1976, hereinafter Esparza Report. The report lists Noriega's race as "caucasian w/ apparent negroid trace."

The pamphlet, *El Criollo de Terraplén,* was written by Major Francisco Porras, who has promoted Noriega's image with compilations of sayings and speeches. Porras, in an interview, provided the information about Mama Luisa's role and Noriega's childhood. Colonel Roberto Díaz Herrera provided additional details and character insights, some based on his conversations with a man who grew up in Terraplén with Noriega and maintained a lifelong relationship with him.

p. 32   Intelligence reports: Esparza Report.

p. 33   Porras stipend: Interview with Gerardo Gonzales.

p. 33   Intelligence connections: The several sources who mentioned

Noriega's high school intelligence connections included a Panamanian who worked with the Panama Canal intelligence service in the 1950s and a congressional staff member who participated in investigations of Panama in the 1970s. Stephen Engelberg and Jeff Gerth of *The New York Times* said in a September 28, 1988, article that U.S. government officials had confirmed that "Noriega had first come to the attention of the United States in the 1950s . . . when he volunteered to inform on leftist students." An anonymous twenty-two-page document provided by Panamanian opposition sources, but whose reliability could not be determined, contains a detailed account of the alleged high school spying. According to the account, entitled *"Hacia Donde Vas, Panamá"* ("Where Are You Headed, Panama"), Noriega was introduced to a forty-five-year-old man said to be a possible source of economic help and a CIA agent. The man at first paid for tips about actions that might result in harm to U.S. citizens in Panama. The man then increased his demands and asked Noriega to join student organizations to gather firsthand information about planned student acts of violence, which the document claims Noriega himself sometimes provoked to give added veracity to his reports.

p. 34 Ridicule, disguising weakness: Interview with Díaz Herrera and his *Panamá: Mucho Más Que Noriega,* pp. 76–77.

p. 35 Letter to Kennedy: Cited in Steve C. Ropp, *Panamanian Politics: From Guarded Nation to National Guard* (New York: Praeger Publishers, 1982), p. 49.

p. 37 Colón rape: Interview with Boris Martínez.

p. 37 Thirty days' restriction: FOIA release, Defense Intelligence Agency (DIA), Biographic Report, Form 1396i, January 1970, 470th Military Intelligence Group, U.S. Southern Command.

p. 37 David rape: Díaz Herrera, *Panamá: Mucho Más Que Noriega,* pp. 78–79, and interview. Díaz Herrera was stationed with Noriega in David at the time and had direct knowledge of the disciplinary action.

p. 38 Repression of Arnulfistas: Esparza Report; interviews with Boris Martínez, who succeeded Torrijos as commander of the Chiriquí military zone, and with Carlos Rodríguez, a close associate of Arias. Noriega's suspension was April 4–13, 1964.

p. 38 Jungle course: FOIA release, U.S. Army School of the Americas, student report for Noriega's course, May 3–21, 1965.

p. 39 Officers' course: FOIA release: U.S. Army School of the Americas, academic records for Manuel Noriega. The officers' course ran from

January to June and the counterintelligence course from October to December 1967.

p. 40 Noriega's U.S. connections: Esparza Report.

p. 41 Racial makeup of Panama: *Area Handbook for Panama* (Department of the Army, 1962), pp. 71–82. The term "mestizo" in Panamanian usage indicates European-Negro as well as European-Indian racial characteristics. Beneath the social upper crust, whose exclusive whiteness gave rise to the derogatory term *"rabiblanco,"* Panama has few rigid racial lines. Even before the Torrijos revolution, Panama was among the most racially mixed and socially integrated societies in Latin America. "Persons regarded as mestizo are found at all social levels, irrespective of the measure in which either white, Indian or Negro blood appears to dominate their ancestry. It is possible to generalize about the correspondence of ethnic factors with class status only to the extent that white elements are more visible at the top of the social pyramid, and recognizably Negroid features tend to cluster near the bottom" (ibid., p. 72). The most distinct racial groups are the approximately 100,000 tribally organized Guayami, Cuna and Choco Indians and the English-speaking Antillean blacks, who make up about 8 percent of the population. The Antillean blacks migrated from the Caribbean islands to Panama as workers to build the canal and have been subject to periodic discriminatory treatment.

p. 41 U.S. investment was $1,325 per capita at the beginning of the decade. In absolute terms, Panama in 1970 was the fourth-ranking country in U.S. direct investment in Latin America and by 1978 had moved into third place, with only the economic giants Brazil and Mexico above her. Ropp, *Panamanian Politics,* pp. 108–10.

p. 42 Arias shootout: Sixteen people were killed, including two National Guard officers shot in cold blood when they tried to serve the National Assembly's impeachment notice to Arias. LaFeber, p. 113.

p. 44 Ouster of Martínez: Interview with Martínez. An excellent account of the military and political maneuvering surrounding the Torrijos government is Renato Pereira, *Panamá: Fuerzas Armadas y Política* (Panama: Ediciones Nueva Universidad, 1979).

p. 45 Suppression of guerrillas: Interview with Díaz Herrera: "There were a dozen [National Guard] dead and you would have to triple that with regard to the guerrillas." See also Pereira, *Panamá,* p. 125.

p. 46 Torrijos interview: Medoro Lagos, *El General Volvió, Segunda Parte* (Panama City: ERSA, 1988). The book is a republication of his 1972

account of Torrijos's return, *El General Volvió.* It includes interviews
at the time with Torrijos, Noriega, the two pilots and others. Lagos was
a journalist who worked in the public relations department of the
National Guard post in David.

p. 46 Appointment of brother: Ibid., and Pereira, *Panamá.* Luís Carlos
got through to his brother later in the day, according to Lagos, and
said he was "virtually a hostage" and had had no choice but to go along
with the appointment. Luís Carlos Noriega later served in a variety of
government jobs and died in 1984.

p. 46 Paredes interview: *La Prensa,* December 18, 1982.

p. 46 Torrijos's loyalists: They included Captains Lorenzo Purcell and
Elías Castillo and Lieutenant Guillermo Wong, who were in charge of
Panama City's Tocumen Airport, where the National Guard's small
air force was located. Other loyalists included Noriega's brother-in-
law, Lieutenant Aquilino Sieiro, Captain Ricardo Garibaldo and Lieutenant Edilberto del Cid, all of whom later were part of Noriega's inner
circle. Noriega's actions are described in Lagos, *El General Volvió.*

p. 47 Noriega speech: Lagos, *El General Volvió,* p. 75.

CHAPTER 3: OPERATIONAL CONTROL

p. 50 Hijacking: Interview with Augusto Villalaz, who added that the
pilot of the plane was Enrique Pretelt, then working for COPA, the
Panamanian Airlines Company. The incident is mentioned in the Esparza Report and interviews with U.S. intelligence personnel.

As recounted over the years, this and similar incidents of violence
have been ascribed more and more directly to Noriega. One U.S.
source said he was told that Noriega personally executed the high-
jacker with a small automatic pistol. According to a former member
of the 470th, a National Guard source reported that Noriega personally executed another man, a Panamanian-American named Anderson. According to the report, Anderson was kidnapped in Costa Rica
as part of an Arnulfistas guerrilla group and brought back to Panama.
He was hung by his thumbs, then forced to dig his own grave and then
shot. When he sat up in the grave, according to the report, Noriega
allegedly jumped into the grave and stabbed him to death. The killing
was investigated by the 470th and reports were filed, but no action was
taken by Noriega's intelligence contacts to confront him. I was unable
to learn further details of the alleged killing.

p. 51   Body thrown into sea: Statement by Father Pedro Hernández Raba-
        lat, in the Colombian magazine, *Véa,* 1972. The statement was also
        carried by AFP, August 21, 1972, and printed in *El Sol de México.* In
        that account the name is spelled Robadal.
p. 51   Noriega "investigation": Interview with Juan Materno Vásquez,
        July 1988.
           Noriega's role had expanded in later accounts of the incident. Sey-
        mour Hersh, *The New York Times,* May 4, 1988, writes that the U.S.
        Army had reports that Noriega was overheard joking about the mur-
        der. Hersh's account, based on U.S. intelligence sources, differs from
        Rabalat's in that Hersh's sources allege Gallegos was taken up in the
        helicopter immediately after his arrest and was thrown out over land,
        but he did not die until several days later. In Hersh's account, Noriega
        was present in the helicopter.
p. 51   The CIA relationship was described by several U.S. military and
        diplomatic sources whose identities cannot be revealed. The CIA has
        never revealed anything willingly about its long relationship with
        Noriega. The existence of the payments was discussed publicly by
        former ambassador to Panama William Jorden on ABC's *Nightline* in
        February 1988. In an interview with me, Jorden said that Noriega "was
        what is known as an asset, no doubt. In that business he extracted his
        pound of flesh, but I wasn't involved in the CIA payroll, so I don't
        know how much they were giving him, if it was regular, or what. . . .
        No doubt that at some stage in late sixties, seventies that Noriega was
        certainly on CIA payroll." There have been newspaper accounts that
        could not be independently confirmed that put the amount as high as
        $200,000 a year. I am skeptical, based on dozens of interviews with
        U.S. officials, that personal payments to Noriega were in that range.
        It is conceivable that the stories refer to the institution-to-institution
        payments described above.
p. 51   Noriega's official contact with the United States was CIA station
        chief Stanley Burnett, who was replaced in August 1971 by Joe Yoshio
        Kiyonaga, an imposing World War II veteran who had been part of
        the CIA's activist Latin American operations team, with previous
        postings in Brazil in 1960 and El Salvador in 1966. Cf. State Depart-
        ment, Biographical Registry, 1977, for Burnett and Kiyonaga postings.
p. 52   Angueira relationship was described by Boris Martínez and Roberto
        Díaz Herrera in separate interviews and by several U.S. officials. Sanjur

told Panamanian journalist Guillermo Sánchez Borbón about his luncheon meeting with Angueira, but claimed not to have discussed the coup plans.

Former Ambassador Jorden lends credence to Panamanian suspicions of U.S. involvement. In his book, *Panama Odyssey* (Austin: University of Texas, 1984), p. 144, he says, "I uncovered no evidence there was an American plot to remove Torrijos from power, certainly not at responsible policy levels. But some intelligence agents may have given the power-hungry young colonels the impression that a move against Torrijos would not be unwelcome. My suspicion is that something of the sort almost certainly happened, and later events fed that suspicion."

p. 53   Esparza Report: FOIA release, 470th MI, Biographic Report.

p. 54   CIA cooperation: FOIA release, Report on Inquiry into CIA-Related Electronic Surveillance Activities, June 30, 1970, p. 56, defines the CIA's collaboration with BNDD as follows: "1) [to] penetrate the major hard drug collection, refining and distribution networks, and 2) to discover which foreign government and police officials are protecting or assisting the traffickers." The document was obtained from the National Security Archive, a repository for declassified government documents.

p. 55   New treaty negotiations: Jorden, *Panama Odyssey,* ch. 7, recounts the failed 1971 negotiations, which began with the arrival in April of U.S. special envoy Robert Anderson. A major question by the Panamanians, Jorden writes, was, "What does jurisdiction over crimes have to do with running the waterway?" (p. 159).

p. 55   Army reaction: LaFeber, *The Panama Canal,* p. 210.

p. 56   Meeting with Tack and Noriega, plane ride: Interview with Laurence "Gerry" Strickler.

p. 56   Him González wrote the affidavit in 1978, after his release from federal prison. His account of the airplane trip does not differ in any significant details from Strickler's description of the same events. The affidavit is included in *16 Años,* p. 87.

p. 59   Intent to indict Noriega: Interview with Strickler. See also *The Village Voice,* October 11, 1988.

p. 59   Moisés Torrijos's case: "Report to the Senate of Senator Birch Bayh, Chairman Select Committee on Intelligence," a declassified version of Bayh's report to a closed session of the Senate, February 21–22, 1978. The record of that debate was released in expurgated form a few weeks later and is contained in the *Congressional Record,* Senate, 3967–4125. Moisés Torrijos's indictment is discussed pp. 3975ff. Details of the case are also found in a letter to *The New York Times,* September 26, 1973, from Representative John Murphy (Dem.-N.Y.), which was also entered in the *Congressional Record,* House, 8354, September 26, 1973.

p. 60   "Overall operational control": Bayh report, p. 14. The BNDD source was among a group of exiles organized in Miami by former National Guard officer Federico Boyd, who fled to Miami after his involvement in the 1969 coup attempt against Torrijos. In 1974 Boyd told a DEA undercover agent that he was planning to overthrow the Torrijos régime "by assassinating Torrijos and perpetrating a revolt by the Panama National Guard" (Senate debate, *Congressional Record,* 4120). With regard to the accusations against Noriega, Senator Bayh commented in the secret Senate session in 1978 that "It should be taken into consideration that the [Boyd] group could possibly be conducting a provocation operation with this [BNDD] source by making certain information available to him to see if any action is taken on the information by U.S. Government authorities. . . . that is the assessment of the handling agent . . . listed in the document" (*Congressional Record,* 4120). Noriega was frequently mentioned by name in the secret session, but in the more carefully censored Bayh report, he is referred to only as a high official in the National Guard.

p. 60   Briefing at NSC: Interview with Strickler and Bayh report, which says "A similar briefing was later given to two NSC staff members." Strickler declined to identify the two NSC officials he met with. See also *Congressional Record,* 3980–81.

p. 60   The Dean story broke in *Newsweek,* June 18, 1973. The idea was not that farfetched in the context of the times. It was the application to the war on drugs of the same mentality that produced the CIA's Phoenix program to identify and kill suspected Vietcong operatives in South Vietnam. The approach seemed particularly attractive for Latin America. According to Edward Jay Epstein, in *Agency of Fear: Opiates and Political Power in America* (New York: Putnam, 1977), a book on the Nixon administration's war on drugs, the CIA was reporting to the White House that "there were only a handful of kingpin traffickers in Latin America, who could be eliminated very swiftly."

According to Epstein, the White House's Ad Hoc Committee on Narcotics, led by Egil Krogh, that summer was exploring the idea of "clandestine law enforcement" to stop key drug networks overseas.

Epstein quotes Krogh's assistant Jeffrey Donfeld as saying that assassination of traffickers was "a very definite part of the plan."

He cites a memorandum in which Krogh reports on a meeting with
President Nixon, in which the president approved a $100 million,
three-year fund to take "forceful action" against traffickers in the "host
country." The memo noted that the fund "can be used for clandestine
law enforcement activities abroad and for which BNDD would not be
accountable. This decisive action is our only hope for destroying or
immobilizing the highest level of drug traffickers," ibid., p. 143.

p. 61   Ingersoll report: "Briefing Paper on the Republic of Panama," prepared by the Bureau of Narcotics and Dangerous Drugs, November 5,
1971. An excerpt: "Panama is one of the most significant countries for
the transshipment of narcotic drugs to the United States. Its geographic location facilitates the illicit traffic because it is a terminus for
air and sea transport. Additionally, domestic and international telecon
facilities are well developed. The significance of Panama is evidenced
by the fact that during the past twelve months, 641 pounds of heroin
were seized in the United States which had transited through Panama.
This 641 pounds consists of only four single seizures and does not
include seizures of less than 100 pounds.

"As South America is the origin of all of the illicit cocaine in the
United States, it is believed that the transshipment of cocaine through
Panama may be even more significant than heroin. In one case in July
1970, United States authorities seized 201 pounds of cocaine which
passed through Panama prior to entering the United States. In another
case, defendants have stated they can bring up to 200 pounds of cocaine
per month through Panama."

p. 62   Memos on September meeting in *Congressional Record,* Senate,
4122, September 22, 1978.

p. 62   Did not mention Noriega: Interview with Ambassador Sayre, who
was present at the meeting.

p. 63   Assassination option paper: Bayh report, p. 17. The assassination
option was also discussed in the February 22, 1978, Senate closed
session, *Congressional Record,* 3981. The first press account was a
February 23, 1978, *Washington Post* story based on the Bayh report.
The options paper was mentioned deep in the story as a "tidbit." *The
New York Times* story that same day did not mention the assassination
option. My attempt to obtain the document from the DEA through the
Freedom of Information Act was unsuccessful. Jack Blum, the chief

investigator for the Kerry Committee, said he was allowed to inspect the document. Nevertheless, none of the seven current DEA officials I interviewed for this book said they had been briefed about the options paper or about any BNDD intelligence concerning Noriega's drug activities in 1971–72 that led up to the drafting of the paper.

p. 64   Defeo report: Report of June 18, 1975, to the Attorney General (Pursuant to Attorney General's Order No. 600–75, Assigning Employees to Investigate Allegations of Fraud, Irregularity and Misconduct in the Drug Enforcement Administration). The "employees" submitting the report were Michael A. Defeo, Thomas H. Henderson and Arthur F. Norton. Leaked portions were the subject of an October 11, 1988, article by Joe Conason and John Kelly in *The Village Voice*. Among the still-classified portions is a long memorandum, "Classified matters: Panama Materials." A list of documents in the report refers to transcripts of investigators' interviews with all of the BNDD/DEA officials involved in Panama matters in 1971–72. In 1988, according to *The Village Voice* article, Senator Orrin Hatch requested and received a copy of the Defeo report's section on Panama.

p. 64   Murphy visit: Interview with Ambassador Sayre; Jack Anderson column, March 14, 1972, and *Congressional Record,* September 26, 1973 (H-8354f); October 13, 1977 (S-33598) and October 14, 1977 (H-33827); and February 22, 1978 (S-3981).

p. 66   On the approaches to prominent Panamanians: *The Washington Post,* February 22, 1978, citing "informed sources."

p. 66   The later investigation of this period by the Senate Intelligence Committee concluded that the heavy U.S. pressure on Torrijos about Noriega may have had an effect. In the Senate's closed session in 1978, Senator Birch Bayh said, "The Panamanians may also have known of BNDD efforts to neutralize the high National Guard officer [Noriega]. Panama responded both with anger and, eventually, as it turned out, with better cooperation on narcotics enforcement." Senate closed Session, *Congressional Record,* 3982.

p. 68   The political maneuvering surrounding the Moisés Torrijos case and the apparent indifference to the weakness of the evidence were revealed in a top-secret letter made public by the Panamanian government. The letter, dated January 25, 1978, from DEA administrator Peter Bensinger to then Attorney General Griffin Bell, reviewed the facts of the case, concluding that "no evidence whatever was uncovered to link [Moisés Torrijos] to this illicit activity." The letter then described the decision to proceed with the indictment, notwithstanding the "dubious and unproven character of the available information":

"In October 1971, the chief of the CIA field station in Panama, Stanley R. Burnett, reported to Washington on Moisés Torrijos's connection with the drug smugglers. The relevant information . . . was conveyed to John Ingersoll with a note from the [then] CIA Director, Richard Helms: 'The president is informed. The information may be used in the national interests of the United States.'

"Mr. Ingersoll personally instructed our agents in the Panama DO to verify the information. No confirmatory evidence was found.

"However, on the direct instruction of the [then] Attorney General John Mitchell, the information was filed as unimpeachable and led to Moisés Torrijos's indictment . . ."

A copy of the letter was published in *16 Años,* p. 80.

p. 67   Copy of the redacted memo was obtained from reporter Cheryl Arvidson, who wrote an investigative series in 1978 on Panama and drugs. Comments about Moisés Torrijos, excised from Arvidson's copy, are found in Jonathan Kwitney, *Endless Enemies* (New York: W. W. Norton, 1986), p. 344.

p. 67   Ship incident: Sayre interview; Senate closed session, S-3981; Bayh report; Leland Riggs deposition, found in *Panama Canal Treaty (Disposition of United States Territory),* Part 3, Hearings before Senate Judiciary Subcommittee on Separation of Powers (Washington, D.C.: U.S. Government Printing Office, 1977), pp. 481–7. The various versions agree except on the detail of how Torrijos was informed. According to Bayh, a State Department official made a call to Torrijos. "The general got very angry and said, 'My brother has the right to be on any ship he wants to be on,' and hung up the telephone." Sayre says he knows of no telephone call being made.

p. 68   Pressure on Torrijos: Interview with Sayer.

p. 68   Dismissal of Torrijos's indictment: Interview with Carlos López Guevara, Moisés Torrijos's brother-in-law, who traveled to New York to push through the legal work to obtain the dismissal. Torrijos's New York attorney filed a letter with the court that he had received from a State Department official conceding that the prosecution was politically motivated.

p. 69   Agreement: Senate closed session, *Congressional Record,* 3981.

p. 69   *Johnny Express* incident: Interviews with Rómulo Escobar and Ambassadors Sayre and Jorden. Jorden was at the National Security

Council and conveyed the request for Noriega to become involved; see *Panama Odyssey,* p. 257. Also *The New York Times,* April 14, 1972; December 22, 1971. For allegations that Villa was part of a CIA operation, see Warren Hinckle and William W. Turner, *The Fish Is Red* (New York: Harper and Row, 1981), pp. 291–2. Rómulo Escobar interviewed Villa in his prison cell and said Villa admitted that the ships were used by anti-Castro groups for military attacks against Cuba.

There is some indication that Castro exacted a quid pro quo for the release of Villa. Former BNDD agent Gerry Strickler says that he was approached by the State Department Cuban desk officer about the possibility of freeing a Chilean convicted of drug smuggling, Oscar Esquella, who was arrested in 1971 at a Miami airport after cocaine was discovered in his airplane. Esquella was a close friend and political supporter of Chile's socialist president, Salvador Allende. After Villa was released, Strickler inquired about Esquella and found out that he was also released. When he attempted to inquire about the possible exchange, he was told the information was classified above his need to know. Strickler interview, December 1988.

The Noriega trip to Cuba is mentioned in various DOD intelligence reports released under the FOIA, including the Esparza Report.

p. 70 Claiming credit: Noriega interview with freelance writer Lally Weymouth, *The Washington Post,* Outlook Section, October 11, 1987.

p. 71 "Enforcement center": Quotation from 1973 House Subcommittee on the Panama Canal report, *Congressional Record,* H-33827.

p. 71 Heroin laboratory: Senate closed session, *Congressional Record,* 4002, citing a secret DEA study of heroin trafficking in Latin America between 1973 and 1976.

p. 71 Rehabilitation and apology: *The New York Times* article and a blistering reply from Congressman Murphy were published in *16 Años,* pp. 17–18.

BNDD chief Ingersoll acknowledged the apology in testimony before Congressman Murphy's canal subcommittee, according to a Jack Anderson column, August 3, 1972. According to the column, quoting secret, undated testimony, BNDD agent Bill Place was ordered to sign a letter of apology that he said was drafted for him by U.S. Ambassador Sayre. Then, questioned by Murphy about the arrest of Joaquín Him González on the baseball diamond, Ingersoll said angrily, "I doubt if we would arrest another Panamanian citizen in the Canal Zone again, because of the flap that the previous arrest created."

Ingersoll resigned less than a year later amidst a public fight with the administration over drug policy.

CHAPTER 4: THE TREATY GAME

p. 73   Bus incident: Interview with retired General Parker and with an officer of the Canal Zone security forces.

p. 74   For a vivid account of the Panamanian revolution and a dispassionate analysis of the U.S. role, see David McCullough, *The Path Between the Seas* (New York: Touchstone, 1977), pp. 361–86, esp. 379ff: "Without the military presence of the United States . . . the Republic of Panama probably would not have lasted a week."

p. 75   Senator's comment: Ibid., p. 397. The senator was Hernando de Soto Money of Mississippi, a critic of Roosevelt's role in Panamanian independence.

p. 75   Treaty negotiation and terms: Ibid., pp. 387–402. The United States bought out Bunau-Varilla's company for $40 million, at that time the largest lump-sum transfer of money out of the United States.

p. 75   U.S. military installations: A Marine battalion stationed in Panama in 1903 to protect canal construction was joined in 1911 by the U.S. Army's 10th Infantry. The first four permanent bases—Forts Sherman, Randolph and DeLesseps on the Atlantic side and Fort Grant, which includes Fort Amador and a string of fortified islands on the Pacific side adjoining Panama City—were completed by 1912. Three other bases, Forts Clayton, Kobbe and Gulick, were built before World War II, when war defenses vastly expanded the U.S. contingent to sixty-eight thousand troops. In the postwar military reorganization, the installations in Panama were designated a unified command, called the Caribbean Command, in which all military forces—Army, Navy, Air Force—in a geographic area came under a single commander. In 1963, the U.S. installations were given the name U.S. Southern Command, or Southcom, to reflect its military responsibility for Central and South America as well as the Caribbean. In this expanded capacity, Southcom headquarters supervised forty-three U.S. military missions staffed by more than eight hundred military personnel in friendly countries in the area. See "US Southcom History," and "Short History of the United States Army in the Panama Canal Area," documents provided by U.S. Southcom's public affairs office, and *Panama: A Country Study,* Area Handbook Series (Washington D.C.: U.S. Government Printing Office, 1981) p. 198.

p. 76   Riots in 1964: The most objective account of the violence is the investigation conducted by the International Commission of Jurists, *Report on the Events in Panama, January 9–12, 1964* (Geneva: 1964). The toll of American dead and injured is taken from Jorden, *Panama Odyssey,* pp. 47, 63. Jorden also lists fifth and sixth American deaths, a civilian killed by a car whose driver was fleeing the rioting and a soldier killed in a jeep accident while on patrol.

p. 77   For a detailed but decidedly pro-American account of the 1964 rioting, see ibid., pp. 38–66. Jorden is sympathetic to U.S. claims of an outside communist role in the rioting but cites only two pieces of evidence, the CIA report of general Cuban activity in Central America aimed at exploiting any unrest that should arise and "the speed with which communist propagandists [outside Panama] jumped on the Panama story." LaFeber, *The Panama Canal,* pp. 138–40, is more critical of the U.S. handling of the crisis. He dismisses as unfounded the claims of an outside communist leadership role. There is no dispute, however, that the Panama People's party, the communist party, supported the uprising and did what it could to fan the flames once they had started. Five Communists were among the five hundred Panamanian demonstrators arrested during the rioting. The Organization of American States investigation concluded that Cuban agents were not involved, according to ibid., p. 141.

p. 77   Johnson and Nixon era talks: Jorden, *Panama Odyssey,* pp. 172ff.

p. 78   Former ambassador to Costa Rica Frank McNeil said of Noriega, "He fed us every conversation with Fidel. And I'm sure he also fed Fidel every conversation with us." Interview with McNeil. Several U.S. officials who declined to be named also discussed Noriega's reporting on his trips to Cuba. A close aide to Torrijos described the trip to Santiago de Cuba and Torrijos's comments.

p. 79   Scali incident: Jorden, *Panama Odyssey,* pp. 196–7.

p. 79   Jorden's conclusion: Ibid., pp. 197–8.

p. 81   Spy versus spy: Bayh report, February 1978. The broad outlines of the espionage incidents are contained in the 1978 Senate debate on Panama, although important details were deleted from the Senate transcript. The story here is pieced together from that transcript and from interviews with Panamanian and U.S. officials.

In his report, Senator Bayh said: "The interest of the Select Committee in intelligence activities in Panama goes back for more than a year. It was clear to the Committee from earlier oversight activities that intelligence activities intended to support important negotiations could, under some high risk conditions, achieve the opposite. Under some circumstances they could undermine, taint or otherwise endanger the intended outcome of negotiations. When it was clear negotiations were underway in earnest in Panama, the Select Committee decided to review our intelligence activities in Panama with a particular focus on whether there were any high risk activities that if disclosed might affect adversely the outcome of treaty negotiations. . . . The Select Committee concluded that U.S. intelligence activities had no adverse impact on terms of the Canal treaties" (p. 2).

According to a staff member at the time, the Intelligence Committee opened its investigation after receiving a report of possible penetration of U.S. intelligence activities by the Panamanians—the incident described herein.

p. 82   Sergeant's job description: Interview with former U.S. intelligence official in Panama.

p. 82   Description of transcripts: Interview with Gabriel Lewis, at that time Panamanian ambassador to the United States, who said Torrijos described the contents of the transcripts to him.

p. 82   The case was first publicized by CBS News in 1977 and in greater detail by *The New York Times,* June 12, 1986 (by Seymour M. Hersh) and September 27, 1988 (by Stephen Engelberg and Jeff Gerth).

p. 83   "Technical manuals": Hersh.

p. 83   "Communications targets": Engelberg and Gerth.

U.S. Army documents relating to the four Canton Song investigations were released to Engelberg under the Freedom of Information Act. According to the documents, the investigation was conducted by USA Sp[ecial] Op[erations] Det[achment], and USAINTA, of Fort Meade, Maryland, the home of the National Security Agency, which is in charge of the United States's most sophisticated electronic surveillance operations and the agency most directly damaged by the Singing Sergeants leaks.

p. 83   Bush role: Engelberg and Gerth, *The New York Times,* September 27, 1988. In 1988, Stansfield Turner, who headed the CIA under President Carter, said that the agency took Noriega off the payroll in 1977 because of the incident, and that he remained off until the payments were resumed in the Reagan administration.

p. 84   Bombings and Torrijos's reaction: Interviews with William Jorden,

Aquilino Boyd, a member of the Panama Canal Zone security detail
and a member of the Southcom intelligence staff.

p. 85 U.S. soldier with expertise in explosives: Army Intelligence documents released under FOIA. The soldier is identified in the documents
but had denied the accusations and was never prosecuted.

p. 86 Torrijos's response: The text of Torrijos's letter answering the
charges was obtained under the FOIA from the State Department. The
effectiveness of Boyd's mission was evident in testimony by General
David McAuliffe, the chief of Southcom. McAuliffe said bombings
remained unsolved and characterized the reports of G2 involvement as
"lots of rumors." See "Panama Gunrunning," Hearings before the
Subcommittee on the Panama Canal, House Committee on Merchant
Marine and Fisheries, June 6, 7, and July 10, 1979 (Washington, D.C.:
U.S. Government Printing Office, 1980). See also Jorden, *Panama Odyssey,* pp. 335–7.

p. 87 Boyd hitting Bunau-Varilla: McCullough, *Path Between the Seas,* p.
395.

p. 88 Noriega-Bush meeting: Interview with Aquilino Boyd.

p. 89 As late as February 1977, the CIA was still attempting to keep secret
its discovery of the Singing Sergeants leaks. See Senate closed session,
Congressional Record, 3972.

p. 89 Defeo Report: Joe Conason and John Kelly, in *The Village Voice,*
October 11, 1988, argue that Bush saw the report. In October 1988,
Representative Sam Gejdenson of Connecticut wrote to Attorney General Richard Thornburgh asking whether Bush "was . . . briefed on the
substance of the 1975 DeFeo report."

p. 90 "Bush listened courteously": Jorden, *Panama Odyssey,* p. 339.

p. 90 Torrijos a Communist? photo inscription: Boyd interview.

p. 90 House guest: Walters told Gabriel Lewis about Noriega's visit.

p. 92 Jimmy Carter, *Keeping Faith: Memoirs of a President* (New York:
Bantam, 1982), pp. 152–85.

p. 92 Money dispute: The U.S. negotiators were impressed by a meticu-
lous study of the relative costs and benefits related to the canal prepared by the Panamanian finance minister, Nicolás Ardito Barletta.
The study concluded that the United States had benefited by at least
$27 billion over the life of the Canal, while Panama received a net
benefit of only $1.1 billion. Jorden, *Panama Odyssey,* p. 412.

p. 94 The intelligence report is described in Senate closed session, *Con-*

gressional Record S-3972, 3985 and 3996. An informed Senate source identified the agency that monitored the intercepts.

p. 94   Linowitz explanations: Ibid., S-3973.

p. 95   Torrijos's trick: Interview with Gabriel Lewis. NSA and other U.S. officials investigating the Panamanian threat immediately suspected that Torrijos might be playing such a trick since by then they knew Noriega had learned from the Singing Sergeants exactly which telephones were being intercepted by the Americans. According to a U.S. official involved, the intercept that revealed the Panamanian threats was turned over to the Senate Select Intelligence Committee in July 1977, within a few days of its occurrence, and thus began the investigation that was aired in the Senate closed session of February 21 and 22, 1978. That session has long been described as a debate on the Intelligence Committee's investigation into the charges of drug trafficking by Panamanian officials. Actually the intelligence matters were discussed as extensively, but are so heavily censored that the discussion is impossible to follow without outside information. Most of what was intelligible in the sanitized report and transcript of the session related to drugs, and news coverage focused almost exclusively on the drug issue. The original thrust of the committee's investigation, however, was to determine if U.S. intelligence activities in Panama adversely affected the treaty negotiations. The committee concluded that the treaties had not been tainted. The mandate to investigate the drug allegations was added in October 1977 after treaty opponents, led by Senator Robert Dole, accused Torrijos of being involved in trafficking.

p. 96   The annuity had been raised from the original $250,000 in the Hull-Alfaro treaty revision of 1939.

p. 96   Treaty provisions relating to U.S. military activities are the following:

Panama Canal Treaty, Article IV:

"Protection and Defense.

"1. The United States and the Republic of Panama commit themselves to protect and defend the Panama Canal. Each Party shall act, in accordance with its constitutional processes, to meet the danger resulting from an armed attack or other actions which threaten the security of the Panama Canal or of ships transiting it.

"2. For the duration of this Treaty, the United States of America shall have primary responsibility to protect and defend the Canal. The rights of the United States to station, train, and move military forces within the Republic of Panama are described in the Agreement in Implementation of this Article, signed this date. The use of areas and installations and the legal status of the armed forces of the United States of America in the Republic of Panama shall be governed by the aforesaid Agreement."

Treaty Concerning the Permanent Neutrality and Operation of the Panama Canal, Article IV: "The United States of America and the Republic of Panama agree to maintain the régime of neutrality established in this treaty, which shall be maintained in order that the Canal shall remain permanently neutral, notwithstanding the termination of any other treaties entered into by the two Contracting Parties."

Article V: "After the termination of the Panama Canal Treaty, only the Republic of Panama shall operate the Canal and maintain military forces, defense sites and military installations within its national territory."

Amendment to Article IV of the Neutrality Treaty:

"A correct and authoritative statement of certain rights and duties of the Parties under the foregoing is contained in the Statement of Understanding issued by the government of the United States of America on October 18, 1977, and by the Government of the Republic of Panama on October 18, 1977, which is hereby incorporated as an integral part of this Treaty, as follows:

" 'Under the Treaty Concerning the Permanent Neutrality and Operation of the Panama Canal (the Neutrality Treaty), Panama and the United States have the responsibility to assure that the Panama Canal will remain open and secure to ships of all nations. The correct interpretation of this principle is that each of the two countries shall, in accordance with their respective constitutional processes, defend the Canal against any threat to the régime of neutrality, and consequently shall have the right to act against any aggression or threat directed against the Canal or against the peaceful transit of vessels through the Canal.

" 'This does not mean, nor shall it be interpreted as, a right of intervention of the United States in the internal affairs of Panama. Any United States action will be directed at insuring that the Canal will remain open, secure, and accessible, and it shall never be directed against the territorial integrity or political independence of Panama.' "

Agreement in Implementation of Article IV of the Panama Canal Treaty: Article I. "Definitions.

"1) Defense Sites: Those areas, and the installations within them, which the Republic of Panama by this Agreement permits the United States Forces to use for the specific purposes of the Panama Canal Treaty, and as the two Governments may otherwise agree, a list of which is set forth in Paragraph (1) of Annex A of this Agreement."

1903 Panama Canal Treaty, Article XXIII: "If it should become necessary at any time to employ armed forces for the safety or protection of the Canal, or of the ships that make use of the same, or the railways and auxiliary works, the United States shall have the right, at all times and in its discretion, to use its police and its land and naval forces or to establish fortifications for these purposes."

See Congressional Research Service, *Background Documents Relating to the Panama Canal* (Washington, D.C.: U.S. Government Printing Office, 1977).

p. 98   Bayh conclusions on Torrijos: Bayh Report, p. 15.

p. 98   Bayh remarks on Noriega: Senate closed session, *Congressional Record,* S-4003.

p. 98   Noriega cooperating: Senate closed session, *Congressional Record,* S-4010.

CHAPTER 5: CENTRAL AMERICAN CASABLANCA

p. 100   Pastora's arrival and meetings with Torrijos: Interview with Edén Pastora, San José, Costa Rica, December 5, 1988. Notwithstanding Pastora's well-known tendency to recount self-serving tales about himself, it is reflective of the basic friendship he felt toward Noriega that he would tell a humanizing story about someone who in December 1988 was nearly universally reviled in the world press.

p. 101   Hugo Spadafora, *Experiencias y Pensamientos de un Médico Guerrillero* (Panamá: Centro de Impresión Educativa, 1980), pp. 160, 164.

Brigade members were given three weeks of secret training on Panama's Coiba Island. By the time they reached the combat zone in southern Costa Rica in November, only sixty-five remained. According to several reports, the brigade's hard core was made up of Panamanian National Guardsmen who had "resigned" in order to volunteer for the brigade. During their service in the brigade, their families continued to receive support payments from the Panamanian government. Interview with Lieutenant José de Jesús Martínez. Also Ropp, *Panamanian Politics,* p. 127.

p. 105   Carlton and Rodríguez backgrounds: Testimony to the Kerry Committee by Carlton and José Blandón; interviews with acquaintances of both men and with DEA agents who interrogated Carlton.

p. 105   Noriega assigned Lieutenant Felipe Camargo to supervise the operation and handle day-to-day contacts with Pastora. One of the companies involved in the 1978–1979 trafficking, EXACO, was later tied to drug trafficking when one of the planes was found abandoned on a Florida runway with marijuana residue in the cargo bay. "Drugs, Law Enforcement and Foreign Policy: A Report of the Subcommittee on Narcotics, Terrorism and International Operations," April 13, 1989 (hereinafter Kerry Report). The arms operation was described by Carlton in Kerry Hearings II, p. 185, and in his classified deposition (hereinafter Carlton deposition) to the Kerry investigators, a copy of which was released to the author.

p. 107   Caza y Pesca deal: "Panama Gunrunning," Hearings of the Subcommittee on the Panama Canal, House of Representatives, June 6, 7, and July 10, 1979. The hearing record includes Kimbler's affidavit on his investigation, the indictment, and statements from representatives of the State Department and the Nicaraguan government.

p. 108   Murphy committee hearings; Atwood statement: "Panama Gunrunning," p. 6.

U.S. denials of knowledge of Panama's role in the arms pipeline to the Sandinistas have long been greeted with skepticism. I was told by a former senior CIA official with responsibilities for Central America at the time that the CIA had full knowledge. Shirley Christian, *Revolution in the Family* (New York: Vintage, 1985), p. 113, states without attribution that Noriega himself gave the CIA information about the arms supply network in mid-1979.

p. 110   Noriega handled the operation: Army Intelligence reported that Noriega set up to guard the shah a team that had received "extensive VIP protection training in anticipation of this assignment and its members are well-versed in the martial arts, use of hand weapons and patrolling techniques." FOIA release, Intelligence Report, 470th Military Intelligence Group, U.S. Southern Command, December 17, 1979.

p. 110   Eskenazi letter: Printed in *The Washington Post,* March 20, 1988.

p. 110   Pressure to not indict Noriega: Interview with Jerome Sanford, the assistant U.S. attorney who prepared the indictment.

p. 110   Dropped as too old: *The Washington Post,* March 20, 1988.

p. 111   Costa Rican congressional investigation: "Informe Sobre el Tráfico de Armas," Comisión de Asuntos Especiales, Legislative Assembly of Costa Rica, May 14, 1981.

p. 111   Spadafora's role in fighting: Hugo Spadafora, *Las Derrotas Somocista y Comunista en Nicaragua* (San José, Costa Rica: privately published, 1985), pp. 42–3. Just before the offensive, he described the brigade members as "men and women of numerous [political] currents, movements and parties of the center and the left; citizens who are pro and anti-government [of Panama]; former members of the National Guard of Panama and former guerrillas who years before had fought against our Guard; Panamanians of the most diverse socio-economic extraction, which rendered the group a true portrait of the social body of our country." In an interview printed July 2 in *La Estrella,* Spadafora said that there were more than one hundred Panamanians fighting in Nicaragua. Ibid., p. 50. Prior to the final offensive, he said he had fought in battles around the hills of Naranjo and the town of Colón.

p. 112   The plan was described by Colonel Roberto Díaz Herrera. See also Ropp, *Panamanian Politics,* p. 131, on Panamanian military training.

p. 112   Sent Noriega to Cuba: FOIA release, Intelligence Report, 470th MI, August 5, 1979.

p. 112   The account of Noriega's involvement in arms shipments to El Salvador is based on testimony by Floyd Carlton, Kerry Hearings II, 192–8; and that of former Noriega aide José Blandón, Kerry Hearings II, 86, 139–43.

p. 113   Free Zone and arms showroom: Sam Dillon and Andres Oppenheimer, *The Miami Herald,* January 30, 1988. The article is important because its account of the arms trafficking appeared before testimony by Blandón and Carlton. Although the writers interviewed Blandón for the article, details about the showroom came from another source who formerly worked in G2 with Noriega.

p. 114   Carlton rescue of Rodríguez: Carlton testimony, Kerry Hearings II, 193–5.

p. 114   Press coverage of crash: The incident was amply covered by FBIS, which reproduced local press reports and Spanish-language wire service accounts. See FBIS June 16, P2–3; June 17, N1–2, P1–6; June 18, N1–2, P1–4; June 19, P1–2.

p. 115   Torrijos's initiative on El Salvador: NSC Latin American aide Robert Pastor and special ambassador William Bowdler traveled to Panama in the spring of 1980 to discuss El Salvador. The Americans discouraged Torrijos from taking an active role such as the one he had played on behalf of the opposition to Somoza in Nicaragua. They also declined his offer for joint action. Interview with Robert Pastor.

The State Department made a strong demarche to Panama about the discovery of the arms shipment, according to Pastor and another source in the State Department.

p. 115   Reprimand to Noriega: Blandón testimony, Kerry Hearings, II, 140–1.

p. 116   Pérez is quoted by Andres Oppenheimer and Sam Dillon, *The Miami Herald,* February 6, 1988. The article, the result of a three-month investigation of Noriega's economic empire, was a major source for my description.

p. 116   Noriega's salary in mid-1970s: "Panama Gunrunning," p. 203. The hearings reproduced a computer printout of all members of Noriega's G2 and their salaries for April 1975. Names on the list include Luís del Cid, Edgardo López, Enrique Pretelt, Cleto Hernández, Luis Córdoba, and Nivaldo Madriñan.

p. 116   Noriega's salary in 1980: FOIA release, 470th MI, group report (date deleted), lists the following salaries for National Guard officers in 1980:

Florencio Florez: $1,726.40

Rubén D. Paredes, LTC: $1,588.80

Manuel A. Noriega, LTC: $1,537.20

Roberto Díaz H., LTC: $1,498.00

In addition, each officer received a monthly expense allowance of $200.

p. 116   Torrijos's system: See William R. Hughes and Ivan A. Quintero, *Quienes Son los Dueños de Panamá?* (Panama: CEASPA, Serie Panamá Hoy, 1987). The book lists Noriega as president of Explosivos Nacionales (Explonsa); Captain Augusto Villalaz, president of Cameco Azuero de Panamá and director of Azucarera Nacional, S.A., owned by Eric Arturo Delvalle.

The elaborate business connections among the National Guard, the government and private business were analyzed by James Cason, a U.S. embassy political officer, who wrote his findings in a long, classified report. The report itself was denied under the FOIA, but a few of Cason's research memos were released. According to his reporting, Panama's restrictive lumber import quotas from Honduras were assigned to Lieutenant Colonel Rubén Darío Paredes, who got his profits as a silent partner in businesses run by Fernando Manfredo, a former ambassador to the United States. Paredes also had an interest in Transit, S.A., an import company set up as a front for the National Guard that controlled access to the Free Zone. The Transit connection is discussed by José Blandón in his testimony to the Kerry committee and in the Andres Oppenheimer and Sam Dillon article in *The Miami Herald,* February 6, 1988. FOIA release, U.S. embassy memo by Cason, March 25, 1983.

p. 117   Mitterrand contribution: Interview with Díaz Herrera.

p. 117   Polisario contribution: Interview with Barletta.

p. 117   Cuban businesses: Blandón, Part 2, p. 93. The Cuban use of Panama to circumvent the U.S. embargo was known by U.S. officials long before Blandón's testimony, but attracted little attention. See, for example, testimony of Elliott Abrams in March 1986 to the Senate Subcommittee on Western Hemisphere Affairs: "Situation in Panama," Hearings Before the Senate Subcommittee on Western Hemisphere Affairs, March 10 and April 21, 1986.

p. 118   Barbaroja and Cuban activities: Interviews with two former State Department officials who did not want to be named.

p. 118   Libya trip: FOIA release, 470th MI, April 4, 1977. The report says Noriega received a "substantial" amount of money, and that after returning to Panama arranged for favorable articles to be written about the Libyan revolution.

p. 118   Israeli role in Central America: Jane Hunter, *No Simple Proxy: Israel in Central America* (Washington, D.C.: Washington Middle East Associates, 1986).

p. 118   Mike Harari: For espionage assistance to G2: Two U.S. military sources. For Harari's Mossad connection and killing of waiter: *Hadashot,* April 29, 1988 (Israeli newspaper: translation provided by Panamanian embassy in Israel), and articles by David Gardner, *The Financial Times,* May 5, 1988, and Lou Toscano, UPI, January 18, 1988. For arms shipments, see Jane Hunter, *Israeli Foreign Affairs,* February 1988, citing *Hadashot,* April 30, 1987, *U.S. News and World Report,* May 2, 1988, and testimony by Blandón, Kerry Hearings, III, 18–19.

p. 119   Spadafora quotations and details of Mercedes and bodyguard from an article by Alan Riding, *The New York Times,* December 28, 1980.

p. 120   Meeting with Carlton and trip to Libya: "Estos Mataron a

Spadafora," *La Palestra* (Chitre, Panamá: Raul Berbey, editor), September 1986, p. 15.

p. 120   Offer to reform brigade: UPI, May 18, 1981.

p. 120   Pastora's defection and new project: Interview with Edén Pastora.

p. 121   Pastora's returning and Noriega's being cut out of liberation project: Interview with Edén Pastora.

p. 121   Reception clash: Interview with Díaz Herrera, who witnessed it.

p. 121   Profiteering, denunciation: Interview with Spadafora's close friend, Abdiel Juliao.

p. 121   Spadafora wrote about the confrontation in which he accused Noriega of disloyalty in *Las Derrotas,* and mentioned it in a March 15, 1984, interview with *La Prensa.* José Blandón was present at the confrontation and described it in an interview.

p. 122   Pastora spent the night elsewhere: Interview with Edén Pastora.

CHAPTER 6: GUNS TO DRUGS

p. 123   The Nicaraguan support was, however, greatly exaggerated by the Reagan administration, which issued a White Paper in March 1981 purporting to contain captured documents proving that Nicaragua, Cuba and the Soviet bloc were shipping hundreds of tons of arms to El Salvador. An article by the author, *Los Angeles Times,* March 23, 1981 (Pacific News Service), scrutinized the actual Spanish-language documents and found they did not support the most important allegations. For example, the White Paper claims that 800 tons of weapons were promised to the FMLN and 200 tons actually reached them, but the documents indicate that only about 10 tons ever crossed the border into El Salvador. Similar articles questioning the White Paper appeared several months later in *The Wall Street Journal* and *The Washington Post.*

p. 123   In November 1981, Reagan signed National Security Decision Directive 17, authorizing $20 million for covert CIA assistance to the Contras.

p. 124   Cocaine production: In 1970, only about 120 kilos of cocaine were seized in the United States; in 1988, seizures for the first ten months amounted to 76,000 kilos, according to the State Department's International Narcotics Control Strategy Report, March 1989.

p. 124   For the Vietnam argument, see Alfred W. McCoy, with Cathleen

B. Read and Leonard P. Adams II, *The Politics of Heroin in Southeast Asia* (New York: Harper and Row, 1972)

p. 125   Profiles of Escobar, Ochoa and Lehder can be found in Gugliotta and Leen, *Kings of Cocaine,* pp. 24–31. See also Elaine Shannon, *Desperados* (New York: Viking Press, 1988), pp. 98–103.

p. 126   Lehder's operation: Gugliotta and Leen, *Kings of Cocaine,* pp. 42, 47. Much of the information about Lehder's operation was obtained from the testimony of pilots who worked for him at one time or another and were persuaded to cooperate with authorities after their arrest. The testimony is contained in the court transcript, *U.S. v. Carlos Lehder Rivas,* Middle District of Florida, November–December 1987.

p. 126   Increased tonnage: Gugliotta and Leen, *Kings of Cocaine,* p. 83.

p. 128   Like almost every head of state and intelligence chief, Noriega and Torrijos were the targets of regular reports by informants linking them to illegal activity. According to James Mills, *The Underground Empire* (Garden City: Doubleday, 1986), p. 883, Santiago Ocampo, one of the older generation of Colombian cocaine traffickers, gave Torrijos a thoroughbred horse. A DEA agent, Tom Zapeda, in testimony to the Kerry committee, Hearings IV, 728–9, said he personally observed Torrijos and Noriega arrive in Medellín, where they were met by men in unmarked Mercedeses who Zapeda believed were traffickers. The incident occurred "prior to 1978," Zapeda said. In another incident repeatedly resurrected in Panama, Luis Bernardo Londoño, a Colombian arrested in 1977 and accused of drug trafficking, said he had to pay Noriega $140,000 for his release from jail. Londoño wrote a letter about the incident to *El Tiempo* of Bogotá and to two other newspapers in October 1977, and the Panamanian opposition *La Prensa* ran stories about the incident several times.

There is no doubt that Panama's vast international banking center was used for money laundering and tax evasion, but little evidence prior to 1981 points to the direct involvement of Noriega or Torrijos in shielding such operations. Ramón Milián Rodríguez, a convicted money launderer, offered testimony to the Miami U.S. attorney's office implicating Noriega in laundering operations as early as 1979, but his testimony was considered unreliable and implausible. Milián was allowed to testify before the Kerry committee with no mention that his credibility was seriously questioned by U.S. prosecutors and that his testimony had been specifically rejected for use in the indictment against Noriega. See Kerry Hearings, II, 227–8. In his testimony,

Milián alleged that he was working as the chief money launderer for Pablo Escobar when he contacted Noriega in 1979 and that Noriega charged a 1½ percent fee for all money laundered in Panamanian banks.

p. 128   Noriega's and Torrijos's relationships with M-19 are described by Blandón, Kerry Hearings, II, 141.

p. 129   Caquetá is the same province where the Tranquilandia cocaine factory was discovered three years later. Investigators noted at the time that M-19 bases were nearby and suggested that they may have been providing protection for the factory.

p. 129   Report on M-19: FOIA release, USDAO (Defense Attaché's Office in embassy) to DIA, Washington, November 9, 1981. The others suspected, as listed in the report, are "Ministry of Foreign relations official, Carlos Pérez Herrera, who manages the Panama-Kadafy liaison, and Leonardo Kam, who manages the Panama–M-19 liaison. . . . These are big money makers, they said. . . ." In a reference made unclear by an earlier deletion, the report also mentioned that "the location of Explonsa, S.A. (National Explosives control facilities) near Sabanita adds further evidence to likelyhood [sic] that shipment was picked up on the Atlantic Coast."

p. 130   *Karina* incident: The loading in Vacamonte and sinking are described by reporter Knut Royce, in part one of a series on Panama for the Hearst newspapers. See the *San Antonio Light,* June 10, 1985. U.S. officials later claimed that the weapons had been purchased by a Colombian drug trafficker, Jaime Guillot Lara, who had received the money, $700,000, from Cuba. Guillot Lara was indicted on drug charges with four Cuban officials in 1982. See testimony of David L. Westrate, DEA deputy assistant administrator, Senate Foreign Relations Committee, May 14, 1985.

p. 130   MAS campaign: Gugliotta and Leen, *Kings of Cocaine,* p. 93; Milián Rodríguez, in testimony to the Kerry Committee, also described the cartel–M-19 war, Kerry Hearings, II, 247–9.

p. 130   After the recovery of Marta Nieves Ochoa, the new organization went on to the business of expansion. They embarked on a collective investment to build a giant complex of cocaine-processing laboratories on the Yarí River, in Caquetá jungle territory until then controlled by M-19. The factories were needed to handle not only the increased imports of coca from Peru and Bolivia, but also the production of the new Colombian coca plantations that the cartel was building. With the two to three years that a coca plant needs to reach maturity, the cartel production curve was expected to reach a peak in 1984.

U.S. ambassador to Colombia Lewis Tambs later charged that M-19 was working directly with the cocaine cartel and provided protection for the Yarí River laboratories, which were known as the Tranquilandia. Proof for this somewhat unlikely marriage of anticommunist drug entrepreneurs and anticapitalist guerrillas has been elusive, but the theory has strong defenders, and not only among conservatives, notably Jack Blum, the chief investigator for the Kerry committee.

Other analysts make a case for continuing competition and warfare between Colombian guerrillas and the cartel. See Merrill Collett, "The Myth of the 'Narco-Guerrillas,' " *The Nation,* August 13/20, 1988. He says that MAS, after obtaining the release of Marta Ochoa, went on a rampage against leftists, including peasants, union leaders and university professors, and that MAS merged with Colombian military hardliners to become an anticommunist death squad. "In February 1983," he writes, "[Colombian] Attorney General Carlos Jiménez Gómez charged that among those involved in MAS were fifty-nine active duty military officers."

p. 131 Noriega's mediation: This key detail was unearthed by reporters Guy Gugliotta and Andres Oppenheimer of *The Miami Herald.* I am grateful to Oppenheimer for providing me with notes of his unpublished 1987 interview with retired Lieutenant Colonel Julián Melo. Melo said Noriega got to know Ochoa "very well . . . because [M-19] had kidnapped Ochoa's sister and Noriega had acted as mediator." Oppenheimer heard the story from U.S. drug enforcement agents in Colombia and confirmed it with a Panamanian government source. José Blandón, in an interview with the author, provided further details of the M-19–cartel talks in Panama. See Gugliotta and Leen, *Kings of Cocaine,* pp. 92–3.

p. 131 Floyd Carlton is a federal prisoner under the witness protection program. The account here is based on Carlton's testimony to the Kerry committee and his interrogation by DEA investigators. The information to the investigators and to the grand jury is summarized in a classified "Prosecution Memo" from Assistant U.S. Attorney Richard Gregorie to the Justice Department, which I have read.

p. 133 Dummy load: Carlton deposition, p. 60. The 1988 Miami indictment describes the first shipment as loaded with "unidentified cargo in duffel bags."

p. 134   Guatemalan rejection: Christopher Dickey, *With the Contras* (New York: Simon and Schuster, 1985), p. 148.

p. 134   Dismantling brigade: José Blandón in *La Prensa,* September 9, 1985, and in interview with author. Brigade member Santos López Lobon also talked about harassment of brigade members after Torrijos's death, in a statement to Costa Rican investigators following Spadafora's death.

p. 135   Conversation with Noriega and Melo: Interview with Abdiel Juliao. Spadafora also talked about the calls in an interview with Mayín Correa, Radio Continente, December 23, 1981.

p. 136   Spadafora denunciation of Noriega as trafficker: Interviews with Spadafora, including the one on January 18, 1982, are compiled in *Panamá '85: Unidad Nacional, La Única Solución* (2nd ed.), a pamphlet published by Spadafora's family after his death. Also, author's interview with Mayín Correa.

CHAPTER 7: OUR MAN IN PANAMA

p. 138   Foundation of *La Prensa:* Interview with Roberto Eisenmann.

p. 139   Overthrow of Flórez: Interview with Roberto Díaz Herrera.

p. 140   Noriega call to embassy contact: FOIA release, U.S. embassy cable, March 3, 1982, and interview with Ambler Moss.

p. 141   Drafting of Plan Torrijos: Interviews with Díaz Herrera, who verified the authenticity of the document.

p. 143   Noriega's spin: FOIA release, DIA, March 19, 1982, from CORUSAOPSGP, Fort Meade, Maryland (acronym unknown).

p. 143   Moss cables: FOIA release, U.S. embassy, March 5 and 26, 1982.

p. 144   Paredes speech: FBIS, March 12, 1982, p. N2.

p. 146   Paredes statement on presidency: Christopher Dickey, *The Washington Post,* May 17, 1983.

p. 147   Colonel Armando Contreras had agreed, at Noriega's and Paredes's urging, to forego his short stint as National Guard commandant in order to take a prestigious and lucrative civilian post involving oversight of U.S. and Panamanian Canal matters.

p. 147   Training of UESAT by Israelis: Two senior U.S. officers posted in Panama.

p. 147   Noriega's retention of power over G2: FOIA releases, CORUSAOPSGP, Fort Meade, Maryland, March 19, 1982; U.S. embassy, March 3, 1982.

p. 147   Clarridge briefing: Bob Woodward, *Veil* (New York: Simon and Schuster, 1987), pp. 229–33.

p. 148   Fighting against communism in El Salvador: The new Southcom role in Central America is spelled out by General John R. Galvin, "Regional Coalition Vital to Southcom Efforts," *Army,* October 1985, p. 5.

p. 148   Spy ships: George de Lama, *Chicago Tribune,* March 23, 1983.

p. 148   Reconnaissance flights, weapons shipments: Philip Taubman, *The New York Times,* May 23, 1983. The use of U.S. bases was confirmed in interviews with two former U.S. officers and an intelligence analyst based in Panama.

p. 149   Panamanian protests: FBIS, May 16, June 2, 1983. Panamanian tacit permission was mentioned in Taubman's article and in my briefings with U.S. Southcom and intelligence officials.

p. 150   Transporting suitcases: Interview with high Panamanian official who asked to remain anonymous.

p. 150   Rodríguez flight with Blandón: Blandón testimony, Kerry Hearings, II, 112.

p. 150   "You're making peanuts . . .": Prosecution memo recounting Carlton's grand jury testimony.

p. 151   Fort Amador installations: "Short History of the United States Army in the Panama Canal Area," 193rd Infantry Brigade Public Affairs Office, 1985. The coastal defense guns were dismantled after World War II, and the inactivated fortifications remained "as stark monuments to a sound but obsolete strategy—a reminder of the vast changes in defense concepts that had taken place in a comparatively short span of years."

p. 152   Noriega was asked about his frequent references to peace and geometry in a September 1, 1983, Televisora Nacional interview, and he expanded on the theme: "I am referring to the peace that comes from within. A man who is not at peace with himself can neither project nor find it. When such a man ties his inner peace to that of his fellow man, two concentric circles of peace will result. . . . Proof of this [the role of the National Guard in guaranteeing this peace] is the fact that Panama is at peace while the Central American isthmus is an arena for circles and triangles of armed conflict. This is true because we had a man like Torrijos, one who believed that peace does not come from the force of weapons or the edge of a bayonet. Peace comes when those weapons and those bayonets are placed at the service of a people, in brotherhood, united in such a way as to achieve positive development."

p. 154   "You know how it works . . .": Interview with Díaz Herrera.

p. 154   Restrictions on Paredes: Interviews with Major Augusto Villalaz and with an American military officer.

p. 154   Editorial: *La Prensa,* September 8, 1983.

p. 155   Diminutive Darth Vader: FOIA release by DIA of U.S. embassy cable, August 17, 1983.

p. 155   Kalish arrival in Panama and meetings with Noriega: Interview with Kalish and Kalish's testimony to Senate Permanent Subcommittee on Investigations (PSI), January 28, 1988. Kalish's story was corroborated by testimony to the Kerry Committee by his partner Leigh Ritch, February 8, 1988.

p. 155   Background on Kalish and his home and cars in Tampa: Milo Geyelín, *St. Petersburg Times,* February 22, 1988.

p. 158   Party at Canal Commission: Kalish may have been mistaken about where he was. His description of the commission office is generally accurate but also fits Noriega's office at Fort Amador, which also overlooks the Canal and has the kind of plate-glass window described by Kalish. Noriega had frequent parties there, and not at the nearby Canal Commission, which remains under U.S. control until the year 2000.

Quotations, unless otherwise noted, are from interviews with Kalish.

p. 158   *En Pocas Palabras,* May 30, June 14, November 15, 1983.

p. 159   Embassy country team: The meetings were described by two participants.

p. 159   Benefit of the doubt: Other U.S. intelligence agencies, however, had viewed Noriega in a more hostile light. In 1982, according to Steven Emerson's book, *Secret Warriors* (New York: Putnam, 1988), ch. 11, the Army's Intelligence and Security Command (INSCOM) bugged various Noriega residences and offices in an attempt to determine the extent of his arms trafficking to leftist guerrillas in El Salvador and Colombia. According to Emerson's sources, the devices were successfully implanted but produced little information of significant value.

p. 159   Red-carpet visit: Other Panamanians on the trip to Washington included Lieutenant Colonel Elías Castillo, newly appointed head of military operations, G3; Lieutenant Colonel Bernardo Barrera, later to serve as G2; and Noriega's West Point–educated aide and translator, Lieutenant Moisés Cortizo.

Officially, the trip was classified as "self-invited," meaning that Noriega was not a fully U.S.-sponsored guest. For the Washington part of the trip, the United States paid all but transportation costs.

p. 160   "Imagine what you can talk about in a four-hour lunch," Noriega told Díaz Herrera and Marcos Justine, according to Díaz Herrera, *Panamá*, p. 110. Díaz Herrera says that he also learned that Noriega and U.S. officials had a secret meeting in Baltimore to discuss "topics that were not pleasing to Cubans and Sandinistas."

p. 161   PDF reorganization: U.S. military aid provided for in the treaty, $50 million, did not begin to flow to Panama until 1982. Díaz Herrera, who was G3 since 1982 and responsible for force development, was indifferent to U.S. cajoling to get moving on reorganization. Most of the $5 million in U.S. aid accepted in 1982 was squandered on thirteen road-bound armored vehicles armed with antitank guns—which U.S. advisers considered useless for Panama's small-unit defense needs. The U.S. advisers presumed that the primary motive was a kickback from the sale.

With Noriega's ascent, according to U.S. military sources, the restructuring program took off like a rocket. He named a new G3, Lieutenant Colonel Elías Castillo, who was close to U.S. military advisers and enthusiastic about working out the details of developing the defense force. Over the next years, Panama received $5 million (1983), $13 million (1984) and $10 million (1985), with which the PDF created two new combat brigades: the crack Canal defense unit, the Battalion 2000, and the counterinsurgency Brigade Paz. As a result of the restructuring, PDF troop strength was increased from approximately ten thousand to fourteen thousand, for the first time significantly outnumbering U.S. troops in Panama. The PDF consists roughly of 4,500 Army, 500 Navy, 200 Air Force and 8,800 paramilitary police and border guards. (Center for Defense Information Fact Sheet, March 4, 1988.)

p. 161   Use of Kalish's Learjet: Kalish testimony to PSI and interview; flight log for the Learjet, tail number N39292, was compiled by U.S. Customs investigators and obtained by the author. The log has a notation from the pilot, "Gen. Noriega to Vegas 111883." Other details of the trip were provided by one of those on board.

p. 162   The mistress's name could not be learned. U.S. military intelligence reported in 1985 about a Noriega mistress who lived in the Washington area in 1982 and early 1983. Magdelena Kusmisik bore Noriega a son in 1982, and he officially legitimized the boy. FOIA release, Southcom, Quarry Heights, to DIA, Washington, April 7, 1985.

p. 162   Bush was at least nominally in charge of the administration's most important attempts at interagency drug enforcement. In early 1982, he established the South Florida Task Force, the first major response to the burgeoning cocaine trade, and headed its 1983 successor agency, the National Narcotics Border Interdiction System.

p. 162   Money-laundering article: *The Wall Street Journal,* November 3, 1983, by Stanley Penn.

p. 163   Milián arrest due to Panamanian cable: Milián testimony, Kerry Hearings II, 232, and interviews with DEA officers.

p. 163   Meeting on ship boarding: Interview with Bramble. The meeting occurred in late 1982.

Díaz Herrera was present at the meeting and recalls that the Central American topics were paramount at the meeting. Reports, including at least one citing Díaz Herrera (*Newsweek,* October 31, 1988), that Bush asked for Noriega's help with the Contras in exchange for U.S. tolerance of his illegal activities, could not be confirmed, and I consider them highly dubious. In my detailed interviews with Díaz Herrera, he backed off the *Newsweek* report and said he may have made disparaging comments to *Newsweek* about Bush because he was angry that Bush in 1987 had refused his requests for an interview. The exchange on drugs is based on Bush's appearance on ABC's *Nightline,* June 9, 1988. De la Espriella's comment is from a deposition by Bush aide Donald Gregg to the Christic Institute, May 20, 1988.

Bush's comments to Ted Koppel are his most extensive on the subject: "I remember going down, Ted, to Panama, all on instructions from the president, and the secretary of state weighing in, to talk to the then-president of Panama and his defense minister [sic], who was Mr. Noriega, about money laundering, and trying to get the Panamanian banks not to be involved in that. So it's not a question of, was there ever any inkling that an official was involved or that the government might have been condoning things that they should have condemned, but that's quite different than having evidence that a person is, you know, up to his eyeballs in bringing narcotics into the United States." Bush also denied a charge by former NSC aide Norman Bailey that there was a "plethora of human intelligence, electronic intercepts, satellite and overflight photography that, taken together, constitute, not just a smoking gun, but rather a 21 gun barrage of evidence." Bush said he had ordered a check of the National Intelligence Daily (NID)—the intelligence report that Bailey claimed contained the information about Noriega—and found that the material cited by Bailey "has never been in the NID."

CHAPTER 8: MARGIN BY FRAUD

p. 165 Barletta's flight: The flight log for Kalish's plane lists Barletta as a passenger and notes that the flight was a Panamanian Air Force official mission.

p. 166 De la Espriella's comments in Caracas: Interview with Díaz Herrera, who was in Caracas for the inauguration and reported the comments to Noriega.

p. 166 Arnulfo Arias's promise: Interview with Carlos Rodríguez.

p. 167 "First line of defense . . .": Interview with Díaz Herrera.

P. 167 Noriega's formula: Noriega interview with *La Prensa*, October 31, 1983.

p. 167 Barletta's wife, Consuelo, is a lawyer. It has been erroneously reported in the U.S. press that she is a former beauty queen. In fact, her sister is a former Miss Panama.

Although his full last name is Ardito Barletta, he has encouraged the use of the matronymic, Barletta, in preference to the patronymic, Ardito.

p. 167 Shoved down the party's throat: Interview with Díaz Herrera; FOIA release, U.S. embassy cable, January 12, 1984, also describes the meeting based on the account of one of those present.

p. 167 Republican and Liberal negotiations: Interviews with Díaz Herrera, Barletta, Republican Party leader Kaisar Bazán and Esquivel.

p. 169 Campaign experts: *The Washington Post,* May 6, 1984, by Margot Hornblower. She lists consultants Joel McCleary, Tim Kraft and Jay Beck.

p. 169 Barletta's campaign war chest: Interview with Barletta. He said he raised a total of $4.8 million, one half in Panama and one half in the United States, Europe and Japan. After the election, it was revealed that the National Endowment for Democracy, the bipartisan U.S. fund to support democratic and pro-U.S. movements abroad, funneled $20,000 to Barletta's campaign through the AIFLD, the American Institute for Free Labor Development. See *La Prensa,* June 17, 1984, citing articles in *The Washington Post* and *The New York Times.*

p. 169   BCCI account: Deposition of Amjad Awan, a BCCI executive who handled Noriega's account, to the Kerry Committee. Hearings IV, 479–80.

p. 169   IHRE skimming: Interviews and testimony of José Blandón, who managed IHRE for several years.

p. 171   Front companies: Some of Panama's richest law firms, including those of prominent opposition figures, specialized in quick setups of companies. A client seeking to do business in Panama without his name being connected to the transactions can buy an already existing company off the shelf, with a conveniently doctored history of seemingly legitimate transactions going back several years. Or he can create an entirely new company, or a chain of companies, each owning the next one in the chain, to create a maze of masked ownership that is virtually impossible to unravel. The fee to set up a corporation was usually $1,000, and $250 a year to file the routine paperwork to keep the company on the books.

A Senate Permanent Subcommittee on Investigations report in 1985, "Crime and Secrecy," p. 102, cited evidence that at least one hundred thousand such companies were on the books in Panama and perhaps as many as a million. The investigators gave this example: "One witness testified . . . that his Panamanian attorney took a 5-year-old shelf company and turned it into an 'operating company' with a 5-year history of excellent growth. The company came complete with bank recommendations, certified financials and Dun & Bradstreet reports. The witness told the attorney what figures should appear on the most recent year's financial statements."

The business of setting up bogus companies was not restricted to attorneys with allegience to the military. For example, Panamanista leader Guillermo Endara, who was installed as president by the 1989 U.S. invasion, personally arranged in 1976 for a string of paper corporations to be transferred to General Manuel Contreras, then the chief of Chile's secret police, DINA, according to notarized documents on the transfer that I obtained. The companies were linked to a tax-fraud scheme revealed in 1980. *La Segunda,* May 18 and 24, 1980, and *Cosas* (no month, 1980), both Chilean publications.

p. 171   Kalish transactions: Kalish testimony to PSI and interviews with author. Kalish was able to provide documentation for the Boeing and Bell transactions, including the letter of credit and a withdrawal slip for $500,000 from BCCI with a note referring to the Boeing purchase. The $36,000 checks included interest of 2½ points above LIBOR.

p. 172   Kalish party: Details from two women who attended the parties.

p. 172   Terre Lind: Her date with Noriega is based on César's account to Kalish and on her own conversations with Kalish. Lind's picture showed up on *The New York Times* society page several years later.

p. 172   Kalish gifts: PSI testimony and Kalish interviews. Kalish's account of his purchases was confirmed to me by an eyewitness to his shopping in Pretelt's jewelry store.

p. 173   Noriega and Carlton's "last flight": Carlton deposition, 74.

p. 173   "Don't be dumb," and bomb comment: Prosecution memo.

p. 174   Bilonick in Medellín: Prosecution memo, Carlton deposition, 81–2.

p. 174   "Nothing goes on": Carlton deposition, 82.

p. 175   Spadafora at press conference: Interview with Pastora aide Carol Prado.

p. 176   Spadafora's first mission: Interviews with Pastora, Pastora aide Carol Prado and Ari Spadafora, Hugo's wife. Prado gave the location of Spadafora's area of operations as the Maíz and Indio rivers, an area about twenty miles south of the Punta Gorda area.

p. 177   Military dogma: *"Los Indios Nicaraguenses y la 'Bahía Cochinos' de Reagan,"* an essay on the war by Spadafora published in *La República* of Costa Rica, November 24, 1983, and January 4 and 6, 1984. Reprinted in *Las Derrotas,* pp. 105–12.

p. 178   Meeting with ARDE directorate: Interviews with Pastora, Prado and Brooklyn Rivera, and transcript of a tape recording of Spadafora's remarks.

p. 178   Gringo support: Pastora used the term in an interview. He has been reluctant to acknowledge that the American CIA was the supplying agency, but independent accounts have left no doubt that Pastora was receiving CIA support, despite his disclaimers. Among other books providing such evidence, see Dickey, *With the Contras,* pp. 149, 239; and Arturo Cruz Jr., *Memoirs of a Counterrevolutionary: Life with the Contras, the Sandinistas and the CIA* (Garden City: Doubleday, 1989), ch. 6.

p. 179   Pastora's relationship with Noriega: Interviews with Pastora, Prado and Ari Spadafora.

p. 179   Panamanian weapons flights: *Newsweek,* September 3, 1984.

p. 179   Noriega contribution of $100,000: U.S. government stipulation 45 in the trial of *U.S.A. v. Oliver North,* U.S. District Court for the District of Columbia.

p. 179   October trip to Panama: Interview with Ari Spadafora.

p. 180   Spadafora collecting information: Carlton deposition. Many associates of Spadafora have commented on his constant note-taking during this period, but Carlton is the only one who claims to know about its specific content regarding Noriega and drug trafficking. Carlton, in his deposition and testimony, did not claim to have given Spadafora any information during the 1984 meetings, but journalist Miguel Antonio Bernal recalls a conversation with Spadafora at this time in which Spadafora said he was receiving information about Noriega's drug trafficking from one of Noriega's pilots.

p. 184 $5 million: Carlton was unsure whether the figure mentioned by Escobar was $4 million or $5 million. See Carlton deposition, p. 88, and Kerry Hearings, II, p. 197. Other sources providing information about the protection money—Julián Melo in his interview with Andres Oppenheimer; Kalish and Díaz Herrera in interviews with the author; and Blandón in his testimony to the Kerry Committee—were no more definite. The $5 million figure is more frequently mentioned by the sources.

p. 184   Suite of offices: Carlton deposition, pp. 90, 145.

p. 184   Flight to Nicaragua: Carlton deposition, p. 90–4. Under questioning, Carlton did not implicate any Nicaraguan officials in the drug transactions.

p. 185   The U.S. indictment against Noriega treats the bribery in a somewhat different light. Colonel Melo is not indicted or even mentioned. Instead, the indictment describes a $4 million bribe to Noriega from a cartel representative, Boris Olarte, who testified against Noriega in late 1987. The Olarte payment may have been an additional bribe—making the total payments for cartel activities in Panama in the neighborhood of $9 million. I find it unlikely that there were two separate bribes, however, since the two alleged payments would both have been for the protection of the same cartel activities. DEA investigators developed the theory that the Olarte bribe was first and paid for general permission to operate in Panama, including the presence of the cartel leaders fleeing from Colombia. The second payment—that to Melo—was to protect specific activities, that is, transport of specific ether shipments and actual production at the factory. Very little could be learned about the alleged Olarte payment, which Olarte claims he made directly to Noriega. If that is true, it would have been the only known instance of Noriega dealing with Colombian traffickers on criminal business without an intermediary. All other witnesses describe Noriega as extremely careful to shield himself from direct contact with Colombian traffickers.

p. 185   Noriega's cooperation: The official was Frank McNeil, then of the State Department's intelligence and research division, testifying to the Kerry Committee, April 4, 1988, Hearings III, 322.

p. 187   Vote fraud: Interview with Díaz Herrera. Nicolás Barletta acknowledged in an interview that he attended meetings at Díaz Herrera's house during the count, but denied it was for the purpose of rigging the vote.

p. 189   Horse trading: Interview with confidential source directly familiar with the thinking and action of Barletta during this period.

p. 189   Bodyguard for mistress: FOIA release, Southcom Intelligence Report, April 7, 1985.

p. 189   Brown's death: La Prensa, August 8, 1984 (news story and En Pocas Palabras).

p. 189   Wassel Rock: La Prensa, September 23, 1984. The gang member who reached the French embassy told his story privately to embassy personnel, who passed it on as reliable to the U.S. embassy, according to a U.S. political officer. A source close to Barletta also said Brown's gang was under Noriega's orders.

p. 190   Gugliotta interview: The Miami Herald, August 30, 1984. Spadafora's articles on strategy are found in his compilation, Las Derrotas, pp. 115–26.

p. 191   Assassination threat: Interview with Ari Spadafora. Another, perhaps separate version of the assassination threat was recounted by John Hull, an American rancher with close ties to the Contra cause. Hull, in an interview, says he was told by a Contra fighter he knew as "Oscar" that Noriega had called Pastora and had offered to provide $50,000 a month in aid to Pastora's group on the condition that Spadafora be "eliminated." Oscar told Hull he knew of the plot by eavesdropping on conversations between Noriega and Pastora.

p. 193   Spadafora interview: La Prensa, September 4, 1984.

p. 194   Cason report: FOIA release, "The 1984 Panamanian Presidential Election: The Question of Fraud and Voting Irregularities," September

20, 1984, sent as an airgram to the State Department. The State Department at first withheld release of Cason's study in response to my FOIA request on the grounds of national security. Inexplicably, when another batch of documents related to the elections was released several months later, it included the study with only minor excisions.

Here are some excerpts from the report:

> Because of challenges ("impugnaciones") to the results of 372 of the 3902 polling places (mesas), 62564 votes were never counted, equivalent to 9.5% of the polling places and approximately 9% of the 716,761 votes that were tallied. Statistical analysis of the excluded votes, using published government coalition (UNADE) figures . . ., shows opposition presidential candidate Arnulfo Arias would have bested the government's candidate Nicolás Ardito Barletta, by 4334 votes in the contested polling places. Subtracting from this figure the 1713 votes comprising the official margin of victory for Barletta, Arias emerges the winner by 2621 votes. . . .
>
> Several reasons account for these challenges. Opposition party representatives challenged voting results where they felt irregularities were attributable to the government coalition UNADE, but amazingly, the opposition also asked that results be thrown out where it was leading UNADE. Through disorganization and failure to train adequately its thousands of poll watchers, the opposition "shot themselves in the foot." By foolishly challenging their own victory on the grounds that their vote totals would have been even higher had various types of alleged irregularities not occurred, the opposition "threw the baby out with the bath water," eventually (when the votes were never reincluded) losing a substantial number of votes to Barletta, enough in Chiriquí province alone to have beaten him for the presidency. [The reference to Chiriquí is apparently to the contested 4.4 circuit tally, which the opposition won by several thousand votes, but claimed that the tally document had been stolen and altered to reduce Arias' margin of victory.]
>
> Most of the challenges, however, were made by candidates of the government coalition in the PRD and PALA parties. The bulk of the challenges were to tables in Bocas del Toro, Chiriquí and Panamá, areas which sided heavily with Arias. In 234 of the 372 challenged polling places, the opposition was leading the government coalition. . . . The challenged tables were generally consecutively

numbered, especially in Colón, where for example, a Liberal party [UNADE] representative had the votes in tables 417–437 thrown out, resulting in a net loss of 1006 votes to Arias. . . .

In addition to the clear case made above that the opposition received more votes than the government coalition in the May election, there is other statistical evidence which suggests quite persuasively that had the Electoral Tribunal investigated substantive charges contained in challenges, it would have found that Arias' margin of victory was even greater than the 2621 votes calculated earlier. . . . In fact, . . . the Electoral Tribunal . . . discarded all challenges and rejected the votes in question, whether valid or not.

Nevertheless, an official Tribunal investigation into the existence of possible fraud is not absolutely necessary to arrive at some tentative conclusions. Our examination of the published voting data used by the government coalition provides numerous examples of highly improbable voter behavior. Using UNADE's published voting results by table, one finds there are 421 mesas (10.7 % of the total) where there was at least a 100% voter turnout; in many cases, the "turnout" was over 200%. Nationwide the average turnout was 78.6%, not counting the challenged votes. . . . The net result of the voting in these 421 small mesas was 6653 votes in favor of Barletta according to UNADE, and 4503 in his favor according to opposition figures. . . . The only other explanation for the extraordinarily large turnout in these 421 cases is fraud.

Discrepancies in the opposition and UNADE vote count in many tables also suggest that substantial post-electoral manipulation of the real totals took place. In half of the 421 cases under scrutiny here, the opposition and UNADE mesa totals do not agree. . . . Close examination, table by table, shows a pattern which strongly suggests persons systematically altered large numbers of results with the purpose of reducing Arias' totals, boosting Barletta's, or both. . . .

A [deleted] official told us in strict confidence that a small group of Tribunal, PDF and comptroller officials systematically altered the official copy of many acts to give an extra edge to UNADE.

Why was there no investigation into fraud? First because the six parties comprising the government coalition consistently supported by the left-wing parties in the National Vote-Counting Board, outvoted the opposition on all the procedural issues and refused to scrutinize the vote-tally sheets for validity (it merely read them). . . .

The opposition's call for a table-by-table recount was never accepted by civic groups or the electoral authorities, and never took place. If it had, our statistical research and empirical evidence strongly suggests Arias would have been clearly shown to be the winner by over 4,000 votes and probably by much more if fraudulent votes had been adjudicated.

(signed) Briggs.

The report includes eight appendices demonstrating Cason's finding in statistical detail.

p. 195   Fraud unlikely: FOIA release, U.S. embassy cable, April 18, 1984, signed by Briggs.

p. 196   Opposition obsession: U.S. embassy cable, May 3, 1984.

p. 196   No serious consideration: Interviews with Briggs and three other embassy offices.

p. 197   Distribution of Cason report: The report was so little noticed that Richard Wyrough, the State Department's Panama desk officer, maintained in 1988 that he had never seen it and that there had been no "demonstrable fraud" in the 1984 elections.

p. 197   Embassy neutrality: FOIA release, U.S. embassy cable, December 12, 1983.

p. 198   Motley memos: FOIA release, three memoranda, one undated, two dated October 3, 1984.

p. 199   Contadora discussion: FOIA release, U.S. embassy cable, October 11, 1984.

CHAPTER 9: REMEMBER ME WHEN THE BOMB
EXPLODES . . .

p. 201   Harvard visit: FOIA release, 193rd Infantry Brigade, Weekly Intelligence Summary, February 28–March 8, 1985.

p. 202   Surveillance: Interviews with a U.S. military officer who asked to remain anonymous and with a DEA agent.

p. 203   Panamanian laws are extraordinarily protective of commercial and bank secrecy. The identity of owners of numbered bank accounts is protected by law. Fines can be imposed on anyone disclosing to foreign authorities information obtained from commercial documents, and it is forbidden to investigate the private affairs of bank clients. The laws date from the early years of the Torrijos government and gave rise to Panama's international banking center, with over one hundred banks and assets of $35–$40 billion in the mid-1980s. Such "offshore" banking systems as Panama's offer a haven from U.S. income taxes for the wealth of large corporations and individuals. Panama's center, while significant, is small in comparison to the tax-haven banks in the Cayman Islands and the Bahamas. See "Crime and Secrecy," PSI, pp. 101–8.

p. 203   Opposition position on treaty: *La Prensa,* January 17, 1985.

p. 203   Panama claimed credit: *16 Años,* p. 68.

p. 203   Gugliotta and Leen, in *The Kings of Cocaine,* write that the Spanish court may have feared the United States was building a trumped-up political case out of the Ochoa arrest intended to prove the Reagan administration's highly publicized charges that Nicaragua's Sandinista government was involved in drug trafficking with the cartel.

p. 203   *La Prensa* reprints: *Time,* February 25, 1985 (reprinted February 25), and "The Cash Connection" (reprinted March 6); and U.S. Narcotics Control Programs Overseas: An Assessment, House Committee on Foreign Affairs, February 22, 1985 (reprinted March 12).

p. 204   Aid and lending: State Department statistics.

p. 205   Vidal reputation and arrests: Miami Criminal Court records list arrests for possession of marijuana (1976 and 1980) and firearms violations (1973 and 1980). Interview with Carol Prado on talk about terrorist tactics. See also *The Miami Herald,* February 16, 1987, and Leslie Cockburn, *Out of Control* (New York: Atlantic Monthly Press, 1987), pp. 74–6.

p. 205   Spadafora's group: Interviews with Ari Spadafora, Rob Owen, John Hall and Carol Prado.

p. 206   Spadafora's contact with CIA agent Fernandez is mentioned by Owen in an August 2, 1985, memo to North and by Ari Spadafora.

p. 206   Owen memo: May 20, 1985, memo to North, released uncensored to the Christic Institute. A redacted version of the memo, and three others mentioning Spadafora and/or Risa, was made public by the congressional Iran-Contra committee, but deleted the names. In the August 2 memo, Owen writes, "Even Joe [Fernandez] believes they [Spadafora, Felipe Vidal and Risa] can be used and be helpful. . . . These people are qualified and can be trusted, though many people want to discredit them just because they are willing to go inside and take the war to the Sandinistas."

North and Owen arranged for Vidal to have access to State Department humanitarian aid funds for the Contras, administered through

the Nicaraguan Humanitarian Aid Office, and Risa's signature appears
on receipts for goods purchased for the Contras. The plan to lure
Pastora's men away was successfully carried out by Vidal and Risa in
1986 and resulted in Pastora's retirement from the Contra struggle. See
The Miami Herald, February 16, 1987.

p. 206   Plotting to undercut Pastora: Owen's memos to North, April 1 and
August 2, 1985, and Owen interview with author. Owen said he was
providing supplies and money for Spadafora's next trip inside Nicaragua. Pastora aide Carol Prado describes Pastora's perception of the
plot by the CIA and the FDN in a memo, titled in English "Operation
Dry Off Pastora," which he provided to the author. The plan was
finally put into effect successfully in mid-1986, with the participation
of Vidal and Risa, and as predicted virtually the entire fighting force
loyal to Pastora shifted its allegiance to the CIA-controlled FDN.

p. 206   Spadafora's reluctance: Interview with Ari Spadafora.

p. 207   Noriega and the CIA: The content of that relationship has been
shielded in U.S. secrecy. But almost every former U.S. official willing
to talk has testified to the intimacy of Noriega's CIA relationship.
Among the former officials testifying are Southcom Commander Paul
Gorman, Frank McNeil, CIA Director Stansfield Turner and Ambassador William Jorden. Officials speaking not for attribution include
two high-ranking former U.S. officers serving in Panama, a former
CIA employee and a former intelligence officer serving at Southcom.

p. 207   North visit: Memo from North to McFarlane, January 15, 1985,
declassified for the congressional Iran-Contra investigation.

p. 207   Lethal assistance request: Stipulations released in the trial of Oliver
North, number 47.

p. 207   Panamanians involved in bombing: North trial stipulation no. 97
says North told Poindexter in August 1986, "Noriega had helped the
USG [U.S. government] the previous year in blowing up a Sandinista
arsenal." Report of the Investigative Committees Investigating the
Iran-Contra Affair (1987), p. 44, and footnotes 235 and 236. The notes
refer to classified North testimony and to an August 23, 1986, computer
note from North discussing his use of a British paramilitary specialist,
David Walker, to carry out the March 6, 1985, bombing that hit a
military complex, munitions dump and city hospital. No one was
killed. A still classified portion of the North testimony was obtained
by Grenada Television and broadcast in a documentary on Walker in
July 1988. In it, North says, "It's my understanding that Mr. Walker

provided two technicians involved in that. We understand that those two technicians were Panamanians." According to North trial stipulation number 98, referring to the August 23 PROF note to Poindexter, North mentioned the Panamanian role in the 1985 bombing because Noriega had offered to "assassinate the Sandinista leadership for the U.S. government" and the Panamanian role in the bombing showed that "Noriega had the capabilities that he proffered."

p. 207   No training took place: Numerous U.S. officials and Panamanians in positions to know said they knew of no such training, and no other confirmation of any kind has surfaced for Blandón's claim that training took place. Significantly, no Contra personnel, who usually talk openly about such matters, have ever alleged that training took place in Panama. The officials who said they knew of no training and that they consider it unlikely that training could have taken place without their knowledge include former Ambassador Briggs, two former CIA employees, two former Southcom officers and retired Colonel Roberto Díaz Herrera.

p. 208   North enterprise firms registered in Panama: Tower Commission report, and *The Washington Post,* December 21, 1986, by Ward Sinclair. According to Panamanian journalist Miguel Antonio Bernal, Noriega's financial representative in Geneva, Juan Alberto Castillero, assisted in setting up the companies.

p. 209   Battle of One Thousand Days: The mural was seen by several sources. The nineteenth-century Noriega is discussed in the Esparza report.

p. 209   Meetings with Mahlstedt: Interview with one of those present at the meetings.

p. 209   "Unreliable": Interview with former U.S. official.

p. 209   Spadafora's talk of guerrilla warfare: The guerrilla option was discussed at the meetings with Mahlstedt. Robert Owen also said Spadafora talked of forming a grass-roots political movement that could be turned into a guerrilla movement if necessary. Other Spadafora associates, who cannot be identified for security reasons, recounted similar conversations.

p. 210   Carlton operation in 1985: Interview with DEA agent Dan Moritz, who handled Carlton's case in 1985.

p. 210   Watson disappearance: Carlton deposition, pp. 96–102, 143ff., and testimony, Kerry Hearings II, pp. 205–7. Additional details were provided by DEA agent Dan Moritz. The allegation that Contra activists were responsible and used the money for supplies is based on Moritz's interrogations of Alemany Soto and other pilots who worked for Carlton. Carlton himself says only that a Nicaraguan Contra pilot, whose name he cannot remember, flew the drugs to John Hull's farm after Watson was murdered.

p. 211   Hull's involvement: In an interview Hull denied any knowledge of the events or that he knew Carlton or Watson. One Kerry committee witness, drug pilot Gary Betzner, testified that he flew weapons for Contras into Hull's airstrip and cocaine out. Hull is one of the defendants in the Christic Institute's lawsuit, which was dismissed for lack of evidence in 1989.

p. 211   Carlton's organization and trip to Colombia: Interview with DEA agent Dan Moritz; Moritz affidavit reproduced in Kerry Report.

p. 211   Kidnappings and press coverage: *La Prensa,* August 7. See also Sam Dillon, *The Miami Herald,* November 3, 1985. In putting together his story, Dillon had access to Panamanian court documents.

p. 212   Caballero background: Interview with Caballero; see also Kerry Report, 127ff, for DIACSA's Nicaraguan Humanitarian Assistance Office transactions.

p. 213   Exchange with Spadafora: Carlton deposition, p. 134.

p. 213   Cattle's role: Interview with a person directly involved.

p. 213   Meeting with Nieves: Interview with Nieves in Costa Rica. The meeting was first revealed by Brian Barger of the Associated Press in an article December 20, 1985.

p. 216   August 12 speech: FBIS, August 14, 1985.

p. 216   Noriega's trip: Interview with senior U.S. embassy official. Colonel Roberto Díaz Herrera said he did not know for sure what Noriega was doing, but he thought he was undergoing treatment for his allergies and facial scars.

p. 217   Discovery of the body: Costa Rican Office of Judicial Investigations (OIJ), Report, September 19, 1985.

p. 217   *Brigadistas:* The three men, Santos López Lobon, Ricuarte Esquivel Rodríguez and Orlando José Ortega, told a Costa Rican investigator that they were traveling that day because their association with Spadafora had exposed them to persecution by the Panamanian military and they had decided to flee Panama. They told a Costa Rican newspaper, *La Prensa Libre,* however, that they had been fighting with the Miskitos as *internacionalistas* for several months before their trip to Costa Rica on September 13. López Lobón said he had worked for

Spadafora as a bodyguard after the war against Somoza and then was recruited to work in counterintelligence in G2 under Noriega. He said he left G2 shortly after Torrijos's death because he was being harassed. See *La Prensa Libre* (Costa Rica), October 1, 1985, and OIJ interrogation reports.

p. 217   Identification of body: Morales statement to OIJ, January 21, 1986.

p. 218   Scene at Paitilla airport: Author's observations. Humberto López Tironi was widely believed to have been involved in Silverio Brown's gang's attack on opposition protesters, May 7, 1984.

p. 220   Hoffman: Hoffman's CIA work was revealed during the Iran-Contra committee hearings in July 1987 and by José Blandón in Kerry Hearings, February 9, 1988.

Hoffman was flown by the PDF out of Panama on September 23 and was immediately detained for questioning by Costa Rican police, who were zealously pursuing the Spadafora murder investigation. Under questioning, he told a different story: He said two friends, one a Honduran and the other a Salvadoran, were traveling in a bus behind the one in which Spadafora was riding and had seen PDF soldiers at Concepción take him prisoner and put him in a Jeep Wagoneer. The story was similar to the account given by other witnesses. The only reference to his previous account was to say that the Honduran said he was worried because "they are detaining all Central Americans in transit to question them, and there are versions that say that it was a Central American cell [that committed the murder] and others say it was the G2 of Panama." OIJ interrogation report, September 24, 1985.

p. 220   Theory of Díaz Herrera involvement: FOIA release, U.S. embassy cable, September 24, 1985.

p. 220   OIJ investigation: Report dated September 19, 1985.

p. 221   Panamanian investigation: Depositions examined by author. The two men, in reinstating their testimony, said that they had been threatened in the days following the murder and forced to retract their statements that they had seen Spadafora taken off the bus by PDF personnel.

p. 222   Noriega phone call: Interview with Barletta.

p. 222   Barletta's instructions: In a letter to Attorney General Manuel José Calvo dated September 22, he said he had considered naming a special investigative commission, as requested by the family, but added: "As you know, the constitution and the law, which I swore to maintain and defend as president of the republic, do not permit me to do so [name a commission], as the investigation of crimes falls within the sole competence of the Attorney General's office. As a result, I respectfully suggest, Mr. Attorney General, that you designate a commission of persons of the highest capacity and character who would collaborate with you and the constituted authorities in the investigation of this horrible crime, within the framework of our judicial system." The letter is quoted by a U.S. embassy cable, September 24, 1985. The cable noted that the dean of the University of Panama law school and other legal experts had argued that naming an independent commission would be constitutional and that there was legal precedent for it.

p. 226   The events in New York are based on interviews with Barletta, Briggs and Gabriel Lewis. All three mentioned the White House message.

p. 227   Coup attempt: Díaz Herrera and several PRD leaders.

p. 227   Abrams call: Interview with Barletta.

p. 228   Sanchez call: Sanchez testimony, Kerry Hearings IV.

CHAPTER 10: WASHINGTON V. MIAMI

p. 229   Aid suspension and U.S. statement: *The Washington Post,* March 28, 1988.

p. 230   Autopsy report by the OIJ Legal Medicine Department, September 15, 1985. The autopsy indicated that Spadafora had inhaled some of his own blood and that his blood was still circulating at the time his head was severed. That evidence led a Panamanian physician and prominent opposition leader, Dr. Luis Guillermo Casco Arias, to speculate that Spadafora may have received severe blows to the head before being killed by decapitation. Dr. Arias concluded that there was no sexual abuse and that his killers "were not oriented toward much greater torture than decapitation."

The presence of undigested rice and other food in his stomach—which he was known to have eaten at a restaurant about noon the day he died—indicated that Spadafora probably was killed soon after he was last seen in early afternoon.

A lurid description of Spadafora's alleged sexual tortures is contained in an article in *Harper's,* June 1988, based on reporting by Panamanian journalist Guillermo Sánchez Borbón but written in English by an American novelist living in Panama. The central, gruesome detail is that Spadafora's leg muscles were severed in order to keep him from closing his knees during the torture. The alleged cuts to the inner thighs were not mentioned in the autopsy or in Dr. Casco Arias's analysis. The autopsy records no trauma at all to the genitals or anus, although it notes the presence of hemorrhoids. The article's description of eight hours of beatings and torture also appears to be contradicted by the food in his stomach. The rest of the article is somewhat imaginative reconstruction of Spadafora's arrest based on the accounts of the eyewitnesses.

p. 231   Intelligence on Noriega responsibility: Two State Department and two U.S. military sources described the intelligence conclusions. Two Panamanians who later turned against Noriega, Roberto Díaz Herrera and José Blandón, claim that in conversations with them Noriega indicated that the murder had been committed by men under the command of Major Luis Córdoba. To Blandón, Noriega allegedly denied any personal responsibility for the killing. Kerry Hearings II, 118.

p. 231   Critical list: *The Washington Post,* October 7, 1985. The overthrow of Barletta, however, did not make the front page of either *The New York Times* or *The Washington Post.*

p. 231   Continued recognition of Barletta: Frank McNeil prepared statement to Kerry Hearings, III, 322f.

p. 232   State Department policy: Descriptions of U.S. strategy toward Delvalle and Noriega are based on interviews with four senior embassy political officers who served in Panama in 1985 and/or 1986 and with a State Department official dealing with Panama. The officials were speaking on a background basis and cannot be named. Their characterizations did not differ in any significant detail. The policy was not spelled out in any State Department cable obtained under the FOIA, however, and it is rare for the State Department to declassify explicit statements of strategy. An October 15 cable relates a conversation between Delvalle and Briggs: "The ambassador pointed out that our regional interests were undermined by the blow to democracy here. We were also concerned about continuing signs of instability in Panama; the public turmoil over the unresolved Spadafora case; [deleted]."

p. 232   Barletta's defenders: Interviews with Norman Bailey, Constantine Menges and Carlton Turner.

p. 233   McNeil statement to Kerry Hearings III, 323. Connie Bruck, in "How Noriega Got Away," *The American Lawyer,* July/August 1988, provides a detailed account of U.S. actions in this period. She attributes Casey's soft line to innocuous bumbling: "One government official recalls rushing up to a group of CIA men the next day to ask what had happened. 'It didn't go too well, they said. Casey had the talkers [talking papers], but he didn't understand that *he* was supposed to deliver the message. He thought he was supposed to warm Noriega up and then hand him over to the subordinates to get hit by the two-by-four. Then the subordinates took Noriega to lunch, and they—assuming Casey had done him in—were making nice noises to try to make him feel better. It was a disaster. Not only did Noriega not get the message, but he went away feeling like he was a pretty important guy—we bring him all the way up here just to make nice over lunch.' " The story is fascinating, but in light of Casey's subsequent defense of Noriega, which is discussed below, it ascribes a kind of wide-eyed innocence to CIA officials I find hard to accept.

p. 233   Iran-Contra activities at NSC: The National Security Archive, *The Chronology: The Documented Day-by-Day Account of the Secret Military Assistance to Iran and the Contras* (New York: Warner Books, 1987) and *Report of the Congressional Committees Investigating the Iran Contra Affair* (Washington, D.C.: U.S. Government Printing Office, 1987).

p. 234   Purpose of Poindexter's tour: *U.S.A. v. Oliver North,* U.S. District Court for the District of Columbia, stipulations of fact submitted by the U.S. government, stipulation 72.

p. 235   Poindexter was angry: *The Miami Herald,* June 14, 1986.

p. 235   Poindexter meeting: *The Miami Herald,* June 14, 1986 and May 12, 1987, and an unpublished interview by Chardy with Noriega, April 20, 1987.

My own interviewing indicated that Central America, not Noriega's troubles in Panama, was the focus of the brief meeting. A U.S. military officer, who rode with Poindexter on the plane to Honduras immediately following the meeting, said that Poindexter intended the meeting to "get Panama focused on Central America" and to convey reassurance of Reagan administration resolve on Central America. He said that in the "debriefing session" on the plane he was told that Poindexter was disappointed that the meeting was so rushed and that he "didn't feel he got his message across." There was no mention of drugs or of Nicaragua as having been a topic of the meeting, he said.

Briggs's description of the meeting was supported by three State Department officials, none of whom was at the meeting. The State Department, in responding to my FOIA request for documents describing the meeting, said that one document had been found but refused to declassify any part of it.

Gerardo González, a PRD leader, said that he was briefed about the meeting a week after it occurred. Poindexter asked for three things, he said: that Panama should lower its profile in the Contadora talks, reinstate Barletta and cooperate more with the United States in the war against Nicaragua. He said that there was only one unpleasant moment, when one of Noriega's aides blurted out that Poindexter's demands were a violation of Panama's national honor. That incident was also recounted by Captain Francisco Porras, who said the aide was Captain Cortizo.

The North trial stipulation 72 gives an overall conclusion to Poindexter's trip by stating: "Poindexter assured them [those he met with in the five countries, including Panama] that the U.S. government was committed to supporting the armed forces in those countries."

Finally, then Assistant Secretary of State for Latin America Elliott Abrams is also on record about the meeting. Testifying before the House Select Committee on Narcotics, March 29, 1988, Abrams said the following: "In truth, I don't think it is accurate to say that he added Panama to his Central America trip. I think the truth is he added Central America to a Panama trip. The main purpose of the trip was to tell Noriega that we could not tolerate what we believed to be the growing, increasing pattern of PDF corruption and it had to change. That was, I guess, the first serious message to Noriega." Abrams's statement that Panamanian corruption was the main purpose of Poindexter's trip is inconsistent with every other account and is implausible in light of the context of Poindexter's Iran-Contra dealings.

p. 236   Winston Spadafora went first to Costa Rica to follow up on something Hugo Spadafora's wife had told him, but which was not yet public: that Hugo had gone to see DEA agent Robert Nieves. Nieves met with Winston Spadafora and assured him that his brother had provided no specific information about Noriega and that he was confident that the meeting had nothing to do with Spadafora's death. After that meeting, according to Nieves, he wrote his first memo, dated October 17, 1985, to Washington describing the meeting with Spadafora. In the memo he said that he related to Winston Spadafora the "substance" of what Hugo Spadafora had told him: "[that] General Noriega is a major cocaine trafficker in Central America and he is assisted by José Robelo and one Sebastián González. I advised Dr. [sic, referring to Winston] Spadafora that his brother's death . . . had nothing to do with the DEA contact." José "Chepón" Robelo was a Contra pilot working with ARDE. The meeting did not become public until AP reporter Brian Barger interviewed Nieves and referred to the meeting in one paragraph in his December 20 story written with reporter Robert Perry. The story, about possible links between the Nicaraguan Contras and drug trafficking, did not mention Noriega.

p. 236   Helms meeting: Interviews with Winston Spadafora and with Deborah DeMoss, Helms staff member.

p. 238   Abrams's opposition to hearings: Interview with a participant in the conversation. Abrams did not respond to repeated requests to be interviewed for this book.

p. 238   Abrams's testimony: "Situation in Panama," Hearings Before the House Subcommittee on Western Hemisphere Affairs, March 10 and April 21, 1986. On the PDF, Abrams said, "It is corrosive of democratic government when the police and military forces, or PDF, are not dependent exclusively upon public funds provided by elected civil institutions of government. The PDF engages in business-like activities that appear to provide a perceptible part of its operating costs. This seems to have begun in the Torrijos years, with the laudable aim of preserving government revenue for social programs. But it is a long-range problem that Panama must resolve and will find very difficult."

p. 238   Other witnesses appearing before the Helms hearings were: Panamanians Adelaide Eisenmann and Roberto Eisenmann, former ambassador Ambler Moss, professors Richard Millett, Steven Ropp and Norman Bailey, Raymond McKinnon (of the DEA), and anti-Castro activist José Sorzano.

p. 239   Closed hearings: A congressional source who asked not to be named.

p. 239   NSA intercept: The existence of the intercept was mentioned by a U.S. military source who said he read an intelligence report referring to it. Winston Spadafora said in an interview that the intercept was part of the Helms investigation and claimed that he had been allowed to hear a tape of the intercept. A congressional source said that the intercept was part of the secret hearings. The first public mention of the intercept was a *Washington Times* story by James Dorsey, January 15, 1988, which attributed it to Winston Spadafora.

Floyd Carlton, in his deposition to the Kerry Committee, gave an account of the same conversation about a month before the *Washing-*

ton Times story. He said he learned of the conversation, not from an intercept, but from a PDF source with connections to G2. Carlton's account of the conversation is as follows:

> When Hugo was taken to the military base or to the barracks to be interrogated, the famous notebook, the famous proof that he was going to present, was found on him, and then the officer in charge of the barracks . . . called the chief of the military zone, and reported what was happening.
>
> In a very detailed way, this person tells me that the major [the chief of the Chiriquí military zone, which was Córdoba] had a direct line to [Noriega in] Europe, and tells him [Noriega], "We caught the dog, and he has rabies."
>
> So then . . . Noriega answered, "What do you do when a dog has rabies? Well, you cut his head off and you take it to the university to examine him."

p. 240   Hecht and Spencer: Documents obtained from the Foreign Agents Registration Office of the Justice Department indicate that the firm was hired in October 1985, just a month after the Spadafora killing and Barletta ouster, and worked for Panama through November 1986, receiving total fees of $359,627. The Hecht-Spencer connection became an issue in the 1988 campaign, in which Spencer served as vice presidential candidate Dan Quayle's campaign manager, after an article by Allan Nairn, "Noriega's Man in Washington," *The New Republic,* September 26, 1988.

p. 240   Noriega meetings with Casey, Burghardt and North: Interview with Ambassador Bazán.

p. 241   Stories on Noriega: The other major stories were by Marvin Kalb of NBC News and Alfonso Chardy of *The Miami Herald,* both June 13. Hersh's second story, also published June 13, dealt with the inchoate plans inside the BNDD in 1972 to assassinate Noriega—a story that was first revealed at the time of the 1978 Senate debate on the Panama Canal treaties (see above, page 63f). His third story, on the 1984 election fraud, appeared on June 21. It said that the Helms closed hearings were told by the CIA that Arnulfo Arias actually won the election by 30,000 votes and that the State Department "initially concluded" that Arias won by 25,000 votes. Those figures are in line with the claims of the ADO, the opposition coalition, but contradict the Cason report, which

is the only systematic U.S. analysis of the election whose existence has been confirmed (see above, page 194ff.; Cason's study concluded that Arias would have won by at least 4,000 votes). Former Ambassador Briggs, in an interview, said that no such CIA study ever crossed his desk and that he would have known of such a study if it existed.

p. 242   Inter-American Defense Board: The board's meeting and the reception were held at the Inter-American Defense College at Fort McNair.

p. 242   Schweitzer's inquiry: Interview with Schweitzer.

p. 243   Policy review: McNeil testimony to Kerry Hearings, III, 40, and his prepared statement, pp. 324–5.

p. 243   Moritz undercover operation: Moritz affidavit to Miami Magistrate in support of search warrant, January (no day) 1986. The affidavit is reproduced in Kerry Report documents. Also, interviews with DEA agents Moritz, Kennedy and Steve Grilli, and with Assistant U.S. Attorney Richard Gregorie.

p. 245   Carlton's return to Panama: Carlton deposition, 101ff.

p. 246   Carlton contact with Telles: Carlton testimony to Kerry Hearings, II, 210–2. Telles, in an interview, declined to comment on the meeting.

p. 247   Rodríguez businesses reverses: *Extra,* April 2, 1986. The Panamanian opposition tabloid wrote that two Rodríguez businesses, Prodalis, S.A., and Hangar, VIP, had been evicted from the Paitilla hangar by the Panamanian Civil Aviation Board.

p. 247   Conversations with César Rodríguez: Carlton deposition, 158ff.

p. 247   Rodríguez tapes: Prosecution memo; Carlton testimony to Kerry Hearings, II, 212f. Steven Kalish, who was visited in jail by César Rodríguez, said Rodríguez also told him about the tapes.

The *Krill* shipment is one of the counts in the Miami indictment. It is also described in the Prosecution Memo and in interviews with Steve Grilli and Richard Gregorie, based on their interrogation of Carlton. The indictment's allegation that Noriega was an active partner in the *Krill* deal is not based on the testimony of Carlton, who does not believe Noriega was. Another unidentified witness has alleged that Noriega was present at the Holiday Inn at a planning meeting for the shipment. If true, it would be the one known exception to Noriega's 1984 decision to dissociate himself from drug dealers. I favor Carlton's interpretation that Noriega's involvement was to set a trap for Rodríguez.

p. 248   Victims' presence in Medellín and discovery of bodies: *El Especta-dor* (Bogotá), March 26 and 27, 1986, and *El Tiempo* (Bogotá), March 26, 1986.

p. 248   Enrique Pretelt and a Dr. Adriano Solis were allegedly in Medellín around the time of the disappearance, according to *La Prensa,* March 31, 1986. Pretelt later told a reporter that he was "in Chiriquí" when asked if he was in Medellín at the time of the murders. Nubia Pino was said by *Extra,* April 1, 1986, to have been the owner of a country villa near Coronado in Panama. Coronado was one of the airstrips Carlton had used for drug flights.

p. 249   Noriega's responsibility for Rodríguez's death: Carlton, in his deposition to the Kerry Committee investigators, p. 156, said, "My conclusion is that Noriega killed him." In his public testimony, Kerry Hearings, II, 212, he said: "All of us were a danger to General Noriega, because he was trying to project a certain political image. He was trying to clean up his image and we, those of us who at some point had done something illegal for him, we were a danger for him."

p. 249   Carlton arrest: Interviews with Moritz, Nieves and Caballero. Caballero's son, Luis, was also in Panama and Costa Rica in July. Also out on bail, he petitioned the Miami court for permission to travel to Panama on July 19 through 22 and to Costa Rica on July 23 through 27. He was traveling "for purposes of demonstrating the Cessna Caravan I for viewing by various clients including the Governments and American Embassies of Panama and Costa Rica." The travel permission document was reproduced in the Kerry Report. That a man under indictment for cocaine smuggling would be doing business with the U.S. embassies in Panama and Costa Rica was one of many examples of questionable associations between U.S. officials and drug figures in Central America mentioned by the Kerry Report. The Caballeros's company, DIACSA, had been granted two contracts by the State Department's Nicaraguan Humanitarian Assistance Office, and were paid more than $40,000. Both contracts were conferred after Caballero and his son were indicted on drug charges.

CHAPTER II: SHOOTING THE KING

p. 251   Noriega's maxims: The Torrijos saying is from the recollections of Roberto Díaz Herrera. The second is from Noriega's book, *Operaciónes Psicologicas* (Panama: National Guard, 1975), a publication of G2. Noriega is considered to have been the primary author of the seventy-nine-page book, described as part of a series on "National Guard doctrine."

p. 252   Avoid any public posture: Embassy cable, June 17, 1986.

p. 252   Noriega assassination offer and meeting with Oliver North: North trial stipulations 97–99, 101 and 106.

Noriega was involved in another set of negotiations that may have been related to U.S. Central American operations at about the same time. On June 14, the PDF confiscated a Danish freighter, the *Pia Vesta,* with a cargo of 1,500 AK47 assault rifles and 1,440 East German–made rocket launchers. Also on board were thirty-two military transport trucks. The weapons were not listed on the ship's manifest.

The owner of the cargo, Miami-based arms dealer David Duncan, claimed that the weapons shipment was destined for the Contras, via a circuitous route that included Peru, Panama and El Salvador. He said the arrangement had the approval and encouragement of Nestor Sanchez of the Defense Department—something Sanchez denies. According to Duncan, in July and August 1986 he was attempting to persuade Noriega to release the shipment and allow it to proceed to El Salvador, where it was to be stored until its final destination could be arranged. Ultimately, Noriega refused to release the ship or its cargo, and the trucks were seen in Panamanian military parades.

The capture of Duncan's cargo occurred only two days after the appearance of Hersh's first story on Noriega in *The New York Times.* José Blandón, then an aide to Noriega, told CNN reporter Lucia Newman that the confiscation was Noriega's way of retaliating against the Reagan administration, which he was convinced was responsible for planting the Hersh story.

In February 1988, Blandón told an even more elaborate story about the *Pia Vesta* affair to *New York Times* reporters Elaine Sciolino and Stephen Engelberg. Blandón said that the shipment was a trap set by Oliver North to prove that Nicaragua was shipping arms to El Salvador's FMLN rebels. According to North's plan, Blandón said, the *Pia Vesta* cargo was supposed to have been captured in El Salvador, and the East Bloc weapons falsely linked to Nicaragua. Noriega foiled the plan, Blandón said, by capturing the ship in Panama before it arrived in El Salvador.

Testifying before the Kerry committee a few days later, Blandón retracted the story, saying that he knew it only from Noriega, had no independent knowledge and did not necessarily believe it.

Congressional investigators into the Iran-Contra affair scrutinized the *Pia Vesta* affair closely, but found no evidence North had anything to do with it.

See Kerry Hearings II, 164ff; *The New York Times,* February 4 and February 11, 1988; *The Miami Herald,* February 8, 1988, by Alfonso Chardy; and *The Wall Street Journal,* March 9, 1988, by José de Córdoba; Iran-Contra Affair, Appendix B, vol. 24, Depositions; *Caretas* (Peru), December 9, 1986, and July 21, 1986; FOIA release, 193rd Infantry Brigade Weekly Intelligence Summary, August 7–13 (description of trucks in military parade).

p. 253   IBC contract: Foreign Agents Registration Act forms, signed by IBC senior partner (and former State Department official) Francis Gomez. Gomez testified about the contract in a deposition to the Iran-Contra Committee, *Iran-Contra Affair* Appendix G: vol. 12, Depositions, Washington 1988, pp. 550–4. Gomez stated in his testimony that the client, Impulso Turístico, was a private company and the contract is listed on Justice Department forms as a nongovernment entity. The purpose, however, was clearly to help the government, according to the forms: "Specifically, IBC has agreed to evaluate the communications capability of government spokespersons, recommend improvements, obtain reference materials and provide assistance from time to time. IBC will also arrange for interviews, speeches and other events for designated Panamanians, both from the private sector and the government, who visit the United States."

p. 253   Approch to Lawn: Lawn deposition to the Iran Contra Committee, pp. 777–80, in which the reference to Noriega is excised, and Engelberg article, *The New York Times,* Feb. 7, 1988.

p. 253   Casey calls: A source to whom Helms described the calls. Helms has acknowledged the calls from Casey when questioned by reporters.

p. 254   CIA report: *Congressional Record,* Senate, August 6, 1987. Helms called it a "nonreport" that showed the "contempt which the operating level of the CIA has for its own oversight committee . . . [and] the level to which some sectors of the U.S. Government will go to protect an individual who is regarded as 'a U.S. asset.' "

p. 254   Kalish plea bargain: Interviews with Kalish and a directly informed legal source.

p. 255   Carlton extradition and comments about Noriega: Carlton deposition, pp. 119, 157.

p. 256   Suspicion of Delvalle: Interviews with Kaiser Bazán and José Blandón.

p. 256   The IMF approved a $44 million loan in July, clearing the way for disbursement of a $60 million commercial bank loan, involving 150 creditor banks, to reschedule $579 million in debt service due in 1986. *Financial Times,* July 4, 1986.

p. 256   Southcom briefings, Davis meetings with Noriega: A U.S. embassy source with direct knowledge of both meetings.

p. 256   Meese statements on Operation Pisces: Text in FOIA release, State Department cable, May 7, 1987.

p. 257   Operation Pisces cooperation: The Panamanian role was described by DEA Panama officer Fred Duncan during an interview on June 29, 1989, at DEA headquarters. Duncan and two other senior DEA officials, chief of intelligence David Wilson and assistant administrator Maurice Hill, argued strongly for the authenticity of Noriega's cooperation after 1984.

p. 258   Letter of commendation: The letter from DEA administrator John D. Lawn said: "Drug traffickers around the world are now on notice that the proceeds and profits of their illegal ventures are not welcome in Panama. In particular, I would like to thank your Attorney General, Mr. Carlos Villalaz, and Director General Nivaldo Madriñan of the DENI, who directed the operations on May 6 which led to the freezing of millions of dollars in trafficker bank accounts in Panama and the seizure of banking records which will provide enforcement authorities with insight into the operations of drug traffickers and money launderers. Also integral to the success of Operation Pisces was Panamanian Defense Forces Captain Luis Quiel, Chief of the Office of International Liaison and Coordination. Captain Quiel worked closely with our agents in Panama, Miami, Washington, and Los Angeles, and was instrumental in both the planning and operational phases of the investigation."

There is some evidence that Noriega's cooperation with the DEA gave rise to threats to him from the cartel. An intelligence report from the U.S. Defense Attaché to DIA, April 17, 1986, said: "Reportedly the General has been forced to move his headquarters to the small island of Naos [a Panamanian island off Fort Amador connected to the mainland by a causeway] into a 'super' protected bunker with extremely limited access. Also each night around Noriega's residence at

Altos de Golf . . . there are a half dozen radio patrol cars guarding all the sidestreets leading to his residence. Other police cars constantly patrol the surrounding areas." The intelligence report quoted an article in the opposition magazine *Quiubo* (April 17–24, 1986) saying the cartel had threatened Noriega because he had shut down the "Panamanian connection" and was now alerting the DEA about drug shipments to the United States.

p. 258   New opposition and APEDE conference: Interview with Eduardo Vallarino and several other participants, including an officer in the U.S. embassy.

p. 260   Díaz Herrera's supposed 1989 ambitions were the subject of several U.S. embassy and U.S. intelligence cables released under FOIA, including 193rd Infantry Brigade Weekly Intelligence Summary, August 7–13 and October 23–29, 1986. They were also the subject of an insider report in the gossipy *Quiubo,* October 23–30, 1986, which painted a scenario of Díaz Herrera as president in 1989 and Noriega as president in 1994, after he will have erased his negative public image with the help of "international agencies such as the U.S. Drug Enforcement Agency and the U.S. Southern Command, both of which support Noriega."

p. 263   Díaz Herrera's statements: See FBIS, June 9, 1986; *La Prensa,* June 6, 7, and 8, 1986; and interview June 13, 1986.

p. 268   Lewis mediation and flight: Interview with Lewis. Those present at Lewis's house were Colonels Alberto Purcell and Leonidas Macias, television magnate Fernando Eleta, Mario Galindo and Jaime Arias on the antigovernment side, and Carlos Duque and Gabriel Díaz representing the progovernment PRD.

p. 268   Plot to destabilize: *La República,* June 15, 1987.

p. 269   The other senator voting with Dodd was Senator Carl Levin (Dem.-Mich.).

p. 269   Embassy attack and pro-American response by students were described in cables June 30 and July 1, 1986, released under FOIA. The Panamanian Foreign Ministry, as it had always done in the past, deplored the attack and picked up the bill for the damages—$106,000.

p. 270   The briefers' spin was reflected in articles in *The Washington Post* and *The New York Times,* July 2, 1986. It is often the practice in Washington for the same official who gave such a speech to brief reporters about it.

p. 272   North prosecution: See, among many other sources, *The New York*

Times, February 18, 1988, and a profile of Kellner in *The Washington Post,* May 20, 1988.

p. 273 Aizprua's polygraph problem: Interviews with federal investigators.

CHAPTER 12: BULLETS ARE KISSES

p. 277 First story on investigation: Ronald J. Ostrow and Doyle McManus, *Los Angeles Times,* August 4, 1987, followed by a *Washington Post* story the next day that made explicit the erroneous assumption that Milián was a Miami grand jury witness. The third story was also in the *Los Angeles Times,* August 13, 1987. A more substantive leak occurred in a *Miami Herald* story September 17, 1987, by Jeff Leen, which described the witness as a Panamanian pilot and provided details that unmistakably pointed to Floyd Carlton, although he was not named.

p. 278 Doubts about Milián: The report on Milián's first interviews in May 1983 with Customs officers just prior to his arrest is contained in the Kerry Report. The Miami U.S. attorney's office took the unusual step of submitting an affidavit, nine pages long, backing up its conclusion that Milián "is not regarded by this office as a credible witness, and this office has declined to base any court proceedings upon his testimony." The June 8, 1988, affidavit by Assistant U.S. Attorney Stephen Schlessinger, is reproduced in the Kerry Hearings, IV, 404–413.

Milián's allegations were controversial for reasons unrelated to Noriega. He claimed in his Kerry committee testimony in June 1987 that he passed nearly $10 million from the cartel to the Nicaraguan Contras. The intermediary, he claimed, was CIA operative Felix Rodríguez (no relation), one of the managers of Oliver North's arms resupply organization based in El Salvador. See Knut Royce, *Newsday,* June 29, 1987. Felix Rodríguez denied any such involvement with the cartel or Milián. But Milián's charges implicating the CIA and the Contras, which have never been substantiated, bolstered his stature with some investigators outside the government, who have claimed that the attacks on his credibility by officers of the Justice Department were part of a Reagan administration cover-up.

I have not investigated the aspects of Milián's testimony not related to Panama, but based on my research, I concur that Milián is not credible in his allegations about Noriega and in his claim to have laundered $200 million a month in Panama.

p. 280   Díaz Herrera attack: Interviews with Díaz Herrera and with a bodyguard, Gabriel Pinzón. Two embassy cables, both dated July 28, 1987, mentioned reports of deaths during the attack.

Noriega insisted as a condition of release that Díaz Herrera retract his charges against him. Díaz Herrera did so, admitting to an "abnormal mental state" as an extenuating circumstance. Soon after arriving in Caracas, however, he withdrew his retraction and began to denounce Noriega in much the same terms as before. His self-published book, *Panamá: Mucho Más Que Noriega,* is a rambling account of his ordeal and of his relationship with Torrijos and Noriega.

p. 283   Plan Blandón: The meetings were described by Gabriel Lewis and José Blandón in interviews. Blandón is the only source for the claim that Noriega himself initiated the negotiations and agreed to the basic tenets of the plan.

p. 285   Blandón evolution: Assuming that Blandón was telling the truth about his original loyalty to Noriega, the arrest of his oldest son, José, in October may have had a role in turning him against Noriega. Young José was arrested during a police raid on an opposition office and held for almost two days. Blandón said that he was not, as some accounts allege, beaten or otherwise abused.

p. 285   Plan Blandón: "Thoughts on a Panamanian Political Solution," October 27, 1987, reproduced in Kerry Hearings, II, 276–85.

p. 286   Murphy visit: Kerry Hearings, IV, 223–69. Admiral Murphy, who had visited Panama with Bush in 1983, traveled in 1987 with South Korean businessman Tongsun Park. They flew on a private Boeing 707 provided without cost by Sarkis G. Soghenalian, an arms dealer who had been indicted in the Southern District of Florida for alleged illegal shipments of arms and aircraft to Iraq. Soghenalian, in testimony to the Kerry committee, said Park told him that he and Murphy were carrying a U.S. government message to Noriega. Soghenalian testimony, Kerry Hearings, IV, 270ff.

p. 287   Call on Grenada: Interview with U.S. embassy staffer present when Noriega claimed to have made the call at Bush's request. See also *The Washington Post,* October 11, 1987.

p. 288   Ruiz arrest in Panama and Cuban drug ring: Interview with DEA agent Frederick Duncan. Reinaldo Ruiz's arrest began the unraveling of a drug ring connected to Colonel Antonio de la Guardia, a Cuban intelligence officer. The case led to the arrest in June 1989 of a group of high Cuban officials on drug charges in Cuba, including de la Guardia and General Arnaldo Ochoa, one of Castro's top officers and a hero of the Cuban military actions in Angola. A televised trial in Cuba was followed by public executions of Ochoa, de la Guardia and two other Cuban officers. See *The Washington Post,* July 8, 1989, by Julia Preston.

p. 289   *60 Minutes* offer: Interview with Kellner. The program, with an interview with Noriega, Carlton, and Blandón, aired February 7, 1988.

p. 292   Justice Department and White House meetings: Interviews with Gregorie and Kellner.

p. 294   Kellner factor: Interview with Kellner.

p. 294   Offer to drop indictment: After a February 17 meeting with Delvalle in Miami, Abrams informed Justice Department criminal division officials that he "would seek to have the indictment dropped against Noriega if he left the country," *The New York Times* (February 19, 1989) quoted Justice Department spokesman John K. Russell as saying. That version of events is supported by Leon Kellner, who said he was called by Attorney General Edwin Meese to inform him of Abrams's action.

p. 298   Shultz message: The public statement was on March 11. The secret approach to Panamanian attachés is referred to in FOIA release, Panama Task Force Situation Report No. 12, March 22, 1988, summarizing an earlier cable ordering the contacts.

SNATCHING DEFEAT . . . AN EPILOGUE

p. 301   "GAO Review of Economic Sanctions Imposed Against Panama," written statement to the House Western Hemisphere Affairs Subcommittee on International Economic Policy and Trade, by Frank C. Conahan, assistant comptroller general, July 26, 1989. The Noriega government ceased all payments on the foreign debt, saving $250 million in interest and an undetermined amount in principal payments. Government investment was slashed 80 percent by postponing infrastructure and repairs on roads and government facilities. It created accounting techniques that enabled U.S. firms operating in Panama to pay their tax obligations in violation of U.S. sanctions and in effect printed new money by issuing government checks in dollar denominations that were widely accepted as cash.

p. 302   Colonel Herrera Hassán's plan: See Katherine King, "Panama

Colonel Recruited by U.S. for Covert Action, Then Told to Respect Noriega's Human Rights," Reuters, October, 1989. Herrera said that he was being paid $4,500 a month for his work. Of the plot, he told King: "I developed a plan. It was my plan with my people. It would have operated outside U.S. borders. The CIA people thought it was great, and they took it to the Senate Intelligence Committee. When they came back, their attitude had changed. They said 'Will Noriega die?' I said it was possible. And they said, 'Look, you can't do this. You have to be aware of Noriega's human rights.' "

p. 302   Clandestine radio: The plan was leaked to reporter Carla Robbins, *U.S. News and World Report,* May 1, 1989. The Program Development Group's CIA identification is based on my interview with a senior Southcom official.

p. 305   October 1989 coup: Major Moisés Giroldi, a black, was also credited with preventing the September 1985 coup attempt by Roberto Díaz Herrera.

p. 307   Laboa's role: Interview with Laboa, July, 1988.

p. 309   Papal nuncio's views of Noriega: Interview with Archbishop Laboa, July 1988.

p. 312   Noriega's wealth: The 1986 estimate is reported in *The Miami Herald,* June 14, 1986. On August 31, 1989, State Department official Lawrence Eagleberger gave the $300 million estimate in a speech denouncing Noriega. Eagleberger's estimate, however, listed many assets as part of Noriega's fortune that actually are owned by the PDF or businessmen friends of Noriega's, according to *The Miami Herald,* January 21, 1989. The properties, which Eagleberger listed but the *Herald* said could not be traced to Noriega, included the PDF's Boeing 727. Three Learjets and several yachts were registered to people or corporations other than Noriega, according to documents obtained after the invasion. Various bank accounts have been discovered that contain what are thought to be Noriega's personal funds. The largest such account, in the London branch of the International Bank of Credit and Commerce (BCCI in its Spanish acronynm) contained $25 million in 1984, according to Amjad Awan, in Kerry Hearings IV, 461–580. On February 8, 1988—three days after the indictments against him were revealed—Noriega directed Awan's bank to transfer $14.9 million from his London account to the bank's Luxembourg branch.

INDEX

ABOUT THE AUTHOR

John Dinges has written about South and Central America for many years for a variety of publications, including *The Washington Post, Time,* ABC and NPR. He is currently a foreign editor at National Public Radio. He holds a master's degree in Latin American Studies from Stanford University and studied theology at the University of Innsbruck, Austria. He was a recipient of an Interamerican Press Association grant in 1972. His first book, with Saul Landau, *Assassination on Embassy Row* (Pantheon, 1980/McGraw-Hill, 1981) received an Edgar Award. As editor of NPR's special reports on the Iran-Contra Affair, he received the Corporation for Public Broadcasting Public Affairs–Events Coverage Award and the Achievement of Merit Ohio State Award.